E-Learning & Social Media

Education and Citizenship for the Digital 21st Century

A Volume in
International Advances in Education:
Global Initiatives for Equity and Social Justice

Series Editors
Elinor L. Brown, *University of Kentucky*
Rhonda Craven, *Australia Catholic University*
George McLean, *Catholic University of America*

International Advances in Education: Global Initiatives for Equity and Social Justice

Elinor L. Brown, Rhonda Craven, and George McLean, Series Editors

E-Learning & Social Media: Education and Citizenship for the Digital 21st Century (2016)
edited by Elinor L. Brown, Anna Krasteva, and Maria Ranieri

Comparative International Perspectives on Education and Social Change in Developing Countries and Indigenous Peoples in Developed Countries (2015)
edited by Gaëtane Jean-Marie, Steve Sider, and Charlene Desir

Inclusive Education for Students With Intellectual Disabilities (2015)
edited by Rhonda G. Craven, Alexandre J. S. Morin, Danielle Tracey, Philip D. Parker, and Hua Flora Zhong

Poverty, Class, and Schooling: Global Perspectives on Economic Justice and Educational Equity (2014)
edited by Elinor L. Brown, Paul C. Gorski, and Gabriella Lazaridis

Migrants and Refugees: Equitable Education for Displaced Populations (2013)
edited by Elinor L. Brown and Anna Krasteva

Indigenous Peoples: Education and Equity (2013)
edited by Rhonda G. Craven, Gawaian Bodkin-Andrews, and Janet Mooney

Communication and Language: Surmounting the Barriers to Cross-Cultural Understanding (2013)
edited by Alexander S. Yeung, Elinor L. Brown, and Cynthia Lee

Refugee and Immigrant Students: Achieving Equity in Education (2012)
edited by Florence E. McCarthy and Margaret H. Vickers

Ethnicity and Race: Creating Educational Opportunities Around the Globe (2011)
edited by Elinor L. Brown and Pamela E. Gibbons

Religion and Spirituality (2010)
edited by Martin Dowson and Stuart Devenish

E-Learning & Social Media

Education and Citizenship for the Digital 21st Century

Edited by

Elinor L. Brown
University of Kentucky

Anna Krasteva
New Bulgarian University

Maria Ranieri
University of Florence

IAP

INFORMATION AGE PUBLISHING, INC.
Charlotte, NC • www.infoagepub.com

Library of Congress Cataloging-in-Publication Data

CIP record for this book is available from the Library of Congress
http://www.loc.gov

ISBNs: 978-1-68123-428-1 (Paperback)
978-1-68123-429-8 (Hardcover)
978-1-68123-430-4 (ebook)

Printed in the United States of America

CONTENTS

Introduction
Elinor L. Brown, Anna Krasteva, and Maria Ranieri ix

SECTION I: TEACHING AND LEARNING IN THE DIGITAL 21ST CENTURY

1. Enabling E-learning Through Science Literacy for the Digital 21st Century as a Right in Education: The Case of Zanzibar
Zelhia Babaci-Whilhite 3

2. Virtual Reality, Learning Scenarios, and Teaching Science to Learners From Other Cultures: Whose Reality?
Chris Fowler 21

3. Workforce Development Through Technologically Enhanced Learning Experiences (TELEs)
Marquita Walker 43

4. Are K–12 Teachers Ready for Technology-Enhanced Teaching and Learning? A Study on Teachers' TPACK Level in a Provincial City in China
Yuqing Guo, Yan Li, and Min Li 65

5. EDUSAT: Harnessing Educational Potentiality in India
Kshama Pandey and Neetu Sing 93

SECTION II: THE INFLUENCE OF SOCIAL MEDIA ON SELF: IDENTITY-EFFICACY-REGULATION

6. Self-Efficacy and the Role of Technology to Support University-to-Work Transition
Maria Antonietta Impedovo ... 121

7. Building a Presence in the Online Space: An Opportunity and a Challenge for 21st Century Students
Mónica Aresta, Luís Pedro, and Carlos Santos ... 143

8. Information Literacy and Web 2.0 Technologies to Support Learners in Developmental Courses
Katura M. Lesane and Kennesha Bracely ... 167

9. Social Media and Self-Regulation: The Need for Strategies to Achieve High Quality Learning
Gisella Paoletti ... 183

10. Using the Voice of Teen YouTube Users for Web 2.0 Technology Enhanced Classroom Teaching
Sun Hee Jang, Yang Yang, and John Williamson ... 199

SECTION III: FOSTERING CITIZENSHIP & SOCIAL JUSTICE ACROSS SOCIAL MEDIA PLATFORMS

11. Recognition of the Social Different-Social Justice for Learning Within an Individualized, Mobile, Convergent Mass Communication
Ben Bachmair ... 223

12. Unlocking the potential of Social Media for Participation, Content Creation and e-Engagement: Students' Perspectives and Empowerment
Maria Ranieri, Alessia Rosa, and Stefania Manca ... 249

13. Digital Citizenship: Communication Capabilities and Technological Literacy
Carolyn M. Cunningham ... 275

14. Digital Diversity and Belonging in Higher Education: A Social Justice Proposition
Sue Timmis, Wan Ching Yee, and Emma Bent ... 297

15. Video Connections: Media Education and Global Citizenship a New Form of Alliance
Alessia Rosa 321

16. What Teachers Believe About Democracy and Why It is Important—How (Should) We Prepare Students for Democracy and Citizenship: Lessons From Australia
David Zyngier 342

About the Authors 369

External Reviewers 377

INTRODUCTION

Elinor L. Brown, Anna Krasteva, and Maria Ranieri

International Advances in Education: Global Initiatives for Equity and Social Justice is an international research monograph series of scholarly works that focus primarily on empowering children, adolescents, and young adults from diverse education, socio-cultural, linguistic, religious, racial, ethnic, and socio-economic settings to become non-exploited/non-exploitive contributing members of the global community. The series draws on the international community of investigators, academics and community organizers that have contributed to the evidence base for developing sound educational policies, practices, and innovative programs to optimize the potential of all students. Each themed volume includes multidisciplinary theory, research, and practice that provides an enriched understanding of the drivers of human potential via education to assist readers in exploring, adapting, and replicating innovative strategies that enable ALL students to realize their full potential.

Among these strategies are the integration of digital technologies (DT) and information and communication technologies (ICT) into contemporary education platforms. However, technology must be more than just a tool to deliver content and stimulate engagement; it must become a means to broaden access to learning, advance equity, promote social justice, and encourage social inclusion. Especially reaching out to address the academic and social needs of rural, impoverished, marginalized, and displaced

E-learning & Social Media:
Education and Citizenship for the Digital 21st Century, pp. ix–xiv

populations. Though the digital-divide continues to hinder educational attainment for underprivileged populations, ICTs are providing significant opportunities to deliver literacy and basic skills instruction to disadvantaged segments of the global population as well as engage, motivate, and customize learning to address local needs.

Nonetheless, the availability of ICT is not a deterministic process. Other societal, cultural, political and contextual factors are of fundamental importance to acceptance and integration that enables people to benefit from technology. The relationship between educational access, instructional delivery and ICT should be considered in more complex terms. In particular, digital technologies should be viewed as instructional tools that improve access to educational opportunities, strengthen cultural resources, promote social and economic equity, and provide students with the knowledge and competencies to prepare them for a future that cannot be predicted. Therefore, developing ICT and media capabilities that instills citizenship and stewardship in today's students is crucial to gleaning the social and cultural advantages of a contemporary global society that encourages full and equal citizenship.

Citizenship education refers to two understandings of citizenship: as belonging and as engagement. The first is focussed on national identity and upholds the values of justice and democracy, as well as language and culture as the roots bridging the personality of children to the community of solidarity and shared norms. The second understanding of citizenship complements the 'roots' with 'roads', with the choices made by the individual, with the capacity to form and develop the child's personality into the actor and author of his/her educational, professional and life projects. The adolescent prepares to become an active, committed, and engaged citizen with critical thinking and capacities for responsible action. Digital citizenship expresses the transformations of both belonging and engaging in the information society and contributes to the development of generation "Y" with the aspiration to innovate and experiment, to explore the possibilities of the new digital world, to question authorities and sources of knowledge and power. Education addresses digital citizenship by opening more venues and avenues for the exploration of citizen rights and responsibilities. The intersection of social media and citizenship education is becoming a powerful global tool for empowerment.

Volume 10, *E-learning & Social Media: Education and Citizenship for the Digital 21st Century,* addresses the use of technology in: developing and expanding educational delivery systems to reach rural populations, providing access to equitable education opportunities for disadvantaged and marginalized populations, and encouraging student civic engagement. The volume evaluates e-learning programmes (distributed through the Internet, via satellite and hosted on social media) that promote equitable education for disadvantaged populations; examines the challenges and benefits of social media on student self-identity, collaboration, and academic engagement; shares promising practices associated with technology in education and e-citizenship in the 21st century, and advances the discussion on blending global citizenship education and social media that raises student awareness, accountability and social justice involvement.

In this volume, Section I consists of five chapters examining: teachers' classroom technology proficiency, the use of technology to present content in cultural and community contexts, and innovative distance learning platforms and software. The opening chapter by Zehlia Babaci-Wilhite, addresses the benefits of infusing the local languages and cultures of Zanzibar into the instructional process as a method of teaching both global and local science in the digital age. The chapter examines formal and informal strategies and how the use of technology, local language, and culture facilitate cognitive development and the understanding, acceptance, and incorporation of new knowledge. Chapter 2, by Chris Fowler, examines science education in developing countries and concurs that to be effective teachers must deliver science instruction that is authentic, relevant, and culturally sensitive. Dr. Fowler presents a conceptual framework for teaching science that considers the cultural needs of the learner and the social issues of the community through the use of Virtual Worlds (VWs) technology.

In chapter 3, author, Marquita Walker, provides a strong case for investment in workforce "soft skills" training to increase worker productivity, reduce unemployment, and decrease workplace prejudices in the United States. The author has developed flexible online Technologically Enhanced Learning Experiences (TELEs) that provide interpersonal skills training for the jobless and underemployed as well as potential employers. Chapter 4, authored by Yuqing Guo, Yan Li, and Min Li, analyses K–12 teachers' use of information and communication technologies (ICTs) in Hangzhou, China. The authors used the technological, pedagogical, and content knowledge (TPACK) model to ascertain the specific skills, knowledge, and personal attributes needed for instructional competence in the use of ICTs in the 21st century Chinese classroom. Section I concludes with chapter 5, by authors, Kshama Pandey and Neetu Singh who present an overview of the present and future directions of EDUSAT, a satellite based online teaching and learning platform that promotes academic equity across India. The authors provide a powerful case for the further development of satellite-based distance learning tools as a means of providing access to equitable education for rural and urban disadvantaged populations.

The five chapters in Section II investigate the impact of social media on identity, self-regulation, self-efficacy, academic achievement, and workforce readiness. Chapter 6, by Maria Impedovo, explores the role of self-efficacy and social media in supporting students' transition from academia to workforce. The author conducted in-depth interviews with Eastern European Italian university students between the ages of 25 and 30 and found that students' personal perspective and self-efficacy, coupled with social networking and Internet participation positively effects their transition from school to work. In chapter 7, Mónica Aresta, Luís Pedro, and Carlos Santos, explore the construction and dissemination of personal, professional, and academic identities in Internet environments. Through surveys, interviews, and the analysis of 3,692 messages on three social media platforms, the authors found that interactive participation in social media settings provide users with opportunities to communicate and explicate their skills, abilities, experiences, and personal characteristics. Additionally, the authors share an innovative model designed to analyze the creation of identity in online environments.

In chapter 8, Katura Lesane and Kennesha Bracely share innovative strategies that assist students enrolled in developmental college classes in acquiring 21st century workforce skills while preparing them to matriculate to credit bearing courses. The authors combined information literacy and web 2.0 technologies to support and encourage academic engagement, independence, and self-efficacy through student generated communication, collaboration, reflection, and peer debriefings. Chapter 9, by Gisella Paoletti, examines the intellectual cost of social media in an academic context. Paoletti's research indicates that students are constantly and impulsively dividing their attention between social media (i.e., text-messaging, face-time, Facebook, and Twitter) and academic engagement (i.e., studying, listening, participating, learning), and proposes that to minimize the potential cognitive costs for these task-switching practices, students must cultivate self-regulation strategies. Section II closes with chapter 10, by Sun Hee Jang, Yang Yang, and John Williamson. The authors posit that Web 2.0 technologies (i.e., social media, YouTube, blogs, wikis), though pervasive, can be effective teaching tools in the classroom. The authors suggest that teachers must consider the relationship between the six dimensions of student learning styles and Web 2.0 characteristics when developing teaching and learning strategies for today's students.

Section III consists of six chapters focused on how social media platforms are used to promote social justice, foster civic engagement, and encourage global citizenship. Chapter 11, by Ben Bachmair, advances the conversation on social justice and democratic education through an in-depth dialogue on the dramatic and ever broadening role of social media and mass communication in the formal learning environment and the associated individual social risks to minority cultures. The author proposes that educators should concentrate on using social media as a cultural resource to minimize stratification that furthers social inequality.

Bachmair provides examples of school projects to explain the three areas of social justice (institutional prerequisites of justice, agency and life orientation, and communicative intention). Chapter 12, by Maria Ranieri, Alessia Rosa, and Stefania Manca, evaluates an instrument developed to assess the attitudes of adolescents toward participation in, adoption of, and contributions to various social media platforms. The authors provide a detailed description of their instrument, and advance the conversation on citizenship education, the links between active social media interaction, civic engagement, and youth empowerment.

Carolyn Cunningham, author of chapter 13, advocates that as social media broadens the spectrum for democratic participation, communication capability becomes an important component in defining technological literacy when fostering technological equality and the use of social media as an instrument for democracy. Cunningham argues that technology literacy underscores cognizance, clarity, and flexibility as the role of technology in society and that possessing communication capability affords individuals the freedom to pursue their potential of self-actualization, self-determination, and self-governance. Chapter 14, by Sue Timmis, Wan Ching Yee, and Emma Bent focuses on social justice as it relates to social equity in undergraduate education. The authors' research findings indicate that digital media can be inclusive and support a sense of belonging for diverse and underrepresented students attending universities, but can also be pervasive and exclusive. However, their research concludes that the role of digital technology in university environments is to provide alternative spaces for student social identity development and peer discourse.

In chapter 15, author Alessia Rosa promotes global citizenship, media literacy, and digital equity through an innovative project that used video and social media to link Kenyan youth with their Italian peers. Kenyan and Italian students shared personal perceptions of life in their respective countries, which raised awareness and stimulated reflection and cultural mobilization among the students. The teachers used the experiences to provide peer-to-peer digital spaces for sharing, developing cognitive skills, and to construct meaning through digital storytelling and cartooning. The final chapter, by David Zyngier, reports on empirical and qualitative research in over 25 countries that describes how democracy is being interpreted in 21st century civic and citizenship education and how this narrow interpretation is fostering youth apathy and disengagement in global citizenship and the democratic process. The author argues that the use of social media and digital literacy will broaden student awareness, analysis, reflection, and participation in educational experiences that facilitate meaningful societal transformation through "thicker democracy."

This volume holds great potential to further the dialogue on: the benefits and challenges of integrating social media into the contemporary academic curriculum, moving toward global educational equity through a broad spectrum of technology platforms, and promoting global social justice awareness and engagement through democratic citizenship education. The chapters provide examples of replicable programs and projects for communities, classrooms, and in political arenas around the globe. The editors, Elinor L. Brown, Anna Krasteva, and Maria Ranieri enthusiastically recommend this volume and the series to educators, politicians, community workers, corporations, administrators, and individuals for use in both professional and personal practices.

SECTION I

TEACHING AND LEARNING IN THE DIGITAL 21st CENTURY

CHAPTER 1

ENABLING E-LEARNING THROUGH SCIENCE LITERACY FOR THE DIGITAL 21ST CENTURY AS A RIGHT IN EDUCATION

The Case of Zanzibar

Zehlia Babaci-Wilhite

ABSTRACT

This chapter will address how to incorporate global and local learning and sustain mother tongue instruction through a science literacy program in the digital age in Zanzibar. Further, it will argue that this sustenance of learning in mother tongue education based in local knowledge ought to be defined as a right in education. I will frame my argument with the theories that reflect and reports on commentary and history compiled from the perspectives of both the dominant and nondominant cultures. The author envisions education as a set of processes intended to enhance multicultural dimensions

E-Learning and Social Media:
Education and Citizenship for the Digital 21st Century, pp. 3–19

in glo-local learning where e-learning has to be taken into consideration within education in order to enhance citizenship for the digital 21st century. This is a radical departure from most mainstream educational research and practice, which is designed to enhance global rather than local learning by using a science model in which reading, writing, and language are employed as tools to foster the development of glo-local knowledge and inquiry in science. I first examine key assumptions about knowledge that inform mainstream educational research and practice. I then argue for an emphasis on the contextualized dimension of learning as a right in education. This means accounting for contextualized knowledge and reversing the current trend in the digital age of decontextualization. I introduce a new model of learning involving alternative assumptions about the value of local knowledge and local languages in the teaching and learning of science subjects using the seeds of science and roots of reading model. I insist that this will form a new platform for innovation with a unique mix of local and global knowledge in understanding and reaching technology for learning in a digital age.

INTRODUCTION

This chapter will address how to incorporate global and local learning and sustain mother tongue instruction in the digital age through a science literacy model in Zanzibar,[1] Tanzania. Further, it will argue that this sustenance of learning in mother tongue education based in local knowledge ought to be defined as a right in education. The chapter explores the formal and informal learning of science and how it facilitates the learning process as well as cognitive learning in the development of new knowledge. I draw on my own research on the teaching of science subjects in Zanzibar and on a review of research on problems with the learning of science due to decontextualized teaching and learning in Africa. The chapter will give attention to the conjunction of several aspects to improve the quality of learning through science literacy using e-learning in mother tongue education and local curriculum within the digital age. The introduction of e-learning rooted in the seeds of science approach will form a new platform for innovation based on a unique mix of local and global knowledge. It will provide teachers and students with the capacity to understand and deploy new technologies for learning.

There has been a tendency in academic approaches to science literacy to regard literacy as an end unto itself, ignoring structures that undercut disciplinary learning, comprehension, critical literacy and strategic reading (Cervetti, Pearson, Bravo, & Barber, 2005). Therefore I will argue along with Cervetti et al. (2005) that literacy will be better achieved through subjects such as science as developed in the Seeds and Science/Roots of Reading (S/R) program which can be adapted and developed in e-learning and made accessible on a larger scale in Zanzibar and elsewhere in Africa.

There is no single theory that encompasses the complex web of epistemological issues embedded in formal and informal knowledge in education. Some of the strands of theory that have been important for framing this chapter are the role of education in society, the role of language in education, as well as the knowledge embedded in local culture. The central theoretical focus in the chapter is on the explanatory power of theories related to education for self-reliance and pedagogy of nondominant groups. The theoretical framework I will put forward incorporates the importance of local context within its cultural identity, emphasizing the development of local capacity on local terms. Such a multiple approach emphasizes the importance of indigenous concepts, articulated in their natural environment. The argument in the chapter draws heavily on the work of three educational theorists. The first is Julius Nyerere and his theory of self-reliance, developed and applied in Tanzania in the 1960s and 1970s. Though his theory no longer governs educational policy in Tanzania, I will argue that it has relevance today in Zanzibar's efforts to achieve equal access and fairness in education and in the society at large. The second theory important to the analysis is Paulo Freire's theory on formal versus informal educational pedagogy. Freire's theory has implications for the language used in schooling and in the society. The third is David Pearson's approach of viewing the role of language and literacy in supporting disciplinary learning, which can be achieved by using literacy skills to think critically and flexibly across many domains of knowledge and inquiry. In line with Pearson, Jacqueline Barber (2005) argues, "Inquiry is curiosity-driven.... It involves reading books to find out what others have learned.... Inquiry requires the use of critical and logical thinking.... Good readers inquire information gathered from text" (p. 1) Furthermore, Cervetti et al. (2005) revised the concept-oriented reading instruction (CORI), which provides a rich and compelling context for teaching reading strategies, but failed to examine the conceptual learning of science. Therefore, Pearson and Barber's approach to improve literacy through inquiry science (or other subject matter foci) serves as the "real-world" interaction ingredient for the CORI model to achieve better results for science as well as literacy.

I will conclude with the notion that *human rights in education* is intimately connected to the life of the people (Babaci-Wilhite, Geo-JaJa, & Lou, 2012), and their language should be a part of the language of education. In short, language plays a critical role in cognitive learning and in the development of critical thinking and new knowledge (Babaci-Wilhite & Geo-JaJa, 2011). Drawing on my research in Zanzibar, I will argue that e-learning can be a bridge to improved teaching and learning as long as it is contextualized in mother tongue education. This can make a positive contribution to efforts to achieve rights in education in Zanzibar and East Africa.

RETHINK EDUCATION IN KISWAHILI: THE LINGUA FRANCA IN EAST AFRICA

In Zanzibar, Kiswahili and English are both official languages, although Kiswahili is understood by the entire population and spoken as mother tongue by the vast majority (Mbaabu, 1996). Many scholars believe that Zanzibar is the birthplace of Kiswahili,[2] which is the lingua franca of Tanzania and East Africa, and the language (mother tongue) of Zanzibar. About 80 million people in 14 countries in East and Central Africa speak Kiswahili. Kiswahili is one of the five official languages of the African Union alongside English, French, Portuguese, and Arabic. Kiswahili has been occasionally used as a working language at UNESCO meetings as far back as 1986. It has, however, never been an official working language of the UN or UNESCO. Haroub Othman (2008, p. 7) argues, "Kiswahili is no longer the language of Tanzania or East Africa; it is the language of the entire African continent, having been adopted by the African Union as one of its official languages."

Kiswahili plays a major role in Tanzania's robust media. Most newspapers in Tanzania are in Kiswahili. The public broadcasting service television TVT (Televisheni Ya Taifa) now TBC (Tanzania Broadcasting Cooperation) send most of their programs in Kiswahili. The radio networks of Radio Tanzania Dar-es-Salaam (RTD) are also state-run and use Kiswahili. It is important to note that from 2007 the state has owned both TVT and RTD. They are both very popular and are both under the umbrella of Tanzania Broadcasting Corporation. However, privately owned media are more important, since they control more than 11 daily newspapers, over six television stations, and more than six FM radio stations. One of them, RFA (Radio Free Africa) reaches the Great Lakes Region Congo DRC, Rwanda, and even Burundi. This demonstrates the importance of cross-border languages.[3]

Julius K. Nyerere, the first president of Tanzania, with his educational vision, insisted on the need for rethinking the relationship between general education and formal education. He wrote:

> We have not until now questioned the basic system of education, which we took over at the time of Independence. We have never done that because we have never thought about education except in terms of obtaining teachers, engineers, administrators, etc. Individually and collectively we have in practice thought of education as training for the skills required earning high salaries in the modern sector of our economy. (Nyerere, 1968, p. 267)

In line with the ideas of Freire (1970/1993), Nyerere believed that education should be an integral part of daily life not separated from it. Education should address the needs of both the local people and the country. According to Joseph Ki-Zerbo (1990), an historian from Burkina Faso, these points about cultural learning and local needs have not been adequately addressed in Africa. The problem today is that African countries are adopting the standards of the world without inclusion local culture in education (Geo-JaJa, 2011). Furthermore, Nyerere wrote, "Colonial education in this country was therefore not transmitting the values and the knowledge of Tanzania society from one generation to the next; it was a deliberate attempt to change those values and to replace traditional knowledge by the knowledge from a different society" (Nyerere, 1968, p. 47). To motivate the active mind, one has to take into consideration the variations in different societies, differences in knowledge, and different ways of teaching to achieve quality education. If education is conceived of as imparting knowledge about the world, then schooling should be regarded as only one aspect of education, since it does not cover all forms of knowledge. This point is highly relevant for media and media education, because popular media use Kiswahili as its medium whereas media education uses English.

According to Freire, much of the knowledge that forms the basis for schooling has its origins from another place and another time: "Knowledge emerges only through invention and re-invention" (Freire, 1970/1993, p. 53). The students who catch on to this form of learning will be successful in school but might actually have less knowledge in the broad sense of the word than one who does not attend school. However, education is most often equated with schooling.

The language issue in Tanzania is deeply related to the conceptualization of education and the debate around whether or not education should encompass the local cultural context. Freire (1970/1993) and others scholars such as Martha Qorro (2004) and Kwesi-Kwaa Prah (2005) argue that using a local language as medium of education fosters the broader view of learning that softens the barriers between real-life and classroom experience. Freire proposed a similar theory about the importance of local knowledge and its relationship to empowerment. Pearson's approach to literacy has relevance for the language debate in Tanzania. His approach aims to develop students' potential to use the information one gains from reading and apply it to new situations, problems, or projects (Cervetti, Barber, Dorph, Pearson, & Goldschmidt, 2012; Pearson, Moje, & Greenleaf, 2007). The S/R model acknowledges that knowledge and wider vocabulary are a consequence as well as a cause of reading comprehension (Cervetti et al., 2012; Pearson et al., 2007). Therefore, learning through Kiswahili in Zanzibar will improve literacy as well as the science subject. Language is not everything in education, but without language, everything is nothing in education (Wolff, 2006).

THE NEGLECT OF LOCAL KNOWLEDGE IN THE WAKE OF GLOBALIZATION

In Zanzibar and elsewhere in Tanzania, reforms and policies connecting local cultures to education have been neglected. According to Samoff (2007, p. 60), "effective education reform requires agendas and initiatives with strong local roots." In other words, local knowledge (also referred to as indigenous knowledge) should be included in the curriculum (Brock-Utne, 2002; Semali & Khanjan, 2012). This knowledge should be conveyed in local languages, which is critical to the preservation and development of local knowledge. The choice of the Language of instruction is extremely important not only because of the implications for quality learning, but also because of the intimate ties between language, culture and identity (Babaci-Wilhite, 2013; Brock-Utne, 2005). Local knowledge and languages are being severely strained through globalization, which is a shorthand way of describing the spread and connectedness of production, communication and technologies across the world. Appadurai (1990, p. 17) argues that

> The critical point is that both sides of the coin of global cultural process today are products of the infinitely varied mutual contest of sameness and difference on a stage characterised by radical disjunctures between different sorts of global flows and the uncertain landscapes created in and through these disjunctures.

Furthermore, he claims that what is taking place through globalization is a process of cultural mixing or hybridization across locations and identities. We cannot think simplistically about the unidirectional nature of global flows of products and culture, but when it comes to languages there is no doubt that the flow is unidirectional from the global North to the South. This process has its roots in earlier stages of imperialism and continues to the present.

Geo-JaJa and Yang (2003) describe Western imperialism in Africa in four stages (a) slave trade, which extracted labor and disrupted local societies (b) colonialism, which divided the continent without regard to ethnicity and cultural boundaries, (c) neo-colonialism, which imposed political and economic pressure, and (d) the globalization of the neo-liberal ideology, bringing free trade regimes that shrink space, time, and borders through new information and communication technologies (NICT). Over the course of the past two decades, imperialism, globalization, and marketization have impacted education in developing countries. Throughout each of these phases, languages of the powerful have been exported to and replaced local languages in education. Prah (2005) supports this view when he writes that globalization is the continuation of the process of imperialism and implies hegemony at one end and denationalization at the other, processes which are often conveniently forgotten in establishing languages to be used in African curriculum.

Knowledge is equated with what the learner is taught in schools. That knowledge that forms the basis for school curricula is decontextualized. The educated person is one who has mastered sets of facts, propositions, models and cognitive skills that are fundamentally separate from the context in which they were learned. Stanton Wortham and Kara Jackson (2012) argue that educational approaches differ in their methods for improving student knowledge, ranging from directives to more discovery-oriented pedagogies, but mainstream approaches all assume that student skills and representations are the target of educational interventions.

Knowledge is also typically viewed as relatively stable. In mainstream approaches to education, schooling often involves the transmission of isolated, portable bodies of knowledge. Schools make sense as institutions only because stable knowledge and reasoning procedures can allegedly transfer, and have value in other contexts where students will use the knowledge they learned in school. Because the context is not integral to the knowledge or skill, the isolated bodies of knowledge often hold little meaning for anyone other than the members of the community who generated that knowledge. The problems students solve in school are thus problems of the disciplinary communities from which the knowledge originated. This often makes schooled knowledge and skills less useful outside of schools. Moreover, given the decontextualized, insular nature of the knowledge being passed on, there is generally little opportunity for students to question the claims on which the knowledge is based.

GLO-LOCAL LEARNING AS A RIGHT IN EDUCATION

I have argued in recent publications that contextualization of education and the use of a local language of instruction should be considered a right in education. Article 26 of the United Nations Declaration of Human Rights (1948) states that everyone has the right to education. It says little about the nature, kind, and quality of education. Rights in education imply that rights are not ensured unless the education offered is of high quality. The UN called for a mainstreaming of human rights to encourage the government's responsibility to insure the rights-based approach. The rights-based framework includes the principle that every human being is entitled to decent education and gives priority to the intrinsic importance of education, implying that governments need to mobilize the resources to offer quality education (UNICEF, 2003, p. 8). Katerina Tomasevski (2003) advocates that education should prepare learners for participation: "it should teach the young that all human beings—themselves included—have rights" (p. 33).

The rights-based approach had its origins in 1993 when the United Nations (UN) held the World Conference on Human Rights in Vienna. During this conference the Vienna Declaration and Program of Action were conceived, linking democracy, human rights, sustainability, and development (Hamm, 2001, p. 1007). In 1997, the Secretary General to the United Nations called for a mainstreaming of human rights into all work of the UN and in 2003, various organizations and agencies met to develop the government's responsibility to insure the rights-based approach. The rights-based approach is crucial for developing countries since this approach works to shift the paradigm away from aid and towards moral duty imposed on the world through the international consensus of human rights. Human rights rhetoric was used to develop a "mode of operation" to describe someone's manner of working, or their method of operating or functioning, as a driving force to bring effectiveness to human rights (Nelson-Dorsey, 2003).

Robeyns (2006) argues that "the rights-based approach model of education is that, once the government agrees that children should have the rights to be educated, it may see its task as being precisely executing this agreement, and nothing more" (p. 77). Furthermore, she claims that "well-developed rights-based educational policies will state precisely which rights are guaranteed to whom, and what the government has to do to ensure that rights are not only rhetorical, but also effective" (p. 77).

Education has the potential to empower, if teaching and learning give nourishment and self-respect that in turn bring confidence to teachers and learners. I agree with Robeyns (2006, p. 77) when she writes, "It will be necessary that the government goes beyond its duties in terms of the rights-based policies, to undertake action to ensure that every child can fully and equally enjoy her rights to education," which implies that teachers are well-trained and well-paid, teaching material is provided, and a good curriculum and pedagogy is developed.

Education is another tool to increase human rights effectiveness as it increases human capabilities, functions, and opportunities in societies. This further leads to the linkage between human rights and development, and enables policy makers and developers to incorporate the rights-based approach within the "common understanding" of a human rights-based approach, assuring these principles: indivisibility, equality, participation, and inclusion (UNDP, 2006, pp. 17–18).

Rights are defined as entitlements that belong to all human beings regardless of race, ethnicity, or socioeconomic class (Nussbaum, 1998, p. 273). All humans therefore are rights holders, and it is someone's duty to provide these rights. "Human rights in education" is a powerful notion as it is intimately connected to the social, occupational, political, cultural, religious, and artistic life of the people (Babaci-Wilhite Geo-JaJa & Lou, 2012). UNESCO's convention in 2005 on the protection and promotion of the diversity of cultural expressions emphasizes the importance of linguistic diversity. Language as part of culture should be part of what Skutnabb-Kangas (2000) calls language as a human right in the education sector. Article 26 of the United Nations Declaration of Human Rights (1948), in education as a human right, states that: "Everyone has the right to education. Education shall be free.... Education shall be directed to ... the development of human personality and to the strengthening of human rights and fundamental freedom" (Universal Declaration of Human Rights, 1948, Preamble). The globalization trends for language in education outlined above, in which local curricula are decontextualized are in contravention of the tenets of the rights-based approach to language in education. This approach is based on the premise that the use of a local curriculum should be regarded as a right in education.

In an increasingly interdependent global world it is important to facilitate the mastery of foreign languages, as well as mastery of subject matter. The policies for developing countries should also be context sensitive and, in addition, one that permits developing countries to remain a partner in the global society. Therefore, I envision education as a set of processes intended to enhance glo-local learning. This is a radical departure from most mainstream educational research and practice, which is designed to enhance global rather than local learning. An innovation with a unique mix of local and global technologies for learning with a value of local knowledge, local languages, local teaching, and learning of science subjects can be the bridge which will be discuss in the next section.

ADAPTING OF THE SEEDS AND SCIENCE/ROOTS OF READING MODEL TO IMPROVE LITERACY IN ZANZIBAR

I argue that these important issues of improving science learning and enabling rights in education can be addressed by applying the seeds of science/roots of reading (S/R) model to Zanzibar education to resolve the problems with the quality of teaching and learning science associated with poor quality of teachers and inadequate teaching aids and facilities. The aim of S/R model is to make sense of the physical world through firsthand experiences while addressing foundational dimensions of literacy. S/R has assembled science and literacy experts to study, enact in the form of curriculum, and test the limits and potential of the science-literacy interface answering how reading and writing can be used as tools to support inquiry-based science learning, and what benefits accrue to reading and writing when they are embedded in inquiry based science as well as what skills, strategies, and possesses are shared in these subjects.

This has the potential to bring the needed outcomes, results, and accomplishments that will improve science, as well as the process of teaching and learning science. The emphasis will be moved from rote memorization to deep understanding.

Pearson and Hiebert (2013) argue that in the effort to promote understanding, existing background knowledge matters, which refers to Goldenberg (2008, p. 18) who claims:

> Beginning reading instruction is guided by neither a theory nor a goal of knowledge development. In fact, just the opposite: children are presented with texts—mostly narrative—chosen to reflect their existing background knowledge, the assumption being that they can use that knowledge to comprehend familiar content.

This reflects the current situation in Zanzibar. As argued above, engagement with local language and local knowledge are necessary to facilitate the teaching and learning process. Furthermore each outcome in the pathway of change is tied to an intervention, revealing the complex web of activity that is required to bring about change (Cervetti, Pearson, Barber, Hiebert, & Bravo, 2007; Cervetti et al., 2012). These principles of learning address the connections between early, intermediate, and long-term outcomes and the expectations about how and why the proposed interventions will bring them about (see Cervetti et al., 2007). In short, the S/R model aims for deep understanding, a program of planning and evaluation, and a commonly understood vision of the long-term goals and on how they will be reached, as well as what will be used to measure progress along the way.

The S/R model requires participants to be clear on long-term goals, identify measurable indicators of success which has been achieved according to Cervetti et al. (2007) through practices known to meet the linguistic needs, such as using graphic representations of abstract concepts (see Pearson & Hiebert. 2013). This fundamental concept builds a curriculum that puts literacy instruction such as "texts, routines for reading, word-level skills, vocabulary, and comprehension instruction" work in the service of acquiring the knowledge, skills, and dispositions of inquiry-based science (Cervetti et al., 2007). When it comes to Zanzibar a "here to there" strategy is direly needed, given problems with teacher competence, support materials, and confusion about the importance of local language and context. The S/R model is designed to be a core science program that addresses all aspects of science proficiency, while simultaneously serving as a supplementary literacy program. It focuses on reading comprehension, vocabulary development, and inquiries. The implementation of the program takes on learning goals in literacy and science by providing students with explicit instruction, opportunities for practice, and increasing independence in using literacy strategies to make sense of and communicate about the natural world.

The multimodal approach of the S/R approach provides students with access to every essential concept to be learned in a unit through a range of different learning modalities called the Do-it; Talk-it; Read-it; Write-it approach. Through experiences, students are engaged with the essential concepts learned, making it easy to understand them by reading, writing, and discussing them. These multiple modalities provide opportunities for students to apply, deepen, and extend their knowledge of the learned concepts.

This effective research-based curriculum offers students an explicit focus on disciplinary literacy and in the specialized knowledge and skills involved in reading, writing, and talking about science, sorely needed in Zanzibar. The program promotes substantive science knowledge and inquiry skills and involves students in deep forays into learning about the natural world by searching for evidence through firsthand experiences (hands on activities) and secondhand experiences (text) in order to construct more accurate, nuanced, and complete understandings of the natural world. Furthermore, students engage in written and oral discourse with the goal of communicating and negotiating evidence-based explanations, and evaluating and revising explanations based on that evidence.

The S/R approach engages students in using literacy in the service of inquiry science. For example, students predict what objects are attracted to a magnet and test their predictions. Then, in an attempt to understand surprising results, students search for evidence in text about the metal composition of the objects they tested. Based on this new evidence, students make claims about what sticks to magnets and write explanations incorporating their claims and evidence. This synergistic approach to integrating science and literacy is in contrast to less authentic approaches to integration, in which students conduct first-hand investigations about X, read about X, and then write about X, what is called additive approaches to integration. These simply add on literacy tasks to a science curriculum or vice versa, and do not provide explicit instruction in how to read and write science text (Pearson, Moje, & Greenleaf, 2007). Recent studies have shown that students exposed to the program made significantly greater gains on measures of science understanding, science vocabulary, and science writing (Cervetti et al., 2012).

ADAPTING THE SEEDS OF SCIENCE/ROOTS OF READING USING A DIGITAL DEVICE

The S/R model links firsthand experiences, discussions, and writing to the ideas and language in informational texts to foster development of core science knowledge and literacy skills (Afflerbach, Pearson, & Paris, 2008; Cervetti, Pearson, Bravo, & Barber, 2005). The model would address how reading and writing can be used as tools to support inquiry based science in Zanzibar and how to support their implementation in today's complicated curricular landscape in Zanzibar using a digital device. The computer has been the digital device that has been used in education to facilitate learning. However, it is revealing to note that 80 percent of the world's population has no access to basic infrastructure facilities that are regarded as commonplace in the industrialized world, and that there are reported to be more computers in New York alone than in the whole of Africa (DFID, 2000 quoted by Crossley & Watson, 2003). "If every city resembled New York, everyone could access the 'other society's' education systems to discover what can be learned that will contribute to improved policy and practice at home" (Arnove, 2003, p. 6). However, the main digital device used in classrooms is no longer a computer. In 2012, the U.S. Department of Education and the Federal Communications Commission encouraged the development of digital textbooks and digital learning in K–12 public education. According to Pew Research Internet Project (PRIP), the rise of E-Reading (2012) has increased and 50% of U.S. adults owns a tablet computer and/or an e-book reader. Furthermore, PRIP showed the interest of using these devices in schools by giving that most teachers and students support tablets for the following reasons:

- much lighter than print textbooks
- improve standardized test scores
- hold hundreds of textbooks
- save the environment by lowering the amount of printing
- increase student interactivity and creativity
- cheaper than print textbooks.

The counter arguments are that tablets are:

- expensive
- too distracting for students
- easy to break
- costly/time consuming to fix
- quickly outdated as new technologies are released

Several states in the U.S. have begun transitioning their instructional materials from paper textbooks to digital learning according to the "Digital Textbook Playbook" such as:

- California in 2009 (launching a free digital textbook initiative) with

    1. San Diego United School district distributing 78,000 digital textbooks to teachers and students since 2011 and 26,000 iPads in 2012
    2. Los Angeles United School district (the second-largest school district in the country) purchasing 655,000 iPads for all K–12 students.

- West Virginia in 2009 (replaced social studies print textbook purchases with digital textbooks).
- Florida in 2015 (mandated that all K–12 instructional materials are required to provided in electronic format)
- Georgia state law requiring that electronic copies of K–12 be made available for use by students.

In the African context with no books and no support materials in teaching and learning, tablets can be very useful and adaptable. The American Association of Publishers argues that the average net unit price of a K–12 print textbook has been $65 in 2010 and that digital textbooks on average cost $50–60. The cost of tablets in the U.S. was on average $489 in 2011 to $343 in 2013 and projected to be $263 in 2015. The implementation costs for e-textbooks on iPad tablets are higher than new print textbooks due to Wi-Fi infrastructure, training teachers and administrators how to use the technology, and annual publisher fees to continue using e-textbooks. Advances in technology have long been changing the way scholars work in terms of teaching and administrative duties, and the trend is growing globally. Zanzibar, with high demands in literacy and technology, the use of tablets has a huge potential to improve to teaching and learning as long as the content is contextualized. I propose that the S/R based model of instruction developed and taught through a tablet will contribute to the sustainability and development of science literacy in Zanzibar. Its application can be a major step in correcting violations of children's rights in education due to the weak learning environment pointed out above, especially the lack of trained teachers and support materials. This will contribute to a solid curriculum grounded in thorough teacher preparation and quality support materials. An application of the S/R model has the potential to contribute to a realization of science learning that ensures every child's rights to quality education.

CONCLUSION

Language is crucial to the learning process inside and outside of schools. Mother tongue instruction is the tool of learning, and therefore, what tool could be more easy to use than the local language as a language in all forms for education. In this chapter, I have reviewed the theory relevant to understanding the importance of language and culture in learning as well as the need to encompass both formal and informal learning in Zanzibar where the choices are between globally powerful and local languages. The theory of self-reliance stresses the importance of the curriculum being grounded in the local context and mediated through a local language. Such an approach emphasizes the importance of indigenous concepts, articulated in their natural environment. Education is more than schooling, therefore rethinking in reteaching is crucial. Kiswahili, the local language, needs to be valued and preserved, and students need to be prepared for the world in a language of instruction, which promotes understanding.

The S/R model represents an opportunity to apply a well-tested science curriculum to the Zanzibari teaching of science that has the benefit of considerable empirical testing. Furthermore, the S/R program leads to improved literacy, scientific knowledge, and personal efficacy for students and greater professional efficacy for teachers (see Cervetti et al., 2007; Pearson, 2007). The adaptation of the S/R model adapted to the local context through a tablet will give easy access and contribute to rights in education and to children's confidence in their community as well as their ability to understand and engage with the world on their own terms. We owe this to children in order to promote social justice locally and globally.

NOTES

1. Tanganyika and Zanzibar united in 1964 to form the United Republic of Tanzania
2. During an interview in February 2012, with the Vice Chancellor at the State University of Zanzibar (SUZA) who expressed that the Zanzibari Kiswahili is the Oxford of Kiswahili (reference to Oxford English) the purest.
3. www.pressreference.com/Sw-Ur/Tanzania.html-43k

REFERENCES

Afflerbach, P., Pearson, P. D., & Paris, S. G. (2008). Clarifying differences between reading skills and reading strategies. *Research Based Classroom Practice*, *61*(5), 364–373.

Appadurai, A. (1990). Disjuncture and difference in the global culture economy. *Theory, Culture & Society, 7*(2), 295–310. doi:10.1177/026327690007002017

Arnove, R. F. (2003). Introduction—Reframing comparative education: The dialectic of the global and the local. In A. Robert & C. Torres (Eds.), *Comparative education: The dialectic of the global and the local* (pp. 1–22). Lanham, MD: Rowman & Littlefield.

Babaci-Wilhite, Z. (2012). A right based approach to Zanzibar's language-in-education policy. Special Issue on Right based Approach and Globalization in Education. *World Study of Education, 13*(2), 17–33.

Babaci-Wilhite, Z. (2013). The new education curriculum in Zanzibar: The rationale behind it. In Z. Desai, M. Qorro, & B. Brock-Utne (Eds.), *The role of language in teaching and learning science and mathematics: LOITASA phase two research* (pp. 127–151). Cape Town, South Africa: African Minds.

Babaci-Wilhite, Z., & Geo-JaJa, M. A. (2011). A critique and rethink of modern education in Africa's development in the 21st century. *Journal of the School of Education* (pp. 133–154). Dar es Salaam, Tanzania: University of Dar es Salaam.

Babaci-Wilhite, Z., Geo-JaJa, M. A., & Lou, S. (2012). Education and language: A human right for sustainable development in Africa. *International Review of Education, 5*. 619–647.

Barber, J. (2005). *The seeds of science/roots of reading inquiry framework*. Retrieved from http://scienceandliteracy.org/sites/scienceandliteracy.org/files/biblio/barber_inquirycycle_pdf_54088.pdf

Brock-Utne, B. (2002). Stories of the hunt—Who is writing them? In C. H. Odora (Ed.), *Indigenous knowledge and the integration of knowledge systems: Towards a philosophy of articulation* (pp. 237–257). Claremont, South Africa: New Africa Education.

Brock-Utne, B. (2005). The continued battle over Kiswahili as the language of instruction in Tanzania. In B. Brock-Utne & R. Hopson Kofi (Eds.), *Languages of instruction for African emancipation: Focus on postcolonial contexts and considerations* (pp. 51–87). Cape Town: CASAS and Dar es Salaam: Mkupi na Nyota. Also published by African Books Collective in Oxford. UK.

Cervetti, G. N., Barber, J., Dorph, R., Pearson, P. D., & Goldschmidt, P. G. (2012). The impact of an integrated approach to science and literacy in elementary school classrooms. *Journal of Research in Science Teaching, 49*(5), 631–659.

Cervetti, G. N., Pearson, P. D., Bravo, M. A., & Barber, J. (2005). *Reading and writing in the service of inquiry-based science*. Oakland, CA: Regents of the University of California.

Cervetti, G. N., Pearson, P. D., Barber, J., Hiebert, E. H., & Bravo, M. A. (2007). Integrating literacy and science the research we have, the research we need. In M. Pressley, A. K. Billman, K. Perry, K. Refitt & J. Reynolds (Eds.), Shaping literacy achievement (pp. 157–174). New York, NY: Guilford.

Crossley, M., & Watson, K. (2003). *Comparative and international research in education—Globalisation, context and difference*. London, UK: Routledge Falmer.

Freire, P. (1993). *Pedagogy of the oppressed*. London, UK: Penguin. (Original work published 1970)

Geo-JaJa, M. A., & Yang, X. (2003). Rethinking globalization in Africa. *Chimera. 1*(1), 19–28.

Geo-JaJa, M. A. (2011, May). *What Education of Classroom for Keeping Pace with 21st Century Inclusive Development in Africa?* Paper presented at Stave University of Zanzibar, Tanzania.

Goldenberg, C. (2008). Teaching English Language Learners, What the Research Does-and Does Not-Say. *American Educator, 32*(1), 8–22.

Hamm, B. (2001). A human rights approach to development. *Human Rights Quarterly, 23*(4), 1005. doi:10.1353/hrq.2001.0055

Ki-Zerbo, J. (1990). *Educate or perish: Africa impass and prospects.* Dakar, Senegal: BREDA with WCARO (UNESCO-UNICEF, Western Africa).

Mbaabu, I. (1996). *Language policy in East Africa.* Nairobi, Kenya: Educational Research and Publications (ERAP).

Nelson, P., & Dorsey, E. (2003). At the nexus of human rights and development: New methods and strategies of global NGOs. *World Development. 31*(12), 2013–2026. doi:10.1016/j.worlddev.2003.06.009

Nussbaum, M. (1998). Capabilities and human rights. *Fordham Law Review* 66(2). Retrieved from http://heinonline.org/HOL/Page?handle=hein.journals/flr66&div=18&g_sent=1&collection=journals

Nyerere, J. K. (1967). Education for self-reliance. In J. K. Nyerere (Ed.), *Essays on socialism* (pp. 44–75). Dar es Salaam, Tanzania: Oxford University Press. (Reprinted in 1968)

Othman, H. (2008, May). *Democracy and language in Tanzania.* Paper presented at the Conference on the Implications of Language for Peace and Development, Institute for Educational Research, University of Oslo, Norway.

Pearson, P. D. (2007). An endangered species act for literacy education. *Journal of Literacy Research, 39*(2), 145–162.

Pearson, P. D., & Hiebert, E. H. (2013). Understanding the common core state standards. In L. Morrow, T. Shanahan, & K. K. Wixson (Eds.), *Teaching with the common core standards for English language arts: What educators need to know* (Chapter 1: Grades PreK–2; Book 2: Grades 3–5) (pp. 1–21). New York, NY: Guilford Press.

Pearson, P. D., Moje, E., & Greenleaf, C. (2007). Literacy and science: Each in the service of the other. *Science, 328*(5977) 459–463.

Pearson, P. D., Moje, E., & Greenleaf, C. (2010). Literacy and science: each in the service of the other. *Science, 328,* 459–463.

Pew Internet & American Life Project. (2012, April). *The rise of e-reading*. Retrieved from http://libraries.pewinternet.org/2012/04/04/the-rise-of-e-reading/

Prah, K. K. (2005). Language of instruction for education, development and African emancipation. In B. Brock-Utne, & R. K. Hopson (Eds.), *Languages of instruction for African emancipation: Focus on postcolonial contexts and considerations* (pp. 23–87). Cape Town, South Africa: CASAS and Dar es Salaam, Tanzania: Mkuki na Nyota.

Qorro, M. A. S. (2004). Popularising Kiswahili as the language of instruction through the media in Tanzania. In B. Brock-Utne, Z. Desai, & M. Qorro (Eds.), *Researching the language of instruction in Tanzania and South Africa (LOITASA)* (pp. 93–116). Zanzibar, Tanzania: African Minds.

Robeyns, I. (2006). Three models of education rights: Rights, capabilities and human capital. *Theory and Research in Education, 4*(1), 69–84.

Samoff, J. (2003). Institutionalizing international influence. In R. F. Arnove & C. A. Torres (Eds.), *Comparative education: The dialectic of the global and the local* (pp. 52–91). Lanham, MD: Rowman & Littlefield. (Reprinted in 2007)

Semali, L., & Khanjan, M. (2012). Science education in Tanzania: Challenges and policy responses. *International Journal of Educational Research, 53*, 225–239.

Skutnabb-Kangas, T. (2000). *Linguistic Genocide in Education or Worldwide Diversity and Human Rights?* Mahwah, NJ: Lawrence Erlbaum Associates.

Tomasevski, K. (2003). *Education denied: Costs and remedies*. London, UK: Zed Books.

UNDP. (2006). *Human development report.* New York, NY: United Nations.

United Nations International Children's Emergency Fund (UNICEF). (2003). The state of the world's children 2004: Girls education and development. New York, NY: UNICEF.

United Nations. (1948). *The universal declaration on human rights*. Adopted by the General Assembly on 10 December 1948. Geneva: United Nations.

Wolff, H. (2006, March). *Optimizing learning and education in Africa—The language factor. A stock-taking research on mother tongue and bilingual education in sub-Saharan Africa*. Paper presented at the Association for the Development of Education in Africa (ADEA): UNESCO Institute for Education—Deutsche Gesellschaft für Technische Zusammenarbeit. ADEA 2006 Biennial Meeting, Libreville, Gabon.

Wortham, S., & Jackson, K. (2012). Relational eduction: Applying Gergen's work to educational research and practice. *Psychological Studies, 57*(2), 164–171.

CHAPTER 2

VIRTUAL REALITY, LEARNING SCENARIOS, AND TEACHING SCIENCE TO LEARNERS FROM OTHER CULTURES

Whose Reality?

Chris Fowler

ABSTRACT

This chapter proposes that technology can be used to design culturally sensitive and authentic science education, but not all technology is suitable or desirable. Virtual worlds (VWs), however, possess many of the technical affordances and learning benefits that could be used to enhance the teaching of science to learners from different cultures. VWs, by definition, reflect the cultures or subcultures of their designers. Consequently, when VWs are used to teach across cultures it will usually require some form of "border crossing" for the learners. In particular, the cultural gap between a learners' everyday world and the world of science can result in unauthentic and ineffective teaching and learning. The world of pedagogy, on the other hand, should mediate between the everyday world and the world of science. It performs

E-Learning and Social Media:
Education and Citizenship for the Digital 21st Century, pp. 21–42

a critical function of correctly aligning the worlds, and in doing so helps to prevent misconceptions and to identify and explore alternative explanations. How to design the pedagogical world is discussed both in theoretical and applied terms. The theoretical aspect is based on Mayes and Fowler's (1999) learning framework and its various enhancements (e.g., Fowler, 2014), and has a strong emphasis on incorporating pedagogical principles into the technical design of the VW. The applied aspects focus on the use of learning scenarios as the bridging mechanism between the worlds.

INTRODUCTION

Science is not value free and is viewed by many researchers (e.g., Baimba, Katterns, & Kirkwood, 1993) as a subculture of Western societies and may conflict with other cultures' conceptions of science. Some of these "other cultures" are not only non-Western, but are also part of the developing world. Education is one critical way of reducing the scientific and technological divide between the developed and developing world (MacLeod, 2005). Improved standards in science and technology are seen by many (e.g., Grossman & Helpman, 1994) as a necessary condition to encourage innovation, which in turn stimulates economic growth, a precursor for poverty reduction, and generally increases the well-being of the citizens in developing countries. The question arises: How best can this be achieved?.

This chapter proposes that authentic and culturally sensitive teaching and learning of science can be achieved through the use of technology. However, not all technology is suitable or available, and even suitable and available technology needs to be designed with the cultural needs of the learner in mind. Virtual worlds (VWs) offer one technological solution that might help improve the teaching of science in developing countries. This chapter will provide a conceptual framework that can inform pedagogical and technological design of VWs for science teaching based on an awareness and sensitivity to key cultural and social issues. However, this chapter does not attempt to report or discuss any empirical evidence that such designs actually benefit teaching and learning.

TEACHING SCIENCE TO LEARNERS FROM OTHER CULTURES

There is a considerable body of research (e.g., Cobern, 1996a) exploring and explaining why indigenous or non-Westernized children have problems learning Western science. The term indigenous normally refers to native or aboriginal people (e.g., Battiste, 2002; Snively & Corsiglia, 2001). However, in this chapter, indigenous refers to any social group or culture that possess their own complex technology, language, and social practices and is not restricted solely to aboriginal people.

There are many theories or approaches that attempt to address cultural differences in cognition and behavior ((see Cooper & Denner, 1998) for a succinct review). The older cognitive deficit theories (see McShane & Berry, 1988) of why indigenous people struggle to acquire Western concepts and perform poorly on Western tests have been replaced by more anthropological approaches with their greater emphasis on the socio-cultural context of teaching and learning. These approaches view science as a cultural activity (see Hammond & Brandt, 2004) that can be incongruent with the learners' own cultural perspective. A Western science perspective may not, therefore, fit well with a non-Western learner's world view (Aitkenhead, 1997, 2006). Anthropological approaches include world views (Cobern, 1993, 1996b), collateral learning (Jegede,1995), and border crossing (Maddock, 1981). However, as McKinley (2007) argues, one difficulty with the anthropological approach is that it asks the question "What makes teaching and learning effective for indigenous children?" but not "What makes an effective indigenous learner and teacher of science?" It is this latter question that this chapter will attempt to answer through exploring the use of VWs in teaching science to learners from other cultures.

Most of the above approaches can be thought of as 'gap' models. In the cognitive deficit approach, a quantitative gap is proposed between Western and non-Western thinking, and by "filling" the gap, for example through education, the deficit can be reduced. The anthropological approaches are more qualitative, and thus have a greater emphasis on negotiation or bridge building to cross the gaps between two qualitatively different perspectives. The emphasis is on adapting or making sense of the two (or more) co-existing worldviews.

Sutherland and Swayze (2012) identify four key areas of conflict or potential gaps. First, there is the learning environment itself, where there is a gap between the place of everyday (informal) learning and (formal) learning in the classroom. The creation of culturally relevant learning environments can result in better student engagement (Nelson-Barber & Estrin, 1995). Second, there can be a gap between objects familiar to the learners in the everyday world, with those less familiar ones used in science textbooks or the science classroom. The use of culturally relevant material has been shown to improve the performance and motivation of Aboriginal children learning science (Atkinhead, 1997; Brayboy & Castagno, 2008). Thirdly, it is recognized that there is a strong relationship between language and reality. If the language of science differs markedly from the language of the everyday world, then misconceptions can arise. The fourth area is less obvious, and is about self-identity. This concerns the students' view of the kind of person they need to be to effectively engage in scientific activities. As Brown, Reveles, and Kelly (2004), and others note, many students do not feel comfortable about taking on the identity of being a scientist. These four areas arguably describe the learner's "sense of place," and this is a key concept for all learners, but more particularly for the indigenous learner (Chinn, 2007).

It is not only learning that takes place within a socio-cultural context, but also teaching, curriculum design, and with the increasing use of sophisticated learning technologies, the design of learning systems. Curricula and systems are created by people, to be taught and learnt from by people, and these people exist "within temporal, political, economic and cultural contexts" (Ornstein & Hunkins, 2004, p. 62). Designers of learning systems are therefore in danger of introducing their own cultural biases when making their design decisions. In this sense, designers are not unlike teachers and need to be sensitive and responsive to the cultural effects that their design decisions have on their users (see also Villegas & Lucas, 2002).

One consequence of designers not being fully aware of their own cultural bias comes from the tendency to emulate familiar, non-technological practices in the design of computerised learning systems. A seemingly trivial but notable example of emulation comes from the development of the early versions of smart boards. These were, in essence, sophisticated blackboards, and although they may be more efficient and effective than the originals, they are still mainly used to emulate a "chalk and talk" pedagogical approach. In these design situations, the designer is not only been constrained by the technology but also by the pedagogy, and both are socio-cultural in nature. System designers therefore also have to cross the border of technical to pedagogical design. This chapter will also try to address how learning designers can successfully cross this border.

THE WORLD OF PEDAGOGY

Teaching and learning is the essential bridge between the learner's everyday world and, in this case, the conventional world of science. Building this bridge is what good (science) teachers have done for generations. The teacher, therefore, plays a critical role in the process of enculturation (see Contreras & Lee, 1990; Hawkins & Peas, 1987) that will allow the learner to smoothly and successfully cross the cultural border between their everyday world and the world of science. Aitkenhead (1996, 1997) in developing Costa's (1995) observations of how successful learners were moving from their family subculture to the one found in the science classroom, describes four types of border crossing: smooth, managed, hazardous, and impossible.

A smooth border crossing will occur when there is strong overlap or congruence between the two world views. However, for the majority of students the transition is not a smooth one. The larger the difference between the worlds, the more hazardous the crossing becomes. If the difference is small, the crossing can be managed and the learner appears to have assimilated the scientific knowledge. They can "play the game" in terms of achieving social goals like talking knowledgeably to their science teacher or passing examinations, even though they see this scientific knowledge as irrelevant or contradictory to their everyday experiences. Where the two worlds or subcultures become more divergent, the crossing becomes more hazardous. The crossing is hazardous because, although the learner is often motivated to do well, they often lack the academic wherewithal to make the transition. Finally, when the worlds are discordant, the learner can see no relevance or benefit in crossing or attempting to cross the border. The crossing appears to be impossible.

Jegede (1995) extended the notion of border crossing to include the cognitive experience in his theory of collateral learning. Border crossing will often be required when two or more contrasting constructs exist simultaneously in the individual's long term memory. The interaction and resolution of the conflicting constructs can, Jegede argues, result in four types of collateral learning: parallel, simultaneous, dependent, and secured. In parallel collateral learning there is no interaction between the constructs—they remain distinct and thus make border crossing impossible. The other extreme occurs when the constructs interact and resolutions are found. A person is able to find reasons to hold both constructs, or one construct begins to assimilate the other, and new constructs emerge. This cognitive process is called secured collateral learning and makes for a smooth border crossing. Dependent and simultaneous collateral learning lie between parallel and secured. In dependent collateral learning, the learner is able to modify one of the constructs without radically changing the other, while simultaneous collateral learning involves learning a concept by using two or more worldviews at the same time. Similarities and differences derived from the different world views are used in the learning of the new concept. Both dependent and simultaneous collateral learning can be associated with managed and hazardous border crossing (Jegede & Aikenhead, 1999).

With respect to the teacher, Jegede and Aitkenhead (1999) built upon Stairs' (1995) notion of the "teacher as a culture broker." In this conception, the teacher is like a tourist guide taking the students to places of interests (scientific concepts and facts), explaining what to look for, and how it relates to their everyday life. In other words, a key role of the teacher is to bring about this alignment. There are many examples in the literature of different teaching and learning strategies that may help border crossing (e.g. Solomon, 1992, Snively,1995, Somerville & Perkins, 2003, and Riggs, 2005). These strategies can be distilled to some very basic principles:

1. Content and resources must be familiar and meaningful.
2. Curricula must be appropriate and sensitive to cultural identity.
3. Communications should use culturally familiar terms and meanings that encourage dialogue and reflection.
4. Constructional tasks and problem solving activities should have relevance in everyday world.
5. Context or place of learning is culturally acceptable and motivating.

These five "C's" should ensure that the design of any learning and teaching experience is authentic, inquiry led, and enjoyable.

In the teaching and learning of science, there are, therefore, three worldviews that need to be considered. In addition to the world of science and the everyday world of the learner, there is also the pedagogical world which is mainly the domain of the teacher. The pedagogical world mediates the world of science and the everyday world. Effective teaching and learning are only likely to occur if these three worlds are correctly aligned (cf. Biggs, 2003). A key role of the teacher is to bring this alignment about. Where misalignments exist, conceptual change will be more difficult and misconceptions are likely to arise. In these situations, the teacher needs to help the learners "accommodate" the new concepts perhaps by reorganizing or replacing their central concepts (cf. Posner, Strike, Hewson, & Gertzoy, 1982).

The problem becomes more complex if it is assumed that there are multiple versions of each world: the everyday, scientific, and pedagogical worlds. For example, within the world of science, different or alternative explanations can co-exist (e.g., Newtonian, Einsteinian, and Quantum physics); and within one classroom there can be many ethnic and social groups each with their own distinctive culture or subculture. Likewise, teachers can differ in their overall philosophy or approach (e.g., instructional or constructional) to their teaching. Multiple versions *within* a world provide alternative conceptions, not misconceptions. Misconception will arise if misalignments occur *between* the different versions of the three worlds (see Figure 2.1). Most, but not all, misconceptions reside with the learners, but teachers too can hold such misconceptions (e.g., Sheehan, Childs, & Hayes, 2011). A misconception may arise from, for example, drawing the wrong "scientific" conclusions from everyday observations, confusions in the use of linguistic terms which have different meanings in their respective worlds, or the use of inappropriate metaphors. Teachers and other respected members of the community can too be a source of misconceptions (see Table 2.1 for some Western examples).

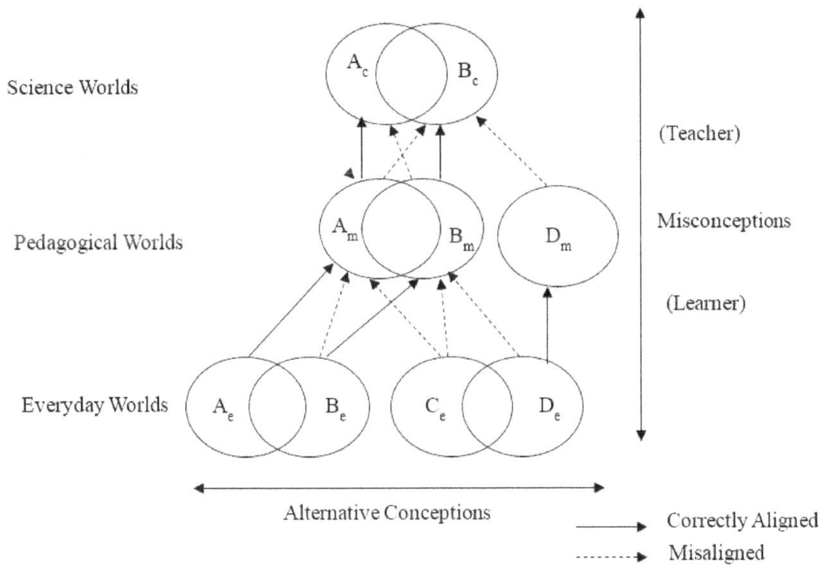

Figure 2.1. Aligning the worlds.

Table 2.1. Misalignments Between Worlds: Some Western Examples

Categories of Misalignments	*Description*	*Misconception Examples*
Metaphorical	Metaphors and models from everyday life used inappropriately to explain scientific concepts.	Electrons circle atoms like planets circle the sun (e.g., Bohr's model—displaced by quantum mechanics).
Social	Respected actors in the learner's life (e.g., teachers, parents, peers) communicate scientific misconceptions.	Teachers and parents confusing respiration with breathing. (One is about inhaling oxygen and exhaling carbon dioxide, the other the metabolic process of turning oxygen into energy.)
Linguistic	Where the language in everyday use causes the confusion.	Mass and weight are used interchangeably. (Mass is about the amount of matter contained by an object, weight is measure of the force of gravity on the object.)
Observational	The wrong scientific conclusion is drawn from the real world observation.	Lighter objects have more buoyancy (but heavy metal objects can float).

Within this multi-world description, the role of the science teacher becomes even more complex. "Knowing your student," that old adage, not only means knowing what they know so the appropriate version of the science world can be chosen, but also knowing the student's everyday world, so that the scientific world can be taught in an authentic way that matches and meets the cultural needs of the learner. This matching includes the use of appropriate resources and language. Knowing the student also means providing support and help in them forming an appropriate self-identity. Failure to take these factors into account is likely to result in misalignments and a subsequent failure to learn effectively, or, make a border crossing a hazardous or impossible one. Knowledge of what students know, who students are, and their cultural background is a necessary but not sufficient condition for effective teaching and learning. There are a multitude of other factors like personality, motivation, or learning styles, that can affect teaching and learning, but they cannot be dealt with in this chapter.

How the teacher deals with this complex variety of interacting factors is challenging. Effective teachers intrinsically appreciate these issues and attempt to adopt strategies to overcome them (see, e.g., Killen, 2002, on teaching strategies for outcome-based education). A question arises as to whether or not technology can help create a more effective pedagogy to help learners meet their learning outcomes. Over 25 years ago, Hawkins and Peas (1987) were one of the first to recognize that technology could provide a bridge between the learner's everyday life and the world of science. In the late eighties, the technology available was limited; the World Wide Web was in its infancy, computers were slow and expensive, and software was still unfriendly. Since then the technology has developed, particularly in the use of virtual reality, but is the gap between the world of science and the everyday world being bridged?

DESIGNING VIRTUAL WORLDS

A VW is a computer simulated environment that has eight defining characteristics:

1. The illusion of being in three dimensions (3-D).
2. Persistent—it is still there even when the user leaves the VW.
3. It happens in real time.
4. It is multi-user (often massive numbers of users).
5. The user has a representation (avatar) in the VW.
6. The experience can be highly interactive (e.g., touching, flying, creating, etc.).

7. It is a social environment where users can communicate with each other (originally using real time text but increasingly now using speech).
8. The rules are loosely based on "reality'" (unlike games like World of Warcraft where rules are based on "fantasy").

The most commonly used VWs, like Second Life (see Figure 2.2), are delivered on a personal computer and therefore cannot be fully immersive (unlike those found in multi-projected cave automatic virtual environments, or a CAVE). Immersion is a technological description of properties that arise from an interaction of representational fidelity and learner interaction (Dalgarno & Lee, 2010), and can result in users experiencing a psychological state of "being there" or presence (psychological immersion). Both fully and semi-immersive systems can induce a sense of presence, but this chapter will focus on only the semi-immersive and desktop based VW.

Figure 2.2. An example of a learning environment in Second Life.

At first sight, VWs appear to address Sutherland and Swayze's (2012) four areas of concern (that is the learning environment, object familiarity, the use of language, and self-identity). The VWs are worlds albeit artificial ones, and therefore can be designed or crafted to produce a valid learning environment. In contrast, most learning management systems (LMS, e.g., Blackboard Collaborate or Moodle), which are currently the most commonly used virtual learning environments, bear very little resemblance to the everyday world. They are persistent and can have multi-users, but they not very interactive (pointing and clicking only). Users have limited representation, social aspects are limited to "chat rooms" which are often not in real time, and communications are mostly text based. Basically LMS's are impoverished learning environments when compared to the potential of a well-designed VW.

With respect to Sutherland and Swayze's (2012) second and third concerns regarding the use of culturally relevant materials and language, both LMS and VWs can accommodate this requirement. However, the LMS is constrained to mainly curriculum content, and this is often poorly localised (see, e.g., Luk-Fong, 2005) to meet the indigenous learner's needs. In contrast, the VW contains both educational and non-educational content that create a more culturally familiar learning context. This combination is important if, as Brown, Collins, and Duguid (1989) argue, learning is contextually situated. The use of the pedagogical world to help decontextualize learning, thus enabling the transfer of skills and knowledge from one context to another, is an important pedagogical function that is difficult to achieve in the traditional LMS.

Finally, Sutherland and Swayze (2012) argue for the importance of self-identity in learning science. There are no avatars in a LMS, although users can choose their own names and use photographs or images to represent themselves, so people are restricted in the ways they can express their individuality and identity. This compares unfavorably to the VW where, like in the real world, the learner through a customized avatar can use a rich range of visual cues (e.g., how they look and dress) that can project roles or other socially relevant information about who they are and who they want to be.

VWs, of all the possible virtual learning environments, therefore, arguably offer the greatest opportunities to build an effective world of teaching and learning. However, although educational VWs do exist (see Patrick, 2008; Erard, 2007), most emulate the existing physical characteristics and teaching practices found in our schools and universities. In some situations, the pedagogical VW should resemble the physical world (e.g., a virtual laboratory), but at other times the pedagogy demands more innovative processes and procedures that may not directly resemble something that can be experienced in the real world (e.g. interacting with a virtual molecule).

When designing a virtual world, the designer needs to take into account both what the technology is capable of doing and what the user requires or needs from that technology to learn effectively. System designers, therefore, separate out what users need from the design of the technology to meet those needs or requirements. The former, user needs, should be technology independent. Clearly, the closer the technology comes to meeting the needs, the greater the utility of the design. The word "utility" is purposively chosen, because technically meeting user needs does not always result in "usable" solutions. A good design should result in both a valued and usable system. However, usability is not being directly addressed in this chapter.

Dalgarno and Lee (2010) suggest five technical affordances offered by VWs that can benefit learning. The five affordances and their benefits are:

1. Spatial knowledge representation that results from the ability to move freely around the VW, experience objects from multiple perspectives and be able to touch, move or generally manipulate objects in the VW.
2. Experiential learning in circumstances not normally possible in the real world. This may be because of health or safety reasons (e.g., being able to "handle" radioactive materials in a VW laboratory) or for reasons of expense or accessibility (e.g., a virtual proton collider). These types of VWs often take the form of simulations or micro-worlds (see Reiber, 1992).
3. Engagement resulting from the intrinsic levels of motivation that can result from the freedom of choice and personal control that exists within VWs.
4. Transfer of knowledge and skills that can result in the close correspondence between actions and events taking place in a VW with those that take place in the real world. The learning context or situation is therefore very similar in both worlds, and this can facilitate the transfer of skills and knowledge (see Brown, Collins, & Duguid, 1989).
5. Collaborative learning that can result from the highly social nature of the VWs as a result of their support of multi-users. According to social constructivist views of learning, conversation and discourse are the cornerstones of collaboration and social negotiation in learning (see Jonassen, 1999; Lave & Wenger, 1991; Vygotsky, 1978).

Fowler (2014) argues that the Dalgarno and Lee (2010) model needs to be extended to include user requirements or more specifically pedagogical requirements. This chapter will describe just enough of Fowler's extended model to enable the reader to understand how the concept of learning scenarios can be used to ensure that authentic or culturally sensitive learning takes place in the pedagogical world. A complete description of the extended model can be found in Fowler (2014).

Fowler adopts Mayes & Fowler's (1999) three learning stages as a starting point. Each of Mayes and Fowler's stages, namely conceptualisation, construction, and dialogue, have certain pedagogical requirements or affordances associated with them. The first stage, conceptualization, is when the learner first comes into contact and initially explores new concepts. Learning at this stage is likely to improve through providing multiple representations of the concept and through the use of metaphors, thus enriching the options available to the student for grasping the concept being presented. In a traditional University, for example, the lecture was the place for conceptualization.

The second stage is more concerned with activity. It adopts the constructivist approach that learning can improve from the "doing." The emphasis moves away from the representation of the concept to the actions that can be carried out on the concepts. These actions are, for example, the tasks or activities traditionally found in a science laboratory or a field study.

The final stage, dialogue, is where the learners can further test their understanding through engaging in debates and discussion with their peers and others. This stage recognizes the social nature of learning, and that new concepts may emerge and the cycle repeats itself. Traditionally, this kind of dialogue took place in tutorials.

Each of these learning stages can be thought of as needing teaching and learning "spaces" within the VW, and each one would have its own pedagogical and design constraints. For example, in the conceptualization space, users need to be able to present concepts, preferably using multi media. Conceptualization is also about exploring the concept more fully. Here the ability to use multiple representations of the same object is an important attribute of the VW. For example, in understanding how matter (e.g., water) can exist in different states (e.g., solid, liquid, or gas) and what causes the states to change (e.g., temperature) can easily be simulated in a VW. A more interactive version could even allow students to manipulate atoms to create new molecules, and visualize the energy changes that result from making and breaking molecules.

At the construction stage the emphasis is more on doing, and it requires a much greater degree of realism. The correspondence between the actions in the VW and the everyday or real world should be as close as possible (behavioral realism, see Fowler (2014)). This requires models of the real world where most, if not all, of the main parameters are incorporated. For example, the model could be of a weather system, where parameters like temperature, air pressure, land typography, and so forth, could be used to model likely rainfall. The simulations used in the conceptualization stage tend to be fixed, abstract, and controlled by the teacher, whereas the modelling in the construction stage is much more dynamic, concrete, and controlled by the learner.

The dialogue stage assumes a certain degree of expertise, so that the learner can engage in meaningful debate and discussion about their understanding of concepts. To be effective, the dialogue needs to flow, so it should be in real time. It also needs to be spontaneous so vocal, rather than text-based, dialogue is preferred. Emotion and passion can also be important, and the use of avatars can help communicate these and other important non-verbal cues. Although this called the dialogue stage, it is not the only stage where dialogue will take place. Fowler and Mayes (1997) point out that the different types of dialogue take place at each stage. For example, at the conceptualization stage dialogues seeking clarification or confirmation of understanding are expected and encouraged, and at the construction stage dialogues of co-operation and collaboration are needed.

In a formal learning context it is important to recognise the role of intended learning outcomes (what the learner needs to achieve) and actual learning outcomes (what the learner actually achieves). Mayes and Fowler's learning stages form part of the transformational process to move from intended to actual learning outcomes. However, the question of how a teacher can make this process more culturally sensitive, and thus more effective, is not addressed by these learning stages. As already noted, there is increasing literature on the importance of developing and using indigenous resources in the design of learning. McLoughlin and Oliver (2000), for example, stress that resources should be selected that reflect the multi-cultural nature of societies, the cultural diversity in the way people learn, and promote equity in learning outcomes. They pose a number of questions (e.g., "What kind of learning environment is most familiar to the students?") that designers need to consider, but provide very little information about how the responses can, in practice, be incorporated into the learning design.

THE ROLE OF LEARNING SCENARIOS

One possible mechanism for the incorporation of indigenous resources into the design solution for VWs is through the use of learning scenarios. A learning scenario is a description of learning that has taken place (i.e., in the everyday world), should take place (i.e., in the world of science), or will help it take place (i.e., in the pedagogical world). They can be records of "natural" pre-existing behaviors, newly created exemplary behaviors, or sets of authentic tasks or activities that can be enacted by learners. The assumption is that scenarios based closely on the learner's everyday world will be more culturally sensitive, and therefore result in more effective learning

The type of learning scenario constructed will arguably be different according to the student's learning stage. For instance, at the conceptualization stage, the learner requires scenarios that help explain and explore the scientific concept being discussed. These scenarios should draw upon the student's everyday experiences as their starting point, drawing out similarities and differences in how the concept is perceived in the world of science compared to the everyday world (see, e.g., Rogoff, 2003). Such scenarios could be constructed by the teacher, and thus the teacher must be aware of the everyday world experienced by the learner. However, such scenarios could also be created by the learners, or co-constructed by the learner and teacher. Indeed, by beginning the conceptualization stage by asking students to create their own scenarios of the scientific concepts operating in their everyday world would provide the teacher with information about the learner's culturally familiar items and whether significant misconceptions or alternative conceptions pre-exist. This could be the teacher's starting point for crossing the border between traditional and scientific explanations.

At the construction stage, the emphasis is on activities or tasks, and the teacher could start with scenarios drawn from the use of indigenous technologies, cooking or making wine at home, for example (see George, 1988). For instance, the student could be asked to write a scenario where a particular chemical reaction could be demonstrated using both local sources of the chemical and/or indigenous technologies. The students could then be expected to enact in the VW both the indigenous and more Western scenarios, and reflect on similarities and differences.

Learners at the dialogue stage have normally mastered the concept and are able to engage in meaningful dialogues concerning the extension and generalization of the concepts, and indeed new concepts may emerge at this stage. One interesting activity at this stage may be to get the learners to reflect and discuss the change in use of language as learning progressed through the other stages. The use of the vernacular should diminish, and the language used should become more "scientific." Their own discussions can also can be recorded and compared to the indigenous or everyday dialogues previously used, and be 'reused' to create learning resources for new students. The scenarios in this case are descriptions of learning that have already taken place.

Scenarios can and should also be used for assessment. This not only refers to the scenarios created by the learners, but also recording and assessing teacher created scenarios that are enacted in the VW. As noted earlier, the enacted scenarios are particularly important at the construction stage of learning.

The use of learning scenarios in VWs assumes that certain tools are available and can be easily used by both teachers and learners. First, there is a need for tools for learners and teachers to easily create or modify content within the VW. The creation of appropriate open source warehouses (e.g., http://openwonderland.org/) containing modules or objects that can be shared and downloaded by users for creating or extending their own VWs is becoming more commonplace. However, it is important that future warehouses contain culturally authentic virtual objects with appropriate metadata to assist their selection. If culturally authentic objects are available to learners, then this would also encourage students to compare and discuss objects chosen or constructed to represent defining characteristics of their everyday worlds. Such discussions around essentially the same scenario but populated with different objects drawn from different cultures could also assist learners in understanding the basis for cultural differences, and reduce prejudice.

Second, there is a need for tools that can record and replay scenes with the VW. Such tools are necessary for encouraging reflection where learners are able to comment or annotate different scenes within a scenario. Recording devices are also important for capturing behaviors for assessment purposes.

There are a number of propriety tools (e.g., Unity-3D) that are used to create high-quality commercial VWs for applications such as games or engineering design but these can be expensive, and are mainly designed to support single user simulations. Nevertheless, they are favored by some researchers with a notable example being Pena-Rios's (2013) blended-reality tool which acts as a virtual laboratory for science and engineering students. The tool allows groups of VW users to collaborate around the construction of embedded-computing products, such as robots. Open source tools provide a lower cost entry point for would-be VW developers, a popular examples being OpenSim (see http://opensimulator.org), RealXtend (see http://realxtend.org) and Meshmoon (http://www.meshmoon.com). However, the development of VWs using these open source tools still require a level of expertise that most teachers and learners are unlikely to possess.

PUTTING IT INTO PRACTICE

When considering using VWs in teaching, a number of issues need to be considered. First there is the question of the kind of learning experience being offered to the students. The key dimension here is the proposed amount of teacher-student contact. In distance learning, the teacher is physically separated from the learner, and in its purist form no face-to-face contact will take place. The ability of VWs to give a strong sense of place and presence, plus the high levels of interactivity make them ideal for distance learning. At the other end of the continuum, most teaching (though not necessarily all learning) takes place in the classroom or face-to-face. Technology generally, and VWs specifically, can be used, but they do not replace face-to-face teaching, but supplement it. Finally, there is the option of blended learning where, in its strongest form, some, but not all of the face-to-face teaching is replaced by technology. In practice this means selected, but not all, face-to-face classes are replaced by online sessions.

Clearly there are many things that need to be considered in deciding what teaching and learning can be replaced and with what technology. For example, in the 1980s the U.K. Open University (OU) used technology (mainly CDs and paper) as the platform for delivering "conceptual" material (e.g., mailing out text books, books of readings, etc.). However, at that time there was very little available and affordable technology to support the construction stage of learning, and in many of the science subjects students had to attend summer schools to undertake their practical work. Similarly, technology was not used initially for the dialogue stage of learning, and this was carried out face-face through tutorials arranged to take place in or near the student's locality (e.g., their local University). Indeed many of the distance learning models being used in developing countries still follow the old UK OU format mainly because of the cost and lack of availability of the appropriate technology (see, e.g., the experiences of the Institute of Distance Learning at the University of Swaziland—Fowler, Vilakati, & Sukati, 2013; and Sukati, 2010).

The OU example above also illustrates that the choice of what technology to use or how it will be used will vary according to Mayes and Fowler's three learning stages (conceptualization, construction, and dialogue). For instance, Barnhardt and Kawagley (2005) describe the fishing practices of native Alaskans and how their knowledge can be used in the teaching of science. The native Alaskan is using observational skills passed down through the generations to choose an optimum spot or eddy to place their fishing nets in the river. The choice involves understanding the river currents, the state of the river (particularly upstream), the amount of traffic (passing boats and people), other conditions that may impact the path the fish take, and the security of the fishing net. All this indigenous knowledge can be the starting point for introducing and exploring Western scientific concepts like, for example, elementary fluid mechanics. VWs are particularly good for recording and sharing knowledge. This could achieved through, for example, learners' filming the fishing process, writing a narrative illustrated with still pictures, or a voice recording describing the activity. All of these learning scenarios could be digitised and made available as resources in the conceptualization space.

In another example, George (1995) observed that some people from Trinidad and Tobago believe that the regulation of body heat is an important factor in healthy living. Changes, particularly excessive body heat, can result in various ailments. Herbert (2008) used these traditional beliefs as the basis for exploring more conventional (i.e., Western) scientific concepts. She asked learners how they would explain "catching a cold" or "adolescents suffering from pimples" using the heated body principle. The everyday explanation was that colds were caught as the result of sudden and unexpected changes in body temperature, like bathing in a cold river after being out in the sun. Adolescents were thought to suffer from excess heat as part of the process of growing up, and when combined with dirt on the skin, pimples would result. In this situation a VW could be used to provide an interactive forum involving avatars where these explanations could be discussed and inconsistencies or new facts can be raised or introduced by the teacher, until the students realize the limitations of their everyday explanatory system and the need to take on new concepts (e.g., germ and virus). The exploration of these emerging abstract new concepts would particularly benefit from the use of a VW.

Finally there may be examples of where a VW is created not only to teach and learn about science, but also to engage the students in debates about wider issues. These issues could include questions of ethics, or morality of undertaking certain actions, or the societal and/or environmental impact of certain interventions. The most powerful examples are found in the social or applied sciences rather than the traditional physical or natural sciences. For example, in the social sciences, the ability to customize avatars allows for the possibility of creating an avatar of a different sex, age, or religion from its creator, allows one to observe the reactions of others to their avatar in the VW (e.g., Diehl & Prins, 2008; Eastwick & Gardner, 2009; and Peck, Seinfeld, Aglioto, & Slater, 2013). In the applied science there are opportunities of building VWs to simulate planned interventions, such as the building of a dam. Such simulations could run within the virtual world, and participants would be encouraged to discuss and explore not only the engineering and scientific principles, but also the effects of changing different parameters on, for example, soil erosion, or climatic changes, or explore their impact on the attitudes and beliefs of critical stakeholders.

SUMMARY AND CONCLUSIONS

Increasing globalization and the massification of education has both advantages and disadvantages, particularly for people from the developing world. On the plus side the economic growth that is likely to result will alleviate poverty and improve health. On the negative side, these rich and diverse cultures and subcultures could become subsumed or harmonized by Western based attitudes, beliefs, and practices. The balancing trick is to find ways where education, in particular, can build upon traditional beliefs and concepts to illustrate more conventional science without replacing the traditional system. The two systems can coexist as alternative explanatory systems. VWs, if properly designed, offer an educational platform that can allow and exploit the coexistence of more than one reality—"ours" and "theirs," The current VW technology, however, requires relatively high end personal computers, servers, and reliable broadband infrastructure. This may not be available or affordable in some parts of the developed world and in many developing countries.

The use of VWs to encourage learners to debate wider social and moral issues should not be underestimated. This use of VW has the additional benefit of encouraging "good" citizenship through the learners participating in key debates, appreciating and tolerating other people's views, and respecting other people's property and the environment in general.

The effectiveness of VWs for teaching and learning is still largely untested. The next step should be to design a science curriculum for a mixed cultural group that can be implemented in a VW. Such future work would not only demonstrate whether real learning benefits result, but also would strengthen the methodology that teachers need for effective implementation and teaching with VW technology. Further, such work needs to more fully explore the financial costs and benefits of adopting a VW approach en masse, particularly for a developing country. In this respect it is important to note that any such methodology is basically a pedagogical one that can define the learning and teaching requirements without necessarily specifying any particular technical solution. Indeed, the developing world may not be able to afford the significant costs of building and servicing a broadband infrastructure to support the use of VWs, and therefore look for cheaper but pedagogically effective indigenous solutions to meet their educational needs. Therefore the 'West is best' mantra needs careful consideration when thinking about the educational needs of developing countries or even subcultures within Western societies. On the other hand, VWs, when and if they become affordable and available, offer the possibility of more than reality (or culture) co-existing within the same learning context. "Whose reality" in a VW should therefore no longer be a question of "ours" or "theirs" but the need for both to enhance teaching and learning.

ACKNOWLEDGMENTS

I would like to thank Orlena Broomes, Michael Gardner, and Vic Callaghan for their insightful comments on early drafts of the chapter.

REFERENCES

Aitkenhead, G. S. (1996). Science education: Border crossing into the subculture of science. *Studies in Science education, 27,* 1–52.

Aitkenhead, G. S. (1997). Toward a First Nations cross-cultural science and technology curriculum. *Science Education, 81*, 217–238.

Aitkenhead, G. S. (2006). *Science education for everyday life: Evidence-based practice*. New York, NY: Teacher College Press.

Baimba, A., Katterns, R., & Kirkwood, V. (1993). Innovation in the science curriculum : A Sierra Leone case study. *International Journal of Science Education, 36*, 269–287.

Barnhardt, R., & Kawagley, A. O. (2005). Indigenous knowledge systems and the Alaskan Native ways of knowing. *Anthropology & Education Quarterly, 36*, 8–23.

Battiste, M. (2002). *Indigenous knowledge and pedagogy in First Nations Education: A literature review with recommendations.* Ottawa, Ontario, Canada: Indian and Northern Affairs.

Biggs, J. B. (2003). *Teaching for quality learning at university.* Buckingham: The Open University Press.

Brayboy, B. M. J., & Castagno, A. E. (2008). How might Native science inform "informal science learning"? *Cultural Studies of Science Education, 3*, 731–750.

Brown, J. S., Collins, A., & Duguid, S. (1989). Situated cognition and the culture of learning. *Educational Researcher, 18*(1), 32–42.

Brown, B. A., Reveles, J. M., & Kelly, G. J. (2004). Scientific literacy and discursive identity: A theoretical framework for understanding science learning. *Science Education, 89*, 779–802

Chinn, P. W. U. (2007). Decolonizing methodologies and indigenous knowledge: The role of culture, place and personal experience in professional development. *Journal of Research in Science Teaching, 44*, 1247–1268.

Cobern, W. W. (1993). Construction of knowledge and group learning. In K. Tobin (Ed.), *The practice of constructivism in science education* (pp. 51–70). Hillsdale: Lawrence Erlbaum Associates.

Cobern, W. W. (1996a). Constructivism and non-Western science education research. *International Journal of Science Education,4*, 287–302.

Cobern, W. W. (1996b). Worldview theory and conceptual change in science education. *Science Education, 80*, 579–610.

Contreras, A., & Lee, O. (1990) Differential treatment of students by middle school science teachers: Unintended cultural bias. *Science Education, 74*, 433–444.

Cooper, C. R., & Denner, J. (1998). Theories linking culture and psychology: Universal and community-specific processes. *Annual Review of Psychology, 49*, 559–584.

Costa, V. B. (1995). When science is "another world": Relationships between worlds of family, friends, school and science. *Science Education, 79*, 313–333.

Dalgarno, B., & Lee, M. (2010). What are the learning affordances of 3-D virtual environments? *British Journal of Educational Technology, 41*, 10–32.

Diehl, W. C., & Prins, E. (2008). Unintended outcomes in Second Life: Intercultural literacy and Cultural Identity in a virtual world. *Language and intercultural Communications, 8*, 101–118.,

Eastwick, P. W., & Gardner, W. L. (2009). Is it a game? Evidence for social influence in the virtual world. *Social Influence, 4*, 18–32.

Erard, M. (2007). A Boon to Second Life Language Schools. MIT Tedchnology Review. Retrieved from http://www.technologyreview.com/news/407667/a-boon-to-second-life-language-schools/

Fowler, C. (2014). Virtual reality and learning: Where is the pedagogy?. *British Journal of Educational Technology*. doi:10.1111/bjet.12135

Fowler, C. J. H., & Mayes, J. T. (1997). Applying Telepresence to Education. *BT Technology Journal, 15,* 189–196.

Fowler, C. J. H., Vilakati, N., & Sukati, C. W. (2013). From Distance Learning to e-Learning: Experiences and Challenges from the University of Swaziland. In C. I. O. Okeke & C. B. S. Mndebele (Eds.). *Education reforms in the SADC Region*. Rosemead, CA: SAP.

George, J. (1988). The role of native technology in science education in developing countries: A Caribbean perspective. *School Science Review, 69,* 815–820.

George, J. (1995). Health education challenges in a rural context: A case study. *Studies in Science Education, 25,* 239–262

Grossman, G. M., & Helpman, E. (1994). Endogenous innovation in the theory of growth. *The Journal of Economic Perspectives, 8,* 23–44.

Hammond, L., & Brandt, C. (2004) Science and cultural process: Defining an anthropological approach to science education. *Studies in Science Education, 40,* 1–47.

Hawkins, J & Peas, R. D. (1987). Tools for bridging the cultures of everyday and scientific thinking. *Journal of Research in Science Teaching, 24,* 291–307,

Herbert, S. (2008). Collateral learning in science: Students' responses to a cross-cultural unit of work. *International Journal of Science Education, 30,* 979–993

Jegede, O. J. (1995). Collateral learning and the eco-cultural paradigm in science and mathematics education in Africa. *Studies in Science Education, 25,* 97–137

Jegede, O. J., & Aikenhead, G. S. (1999). Transcending cultural borders : Implications for science teaching. *Research in Science and Technology Education, 17,* 45–67.

Jezewski, M. A., & Sotnik, P. (2001*). Cultural brokering: Providing culturally competent rehabilitation services to foreign-born persons.* Buffalo, NY: Center for International Rehabilitation Research Information & Exchange.

Jonassen, D. (1999). Designing constructivist learning environments. In C. M. Reigeluth (Ed.). *Instructional design theories and models: A new paradigm of instructional theory* (Vol. 2, pp. 371–396). Mahwah, NJ: Lawrence Erlbaum Associates.

Killen, R. (2007). *Teaching strategies for outcomes-based education*. South Africa: Juta and Company.

Lave, J., & Wenger, E. (1991). *Situated learning: Legitimate peripheral participation.* Cambridge, UK: Cambridge University Press.

Luk-Fong, P. Y. Y. (2005). Globalisation and localisation enmeshed: Towards a framework for the development of guidance curriculum in Hong Kong. *Globalisation, Societies and Education, 3,* 83–100.

MacLeod, H. (2005). What role can educational multimedia play in narrowing the digital divide? *International Journal of Education and Development using Information and Communication Technology, 1,* 42–53.

Maddock, M. N. (1981). Science Education: An anthropological viewpoint. *Studies in Science Education, 8*, 1–26.

Mayes, J. T., & Fowler, C. J. H. (1999). Learning Technologies and Usability: a Framework for Understanding Courseware. *Interacting with Computers, 11*, 485–497.

McLoughlin, C., & Oliver, R. (2000). Designing learning environments for cultural inclusivity: A case study of indigenous online learning at tertiary level. *Australian Journal of Educational Technology, 16,* 58–72

McKinley, E. (2007). Post colonialism, Indigenous students and Science Education. In S. K. Abel & N. G. Lederman (Eds.), *Handbook of Research on science education* (pp 199–227). Mahwah, NJ: Lawrence Erlbaum Associates.

McShane, D., & Berry, J. W. (1988). Native North Americans: Indian and Inuit abilities. In S. H. Irvine & J. W. Berry (Eds.), *Human abilities in cultural context* (pp. 385–426). Cambridge, UK: Cambridge University Press.

Nelson-Barber, S., & Estrin, E. T.(1995). *Culturally responsive mathematics and science education for Native students.* San Francisco, CA: Far West Laboratory for Education Research and Development.

Ornstein, A., & Hunkins, F. P. (2004). *Curriculum: Foundations, principles and issues.* Boston, MA: Pearson.

Patrick, M. (2008). Universities use second life to teach complex concepts. *Government Technology*. Retrieved from http://www.govtech.com/education/Universities-Use-Second-Life-to-Teach.html

Peck, T. C., Seinfeld, S., Aglioto, S. M., & Slater, M. (2013) . Putting yourself in the skin of a black avatar reduces implicit racial bias. *Consciousness and Cognition, 22*, 779–787.

Pena-Rios, A., Callaghan, V., Gardner, M. R., Alhaddad, M. (2013, November). *Reality interactions within an immersive blended reality learning space.* Immersive Education 2013 (iED'13), London, UK: King's College.

Posner, G., Strike, K., Hewson, P., & Gertzoy, W. (1982). Accommodation of scientific conception: Toward a theory of conceptual change. *Science Education, 66*, 211–227.

Rieber, L. P. (1992). Computer-based microworlds: A bridge between constructivism and direct instruction. *Educational Technology Research & Development, 40*, 93–106.

Riggs, E. M. (2005). Field-based education and indigenous knowledge: Essential components of geoscience education for native American communities. *Science Education, 89*, 296–313.

Rogoff, B. (2003). *The cultural nature of human development.* New York, New York: Oxford University Press.

Sheehan, M., Childs, P. E., & Hayes, S. (2011, Sept. 1-3). *Identification of Irish preservice science teachers' misconceptions in chemistry.* ESERA: Science Learning and Citizenship.

Solomon, J. (1992). *Getting to know about energy*. London, UK: Falmer.

Somerville, M., & Perkins, T. (2003). Border work in the contact zone: thinking indigenous/non-indigenous collaboration spatially. *Journal of Intercultural Studies, 24*(3), 253–266.

Snively, G. (1995). Bridging traditional science and Western science in the multicultural classroom. In G. Snively & A. MacKinnon (Eds.). *Thinking globally about mathematics and science education* (pp. 53–75). Vancouver, Canada: Centre for the Study of Curriculum & Instruction, University of British Columbia.

Snively, G., & Corsiglia, J. (2001). Rediscovering indigenous science: Implications for science education. *Science Education, 85*, 6–34.

Stairs, A. (1995). Learning processes and teaching roles in Native education: Cultural base and cultural brokerage. In M. Battiste & J. Barman (Eds.), *First Nations education in Canada: The circle unfolds* (pp 139–153). Vancover, Canada: University of British Columbia Press.

Sukati, C. W. (2010). *In pursuit of Quality: UNISWA Lecturer's Perception on the Academic Performance of Conventional and Distance Education Students.* In the Proceeding of the 6th Pan Commonwealth Forum, India, 2010. Retrieved November 3, 2011, from http://www.pcf6.net/pages/full%20paper.php

Sutherland, D., & Swayze, N. (2012). Evaluating indigenous science education programs: Applying the Ininiwi-kiskanitamowin Indigenous Science Education Model to an informal education program. In R. Jorgensen, P. Sullivan, & P. Grootenboer (Eds.), *Pedagogies to enhance learning for indigenous students: Evidence-based practice* (pp. 175–193). Singapore: Springer.

Villegas, A. M., & Lucas, T. (2002). Preparing culturally responsive teachers rethinking the curriculum. *Journal of teacher education, 53*, 20–32.

Vygotsky, L. S. (1978). *Mind in society*. Cambridge, MA: Harvard University Press.

CHAPTER 3

WORKFORCE DEVELOPMENT THROUGH TECHNOLOGICALLY ENHANCED LEARNING EXPERIENCES

Marquita Walker

ABSTRACT

Local and global economies face serious economic and social costs in lost productivity as a result of the mismatch between workers' skills, employers' needs, and cost effective training programs for workforce development. Direct investments in workforce development and training have declined while the need for skilled labor has increased (Holzer, 2008). Skilled labor, which requires increased technical and people skills, places groups of individuals disadvantaged because of ethnicity, race, gender, decreased education, or poor basic skills in a precarious position as they face the challenge of competing for jobs in a global labor market requiring at least some postsecondary education and training. This inability to function well in the labor market contributes to low employment and earnings thus placing these disadvantaged groups in distressed situations as family providers. Increased investments in workforce development and training will contribute to the reduction of unemployed workers. Technologically enhanced learning experiences (TELEs) provide a flexible learning solutions tool to address this

E-learning and Social Media: Education and Citizenship for the Digital 21st Century, pp. 43–63

disparity. TELEs are online training modules, providing initial and long-term support for workers to upgrade their occupational and interpersonal skills to regain lost earnings, reintegrate into the workforce, and increase the supply of skilled workers employers need to remain competitive in the current economy.

INTRODUCTION

The need to produce a skilled workforce for the 21st century is paramount if the United States is to maintain its competitive edge in the marketplace. Development of a workforce capable of staffing current and future technical and green jobs requires a multi-faceted approach to training, which addresses workers' hard and soft skills. Limited training resources force state-run career centers, community colleges, technical institutes, four-year colleges, and private educational providers to wisely invest in training which fulfills employer demands for competent workers. This necessitates aligning employer demands with worker competencies for specific technical skills as well as soft or interpersonal skills. Aligning the interests of employers, the demand side of the labor market, and workers, the supply side of the labor market (Manyika, Lund, Auguste, Mendonca, & Ramaswamy, 2011) necessitates creating a venue which leverages the ability of workers to find meaningful information and employers to find skilled workers. The capacity of public and private organizations to align training programs with training needs is paramount if the U.S. labor pool is to "attract and retain employers, help reduce unemployment, and allow for fulfillment of societal needs" (Salas, Tannenbaum, Kraiger, & Smith-Jentsch, 2012, p. 75). The ability of workers to choose training programs resulting in increased earnings in the economic landscape is predicated on the notion that workers receive, or have access to, reliable and meaningful data which evaluates the success of training programs, provides options that fit workers existing skills, and meets current employer needs (Jacobson, & LaLonde, 2013). Technologically enhanced learning experiences (TELEs) are a training tool for workforce development which incorporates a cost-effective, flexible learning solution approach. TELEs are online training modules providing initial and long-term support for workers wishing to upgrade their occupational and interpersonal or people skills to regain lost earnings, reintegrate into the workforce, and increase the supply of skilled workers employers need to remain competitive in the current economy.

TRAINING NEEDS

The economic downturn experienced in the U.S. since 2007 has created a glut of unemployed workers who need to upgrade their marketable skills in order to reintegrate into the marketplace. The Department of Labor (2014) reflects 9.6 million people as unemployed in August, 2014 and Hotchkiss, Pitts, and Rios-Avila (2014) posits there is a pronounced skills mismatch between employers and employees after the Great Recession. The unprecedented number of unemployed without marketable skills contributes to a stagnant economy and presents challenges and opportunities for training and retraining the current and future workforce. Training and retraining workers in marketable skills includes upgrading technical skills, as well as people skills. A growing body of research has documented the need for increased training in people skills, also known as interpersonal or soft skills, for workers who wish to take the technical and green jobs of the future, the unemployed who wish to upgrade their skills for reintegration into the workforce, and adult learners who wish to engage with post-secondary level curriculum, receive feedback, and complete soft skills certification (Burrus, Jackson, Xi, & Steinberg, 2013; Goldstein & Ford, 2002; Salas et al., 2012). As firms compete in the marketplace, the investment in human capital through rigorous interpersonal training produces more dividends and profits for firms than does investment in finance, products, or markets (Boudreau & Ramstad, 2005). The driver behind increased product or service sales is improved relationships between labor and management, customers and the company, and the marketplace and company stakeholders. Employers that invest in soft skills training have an advantage in their line of business because their employees are better able to deal with intra-workplace conflict, engage in positive labor-management relationships, and contribute to the productivity and efficiency of the firm (Salas et al., 2012).

Continual investment in the workforce then is central to the firm's competitive advantage in the marketplace (Huselid & Becker, 2011). Workplace organizations have spent approximately $164.2 billion in worker training in 2012 ("State of the Industry," 2013), and the trend in training, learning, and development has been to use increased technology (Patel, 2010). According to Salas (2012), training research shows "training works" and "the way training is designed, delivered, and implemented matters" (p. 74). Since substantial evidence exists that workplace training works if well-designed (Wang & Hannafin, 2005), it makes sense to view training as an investment in future productivity of the firm, as well as an investment in the human potential of the workforce. Firms that invest in workers' human capital should do so based on evidence documented through training research in order to make informed investment decisions "about the science of training effectiveness" (Salas et al., 2012, p. 92).

Soft or interpersonal skills are critical in workforce development and are a significant contributor to workplace success (Bedwell, Fiore, & Salasi, 2011; Goleman, 1995). Employers require current and potential workers to successfully complete technical tasks as well as interact with other workers, managers, customers, and additional stakeholders. Interpersonal skills rank as one of the most important requirements for personal and organizational success. Much of the research in interpersonal skills occurs in the healthcare industry because administrators and educators believe healthcare providers should have an "excellent bedside manner" (Bedwell et al., 2011, p. 4), but local, state, national, and international firms are becoming more interested in their workers' abilities to develop and maintain relationships, collaborate within and across global boundaries, and communicate verbally and nonverbally with all interested parties.

The multidimensionality of interpersonal skills has been segregated into two broad categories, interpersonal communication and relationship building (Klein, DeRoouni, & Salas, 2006). Klein (2006) develops these categories from research on interpersonal skills derived from a trait-based approach, which contends individual behaviors can be learned or are inherent, and a situational approach, which contends the environment or social situation encourages the continuous correction of social performance based on others' reactions. Interpersonal communication and relationship building are essential for successful workplace organizations.

DELIVERY SYSTEMS

Delivery systems which enable workers to train and retrain for current and future jobs are expensive and time consuming. Technologically enhanced learning experiences (TELEs) are one solution which holds the promise of flexibility, cost containment, and the reduction of environmental footprints. The evolution of TELEs began in the 1990s when interest in learning minus formal instruction first surfaced. Known as "informal learning, self-choice learning, spontaneous learning, resource-based learning, and self-directed learning" (Hannafin, Hill, Land, & Lee 2014, p. 642), student-centered open learning environments (SCOLEs) as hybrid learning environments, such as blended face-to-face and online courses, provided choices for students to address individual, unique, and specific learning interests as defined by their needs. SCOLEs allowed the student to determine his or her own learning goals and which resources were needed to support those learning goals. The interest in self-directed learning increased as higher education and training costs skyrocketed, monies for government-assisted educational funding decreased, and environmental concerns surfaced. The need to design learning experiences to meet the specific needs of learners in the classroom as well as in the workplace begat the idea of creating learning environments which addressed very specific learning needs for very specific situations. TELEs can provide an online learning buffet of customized courses and training sessions which address the identified unique and specific needs of learners.

Wang and Hannafin (2005) define TELEs as "technology-based learning and instructional systems through which students acquire skills or knowledge, usually with the help of teachers or facilitators, learning support tools, and technological resources" (p. 5). TELEs are electronic interactions between students and instructors or facilitators which foster learning in a distributed learning environment situated within specific contextual parameters of workforce development, such as workplace relationships or workplace communication. TELEs are grounded in "design-based research which blend[s] empirical research with theory-based design of learning environments" (Swan & Matthews, 2012, p. 1). Design-based methodologies should consider aligning learning environments with "strategies for developing and refining theories" (Wang et al., 2005, p. 12) which could improve the curriculum and delivery of TELEs and evaluation of learning outcomes. Design-based research contributes to the creation and development of knowledge in learning environments (Collective, 2003).

What separates TELEs from traditional instructional design approaches is the fusion of research and design. Traditional instructional design acknowledges a relationship between research and design, but research and design function as separate entities. Generally, traditional instructional design is predicated on existing theory and the design's effectiveness is tested after delivery. In TELEs, theories are mediated and refined through practical application of design, resulting in synergy between research and design. This interaction between research and design, researchers and practitioners, and learning environments and learning theories produces data which either supports or rejects the existing theory and may require design changes. Inconsistencies or flaws quickly become visible and adjustments are made to the design, so "design is embodied in research, and research is embodied in design" (Wang et al., 2005, p. 13). This then is the nature of the TELE.

TELEs are designed to teach behavioral skills through virtual interaction and provide to employers a quality and flexible learning solutions tool. Current research reflects that soft skills such as self-confidence, self-control, and commitment create successful employees and more successful firms (Goleman, 1995). Antidotal evidence suggests the horizontal, team driven, and collaborative partnerships in today's workplace require leaders and followers to cooperate. Creating competent workers within the workplace requires a firm's long-term investment, because changing behaviors is a long-term process. TELEs provides to businesses initial and long-term support which focus on the broader parameters of organizational and behavioral changes and help businesses understand how those competencies work together to create employees who can manage themselves and relate to others.

Because teaching soft skills involves changing individual behavior to effectively engage with management, workers, customers, and other stakeholders, learners who master soft skills provide for the firm a proactive, engaged, and knowledgeable workforce who think-on-their-feet, respond quickly and creatively to problems, and contribute to an atmosphere of cooperation and collaboration in the workplace (Salas et al., 2012). Firms who invest in soft skills worker training have an advantage in the marketplace because their employees are better able to deal with intra-workplace conflict, engage in positive labor-management relationships, and contribute to the productivity and efficiency of the firm. Interactive training modules provide essential instruction in soft skills such as interpersonal communication and relationship building, which contribute to the development of a well-rounded employee who appreciates different perspectives, brings creativity and ingenuity to the work process, and solves problems in an amenable and efficient manner. As a result, this worker becomes an invaluable asset to the employer. The use of TELEs by employers to upgrade workers' emotional IQ provides a competitive advantage by decreasing training costs and time, providing easier access to course material, and reducing carbon footprints. TELEs:

- Are web-based, user-friendly, and tailored to adult learners.
- Are available 24/7, reduce the cost of education and associated materials for the employer and the employee, alleviate travel to and from an educational institution, and negate child/elder care costs.
- Are interactive thus allowing for active learning rather than passive learning.
- Are grounded in theoretically based principles of adult learning suited to different learning styles.
- Allow students to manage their own time, remain on task at their own pace through the use of asynchronous electronic blogs, posts, and video chats, and revisit unclear or unfamiliar material.
- Include testing components with instant feedback.

DESIGNING TELEs

Designing TELEs for soft skills training presents special design challenges. A flexible timeframe for completion is paramount in addressing the needs of learners whose work, familial, and community obligations often limit the amount of time available for studies. TELEs for soft skills training do not necessarily conform to the standard U.S. educational system's semester which usually lasts from 8 to 16 weeks. Rather, the length of a TELE is based on the amount of time required for students to gain competencies within content area. The timeframe may be different for each learner, so the design and delivery of the content must be malleable enough to ensure learning takes place. This means designing and delivering focused content specific to the learner's need in a timeframe consistent with the learner's availability.

Digitally connecting the theoretical application of adult learning with retraining for disadvantaged workers is one strength of TELEs. The use of TELEs as a newer digital phenomenon providing educational opportunities through e-learning provides for adult learners, who may be less confident than younger workers, a more flexible, shorter-term approach to training and learning (Bowman & Kearns, 2007). One weakness of TELEs for soft skills training in workforce development is the longer assessment and evaluation period required to document changed behavior, evidence that learning has occurred. I discuss more about how learning is evidenced through changed behavior later in this chapter.

It is important to define some of the terms used when exploring training issues as they relate to workforce development. The training research literature refers to training as "a systematic approach to learning and development to improve individuals, teams, and organizational effectiveness" (Goldstein et al., 2002, p. 452). This suggests a continual, logical, and methodical engagement or interaction strategy in which humans have opportunities to acquire tertiary qualifications for advancement in their workplace lives. Individuals engaged with learning opportunities in the workplace are involved in an interrelationship between workplace culture, practice, and expectation (Alvesson & Willmott, 2002) and their own set of experiences and education (Billet, 2006; Wenger, 1998). Consequently, "learning is both a component and an outcome of individuals' engagement in work" (Weedon & Tett, 2013, p. 13).

The ability of individuals to learn is impeded by many obstacles: situational, such as job, family, or household; institutional, such as cost, appropriate courses, and scheduling; and dispositional, such as "perceptions like little to gain by participating, concerns about own ability to succeed, belief that one is too old to go back to study, and bad previous experience with schooling" (Rubenson, & Desjardins, 2009, p. 192). Structural barriers embedded in market-based government policies regulating funding for training in adult education programs often contribute to inequities which determine eligibility and compensation issues (Rubenson et al., 2009). As a result of macro structural and micro situational, institutional, and dispositional barriers, adult learners face challenges in the acquisition of tertiary qualifications and may embrace an opportunity to engage with and acquire educational credentials via TELEs.

The term competencies is often used as a synonym for skills (Burrus et al., 2013). Competencies "can be defined as the ability to perform and sequence actions to attain a specific goal" (Evers, Rush, & Berdrow, 1998) and the "strategies and procedures for acquiring and working with the knowledge that comes with experience and practice" (Tippins & Hilton, 2010, p. 9). References to competencies extend to those skills considered important for most jobs. Though certain technical competencies or skills may be specific to one particular industry or job, interpersonal competencies or skills are ubiquitous to most industries and jobs. Competencies outline and clarify the specific goals of an educational experience. Developed over the course of the last 70 years, the Department of Labor analyzed thousands of jobs, working conditions, workers' interests and temperaments, and training times which resulted in the *Dictionary of Occupational Titles* (DOT), a guide for matching employer needs with worker skills. As the occupational landscape began to change in the 1970s from one reflecting a manufacturing economy to one reflecting a service economy, the DOT became outdated and needed revision. The necessity of more comprehensive data which informed workers of the necessary competencies to succeed in the highly skilled and technical current job market was recognized and resulted in the creation of *The New DOT: A Database of Occupational Titles for the Twenty-First Century* (O*Net) (Dye & Silver, 1999). The online database provides national occupational benchmarks and aids in a standardized terminology for employers and workers. Based on O*NET analysis, the five most important competencies for the 21st century workforce are complex problem solving, fluid intelligence, teamwork and cooperation, persistence and innovation, and oral and written communication skills (Burrus et al., 2013). These competencies, with the exception of teamwork, are all related in higher wages (Burrus et al., 2013).

Another important term to define is student, or learner. We generally think of traditional students as individuals, ages 18–24, moving from secondary education into higher education and non-traditional students as adults who have had some experience in the workforce and have returned to school to upgrade skills, complete previously interrupted education, or for personal satisfaction. Government policies providing funding for higher education through the Workforce Investment Act (WIA, 1998), The Servicemen's Readjustment Act of 1944, more commonly known as the GI Bill ("Employment and reemployment rights of members of the uniformed services"), or other training programs encourage nontraditional students to return to higher education. Such an investment in human capital returns dividends in the form of increased wages from which higher taxes can be extracted, creates a knowledgeable citizenry who make informed decisions, and contributes to the overall public good of the country.

As the economic environment became less stable in the Great Recession of 2007, traditional students unable to find work after graduation continued their education into advanced degrees, and nontraditional students unable to find work because of job loss or skill deficiency entered higher education. The idea of traditional and nontraditional students became blurred as learning environments filled with students of all ages and skill levels. The more appropriate term, learner, seemed to better describe the typical individual inhabiting the learning environment in a knowledge-based economy. A learner is defined as one in whom a change occurs and who continually engages with new knowledge throughout his or her life depending on the situational context of the environment (Knowles, Holton, & Swanson, 1998). This definition suggests learning is a lifelong pursuit, and a learner is one who continually engages in that pursuit. For our purposes, we will interchangeably use the term student and learner.

The term learning also requires some explanation. Learning implies a learner has acquired new information which causes a change in behavior, or the acquisition of knowledge, skills, and attitudes (Knowles et al., 1998). Learning then takes place within the learner, and changed behavior or acquisition of knowledge, skills, and attitudes is evidence learning has occurred. "Learning is the process of gaining knowledge or expertise" (Knowles, Holton, & Swanson, 2005a, p. 17). The onus of learning takes place within the learner, not the educator or the instructor. The multiple interpretations given to the term learning by learning theorists describe learning as a process (Crow & Crow, 1963), a product (Haggard, 1963), and a function (Harris & Schwahn, 1961). All agree learning shapes, changes, or controls behavior (Knowles, 2005b). Subsequent learning and cognitivist theorists suggest learning includes competency development (Bruner, 1966), personal involvement, and evaluation by the learner (Rogers, 1969). This worldview suggests that learning hinges on the philosophy that learning is organic, proactive, and relational, and is the interpretation most relevant to the development of TELEs.

FRAMEWORK FOR THE DEVELOPMENT OF TELEs

The framework for the development of TELEs is based on the principles of adult learning theory, training transfer and its assessment, the design of competencies that link specific skill performance with specific curricula content and job descriptions, and continued support once formal training ends. The impact of TELEs on learning relies on the assessment of learning outcomes through quantitative and qualitative metrics which assess the effectiveness of knowledge, skills, and abilities (KSAs) acquisition. Training needs for workforce development should be "purposeful, outcome-based, strategic, and based on the contextual need of the work environment and on sound principles of adult learning (Koo & Miner, 2010, p. 254). This necessitates a collaborative relationship between the entity responsible for designing workforce development training and the firm wishing to upgrade its workers' KSAs. The academy must be able to identify how best to translate research into practice in order to enhance the curriculum through evidence-based workforce development training, and the firm must identify specific training needs necessitating specialized and focused training programs. This exchange results in a two-directional partnership between academies and firms which addresses the continual changing needs of firms as they respond to market forces dictating malleable workforce KSAs, and current evidence-based research in designing, delivering, and evaluating theoretically-sound, high-quality training programs.

Adult Learning Theory

Adult learning theory is an integral part of designing and delivering soft skills training to enhance workforce development. Adults bring to the table a history of education and experiences which influence the way they think, act, and learn (Smith & Smith, 2010). Adults expect relevance in the learning process and learn best when outcomes are clear and integrated into the curriculum (Caffarella, 2002). What they learn today, adults expect to use tomorrow (Koo et al., 2010). Consequently, adults require a variety of learning experiences which simulate "real life" situations (Bransford, Brown, & Cocking, 2000; Knowles et al., 1998; Schon, 1987; Wlodkowski, 2008). If the adult learner is engaged, the likelihood of learning is increased. As mature workers and reliable employees, adults seek to gain competencies which will translate into higher earnings and better benefits (Smith & Smith, 2010). The "adult friendly" curricula, which seek to optimize flexibility, access, and success for working adult learners, are adaptable to mature age workers in the form of shorter courses and a compressed time frame within an e-learning environment. Adult learning theory offers prescriptions for defining the learning environment, engaging the adult learner, and identifying learning activities appropriate for adult learners. Adult learning theory is an important component in the development of competencies which detail the expected outcomes of learning experiences. "Competencies 'facilitate adults' engagement in the learning process" (Koo et al., 2010, p. 256).

A learner-center approach (Wadsworth, 1996) used in developing the adult-friendly curriculum (Smith & Smith, 2010) for soft skill training is theoretically grounded in the Action Research Model developed by Lewin (1946). Action research seeks to find solutions "focused on participative group processes for addressing conflict, crises, and change, generally within organizations" (O'Brien, 1998, p. 8). Therefore, much of the researcher's time is devoted to refining the methodological tools used in collecting, analyzing, and presenting information in an ongoing basis (Lewin, 1946). Situating the continual redesign of TELEs in the action research model allows researchers and instructors to continually adjust or change content design based on existing and new data derived from interactions with learners. The mediation and refinement of this practical application increase the chances of learning transfer and the development of cross-cutting competencies for lifelong learning.

The use of technological tools to enhance learning is contextualized in some transition literature in academics as dimensions of independent learning, group work, motivation and responsibility and numerous initiatives aim[ed] to encourage students to develop in these areas and foster skills such as autonomy, critical thinking and self-directed learning" (Cook, & Rushton, 2008). These jobs require upgraded occupational skills as well as dependability and conscientiousness, which can yield significant returns for a firm over the long term.

Training Transfer

Pressure to change the way learners learn comes from the necessity for a trained workforce, as well as from the academy. As institutions of higher education and intermediaries such as community colleges, career and technical programs, and apprenticeships with limited resources strive to attract, retain, and prepare more students for career paths, new and innovative instructional practices and assessment techniques are needed to maintain a competitive edge in the marketplace. A student's ability to learn from traditional delivery in lecture formats is minimal (Fink, 2013), and requires rethinking instructional curriculum, delivery, and certification of learning. As reduced resources from government coffers shrink, an increase in the emphasis on objective measurements of learning transfer, documented through performance-based testing and accountability programs, ties funding to performance measures. This complicates the issue of measuring soft skills transfer because of the intangible nature of the skills. As society moves into a knowledge-based economy, traditional ways of teaching are challenged as the needs of students change from simply learning technical skills to the necessity of learning critical thinking and problem solving skills (Dolence & Norris, 1995). This transition is difficult for instructors and students alike who must adapt to new ways of teaching and learning. As teaching shifts to a learner-centered approach from an instructor-centered approach, old ways of presenting information through lectures within a classroom are being replaced with active and virtual learning environments which engage students in interactive and hands-on-learning. Facilitating these types of learning environments within a virtual environment means institutions of learning, instructors, and students must adapt to new ways of approaching learning. TELEs engender a virtual space which offers to students an array of learning opportunities designed to introduce specific marketable skills as well as complement existing skills. The creation of TELEs requires structural changes on the part of educational institutions which must now explore new online delivery systems, provide increased faculty support for training in instructional design, and evaluate the success of such systems.

Workers should be able to transfer the training they receive to their job or job performance. Training designed and delivered to workers should produce some measurable output in the form of direct organizational performance such as reduced errors (Senders & Moray, 1991), acquisition of new skills (Hill & Lent, 2006; Satterfield & Hughes, 2007), increased team performance (Edkins, 2002; Morey et al., 2002; Salas, Burke, Bowers, & Wilson, 2001b; Salas et al., 2012), or indirectly to organizational performance in the form of reputation (Clardy, 2005; Darch & Lucas, 2002) and social capital (Brown & Van Buren, 2007). These measurements are then used to determine whether sustainable changes in behavior or cognition occurred and if the training investment was beneficial to the firm and society.

Measuring soft skills learning transfer is difficult, though measuring the transfer of technical or hard skills such as working with software, equipment, or data, is easily facilitated. Students who learn how to complete some technical processes move into the workforce and can either complete the technical process, which usually involves some sequencing of steps, on the job or not. Objective metrics tell us whether the task was successfully completed. If the technical process was not completed, the employer and the employee immediately know the technical skill was not transferred. Technical skills' transfer, though important, is "insufficient for subsequent success beyond an entry-level position" (Laker & Powell, 2011, p. 113). A more robust skill transfer must take place in the form of soft or interpersonal skills.

Engagement with, and results from, the use of soft or interpersonal skills may not immediately be apparent. Soft skills involve the ability to handle personal interactions with others, manage oneself, take leadership positions, resolve conflict, communicate in written and oral form, and possess emotional intelligence. Employees who wish to move beyond entry level positions within a firm usually require proficiency in these areas (Goleman,

1995; Laker et al., 2011; Mitchell, Skinner, & White, 2010). The ability to learn how to handle oneself in interactions with coworkers, managers, and the public present some challenges to workers who may feel they already have some skills in these areas. Individuals usually believe they have some adequate way of dealing with others and may resist organizational or managerial requirements to adopt new approaches (Salas et al., 2012). Unlike the learning environment for technical skills which can mirror the work environment, the learning environment for soft skills is difficult to recreate because of the seriousness and complexity of real-life situations. Also, unlike the transfer of technical skills in which a worker either completes the task correctly or not, the transfer of soft skills may result in multiple correct solutions depending on situational circumstances. Uncertainty about when to apply new soft skills' approaches and in what context to apply them increases workers' resistance to learning soft skills and increases the likelihood of dissonance during transfer. In order to increase the transfer of soft skills' training to the job, instructors employ multiple techniques within a virtual environment using written, video, interactive case studies, role playing, and team development. The individual student, working at his or her own pace, can virtually interact with avatars within a simulated environment to develop strategies for success, solve problems, and build relationships.

The "transfer problem" (Grossman & Salas, 2011, p. 104) is a long recognized issue for the academy and workplaces. Narrowing the gap between training and workplace performance is a challenging goal, and positive results to date have been minimal (Georgenson, 1982; Saks, 1995; Yamnill & McLean, 2001). Seminal work on training transfer (Baldwin & Ford, 1988) was further refined (Ford & Weissbein, 1997) to reflect three broad constructs: learners, intervention, and work environment (Burke & Hutchins, 2007). According to Burke and Hutchins (2007), learner characteristics which influence training transfer include "cognitive ability, self-efficacy, pretraining motivation, negative affectivity, perceived utility, and organization commitment variables" (p. 271). The intervention construct includes the design and delivery of the training, and the work environment dictates which specific knowledge, skills, and abilities are necessary to perform the job.

TELEs designed for soft skills training in workforce development address the transfer problem in three ways: content design, assessment, and evaluation. First, let's address content design. In a virtual environment, the creation of a social presence within the learning environment is necessary. This is achieved in several ways in asynchronous learning environments. Embedded in the course content are social cues, exchanges, and interactions between the instructor and the learner, and between learners, which simulate the physical presence of a face-to-face classroom.

Interactive discussion boards and community forums in which learners' questions are posed and answered provide opportunities for learners and the instructor to "talk to each other." Inclusion of video-based lectures, voice-over PowerPoints, and podcasts also create an atmosphere of social presence. The most important foundational piece underlying all of these components is the learner's interest in the content. We know the longer a learner interacts with the material, the greater the learning transfer. The key is to capture the learner's attention through various components which appeal to the learner's visual, auditory, and kinetic ways of learning. If the learner's attention is lost, the learning transfer is diminished. Keeping the learner's interest is then paramount in the content design of TELEs.

Including game-like components within the virtual learning environment also increases learner's participation. The literature on gamification, "the process of making activities more game-like" (Werbach, 2014), explores ways learners strategize to achieve goals and develop relationships to advance their interests (Werbach, 2012). This burgeoning field explores new and better methods of capitalizing on ways learners achieve, and many of the techniques in gamification can be superimposed on the design technique in TELEs. For instance, instructors and students might interact through game-like structures in the course, in which avatars simulate work situations involving conflict, aggression, or harassment. Or learners might be required to achieve some level of content mastery before progressing to the next level and receive some sort of reward, badge, or token for completion of each level (Werbach, 2012). These techniques increase learners' self-confidence in task completion as well as problem-solving skills as learners navigate complex simulated environments.

Second, the assessment of learning transfer is important. Assessment is formative and focuses on improving learning transfer. Assessments from learners and workplaces provide the impetus for change (Mayer, 2011). Assessment of learning transfer is predicated on several factors: the length of time the learner engages with the material, the interactivity exhibited by the learner, and learner feedback. Learners' growth and knowledge competence is assessed via a qualification framework connecting learning outcomes or objectives with specific learning assignments or objects. Some training providers establish their own qualifications framework using rubrics and a traditional grading system with which to gauge training transfer, and some training providers are moving toward a standardized qualification framework based on competencies such as those outlined in the Degree Qualifications Profile (DQP, n.d.) established by the Lumina Foundation (Ewell, 2013). Though the DQP speaks to overall curriculum mapping for general education requirements or specific majors, the concept of moving toward competency-based outcomes instead of describing institutional reference points for incremental and cumulative learning, such as historical exploration or math proficiency (Degree Qualifications Profile), has some relevance for assessing competencies in workforce development. Regardless of the type of qualification framework, the learning assessment space allows instructors to alter the learning environment based on their interpretation of the feedback from learners. This interactive process between learners and instructors acts as a feedback loop in which areas of weakness are identified and improvement can be made. Assessment of learning transfer allows the instructor to alter, redesign, or change the course in some way based on this interactive feedback. Integrating assessment efforts with educational planning and instructional design continuously through the learning activity will help develop, test, and disseminate more effective strategies, resulting in greater learning transfer and a more competent workforce.

Third, evaluations are summative and gauge the evidence of cogitative, affective, or behavioral changes in the learner. Evaluations are designed to document achieved competencies. The success or failure of TELEs as a delivery system hinges on some change in the learner which is reflected in the learner's personal life, workplace, or society. This means evaluations must provide some evidence learning transfer has occurred. Instructors evaluating the evidence learners produce through quizzes, exams, worksheets, written papers, group or individual projects, skills and competencies exams, reflective writing, e-portfolio creation, and other graded assignments use their expertise to determine competency within some range of acceptability. Ranges of acceptability, usually from low to high proficiency, are mirrored in rubrics designed to reflect benchmarks in competencies. Evidence of long-term learning transfer is more difficult to produce and requires longitudinal studies which follow learners into the workplace and society.

Linking Competencies to Specific Skills

Linking competencies to specific skills lies at the heart of workforce development. The employment and training administration (ETA) identified specific core competencies of KSAs required of all workers in many occupations (Ennis, 2008; Lucia & Lepsinger, 1999; Rodriguez, Patel, Bright, Gregory, & Growing, 2002). The competencies are structured hierarchically with core or foundational competencies at the bottom of the structure, and competencies more specific to certain occupations located higher on the structure. These competency models are used to align labor market demand with labor market supply by workforce development specialists, workforce investment boards, and education and training providers who link workers with an occupation or industry (Ennis, 2008; Mansfield,

1989; Rodriguez et al., 2002) in which they have the greatest chance of success for career and geographic mobility. Competency models establish a framework in which a common language, expectation, and perspective allows individuals, teams, and organizations to recruit, screen, hire, train, evaluate, and advance competent workers (Ennis, 2008). Competency models allow employers to better align the needs of their firm with the KSAs of their employees, but competency models also allow learners to align their interests with current or potential employers. Learners proactively select from the array of available TELEs those courses which help them fill in the competency gaps as identified by workforce development specialists or potential employers. The idea undergirding linking competencies to specific skills is to provide a "'means' (knowledge, skills, abilities) to and 'end' (to be an effective employee functioning and performing at expected standards)" (Youn Chyung, Stepich, & Cox, 2006). That end is certification of foundational competencies credentialing a learner not only for a position within a certain occupation and potential career advancement, but an opportunity to participate in the global workforce.

CONTINUED SUPPORT

Though workforce training should be planned, systematic, and designed to promote the acquisition of KSAs (Salas & Cannon-Bowers, 2001a), some learners need continued support once formal training has ended. Pedagogically sound opportunities to learn specific and targeted KSAs through the delivery of "instruction, demonstration, practice, and timely diagnostic feedback about their performance" (Salas et al., 2001a, p. 77), "provide benefits to individuals, teams, organizations, and society" (Aguinis & Kraiger, 2009, p. 753) through sustainable changes in behavior and cognition. TELEs are designed to include additional information and training, should learners need continued support. Continued support is available in the form of web-based formal mentoring programs in which learners engage with an instructor in a synchronous online environment, informal mentoring embedded in blogs and chat rooms providing space for a community of learners to ask and respond to questions, and self-directed learning in which learners access a pool of available web-related topical resources in order to strengthen and reinforce interpersonal communication and relationship building skills.

CONCLUSION

The changing nature of the economic environment, limited resources, and demographic changes in the workforce require new and innovative training techniques in workforce development in order for the U.S. to remain competitive in a global economy. Today's workforce must not only have the knowledge, skills, and abilities to meet the changing needs of employers and firms who operate in a diverse and globally-competitive marketplace, but the competencies to adapt to new organizational structures and business models which require better communication and relationship building techniques. Aligning employer needs with worker competencies requires rethinking the delivery of workforce development training to include soft and interpersonal skills as well as technical skills. This necessitates training mechanisms which support the malleable needs of employers and employees. TELEs provide a theoretically-designed, pedagogically-sound, learner-centered approach to training which allows the current and future workforce to acquire, enhance, and adapt soft and interpersonal skills competencies to local, national, and global work environments. TELEs provide an electronically interactive, cost-effective, carbon-reducing training mechanism which allows learners to access material based on their timeframe, work at their own speed, reintegrate with the material for continued support, and receive credentials for competency certification.

REFERENCES

Aguinis, H., & Kraiger, K. (2009). Benefits of training and development for individuals and teams, organizations, and society. *Annual Review of Psychology, 42*, 750–757.

Alvesson, M., & Willmott, H. (2002). Identity regulation as organizational control: Producing the appropriate individual. *Journal of Management Studies, 39*(5), 619–644.

Baldwin, T. T., & Ford, J. K. (1988). Transfer of training: A review and directions for future research. *Personal Psychology, 41*, 63–105.

Bedwell, W. L., Fiore, S. M., & Salasi, E. (2011). *Developing the 21st century (and beyond) workforce: a review of interpersonal skills & measurement strategies*. Stellenbosch University. Retrieved from http://www7.nationalacademies.org/BOTA/21st_Century_Workshop_Salas_Fiore_Paper.pdf and http://scholar.sun.ac.za

Billett, S. (2006). Work, subjectivity and learning In S. Billet (Ed.), *Work, subjectivity and learning: Understanding learning through working life* (pp. 1–17). Dordrecht, Netherlands: Springer.

Boudreau, J., & Ramstad, P. (2005). Talentship, talent segmentation, and sustainability: A new HR decision science paradigm for a new strategy definition. *Human Resource Management, 44*, 129–136.

Bowman, K., & Kearns, P. (2007). *E-learning for the mature age worker.* Australian Government: Global Learning Services.

Bransford, J. D., Brown, A. L., & Cocking, R. R. (Eds.). (2000). *How people learn: Brain, mind, experience, and school.* Washington, DC: National Research Council, National Academy.

Brown, K. G., & Van Buren, M. E. (2007). Applying a social capital perspective to the evaluation of distance training. In S. Fiore (Ed.), *Where is the learning in distance learning? Towards a science of distributed learning and training* (pp. 41–63). Washington DC: American Psychological Association.

Bruner, J. (1966). *Toward a theory of instruction*. Cambridge, MA: Harvard University Press.

Burke, L. A., & Hutchins, H. M. (2007). Training transfer: An integrative literature review. *Human Resource Development Review, 6*(3), 263–296.

Burrus, J., Jackson, R., Xi, N. & Steinberg, J. (2013). Identifying the most important 21st century workforce competencies: An analysis of the occupational information network (O*NET). In J. Carlson (Ed.), *ETS Research Report Series*. Princeton, NJ: Educational Testing Services.

Caffarella, R. S. (2002). *Planning programs for adult learners: A practical guide for educators, trainers, and staff developers*. San Francisco, CA: Jossey-Bass.

Clardy, A. (2005). Reputation, goodwill, and loss: Entering the employee training audit equation. *Human Resource Development Review, 4*, 479-304.

Collective. (2003). Design-based research: An emerging paradigm for education inquiry. *Educational Researcher, 32*(1), 105–114.

Cook, A., & Rushton, B. (2008). *Student transition: Practices and policies to promote retention*. London, UK: SEDA.

Crow, L. D., & Crow, A. (Ed.). (1963). *Readings in human learning*. New York, NY: McKay.

Darch, J., & Lucas, T. (2002). Training as an ecommerce enabler. *Journal of Workplace Learning, 14*, 148–155.

Degree Qualifications Profile. Lumina Foundation. (n.d.). Indianapolis, IN. Retrieved from http://www.luminafoundation.org/publications/The_Degree_Qualifications_Profile.pdf

Department of Labor. (2014). News release: The employment situation. Retrieved from http://www.bls.gov/news.release/pdf/empsit.pdf

Dolence, M. G., & Norris, D. M. (1995). *Transforming higher education: A vision for learning in the 21st century*. Ann Arbor, MI: Society for College and University Planning.

Dye, D., & Silver, M. (1999). The origins of O*NET. In N. G. Peterson (Ed.), *An occupational system for the 21st century: The development of O*NET* (pp. 9–19). Washington, DC: American Psychological Association.

Edkins, G. D. (2002). A review of the benefits of aviation human factors training. *Human Factors Aerospace Safety, 2*, 201–216.

Employment and reemployment rights of members of the uniformed services, Pub. L. No. 103–353, 4301 Stat. (1994, October 13).

Ennis, M. (2008). Competency models: A review of the literature and the role of the employment and training administration (ETA). (P. D. Team, Ed.). Washington DC: U.S. Department of Labor.

Evers, R. R., Rush, J. C., & Berdrow, I. (1998). *The bases of competence: Skills for lifelong learning and employability*. San Francisco, CA: Jossey-Bass.

Ewell, P. T. (2013). The Lumina Degree Qualifications Profile (DQP): Implications for assessment. In C. G. Schneider (Ed.). University of Illinois at Urbana-Champaign: National Institute for Learning Outcomes Assessment.

Fink, L. D. (2013). *Creating significant learning experiences: An integrated approach to designing college courses* (2nd ed.). San Francisco, CA: Wiley.

Ford, J. K., & Weissbein, D. A. (1997). Transfer of training: An updated review and analysis. *Performance Improvement Quarterly, 10*(2), 42–63.

Georgenson, D. L. (1982). The problem of transfer calls for partnership. *Training and Development Journal, 36*, 75–78.

Goldstein, I. L., & Ford, J. K. (2002). *Training in organizations: Needs assessment, development, and evaluation* (4th ed.). Belmont, CA: Wadsworth.

Goleman, D. (1995). *Emotional intelligence*. New York, NY: Bantam Books.

Grossman, R., & Salas, E. (2011). The transfer of training: What really matters? *International Journal of Training and Development, 15*(2), 103–120. doi:10.1111/j.1468-2419.2011.00373.x

Haggard, E. A. (1963). Learning a process of change. In L. Crow (Ed.), *Readings in human learning* (pp. 19–27). New York, NY: McKay.

Hannafin, M. J., Hill, J. R., Land, S.M., & Lee, E. (2014). Student-centered, open learning environments: Research, theory, and practice. In J. M. Spector (Ed.), *Handbook of research on educational communications and technology* (pp. 641–651). New York, NY: Springer.

Harris, T. L., & Schwahn, W. E. (1961). *Selected readings on the learning process*. New York, NY: Oxford University Press.

Hill, C. E., & Lent R. W. (2006). A narrative and meta-analytic review of helping skills training: Time to revive a dormant area of inquiry. *Psychotherapy: Theory, Research, Practice, 43*, 154–172.

Holzer, H. J. (2008). *Economic cost of inadequate investments in workforce development.* Washington, DC: Georgetown University.

Hotchkiss, J. L., Pitts, M. M., & Rios-Avila, F. (2014). A search for evidence of skill mismatch in the aftermath of the great recession. *Applied Economics Letters, 24*(9), 587–592.

Huselid, M. A., & Becker, B. E. (2011). Bridging micro and macro domains: Workforce differentiation and strategic human resource management. *Journal of Management, 37*, 421–428.

Jacobson, L. S., & LaLonde, R. J. (2013). *Using data to improve the performance of workforce training*. Washington DC: Brookings Institute.

Klein, C., DeRoouni, R. E., & Salas, E. (2006). Uncovering workplace interpersonal skills: A review, framework, and research agenda. In G. Hodgkinson (Ed.), *International review of industrial and organizational psychology* (Vol. 21, pp. 80–126). New York, NY: Wiley & Sons.

Knowles, M., Holton, E., & Swanson, R. (1998). *The adult learner: The definitive classic in adult education and human resource development* (5th ed.). Woburn, MA: Butterworth-Heinemann.

Knowles, M., Holton, E., & Swanson, R. (2005a). *The adult learner: The definitive class in adult education and human resource development* (6th ed.). Amsterdam: Elsevier.

Knowles, M. S. (2005b). The adult learner: The definitive classic in adult education and human resource development. In R. A. Swanson (Ed.), *The adult learner*. Amsterdam: Elsevier.

Koo, D., & Miner, K. (2010). Outcome-based workforce development and education in public health. *Annual Review of Public Health, 31*, 253–269.

Laker, D. R., & Powell, J. L. (2011). The difference between hard and soft skills and their relative impact on training transfer. *Human Resource Development Quarterly, 22*(1), 111–122.

Lewin, K. (1946). Action research and minority problems. *Journal of Social Issues, 2*, 34–46.

Lucia, A. D., & Lepsinger, R. (1999). A competency-based model of sustainable competitive advantage: Toward a conceptual integration. *Journal of Management, 18*(1), 77–91.

Mansfield, B. (1989). Competence and standards. In J. W. Burke (Ed.), *Competency based education and training*. Sussex, England: Routledge.

Manyika, J., Lund, S., Auguste, B., Mendonca, L., & Ramaswamy, S. (2011). An economy that works: Job creation and America's future Retrieved February 9, 2014, from http://www.mckinsey.com/Insights/MGI/Research/Labor_Markets/An_economy_that_works_for_US_job_creation

Mayer, R. E. (2011). *Applying the science of learning*. University of CA, Santa Barbara, Pearson.

Mitchell, G. W., Skinner, L. B. J., & White, B. J. (2010). Essentials soft skills for success in the twenty-first century workforce as perceived by business educators. *The Delta Pi Epsilon Journal, 52*(1), 43–53.

Morey, J. C., Simon, R., Jay, G. D., Wears, R. L., Salisbury, M. et al. (2002). Error reduction and performance improvement in the emergency department through formal teamwork training: Evaluation results of the MedTeams Project. *Health Service Research, 37*(1153–1181).

O'Brien, R. (1998). *An overview of the methodological approach of action research*. Brazil: University Federal da Paraiba.

Patel, L. (2010). *ASTD State of the industry report 2010*. Alexandria, VA: American Society for Training and Development.

Rodriguez, E., Patel, R., Bright, A., Gregory, D., & Growing, M. (2002). Developing competency models to promote integrated human resource practices. *Human Resource Management, 41*(3), 309–324.

Rogers, C. R. (1969). *Freedom to learn*. Columbus, OH: Merrill.

Rubenson, K., & Desjardins, R. (2009). The impact of welfare state regimes on barriers to participation in adult education: A bounded agency model. *Adult Education Quarterly, 59*(3), 187–207.

Saks, A. M. (1995). Longitudinal field investigation of the moderating and mediating effects of self-efficacy on the relationship between training and newcomer adjustment. *Journal of Applied Psychology, 80*, 211–225.

Salas, E., & Cannon-Bowers, J. A. (2001a). The science of training: A decade of progress. *Annual Review of Psychology, 52*, 471–499.

Salas, E., Burke, C. S., Bowers, C. A. & Wilson, K. A. (2001b). Team training in the skies: Does crew recourse management (CRM) training work? *Human Factors, 42*, 641–674.

Salas, E., Tannenbaum, S. I., Kraiger, K., & Smith-Jentsch, K. A. (2012). The science of training and development in organizations: What matters in practice. *Psychological Science in the Public Interest, 13*(2), 74–101. doi:10.1177/1529100612436661

Satterfield, J. M., & Hughes, E. (2007). Emotion skills training for medical students: a systematic review. *Medical Education, 41*(935–941).

Schon, D. A. (1987). *Educating the reflective practitioner: Toward a new design for teaching and learning in the profession*. San Francisco, CA: Jossey-Bass.

Senders, J. W., & Moray, N. P. (1991). *Human error: Cause, prediction, and reduction*. Hillsdale, NJ: Erlbaum.

Smith, E., & Smith, A. (2010). Old dogs, new tricks: Training mature-aged manufacturing workers. *Journal of Workplace Learning, 22*(5), 277–291. doi:10.1108/13665621011053190

State of the Industry, American Society for Training & Development. (2013). Alexandria, VA: ASTD

Swan, K., & Matthews, D. (2012). *Improving courses across an online program: A design-based approach.* Paper presented at the 28th Annual Conference on Distance Teaching and Learning.

Tippins, N., & Hilton, M. (Ed.). (2010). *A database for a changing economy: Review of the Occupational Information Network (O*NET)*. Washington, DC: The National Academies Press.

Wadsworth, B. J. (1996). *Paiget's theory of cognitive and affective development: Foundations of constructivism* (5th ed.). White Plains, NY: Longman.

Wang, R., & Hannafin, M. J. (2005). Design-based research and technology enhanced learning environments. *Educational Technology Research and Development, 53*(4), 5–23.

Weedon, E., & Tett, L. (2013). Plugging a gap? Soft skills courses and learning for work. *International Journal of Lifelong Learning*. doi:10.1080/02601370.2013.773572

Wenger, E. (1998). *Communities of practice: Learning, meaning and identity*. Cambridge, UK: Cambridge University Press.

Werbach, K. (2012). *For the win: How game thinking can revolutionize your business*. Philadelphia, PA: The Wharton School, Wharton Digital Press.

Werbach, K. (2014). (Re)defining gamification. Philadelphia, PA: The Wharton School. Retrieved from http://works.bepress.com/cgi/viewcontent.cgi?article=1003&context=kevin_werbach

Wlodkowski, R. J. (2008). *Enhancing adult motivation to learn: A comprehensive guide for teaching all adults* (3rd ed.). San Francisco, CA: Wiley.

Workforce Investment Act. 105th Congress, Pub. L. No. 105-220 § 101, 936 Stat. (August 7, 1998).

Yamnill, S., & McLean, G. N. (2001). Theories supporting transfer of training. *Human Resource Development Quarterly, 12*(2), 195 208.

Youn Chyung, S., Stepich, D., & Cox, E. (2006). Building a competency-based curriculum architecture to educate 21st century business practitioners. *Journal of Education for Business, 81*(6), 307–314.

CHAPTER 4

ARE K–12 TEACHERS READY FOR TECHNOLOGY-ENHANCED TEACHING AND LEARNING?

A Study on Teachers' TPACK Level in a Provincial City in China

Yuqing Guo, Yan Li, and Min Li

ABSTRACT

Over the last few decades, the incorporation of information and communication technologies (ICTs) into daily pedagogical practices has been viewed as a viable solution for the innovation of educational systems. Teachers have been seen as crucial actors in this process, and therefore much emphasis has been put on the necessity to provide them with adequate technological and pedagogical competences through training and lifelong learning. However, while a greater knowledge of teachers' level of skills in technology-enhanced learning would be extremely helpful to deliver effective training courses, up to now, empirical studies on teachers' digital and pedagogical skills have been poor and fragmented, especially in developing and populous countries such as China. The current study attempted to explore this issue in a provincial

E-Learning and Social Media:
Education and Citizenship for the Digital 21st Century, pp. 65–92

city in China, through the assessment of K–12 teachers' levels of skills in technology, pedagogy and content, and by looking into factors that might have influenced the obtained results. The research design was descriptive in nature and Mishra and Koehler's (2006, 2009) technological pedagogical and content knowledge (TPACK) model was adopted as the theoretical framework. Besides determining teachers' level of skills, six hypotheses on possible correlations between teachers' TPACK level and their personal characteristics were investigated. Results of data analysis revealed that: (1) surveyed Chinese K–12 teachers (N = 691) were more competent in non-technology-related TPACK domains than in technology-related TPACK domains; (2) male teachers rated themselves to be more competent in all of the seven TPACK domains than did female teachers; (3) discipline had a significant impact on K–12 teachers' technology-related knowledge domains; (4) age, professional title and teaching experience had a significant impact on K–12 teachers' TK, CK and PCK; (5) online education experience had a significant impact on all seven TPACK domains of the K–12 teachers involved in the study. These results suggested that, regardless of age and the teaching experience, K–12 teachers in China need more training, especially in the area of ICT-pedagogy integration, and that increasing teachers' online educational experience could be an encouraging factor to make teachers more familiar with the use of ICTs in their daily pedagogical practices.

INTRODUCTION

The 21st century witnessed the widespread use of computers and the Internet within educational systems all over the world. As a result, the use of information and communication technologies (ICTs) to support teaching and learning have become an increasingly common practice (see, e.g., van Raaij, & Schepers, 2008). Around the globe, a number of schools and training institutions have implemented various computer-assisted and web-based teaching and learning innovations. Several countries have indeed embraced the vision that integrating digital technologies into current pedagogical practice is a viable way to change education today and, consequently, they have put forward a series of plans or projects to promote the innovation of the instructional system (AI-Qirim, 2011; Miao, 2008). China is one of them.

As the most populous country and the largest educational consumer, policymakers in China are quite conscious about the importance of ICTs and their potential for education. According to the ministry of education of China (MOE), China currently has about 230 million K–12 students and 12.71 million K–12 teachers (MOE, 2012). To promote the integration of technology and education in K–12 schools, since the mid-1990s, the MOE has supported twelve influential national projects. Among them, more than half (seven) are related to infrastructure and educational resources' development, such as *1000 Pilot Networked Campuses* (1996), *Multimedia Courseware Development Project* (1996), *Schools-Connected* (2001), *Digital Resources for Basic Education* (2002), *Distance Education for Rural Schools (Phase I)* (2003), *Classes-Connected* (2010) and *Distance Education for Rural Schools (Phase II)* (2010); two are related to students' computer education, named *100 Experimental Zones of Computer Education* (1996) and *Universalizing Computer Education in Schools* (2000), respectively; two concern teachers' ICT competence development, named *Teacher Training on Computers* (2000) and *Educational Technology Training for Teachers* (2004), respectively; and one is about *Educational e-Administration* (2010).

In 2010, the Chinese Ministry of Education launched a new national plan called *National Medium- and Long-term Plan for Education Reform and Development* (2010–2020), where the introduction and development of ICTs in education were clearly identified as crucial steps in the overall process of the national strategy. The plan listed three major goals in the area of technology in education to be reached by 2020: (1) to reduce the digital divide by strengthening investments in infrastructures, improving broadband coverage, and providing all schools with access to the Internet; (2) to implement platforms for sharing online educational resources and delivering public services to create high-quality educational materials, especially addressed to rural and remote areas, meanwhile, to support the integration of ICTs in education through teachers' training and professional development; and (3) to develop and maintain educational management systems for the digitization of educational management and related services. To achieve these goals, the Chinese government elaborated the Master Plan for Developing ICT in Education in China (2011–2020), which detailed how to effectively integrate ICT tasks and strategies into schools and teaching.

However, despite these important projects, the integration of ICTs into the Chinese education system is still in its early stage. As shown in Figure 4.1, according to the evolution model of ICT-pedagogy integration, which was proposed by UNESCO (2005), China is just moving from the first stage (Emerging stage) to the second stage (Application stage) (Zhu, 2011).

Computers and the Internet are expected to bring a fundamental revolution to current educational systems, while challenges and opportunities always come together when concretely using technologies in traditional schools. Literature records many successful stories as well as precious lessons relating to ICTs in teaching practices (see, e.g., Asia Development Bank, 2009; Shinohara & Zhou, 2006; Wallace, 2004). However, the history of technology and education is also studded with a number of unsuccessful experiences. In his influential studies on teachers and technologies in Western countries, Cuban (1986, 2001) showed that, despite extraordinary

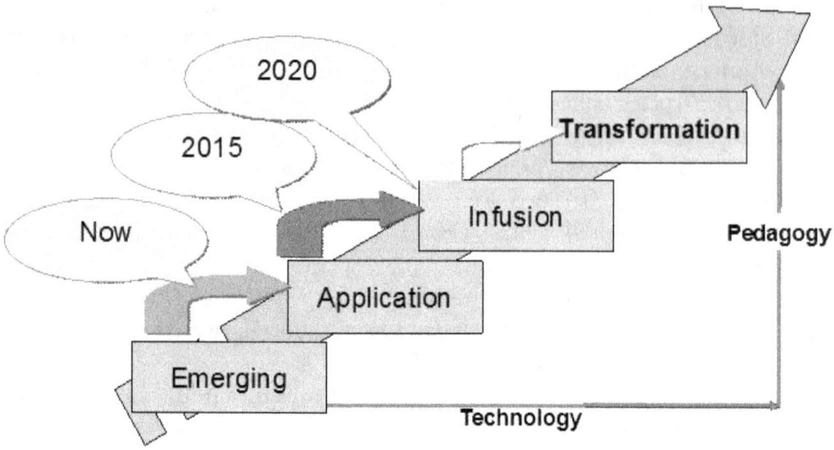

Source: Zhu (2011).

Figure 4.1. China's stage in the Evolution Model of ICT-Pedagogy Integration.

claims about the revolutionary impact of technology-enhanced teaching, computers or the Internet have been used only a little in schools. He explained this result with what he called the "situationally constrained choice" (Cuban, 1986, p. 48), which incorporates the issue of the structure of schools and classroom environment, as well as the teaching culture, including social beliefs and teachers' attitudes. Other scholars underlined that teachers' attitudes and their knowledge about the educational use of ICT were very important factors (Erdogan & Sahin, 2010; Li & Lindner, 2007; Teo, Chai, Hung, & Lee, 2008).

In this light, the issue of teachers' professional development becomes crucial. In Western countries, a great emphasis has been put on teachers' training for a long while, with relatively disappointing results. Some scholars (see, e.g., Anthony & Clark, 2011; Haydn & Barton, 2007) highlighted that the gap between theory and practice impacted negatively on the improvement of teachers' skills. Other scholars (Zhao & Frank, 2003) stressed the ephemeral nature of most teachers' training courses, which are normally concentrated at the beginning of the school year with a few hours and low socio-technical support. All these arguments seem to be convincing. However, in order to design and develop effective training courses, two preliminary elements seem to be of fundamental relevance: Firstly, acknowledging the actual level of teachers' skills and knowledge; secondly, gaining knowledge about the impact of teachers' personal characteristics on their own skills. To date, the number of studies around teachers' level of skills in technology-enhanced pedagogy is still poor. There are also few assessment instruments to measure teachers' skills within the framework of the technological pedagogical and content knowledge (TPACK) model. This latter aims to describe the specific knowledge needed for teachers to teach appropriately in the digital era (Archambault & Barnett, 2010; Chai, Koh, Tsai, & Tan, 2011; Jang & Tsai, 2012; Lee & Tsai, 2010).

The present study intends to provide "a piece of evidence" about Chinese teachers' technological and pedagogical skills, and to investigate the factors that may impact on their ICT-pedagogy integration level. It is based on theory and tools developed within the TPACK framework. Prior to describing our research study, we will provide a brief overview of the literature on the issue of teachers' technological training as well as an introduction to the TPACK model.

THE TPACK MODEL AND THE LEVELS OF INNOVATION

In the literature relating to teachers' training on ICTs in education, several factors are reported as variables influencing the success of training program. Some studies point out factors such as inadequate timing, unrealistic separation between theory and practice, lack of support, generic objectives, and the mismatching between institutional offers and teachers' needs (Teo, Chai, Hung, & Lee, 2008). One of the most critical facets concerns the overstated attention to the very technical aspects, while concrete examples of how to implement pedagogically meaningful classroom digital experiences are still scarce or also trivial in some way (Polly, Mims, Shepherd, & Inan, 2010). In addition, several studies proved that the lack of integration between technology and pedagogy very often determines infrequent use or inadequate applications of ICT in education (Andersson, 2006; Cradler, Freeman, Cradler, & McNabb, 2004; Starkey, 2010). In this framework, one theoretical proposal which takes into account both technology and pedagogy is the TPACK model. Based on Shulman's (1986, 1987) idea of pedagogical content knowledge (PCK), the TPACK model was first developed by Pierson (2001) and then enriched by other scholars during the past decade (e.g., Angeli & Valanides, 2009; Koehler, Mishra, & Yahya, 2007; Thompson & Mishra, 2007–2008). At present, the TPACK framework is commonly represented by a Venn diagram with three overlapping circles, each representing a distinct area of knowledge, named pedagogical knowledge (PK), content knowledge (CK), and technological knowledge (TK) (Mishra & Koehler, 2006, 2009) (Figure 4.2). The framework also suggests that, by combining these types of knowledge, we may obtain four additional types of knowledge: pedagogical content knowledge (PCK), technological pedagogical knowledge (TPK), technological content knowledge (TCK) and technological pedagogical content knowledge (TPACK). According to Mishra and Koehler (2006, 2009):

- PK is knowledge about pedagogical methods that are necessary in the processes of teaching and learning
- CK is knowledge about the actual subject matter that is to be learned or taught, including knowledge of important events, concepts, theories, and procedures within a given field
- TK includes knowledge of operating systems and computer hardware, and the ability to use standard sets of software tools such as word processors, spreadsheets, browsers, and e-mail
- PCK represents the blending of content and pedagogy into an understanding of how particular aspects of subject matter are adapted, represented, and organized for instruction
- TPK refers to the knowledge of the existence and features of the various technologies that can be used for teaching and learning, and vice versa; it also relates to the awareness of how teaching might change as a result of using certain technologies
- TCK concerns the knowledge about the way in which technology and content are deeply related with technological progress, allowing for newer and different representations of contents and influencing the type of technology to be used for teaching; finally
- TPACK includes and goes beyond all the types of knowledge mentioned above since it entails the integration of technological skills and knowledge, instructional methods, educational contents, and pedagogical theories.

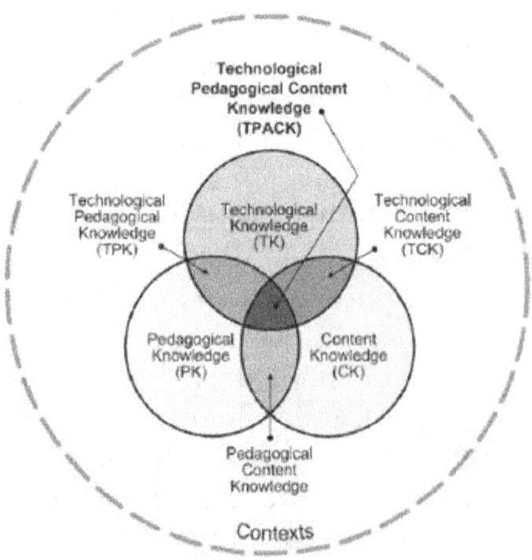

Source: Mishra and Koehler (2006, 2009).

Figuee 4.2. Graphic representation of TPACK.

Although the TPACK framework is well used by researchers around the world, there are still some critical issues that require consideration. Among them, we can mention the fuzzy boundaries associated with the model (Angeli & Valanides, 2009; Cox & Graham, 2009) and the wide definitions of all "core" knowledge (Graham, 2011). Angeli and Valanides (2009) observed that the boundaries among some components of TPACK, such as TCK, TPK, and TPACK, are not very clear and, as a consequence, the distinction and/or the classification of types of knowledge are not always sufficiently accurate. To reduce ambiguity, some scholars developed specific tools to delimit those knowledge areas (Archambault & Barnett, 2010; Schmidt, Baran, Thompson, Mishra, Koehler, & Shin, 2009). Through a factor analysis, Schmidt et al. (2009) created an assessment tool including 47 items to specifically examine and support pre-service teachers' development of TPACK in elementary or early childhood education. Later, Archambault and Barnett (2010) developed a more general tool for measuring different knowledge domains of TPACK. This instrument included 24 items and proved to be a promising tool for measuring each of the areas described by the TPACK. Again, Graham (2011) has recently pointed out that, according to the criteria for theory building, the TPACK framework presents some specific weaknesses in terms of definitions and underlined the need for further theoretical development in this area.

However, the overlooking of the contextual issues is probably one of the most relevant limitations of this model. Indeed, a weakness of the TPACK model is that it focuses only on individual characteristics to the exclusion of contextual factors; as such it "hides" a whole domain—that is, the institutional characteristics—that, as Cuban (1986, 2001) implies, significantly affects what actually happens at school when ICTs come into play. This does not mean that individual characteristics are not relevant, but we need to remember that teachers' personal characteristics are only one component of the complex system of factors influencing educational innovation. In particular, following Kozma's (2003) conceptual framework, we may say that teachers' characteristics belong to the "micro-level" of the complex system of variables impacting on pedagogical innovation. More analytically, Kozma (2003) identified a concentric set of contextual levels which include the classroom (micro-level), the school or local community (meso-level), and state, national, and international entities (macro-level). For each level, Kozma (2003) indicated actors and factors that can mediate change: on the micro-level, they include the classroom organization, teacher characteristics, teachers' experience with ICTs, and student characteristics; for the meso-level, school leaders and parents are identified as possible actors, while the school organization, ICT infrastructure, technical support, and local culture are possible factors; last, national and state policies and international trends are included on the macro-level.

With this mind, this study intended to focus on the micro-level of the Kozma's framework and aimed at exploring teachers' characteristics by applying the TPACK model in the Chinese educational context.

AIMS AND OBJECTIVES

Though the interest in measuring teachers' TPACK level around the world is growing (Archambault & Barnett, 2010; Chai, Koh, Tsai, & Tan, 2011; Erdogan & Sahin, 2010; Jang & Tsai, 2012; Oster-Levinz & Klieger, 2010), few studies have explored it in mainland China, where millions of teachers today are asked to innovate their teaching practices through ICTs. Indeed, despite China having put forward the national educational technology standard for teachers in 2004, until now, there has been no systematic research focusing on Chinese K–12 teachers' competences in educational technology. Therefore, the study aims to examine Chinese K–12 teachers' TPACK levels and explore the factors that may influence them. In particular, the specific objectives of the study include: (1) measuring K–12 teachers' TPACK levels in a selected city by using the already mentioned instrument, proposed by Archambault & Barnett (2010); and (2) verifying a range of hypotheses about the impact of personal characteristics on K–12 teachers' TPACK levels. As far as this second aim is concerned, it should be noted that there are a number of factors that can be considered. Buabeng-Andoh (2012) has recently conducted a wide literature review on factors influencing teachers' adoption and integration of ICTs into teaching, identifying three main categories: First, personal characteristics such as educational level, age, gender, educational experience, and experience with computer for educational purposes (e.g., Schiller, 2003); second, institutional characteristics, meaning accessibility of ITCs in the classroom, technical support, leadership sustainability, and teachers' training (e.g., Vannatta & Fordham, 2004); finally, technological characteristics, which include relative advantage, compatibility, complexity, trialability, and observability as perceived by individuals (Rogers, 2003). Among these variables, the current study focuses on personal characteristics. Indeed, as many scholars have pointed out, personal characteristics are crucial factors, but evidence around their impact is still uncertain. For example, Jang and Tsai (2012) found that teaching subjects and teaching experiences play crucial roles in teachers' TPACK. Other studies (e.g., Wong & Li, 2008) showed that teaching experience influences the successful use of ICTs in classrooms. However, some studies reported that teachers with less experience in teaching were more likely to integrate computers in their teaching than teachers with more teaching experience (e.g., U.S. National Center for Education Statistics, 2000). Other studies came up with the opposite conclusion (Lau & Sim, 2008), claiming that older teachers use computer technology in the classrooms more frequently than the younger teachers.

Another controversial variable is gender. Some studies (e.g., Kay, 2006) documented that male teachers used more ICTs than their female counterparts, while other studies revealed that the gender variable is not a predictor of ICT integration into teaching (Norris, Sullivan, Poirot, & Soloway, 2003). Also, previous online educational experience was found to have an impact on teachers' acceptance of using ICTs in their teaching (Yuen & Ma, 2008).

Considering these variables, the study planned to test the following hypotheses:

Hypothesis 1: There are no significant differences between male teachers' TPACK level (including the TK, PK, CK, TPK, TCK, PCK and TPACK domains) and that of female teachers.

Hypothesis 2: The "age" factor is positively related to K–12 teachers' TPACK level (including the TK, PK, CK, TPK, TCK, PCK and TPACK domains).

Hypothesis 3: The "discipline" factor has a significant impact on K–12 teachers' TPACK level (including the TK, PK, CK, TPK, TCK, PCK and TPACK domains).

Hypothesis 4: The "professional title" factor is positively related to K–12 teachers' TPACK level (including the TK, PK, CK, TPK, TCK, PCK and TPACK domains).

Hypothesis 5: The "teaching experience" factor is positively related to K–12 teachers' TPACK level (including the TK, PK, CK, TPK, TCK, PCK and TPACK domains).

Hypothesis 6: K–12 teachers with online education experience will show a higher TPACK level (including the TK, PK, CK, TPK, TCK, PCK and TPACK domains) than do K–12 teachers who have no online education experience.

METHODOLOGY

The target population was made up of teachers from Hangzhou city. Hangzhou is the capital and largest city of Zhejiang Province, which is located in Eastern China. It is also one of the most developed cities in China, with 807 K–12 schools, 0.91 million K–12 students and 56,283 K–12 teachers (Hangzhou Bureau of Education, 2010). All the schools can access the Internet and the student-to-computer ratio in primary and secondary schools is 6.7:1 and 4.9:1, respectively. According to the table of "Determining Sample Size for Research Activities" (Krejcie & Morgan, 1970), 384 teachers was the minimum sample. In the study, we asked 750 teachers to fill in the survey.

The study is descriptive in nature, adopting a quantitative research design. The survey instrument consisted of two sections. The first one aimed at collecting information about participants' personal characteristics, such as school type (primary school or secondary school), gender (male or female), age (indicated by years), level of education (Associate Degree, Bachelor's Degree and Master's Degree), discipline (Chinese, Mathematics, English, etc.), professional title (senior level, 1st level, 2nd level, 3rd level), teaching experience (indicated by years), and online educational experiences (having or not having).

The second section intended to determine teachers' TPACK level. As mentioned before, Archambault and Barnett's (2010) instrument, based on 24 items, was adopted, translated, and adapted to the Chinese cultural and institutional context. For each of the seven domains of the TPACK model, three or four items were used, such as: "I can face technical problems associated with hardware" (TK); "I'm able to use a variety of teaching strategies to explain concepts to students" (PK); "I'm able to create materials that match with specific provincial/state standards" (CK); "I'm able to implement online environments supporting students in developing new knowledge and skills" (TPK); "I'm able to distinguish between correct and incorrect problem-solving attempts by students" (PCK); "I'm able to use technological representations (i.e., multimedia, visual demonstrations, etc.) to demonstrate specific concepts in my content area" (TCK); and "I'm able to use online assessment tools to change instruction" (TPACK). Participants' responses to each statement were on a 5-point Likert scale, ranging from 1 = Poor at one end to 5 = Excellent at the other, with 3 = Good in the middle. Higher scores in a specific domain mean higher perceived acquaintance or more self-perceived competences in the specific domain of knowledge. The questionnaire underwent expert review and two rounds of think-aloud piloting. The internal consistency (Cronbach's alpha) of each subscale was examined and the alpha values ranged from 0.70 to 0.89, which means that the instrument was reasonable for internal reliability.

Data were collected during the winter semester of 2011 (October-December). With the help of the Hangzhou Bureau of Education, 750 printed surveys were handed out to 25 randomly selected primary and secondary schools. All participants were provided with written information introducing the nature and purpose of the research project. At the same time, all participants were told that they could choose not to fill in part or all of the survey. At the end of 2011, we got 691 useful surveys back and the valid rate was 92%. Data were analyzed by using statistical package for the social sciences (SPSS) 15.0 software. Descriptive statistics were used to describe information about participants' personal characteristics and their overall TPACK level. Kruskal-Wallis analysis and Mann-Whitney test were used to analyze the significant differences in TPACK levels with reference to participants' individual characteristics. Because some participants left some blanks in their survey instruments, the subtotals in some tables would differ from the total number of the useful survey (n = 691).

FINDINGS

Among the 691 participating K–12 teachers, 410 (59.8%) were primary school teachers and 276 (40.2%) secondary school teachers; 194 (28.4%) were male and 490 (71.6%) female. Table 4.1 shows participants' demographics. Data indicate that the majority of participants were 39 years old or younger and had a Bachelor's degree; they teach different disciplines, covering Chinese, Mathematics, English, Computer Education, Science, Music, Painting, Geography, and more. Their teaching experiences and their professional titles noticeably vary among different groups; about four-tenths of the participating K–12 teachers indicated that they had online education experience.

Objective one was to measure K–12 teachers' TPACK level in a selected city in China. As shown in Table 4.2, participating K–12 teachers from Hangzhou city (N = 691) reported being more competent in non-technology-related TPACK domains, as indicated by PK (M = 3.02), CK (M = 2.88) and PCK (M = 2.99), than in technology-related TPACK domains, as indicated by TK (M = 2.46), TPK (M = 2.59), TCK (M = 2.59), and TPACK (M = 2.46).

Objective two aimed at verifying a range of hypotheses about the impact of personal characteristics on K–12 teachers' TPACK level. Regarding Hypothesis 1, as results of Mann-Whitney test (Table 4.3), gender had a significant impact on all seven TPACK domains ($p < 0.05$): (1) TK, z = 10.15; (2) PK, z = 5.56; (3) CK, z = 5.88; (4) TPK, z = 4.13; (5) PCK, z = 5.80; (6) TCK, z = 4.21; (7) TPACK, z = 4.50. Male teachers rated themselves more competent than did female teachers. Therefore, Hypothesis 1 was rejected.

Regarding Hypothesis 2, as results of Kruskal-Wallis analysis indicate (Table 4.4), age had a significant impact on three out of seven of K–12 teachers' TPACK domains ($p < 0.05$): (1) TK, Chi-Square = 10.40; (2) CK, Chi-Square = 7.46; (3) PCK, Chi-Square = 10.04. Generally speaking, the older K–12 teachers were, the more competent they were in CK and PCK, while the less competent they were in TK. However, age had no significant impact on K–12 teachers' other knowledge domains, such as PK, TPK, TCK, and TPACK. Therefore, Hypothesis 2 was partly confirmed.

Table 4.1. Participating K–12 Teachers' Personal Characteristics (*N* = 691)

Personal Characteristics		*N*	%
School type	Primary school	410	59.8
	Secondary school	276	40.2
Gender	Male	194	28.4
	Female	490	71.6
Age	≦ 29	247	36.3
	30-39	336	49.3
	≥ 40	98	14.4
Disciplines	Mathematics	219	32.40
	Chinese	175	25.89
	English	76	11.24
	Computer education	70	10.36
	Painting	29	4.29
	Music	26	3.85
	Science	26	3.85
	Physical education	22	3.25
	Geography	14	2.07
	Politics	9	1.33
	History	6	0.89
	Moral education	4	0.59
Level of education	Associate Degree	54	7.9
	Bachelor's Degree	603	88.5
	Master's Degree	24	3.5
Professional title	Senior level	66	9.9
	1st level	322	48.1
	2nd level	200	29.9
	3rd level	82	12.2
Teaching experience	0–5	193	28.6
	6–10	185	27.4
	11–15	115	17.0
	16–20	109	16.1
	>20	73	10.8
Online education experience	Have	285	41.2
	Have not	240	34.7
	No response	166	24.0

Table 4. 2. Participating K–12 Teachers' TPACK Level (*N* = 691)

	Number of Survey Items	*N*	*Mean*	*Percentiles* 25th	50th (Median)	75th
TK	3	691	2.46	2.00	2.33	3.00
PK	3	691	3.02	2.50	3.00	3.50
CK	3	691	2.88	2.33	2.67	3.33
TPK	4	691	2.59	2.00	2.33	3.00
PCK	4	691	2.99	2.40	3.00	3.40
TCK	3	691	2.59	2.00	2.50	3.00
TPCK	4	691	2.49	2.00	2.25	3.00

Note: 1 = poor; 2 = fair; 3 = good; 4 = very good; 5 = excellent

Table 4.3. Distribution of Participating K–12 Teachers' TPACK by Gender (*N* = 691)

	Gender	*n*	*Mean Rank*	*Sum of Rank*	*Mann-Whitney U*	*Z*	*p*
TK	Male	194	463.18	89,857.00	24,118.00	10.15**	0.00
	Female	490	294.72	144,413.00			
PK	Male	194	407.50	79,055.00	34,920.00	5.56**	0.00
	Female	490	316.77	155,215.00			
CK	Male	194	412.29	79,984.50	33,990.50	5.88**	0.00
	Female	490	314.87	154,285.50			
TPK	Male	194	391.60	75,971.00	38,004.00	4.13**	0.00
	Female	490	323.06	158,299.00			
PCK	Male	194	411.76	79,882.00	34,093.00	5.80**	0.00
	Female	490	315.08	154,388.00			
TCK	Male	194	392.69	76,182.00	37,793.00	4.21**	0.00
	Female	490	322.63	158,088.00			
TPACK	Male	194	396.16	76,854.50	37,120.50	4.50**	0.00
	Female	490	321.26	157,415.50			

Note: 1 = poor; 2 = fair; 3 = good; 4 = very good; 5 = excellent. ** $p < 0.01$

Table 4.4. Distribution of Participating K–12T eachers' TPACK by Age (N = 691)

	Age	*n*	*Mean Rank*	*DF*	*Chi-Square*	*p*
	≦ 29	247	362.01	2		
TK	30–39	336	341.30		10.40**	0.006
	≥ 40	98	287.01			
	≦ 29	247	331.11	2		
PK	30–39	336	345.75		1.07	0.59
	≥ 40	98	349.65			
	≦ 29	247	318.73	2		
CK	30–39	336	345.89		7.46*	0.02
	≥ 40	98	380.35			
	≦ 29	247	340.24	2		
TPK	30–39	336	345.38		0.62	0.73
	≥ 40	98	327.89			
	≦ 29	247	311.52	2		
PCK	30–39	336	352.08		10.04**	0.007
	≥ 40	98	377.31			
	≦ 29	247	338.98	2		
TCK	30–39	336	349.49		2.14	0.34
	≥ 40	98	316.97			
	≦29	247	344.46	2		
TPACK	30–39	336	343.08		0.76	0.68
	≥ 40	98	325.12			

Note: 1 = poor; 2 = fair; 3 = good; 4 = very good; 5 = excellent. * $p < 0.05$; ** $p < 0.01$

As to the impact of discipline, given that Chinese, Mathematics and English are the three most important courses in Chinese K–12 education, and also considering that teachers teaching Chinese, Mathematics, English, and Computer Education were the most numerous groups in the study, we limited this to comparing these four groups' TPACK levels. Regarding Hypothesis 3, as shown by Kruskal-Wallis analysis (Table 4.5), discipline had a significant impact on K–12 teachers' technology-related knowledge domains ($p < 0.05$): (1) TK, Chi-Square = 75.50; (2) TPK, Chi-Square = 11.99; (3) TCK, Chi-Square = 23.92; (4) TPACK, Chi-Square = 9.40. Computer Education teachers declared themselves to be more competent in technology-related knowledge than teachers teaching

Chinese, Mathematics, or English. However, discipline had no significant impact on K–12 teachers' non-technology-related knowledge, such as PK, CK, and PCK. Therefore, Hypothesis 3 was partly confirmed.

Table 4.5. Distribution of Participating K–12 Teachers' TPACK by Discipline (N = 540)

	Discipline	*n*	*Mean Rank*	*DF*	*Chi-Square*	*p*
TK	Chinese	175	236.02	3		
	Mathematics	219	273.58			
	English	76	211.12		75.50**	0.00
	Computer Education	70	407.71			
PK	Chinese	175	252.8	3		
	Mathematics	219	286.72			
	English	76	261.2		5.15	0.16
	Computer Education	70	270.46			
CK	Chinese	175	260.39	3		
	Mathematics	219	276.92			
	English	76	254.04		3.10	0.38
	Computer Education	70	289.81			
	Chinese	175	273.17	3		
	Mathematics	219	259.7			
TPK	English	76	242.62		11.99**	0.007
	Computer Education	70	323.89			
	Chinese	175	248.26	3		
	Mathematics	219	287.98			
PCK	English	76	259.53		7.00	0.07
	Computer Education	70	279.73			

(Table continues on next page)

Table 4.5. (Continued)

	Discipline	*n*	*Mean Rank*	*DF*	*Chi-Square*	*p*
TCK	Chinese	175	256.73	3	23.92**	0.00
	Mathematics	219	255.17			
	English	76	265.76			
	Computer Education	70	353.94			
TPACK	Chinese	175	273.33	3	9.40*	0.02
	Mathematics	218	256.34			
	English	76	256.38			
	Computer Education	70	319.00			

Note: 1 = poor; 2 = fair; 3 = good; 4 = very good; 5 = excellent. * p <0.05; ** p <0.01

Regarding Hypothesis 4, as indicated by Kruskal-Wallis analysis (Table 4.6), professional title had a significant impact on four out of seven of K–12 teachers' TPACK domains ($p < 0.05$): (1) TK, Chi-Square = 10.56; (2) PK, Chi-Square = 19.41; (3) CK, Chi-Square = 34.12; (4) PCK, Chi-Square = 46.59. However, professional title had no significant impact on K–12 teachers' perceived TPK, TCK, and TPACK. Therefore, Hypothesis 4 was partly confirmed.

Table 4.6. Distribution of Participating K–12 Teachers' TPACK by Professional Title (*N* = 691)

	Professional Title	*n*	*Mean Rank*	*DF*	*Chi-Square*	*p*
TK	Senior level	66	279.64	3	10.56*	0.01
	1st level	322	326.48			
	2nd level	200	360.42			
	3rd level	82	355.13			
PK	Senior level	66	402.85	3	19.41**	0.00
	1st level	322	332.75			
	2nd level	200	345.16			
	3rd level	82	268.53			

(Table continues on next page)

Table 4.6. (Continued)

	Professional Title	*n*	*Mean Rank*	*DF*	*Chi-Square*	*p*
CK	Senior level	66	432.51	3	34.12**	0.00
	1st level	322	330.90			
	2nd level	200	345.97			
	3rd level	82	249.98			
TPK	Senior level	66	348.70	3	5.56	0.14
	1st level	322	341.88			
	2nd level	200	339.84			
	3rd level	82	289.24			
PCK	Senior level	66	439.32	3	46.59**	0.00
	1st level	322	338.52			
	2nd level	200	341.79			
	3rd level	82	224.73			
TCK	Senior level	66	366.26	3	6.78	0.08
	1st level	322	339.84			
	2nd level	200	337.65			
	3rd level	82	288.44			
TPACK	Senior level	66	336.82	3	3.41	0.33
	1st level	322	338.90			
	2nd level	200	344.35			
	3rd level	82	299.49			

Note: 1 = poor; 2 = fair; 3 = good; 4 = very good; 5 = excellent. * $p < 0.05$; ** $p < 0.01$

Coming to Hypothesis 5, as shown by Kruskal-Wallis analysis (Table 4.7), teaching experience had a significant impact on three out of seven of K–12 teachers' TPACK domains ($p < 0.05$): (1) TK, Chi-Square = 17.75; (2) CK, Chi-Square = 10.55; (3) PCK, Chi-Square = 17.36. Generally speaking, the more teaching experience K–12 teachers had, the more competent they were in CK and PCK, while the less competent they were in TK (Table 4.9). However, teaching experience had no significant impact on K–12 teachers' perceived PK, TPK, TCK, and TPACK. Therefore, Hypothesis 5 was partly confirmed.

Table 4.7. Distribution of Participating K–12 Teachers' TPACK by Teaching Experience (*N* = 691)

	Teaching Experience	*n*	*Mean Rank*	*DF*	*Chi-Square*	*p*
	0–5	193	361.23	4		
	6–10	185	365.78			
TK	11–15	115	329.05		17.75**	0.00
	16–20	109	291.08			
	> 20	73	290.36			
	0–5	193	318.27	4		
	6-10	185	337.72			
PK	11–15	115	335.23		4.81	0.31
	16–20	109	363.2			
	> 20	73	357.62			
	0–5	193	309.88	4		
	6–10	185	334.97			
CK	11–15	115	333.8		10.55*	0.03
	16–20	109	368.99			
	> 20	73	380.36			
	0–5	193	333.62	4		
	6–10	185	344.55			
TPK	11–15	115	339.24		1.50	0.83
	16–20	109	347.69			
	> 20	73	316.54			
	0–5	193	296.52	4		
	6–10	185	335.99			
PCK	11–15	115	346.8		17.36**	0.00
	16–20	109	385.64			
	> 20	73	367.77			
	0–5	193	324	4		
	6–10	185	370.25			
TCK	11–15	115	325.45		7.91	0.10
	16–20	109	338.61			
	> 20	73	312.16			

(Table continues on next page)

Table 4.7. (Continued)

	Teaching Experience	n	Mean Rank	DF	Chi-Square	p
TPACK	0–5	193	324.26	4	3.32	0.51
	6–10	185	358.5			
	11–15	115	339.74			
	16–20	109	330.39			
	> 20	73	330.99			

Note: 1 = poor; 2 = fair; 3 = good; 4 = very good; 5 = excellent. * p <0.05; ** p <0.01

As far as Hypothesis 6 is concerned, Results of Mann-Whitney test (Table 4.8) show that previous online education experience had a significant impact on all seven TPACK domains (p < 0.05): (1) TK, z =8.50; (2) PK, z =6.61; (3) CK, z =10.80; (4) TPK, z =6.88; (1)TK, z= 8.50; (2) PK, z = 6.61; (3) CK, z = 8.34; (4) TPK, z = 10.80; (5) PCK, z =6.88; (6) TCK, z =9.41; (7) TPACK, z =10.45. K–12 teachers who attended online courses were more competent in all seven domains than teachers without online education experience. Therefore, Hypothesis 6 was totally confirmed.

Table 4.8. Distribution of Participating K–12 Teachers' TPACK by Online Education Experience (*N* = 691)

	Online Education Experience	n	Mean Rank	Sum of Rank	Mann-Whitney U	Z	p
TK	Yes	285	314.19	89,545	19,610.00	8.50**	0.00
	No	240	202.21	48,530			
PK	Yes	285	302.13	86,106.5	23,048.50	6.61**	0.00
	No	240	216.54	51,968.5			
CK	Yes	285	313.11	89,236	19,919.00	8.34**	0.00
	No	240	203.5	48,839			
TPK	Yes	285	327.94	93,461.5	15,693.50	10.80**	0.00
	No	240	185.89	44,613.5			
PCK	Yes	285	304.58	86,806	22,349.00	6.88**	0.00
	No	240	213.62	51,269			
TCK	Yes	285	319.84	91,153.5	18,001.50	9.41**	0.00
	No	240	195.51	46,921.5			
TPACK	Yes	285	326.08	92,932.5	16,222.50	10.45**	0.00
	No	240	188.09	45,142.5			

Note: 1 = poor; 2 = fair; 3 = good; 4 = very good; 5 = excellent. ** p < 0.01

DISCUSSION AND IMPLICATIONS

Although the sample in the study was limited, results enable us to make some considerations on K–12 teachers' levels of technology integration into teaching practices in China and reflect on the role of training for innovation of Chinese educational system. Generally speaking, the study found that surveyed Chinese K–12 teachers rated themselves more competent in non-technology-related TPACK domains, as indicated by PK, CK, and PCK, than in technology-related TPACK domains, as indicated by TK, TPK, TCK, and TPACK. This means that while teachers believe to possess an adequate level of pedagogical and subject content knowledge, they feel less competent in ICT for teaching. However, there were differences among K–12 teachers' TPACK levels when the impact of their personal characteristics was taken into account.

Looking at the variable gender, the study found that male teachers rated themselves more competent in all seven TPACK domains than did female teachers. On one hand, such findings seem to confirm previous studies, which stated that significant differences were found between male and female teachers in favour of males (Erdogan & Sahin, 2010). On the other hand, this result contrasts with other studies which found that there is no significant difference in teachers' TPACK according to gender (Jang & Tsai, 2012). Therefore, it seems that "gender" still remains a controversial factor; more qualitative studies would be useful to understand teachers' attitudes toward ICTs according to gender and to explore, in the school context, what are the social expectations from teachers in the light of this variable.

Discipline had a significant impact on K–12 teachers' technology-related knowledge domains (TK, TPK, TCK, and TPACK), while it had no significant impact on K–12 teachers' non-technology-related knowledge domains (PK, CK, and PCK). The study indicated that computer education teachers were more competent in technology-related knowledge than teachers teaching the three core courses (Chinese, Mathematics, or English). However, they reported similar levels of pedagogical and subject content knowledge, as did teachers from other disciplines. We must be cautious in the interpretation of these data. It is probable that computer education teachers perceive themselves as more skilled in ICTs and therefore believe themselves to be competent in technology and pedagogy integration as well. However, we cannot conclude that teachers in computer education are actually more competent, but just that they are likely to be more confident in their own capacity to use ICTs in daily practices. The difference between these two levels of analysis must be recognized to avoid the trivial conclusion according to which being able to perform technical procedures in the classroom necessarily brings to an effective way of blending technology, subject knowledge, and pedagogy. However, looking at the overall school organization, the presence of teachers who are confident with ICTs could provide support for less confident teachers. This resource should not be overlooked.

Age, professional title, and teaching experience are mutually positively correlated variables. The study found that these three variables had a significant impact on K–12 teachers' TK, CK, and PCK. However, they had no significant impact on teachers' TPK, TCK, and TPACK. Younger teachers indicated a significantly higher level of TK than did their counterparts, while teachers with a higher professional title indicated a significantly higher level of PK, CK, and PCK than did their counterparts. In addition, teachers having more years of teaching experience indicated a significantly higher level of CK and PCK than did their counterparts. No differences in the level of technological pedagogical knowledge, technological content knowledge, or technological pedagogical content knowledge were found between teachers on the basis of their age, professional title, or teaching experience. This result is different, for example, from that of Jang and Tsai's (2012) study, which found that teachers' TPACK differed significantly according to their varying amounts of teaching experience: Teachers with more teaching experience demonstrated higher TPACK than did teachers with less teaching experience (Jang & Tsai, 2012). Our findings indicate that CK and PCK would increase along with age, professional title, and teaching experience, while technology-related knowledge would not increase naturally along with age, professional title, and teaching experience. This seems to suggest that while the direct experience of teaching may have an influence on the improvement of teachers' content knowledge and pedagogical content knowledge, this is not the case with technology-enhanced teaching. There could be more than one explanation for this. Firstly, since technologies always change, teachers' technological skills tend to become rapidly obsolete, while they are expected to use different types of technologies throughout their career. This is the case, for example, for a teacher who started working in '80 and is able to use a computer for teaching, but not an interactive whiteboard. In order to use it, he or she needs to learn how to use this new technology and how to integrate it in his or her teaching practice. Therefore, there seems to be a tension between the teacher's experience and the introduction of new technologies into daily practices. Second, as highlighted by Cuban (1986), the professional culture of teaching makes most teachers resist change rather than adopt it. The profession of teaching has the unique characteristic that teachers, before becoming teachers, have been taught for years, thus experiencing a long "unwilled training." Regardless of their age, they mostly tend to reproduce what they have experienced rather than change it by innovating their practices. To a certain extent, our finding confirms this view. Being a young teacher is not enough to ensure innovation and change.

In addition, interestingly, the study also found that professional title had a significant impact on K–12 teachers' PK level, while age and teaching experience had no significant impact on K–12 teachers' PK level. At first glance, this finding is a little confusing when considering that age, teaching experience, and professional title are three correlated variables. However, looking into the context of Chinese educational and training programs for K–12 teachers, researchers could find some reasonable explanations for this result: Pedagogical knowledge is more about theoretical knowledge relating to teaching strategies. In both pre- and in-service educational and training programs for Chinese K–12 teachers, many contents revolve around pedagogical knowledge. This study confirmed this situation by indicating that, among the seven knowledge domains, teachers rated their pedagogical knowledge as the highest one. It means that, in general, teachers show confidence in their pedagogical knowledge and therefore few differences are likely to emerge among groups of different ages and teaching experiences. Teachers' teaching experience would increase naturally with their age, while their professional titles would not change spontaneously with age increase. To get a higher professional title in Chinese K–12 school systems, besides accumulating a certain amount of years of teaching experience, teachers need to undertake some research programs and publish academic papers. Such research activities might help teachers to develop a deeper understanding of pedagogical knowledge in theory and practice. This contextual information might explain the different impact of age, teaching experience, and professional title on teachers' pedagogical knowledge.

Finally, the study found that previous online education experience had a significant impact on all seven TPACK domains of participants. Indeed, K–12 teachers who had attended online educational or training programs declared to be more competent in all seven domains than did K–12 teachers without online education experience. Such findings confirmed previous studies about the impact of the time factor, which means that to integrate technologies into teaching practice in an effective way, teachers need to become familiar with them through training and appropriate coaching for a certain amount of time (Oster-Levinz & Klieger, 2010; Polly, Mims, Shepherd, & Inan, 2010).

Though we must be careful with the interpretation of these results, what are their implications for Chinese teachers' educational and training programs and the technological innovation of teaching practices?

Our findings suggest that integrating technology into teachers' pedagogical practices is still a big challenge for the Chinese K–12 school system. Although most of the Chinese K–12 teachers have opportunities to receive pre- and in-service training programs (Han & Wang, 2010), their competences in technology-related TPACK domains are still unsatisfactory. Such phenomena might be partly explained by the insufficient high-quality pre- and in-service training programs organized for K–12 teachers (Potter, 2003). Too much theoretical knowledge, lack of practical guidance, lack of interactivities and cultural and pedagogical conflicts were frequently reported in literature as obvious shortcomings of current educational technology training programs (Ding, 2002; Zhu, 2011). The findings therefore imply that innovative teacher education/training programs are necessary to better integrate technology into the instructional process. More practical guidance and interactive activities should be added in current teachers' education programs to help them deepen their understanding about the relationship between technology, pedagogy, and content. What's more, increasing teachers' online educational experiences should be recommended to improve teachers' confidence with ICTs and, consequently, their ability to use technologies in their daily pedagogical practices.

Another consideration refers to the influence that teachers' beliefs may have on the innovation process. As underlined by Zhao and Cziko (2001), when using ICTs in pedagogical practice, teachers' actions and decisions are frequently inspired by pragmatic, rather than methodological, principles. Teachers tend to adopt ICTs when they think they will achieve better results by using them (effectiveness principle), when they realize that using ICTs does not interfere with other important educational goals (disturbing principle), and when they believe they have sufficient skills and resources to manage new situations (control principle). Teachers' beliefs also include the visions they have about teaching as well as their views on their role and of that of their children. They have implicit pedagogies influencing their practice and personal expectations of the role they have to play in the classroom, regardless of instructional theories and principles. Finally, teachers' beliefs also incorporate the ideas they have of their own digital competences and their capacity to integrate them in their practice. All these elements, especially teachers' self-confidence and self-efficacy, must be taken into consideration when planning teachers' educational or training programs. The use of tools based on self-perceived questionnaires, as in the case of the present study, may be of fundamental importance to evaluate this subjective dimension, which is so relevant for educational innovation and school change.

CONCLUSION AND LIMITATIONS OF THE STUDY

In this digital era, the introduction of ICTs in education is one of the most obvious trends that happened in all types of educational settings around the world. Within this process, teachers, as the most influential agents of change, have been viewed as playing a crucial role. To a certain degree, teachers' technological pedagogical and content knowledge level could be looked at as a determinant, as well as a predictor, of a school or a state's degree of informationalization. With this in mind, this study attempted to explore K–12 teachers' TPACK level in a provincial city in China and to investigate the impact of some personal characteristics on these teachers' TPACK level. Although the study found data that may provide food for thought, its findings did not show any cause-and-effect relationships, nor can they be generalized. Due to time and other contextual limitations, the study only explored a small group of Chinese K–12 teachers in an urban city, which is located in an economically developed province. Considering the millions of K–12 teachers in the Chinese basic education system, and the existence of dramatic socio-economic differences among different regions, the results could not provide a whole picture of Chinese K–12 teachers' TPACK level. Further research should be carried out to explore teachers' TPACK level in a larger population or among some specific groups, such as rural teachers, or teachers working for higher education, vocational education, or special education, among other things.

As to the measurement tools used in the study, though they were tested in previous researches and adapted to Chinese situation, there are still some obvious weaknesses. Firstly, the measure of each knowledge domain depends on participants' personal judgment. Although this self-reported knowledge level could, to a certain degree, reflect an individual's actual situation, it still remains a subjective assessment. More objective measurement tools are needed to overcome this shortcoming. Second, those statements used in the instrument just present a general description of the seven knowledge domains of the TPACK model. The instrument did not take into account the differences existing among different disciplines. As is well known, each discipline has its own feature and, therefore, it requires different content knowledge, pedagogical knowledge, and technological knowledge on the part of teachers. Therefore, a discipline-specific instrument might be needed to reflect more authentically and effectively a teacher's actual TPACK level. At the same time, when completing a discipline-specific instrument, teachers might have a better idea of their own strengths and weaknesses in the area of technological pedagogical and content knowledge integration.

ACKNOWLEDGMENTS

A special thank you to Dr. Maria Ranieri who assisted with the writing and reviewing of this work This work was supported by grants from the National Social Science Foundation of China (13CGL113).

REFERENCES

Al-Qirim, N. (2011). Determinants of interactive white board success in teaching in higher education institutions. *Computers & Education, 56*(3), 827–838. doi:10.1016/j.compedu.2010.10.024

Andersson, S. B. (2006). Newly qualified teachers' learning related to their use of information and communication technology: a Swedish perspective. *British Journal of Educational Technology, 37*(5), 665–682.

Angeli, C., & Valanides, N. (2009). Epistemological and methodological issues for the conceptualization, development, and assessment of ICT-TPCK: advances in technological pedagogical content knowledge (TPCK). *Computers & Education, 52*(1), 154–168. doi:10.1016/j.compedu.2008.07.006

Anthony, A. B., & Clark, L. M. (2011). Examining dilemmas of practice associated with the integration of technology into mathematics classrooms serving urban students. *Urban Education, 46*(6), 1300–1331.

Archambault, L. M., & Barnett, J. H. (2010). Revisiting technological pedagogical content knowledge: exploring the TPACK framework. *Computers & Education, 55*(4), 1656–1662. doi:10.1016/j.compedu.2010.07.009

Asia Development Bank (2009). *Good practice in information and communication technology for education*. Mandaluyong City, Philippines: Asian Development Bank.

Buabeng-Andoh, C. (2012). Factors influencing teachers' adoption and integration of information and communication technology into teaching: a review of the literature. *International Journal of Education and Development using Information and Communication Technology (IJEDICT), 8*(1), 136–155.

Chai, C. S., Koh, J. H. L., Tsai, C. C., & Tan, L. L. W. (2011). Modeling primary school pre-service teachers' technological pedagogical content knowledge (TPACK) for meaningful learning with information and communication technology (ICT). *Computers & Education, 57*(1), 1184–1193. doi:10.1016/j.compedu.2011.01.007

Cox, S., & Graham, C. R. (2009). Diagramming TPACK in practice: using an elaborated model of the TPACK framework to analyze and depict teacher knowledge. *Tech Trends, 53*(5), 60–69.

Cradler, J., Freeman, M., Cradler, R., & McNabb, M. (2004). Research implications for preparing teachers to use technology. *Learning & Leading with Technology, 30*(1), 50–55.

Cuban, L. (1986). *Teachers and machines: the classroom use of technology since 1920*. New York, NY: Teachers College Press.

Cuban, L. (2001). *Oversold and underused: computers in the classroom*. Cambridge, MA: Harvard University Press.

Ding, X. (2002, October). *The digital divide and ICT education in China*. Paper presented at the Seventh Programming Cycle of APEID Activities "The Promotion of ICT Education to Narrow the Digital Divide," Tokyo, Japan.

Erdogan, A., & Sahin, I. (2010). Relationship between math teacher candidates' technological pedagogical and content knowledge (TPACK) and achievement levels. *Procedia Social and Behavioral Sciences, 2*, 2707–2711. doi:10.1016/j.sbspro.2010.03.400

Graham, C. R. (2011). Theoretical considerations for understanding technological pedagogical content knowledge (TPACK). *Computers & Education, 57*(2), 1953–1960. doi:10.1016/j.compedu.2011.04.010

Han, J., & Wang, Z. (2010). Capability building in educational technology for teachers in China. *British Journal of Educational Technology, 41*(4), 607–611. doi:10.1111/j.1467-8535.2010.01089.x

Hangzhou Bureau of Education (2010). Educational development in Hangzhou. Retrieved February 22, 2012, from http://www.hzedu.net/Template/govManage3.aspx?id=32979

Haydn, T. A., & Barton, R. (2007). Common needs and different agendas: how trainee teachers make progress in their ability to use ICT in subject teaching. Some lessons from the UK. *Computers & Education, 49*(4), 1018–1036.

Jang, S., & Tsai, M. (2012). Exploring the TPACK of Taiwanese elementary mathematics and science teachers with respect to use of interactive whiteboards. *Computers & Education, 59*(2), 327–338. doi:10.1016/j.compedu.2012.02.003

Kay, R. (2006). Addressing gender differences in computer ability, attitudes and use: the laptop effect. *Journal of Educational Computing Research, 34*(2), 187–211.

Koehler, M. J., Mishra, P., & Yahya, K. (2007). Tracing the development of teacher knowledge in a design seminar: integrating content, pedagogy, and technology. *Computers & Education, 49*(3), 740–762.

Kozma, R. (Ed.) (2003). *Technology, innovation, and educational change: A global perspective*. Eugene, OR: International Society for Technology in Education.

Krejcie, R. V., & Morgan, D. W. (1970). Determining sample size for research activities. *Educational and Psychological Measurement, 30*, 607–610.

Lau, C. T., & Sim, C. H. (2008). Exploring the extent of ICT adoption among secondary school teachers in Malaysia. *International Journal of Computing and ICT Research, 2*(2), 19–36.

Lee, M. H., & Tsai, C. C. (2010). Exploring teachers' perceived self-efficacy and technological pedagogical content knowledge with respect to educational use of the world wide web. *Instructional Science, 38*, 1–21.

Li, Y., & Lindner, J. R. (2007). Faculty adoption behaviour about Web-based distance education: a case study from China Agricultural University. *British Journal of Educational Technology, 38*(1), 83–94. doi: 10.1111/j.1467-8535.2006.00594.x

Miao, F. (2008). ICT-capacity standards for teachers in China. In E. Meleisea (Ed.), *ICT in teacher education: case studies from the Asia-Pacific region* (pp. 53–61). Bangkok, Thailand: UNESCO.

Mishra, P., & Koehler, M. J. (2006). Technological pedagogical content knowledge: a framework for teacher knowledge. *Teachers College Record, 108*(6), 1017–1054.

Mishra, P., & Koehler, M. J. (2009).Teachers' technology pedagogical content knowledge and learning activity types: curriculum-based technology integration reframed. *Journal of Research on Technology in Education, 41*(4), 393–416.

MOE (2012). 2010 *Chinese educational statistical data.* Retrieved February 22, 2012, from http://www.moe.edu.cn/publicfiles/business/htmlfiles/moe/s6200/index.html

Norris, C., Sullivan, T., Poirot, J., & Soloway, E. (2003). No access, no use, no impact: snapshot surveys of educational technology in K–12. *Journal of Research on Technology in Education, 36*(1), 15–27.

Oster-Levinz, A., & Klieger, A. (2010). Online tasks as a tool to promote teachers' expertise within the technological pedagogical content knowledge (TPACK). *Procedia Social and Behavioral Sciences, 2*, 354–358. doi: 10.1016/j.sbspro.2010.03.034

Pierson, M. E. (2001). Technology integration practice as a function of pedagogical expertise. *Journal of Research on Computing in Education, 33*(4), 413–430.

Polly, D., Mims, C., Shepherd, C. E., & Inan, F. (2010). Evidence of impact: transforming teacher education with preparing tomorrow's teachers to teach with technology (PT3) grants. *Teaching and Teacher Education, 26*(1), 863–870. doi:10.1016/j.tate.2009.10.024

Potter, G. (2003). *A comparison of Chinese and Western distance education initiatives: educational goals and instructional practices*. Paper presented on Distance Learning and the Internet Conference 2003. Singapore. Retrieved February 22, 2012, from http://www.cit.nus.edu.sg/dli2003/Presentation/Geoff_Potter.pdf

van Raaij, E. M., & Schepers, J. J. L. (2008). The acceptance and use of a virtual learning environment in China. *Computers & Education, 50*(3), 838–852. DOI:10.1016/j.compedu.2006.09.001

Rogers, E. M. (2003). *Diffusion of innovations*. New York, NY: Free Press.

Schiller, J. (2003). Working with ICT: perceptions of Australian principals. *Journal of Education Administration, 41*(3), 171–185.

Schmidt, D. A., Baran, E., Thompson, A. D., Mishra, P., Koehler, M. J., & Shin, T. S. (2009). Technological pedagogical content knowledge (TPACK): the development and validation of an assessment instrument for preservice teachers. *Journal of Research on Technology in Education, 42*(2), 123–149.

Shinohara, F., & Zhou, N. (2006, June/July). *Research and development of the Asia-Pacific regional guideline of ICT-pedagogy integration and teacher training.* Paper presented in the 18th Annual Japan-U.S. Teacher Education Consortium, Tokyo, Japan. Retrieved from http://www.u-gakugei.ac.jp/~shinohar/projcts/mongol/references/referen/itedsp/justec06.pdf

Shulman, L. S. (1986). Those who understand: knowledge growth in teaching. *Educational Researcher, 15*(2), 4–14.

Shulman, L. S. (1987). Knowledge and teaching: foundations of the new reform. *Harvard Education Review, 57*(1), 1–21.

Starkey, L. (2010). Supporting the digitally able beginning teacher. *Teaching and Teacher Education, 26*(7), 1429–1438.

Teo, T., Chai, C. S., Hung, D., & Lee, C. B. (2008). Beliefs about teaching and uses of technology among pre-service teachers. *Asia-Pacific Journal of Teacher Education, 36*(2), 163-174. doi:10.1080/13598660801971641

Thompson, A. D. & Mishra, P. (2007-2008). Breaking news: TPCK becomes TPACK! *Journal of Computing in Teacher Education, 24*(2), 38–64.

UNESCO (2005). *Regional guideline on teacher development for pedagogy-technology integration*. Retrieved from http://www.unescobkk.org/fileadmin/user_upload/ict/e-books/Draft_Regional_Guidelines/Regional_guidelines.pdf

U.S. National Center for Education Statistics (2000). *Teachers' tools for the 21st century: A report on teachers' use of technology*. Retrieved from http://nces.ed.gov/pubs2000/2000102.pdf

Vannatta, R., & Fordham, N. (2004). Teacher dispositions as predictors of classroom technology use. *Journal of Research on Technology in Education, 36*(3), 253–271.

Wallace, R. M. (2004). A framework for understanding teaching with the Internet. *American Educational Research Journal, 41*(2), 447–488. doi:10.3102/00028312041002447

Wong, E. M. L., & Li, S. C. (2008). Framing ICT implementation in a context of educational change: a multilevel analysis. *School Effectiveness and School Improvement, 19*(1), 99–120.

Yuen, A. H. K., & Ma, W. W. K. (2008). Exploring teacher acceptance of e-learning technology. *Asia-Pacific Journal of Teacher Education, 36*(3), 229–243. doi:10.1080/13598660802232779

Zhao, Y., & Cziko, G. A. (2001). Teacher adoption of technology: a perceptual control theory perspective, *Journal of Technology and Teacher Education, 9*(1), 5–30.

Zhao, Y., & Frank, K. (2003). Factors affecting technology use in schools: an ecological perspective. *American Educational Research Journal, 40*(4), 807–840.

Zhu, Z. (2011, November). *Suggestions on the development of ICT indicators in China*. Paper presented at the "International Expert Meeting on ICT in Education Indicators and E-School Standard," Hangzhou, China.

CHAPTER 5

EDUSAT

Harnessing Educational Potentiality in India

Kshama Pandey and Neetu Singh

ABSTRACT

The universalization of education has become the top priority, especially for developing nations. But the extension of quality education to remote and rural regions becomes a herculean task for a large country like India with a multilingual population separated by vast geographical distances. In this perspective, EDUSAT technology has become very powerful media for the interactive participation between educators and students in urban and rural regions. It is especially configured to meet the growing demand for an interactive satellite-based distance education system employing direct-to-home (DTH) quality broadcasts through an audio-visual medium. EDUSAT, which was launched in 2004, addresses this need by providing many facilities and possibilities, including the eradication of illiteracy in India. This chapter highlights the educational paradigms of EDUSAT including the advantages, challenges, and limitations of providing quality education via a satellite distance-learning platform.

E-Learning and Social Media: Education and Citizenship for the Digital 21st Century, pp. 93–118

INTRODUCTION

Education must reach out to every citizen throughout one's lifecycle. The challenge of the day is to stay updated and to keep the nation updated. Formal education institutions in India face many challenges associated with preparing and imparting quality learning systems. With the increasing globalization and commercialization of India, the educational and vocational needs of students, citizens, and the nation are changing rapidly. In this perspective, a satellite system can establish needed connectivity between urban educational institutions with adequate infrastructure imparting quality education and the large number of rural and semi-urban educational institutions that lack the necessary infrastructure. Besides supporting formal education, a satellite system can facilitate the dissemination of information to rural and remote populations. Thus, in spite of access to skilled teachers, the aspirations of the growing student population in rural areas can be met through the concept of tele-education. This strongly reflects India's commitment to use digital technology for national development, especially for educating the population in remote and rural locations.

Recognizing the importance of education in national development and the challenges faced in the field of education on a number of fronts, like the adult and continuing education, school education, higher education, and professional education, it was felt that a promising technology, such as a satellite based system, could provide an optimal solution in achieving the necessary growth and appropriate quality in education and also its reach in remote parts of the country. Therefore, Indian Space Research Organization (ISRO) has launched a communication satellite called GSAT-3 for exclusive use of the education sector. It has envisaged the development of a nation-wide education network called EDUSAT with the aim of providing a sustainable distance education service in India using the GSAT-3 satellite. *GSAT-3, known as EDUSAT, is meant for distant K–16 classroom education.* This is the first dedicated "Educational Satellite" that provides the country with satellite based two-way communication for delivering educational materials.

The universalization of education has become the top priority, especially for developing countries. But the extension of quality education to remote and rural regions becomes a herculean task for a large country like India with a multilingual population separated by vast geographical distances. In this viewpoint, EDUSAT is the satellite exclusively devoted to meet the demands of the educational sector. EDUSAT, launched on September 20, 2004, is the first Indian satellite built exclusively for serving the educational sector. It is mainly intended to meet the demand for an interactive satellite based distance education system for the country.

EDUSAT: AN INTRODUCTION

EDUSAT meets the educational need for an interactive satellite-supported learning platform that acts as an interface between face-to-face and open flexible learning. It is an improved version of the satellites launched under the Indian national satellite (INSAT) series and has several new features/ technologies. It has been specially configured for the audio-visual medium, employing digital interactive classroom and multi-centric systems. It carries multiple regional beams covering different parts of the country: five Ku-band transponders with spot beams covering Northern, Northeastern, Eastern, Southern and Western regions; one Ku-band transponder with its footprint covering the mainland region and six extended C-band transponders with their footprint covering the entire country (Figure 5.1). The satellite facilitates a variety of telecommunication, transmission, and retrieval of data formats. The most remarkable feature of EDUSAT is its capability to create a network of all schools/colleges/universities through the national and regional hubs. It facilitates a link between urban educational institutions imparting quality education to rural and semi-urban educational institutions which lack necessary resources and infrastructure.

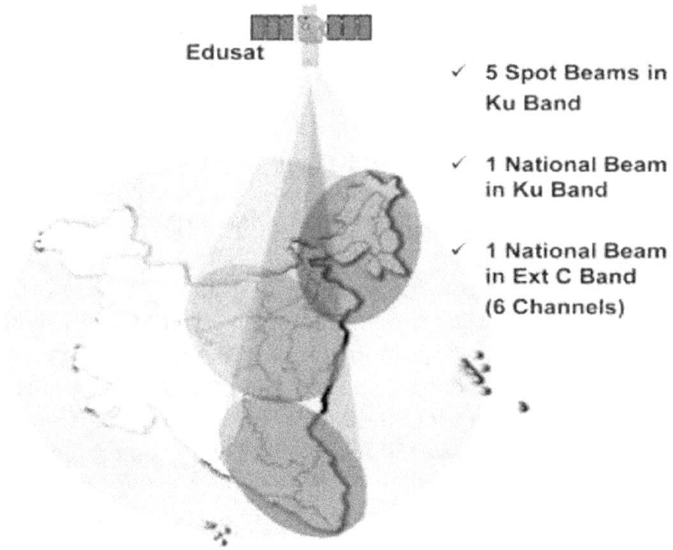

Source: ISRO, India.

Figure 5.1. EDUSAT coverage in India.

HISTORICAL PERSPECTIVE AND ORIGIN OF EDUSAT

Over a period of the last 30 years, ISRO has initiated several projects/programs to cater to the country's need for education, training, and general awareness among the rural poor. The specific factors that formed the basis of the launch of the EDUSAT were: An acute shortage of qualified teachers; the student dropout rate; the need to provide formal and in-formal continuing education, reduce illiteracy among the population, provide effective teacher training and scholarly research; and provide access to education in remote areas of the country. The program to utilize EDUSAT was known as the EDUSAT Utilization Program (EUP). EUP was to be utilized by various national and regional users.

KEY FEATURES OF EDUSAT

It is essentially intended to meet the requirement for an interactive satellite based e-learning and distance based education system for the country. It strongly displays the commitment of India to use space technology for the development of the nation, especially in the field of education, by educating the maximum possible population residing in the remote and rural geographical locations. EDUSAT is configured to cope with the demand of interactive e-learning systems through audio and video mode broadcast throughout the country. With the success of the INSAT-based educational services, a need was felt to launch a satellite dedicated for educational service, and ISRO conceived the EDUSAT project in October 2002. EDUSAT is the first exclusive satellite for serving the educational sector. It is specially configured to meet the growing demand for an interactive satellite-based distance education system for the country through the audio-visual medium, employing direct-to-home (DTH) quality broadcast.

The 1950 kg EDUSAT is launched from Satish Dhawan Space Centre (SDSC) SHAR, Sriharikota, into a geosynchronous transfer orbit (GTO) by ISRO's geosynchronous satellite launch vehicle (GSLV). From GTO, EDUSAT will reach the 36,000 km high geostationary orbit (GSO) by firing, in stages, it's on-board liquid apogee motor (LAM). This is a geosynchronous satellite developed on I-2K bus. GSAT-3 is co-located with METSAT (KALPANA-1) and INSAT-3C at 74° East longitude.

EDUSAT carries five Ku-band transponders providing spot beams, one Ku-band transponder providing a national beam, and six Extended C-band transponders with a national coverage beam. It will join the INSAT system that already has more than 130 transponders in C-band, extended C-band, and Ku-band providing a variety of telecommunication and television services. Main features of EDUSAT are given in the Table 5.1.

Table 5.1. Installation, Commissioning, and Integration of SITs

MAIN FEATURES OF EDUSAT	
Mission	Education
Spacecraft Mass	1950.5 Kg mass (at Lift - off) 819.4 Kg (Dry mass)
Onboard power	Total four solar panel of size 2.54 M x 1.525 M generating 2040 W (EOL), two 24 AH NiCd batteries for eclipse support
Stabilization	3 axis bodies stabilized in orbit using sensors, momentum and reaction wheels, magnetic torquers and eight 10 N & 22N reaction control thrusters.
Propulsion	440 N Liquid Apogee Motor with MON - 3 and MMH for orbit raising
Payload	• Six upper extended C - band transponders • Five lower Ku band transponders with regional beam coverage • One lower Ku band National beam transponder with Indian main land coverage • Ku beacon • 12 C band high power transponders with extended coverage, covering southeast and northwest region apart from Indian main land using 63 W LTWTAs
Launch date	September 20, 2004
Launch site	SHAR, Sriharikota, India
Launch vehicle	GSLV-F01
Orbit	Geostationary (74°E longitude)
Mission Life	7 Years (minimum)

Source: http://www.isro.org/satellites/edusat.aspx

TECHNOLOGICAL CAPABILITIES OF EDUSAT: AN EDUCATIONAL NETWORK

Seven different educational organizations have been provided bandwidth on the national beam of the EDUSAT network. These are noted in Table 5.2 including the number of nodes installed at those locations. The national beam network operates at Ku-Band (14/11 GHz) frequency. One of the transponders of the geo-stationary satellite, GSAT-3(740E), for example, is utilized to operate this broad footprint, as is shown in Figure 5.1. State networks receiving one of the regional beams continue to be upgraded.

Schools in different states are connected through Sarva Shiksha Abhiyan (SSA), the Education for All project. The tribal area of Madhya Pradesh has been covered in the Indira Gandhi National Open University national beam. A pilot project was inaugurated to network 800 primary schools, 100 secondary schools, and 75 higher secondary schools, with a hub at Sidhi district headquarters. UGC terminals were also been installed in several colleges/universities in the remote areas.

Table 5.2. National Agencies With Its Networking Coverage

Customer Name	*Total of Nodes for Each Agency*	*Installation and Commissioning Completed*
Indira Gandhi National Open University	134	129
National Council of Educational Research & Training/ Central Institute of Educational Technology	100	71
ARVN	11	11
Indian Space Research Organization	9	9
University Grants Commission/CEC	58	50
All India Council of Technical Education	103	83
Department of Space and Technology	20	10
Total	441	406

EDUSAT is already providing a wide range of educational delivery modes like one-way TV broadcast, interactive TV, video conferencing, computer conferencing, web-based instructions, and more.

Sixty four networks have been setup so far, out of which 10 networks use national Ku-band beam and 36 networks are operational on regional Ku-band and Extended-C band national beams. There are more than 3,386 interactive classrooms and 31,313 receive only classrooms totaling close to 34699 classrooms. Networks have already been setup in 24 states covering almost entire country including all islands (Andman & Nicobar, Lakshdweep), North-Eastern states and Jammu & Kashmir. Implementation in remaining states is under progress.

OBJECTIVES OF EDUSAT: A LEARNING DEVICE

The General Objectives of EDUSAT are included as follow:

- To educate the nation
- To provide education on demand
- To make education accessible at home
- Providing support to formal and non-formal education
- Teachers' training program
- Increasing access to quality resource persons
- Enhancing community participation
- Taking education to remotest corner of the country

The specific objectives of EDUSAT are included as follow:

Primary and Secondary Education

1. To increase the rate of school enrollment
2. To increase female literacy
3. To remove gender disparity.
4. To arrest the rate of drop out
5. To improve the quality of teaching
6. To improve the quality of learning
7. To empower students
8. To empower girl students
9. To enhance the level of students' performance
10. To bridge the gap between students and teachers
11. To make learning participatory
12. To increase learning resources
13. To create school database
14. To reform the evaluation process
15. To train teachers in student centric learning
16. To bridge the gap between schools and the community
17. To facilitate participation of parents

Distance Education

1. To provide quality based open distance learning
2. To improve the teaching-learning process

3. Networking among open universities to exchange content and databases
4. Networking among open and regular universities to link campuses and classrooms
5. To promote radio counseling
6. TV broadcasting
7. Radio broadcasting
8. Teleconference
9. To facilitate open education through ICT networking of students and teachers by creating ICT equipped study centres in rural, backward, and remote places
10. To establish virtual classrooms for imparting education electronically
11. To eradicate adult illiteracy by promoting continuous learning among un-enrolled persons such as farmers, artisans, labourers, housewives, and others
12. To bridge the digital divide by enhancing access to learning resources
13. To increase women's education
14. To empower women
15. To train teachers of primary and secondary schools

Professional Education

1. To achieve quality and excellence in technical education
2. Networking of institutions-engineering, medical, management
3. Online counseling for students seeking professional education
4. Resource sharing among professional colleges through video conferencing and networking of classrooms
5. To create digital libraries
6. To facilitate web-based learning
7. To train teachers in technical education
8. To improve instructional inputs
9. To improve methods of teaching and learning
10. To bring about changes in the methods of evaluation
11. To make professional education accessible to disabled and other weaker sections of the society
12. To empower women
13. To impart professional skills to women

According to DECU-the Development and Educational Communication Unit, of ISRO, the EDUSAT generally aims at using Satellite-based Educational Program;

1. To provide effective teacher training
2. To supplement the curriculum based teaching
3. For greater community participation and monitoring
4. To provide access to quality resource persons
5. To strengthen distance education
6. To take education to all parts of the country
7. To provide access to new technologies

EDUSAT AND ITS CAPABILITIES

EDUSAT has enormous capacity for providing a variety of options for broadcast/telecast/interactive modes and online communication networks at the national, regionaland state levels. The technological capabilities of EDUSAT are depicted in Figure 5.2.

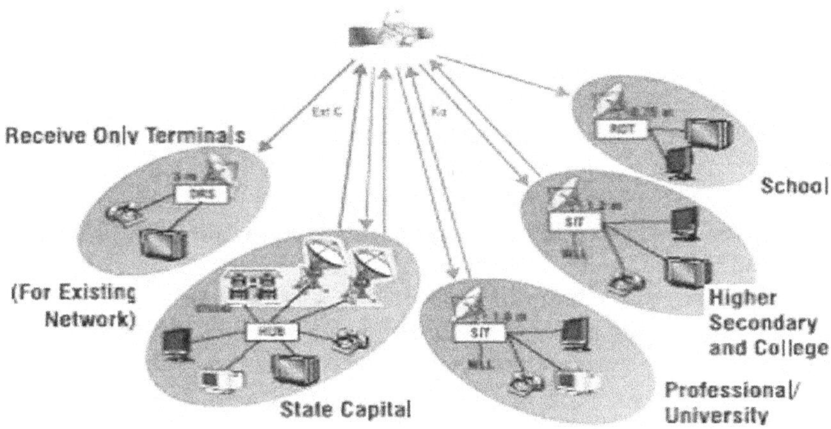

Figure 5.2. Technological capabilities of EDUSAT.

EDUSAT APPLICATION TECHNOLOGY CONFIGURATION

Technological innovations create demand for improved designs. The mission has always been for improved performance, which is particularly true in telecommunication, where technological advancement has prompted demand for improved and higher competencies for carrying information. Starting in the mid-19th century, the electric telegraph spread around the world and provided faster communication, but it remained an asynchronous communication system. The telephone, another 19th century invention, provided the main synchronous interactive communication system by using a communication channel capable of carrying the human voice both ways in real time. The 20th century witnessed a parallel technological development, first with radio, which in its initial phase provided wireless communication for ships at sea and then triggered broadcasting and, in the current times, has placed mobile telephones in the hands of people around the world. Thereafter video technology arrived among us. These technologies possess vital features. It teaches us, entertain us, and bring our fantasies to life. Video along with audio adds realism to human communication. Television, as the next great innovation, is currently in the transition between one-way broadcasting and two-way interactive services, made possible by digital technology. Many of the advantages of digital technology have been enabled by the development of the modern radio communication systems of mobile telephony, satellite networks, and digital video broadcasting. The convergence of television and computers has been a major step in the enhancement of digital video broadcasting. Today, digital TV broadcasts are just long streams of bits that can contain any data broadcasters want to add to their signal. Data is sent along with the video and audio. For the last few decades, television has changed the way viewers see the world and how they learn and communicate. Broadcasting has traditionally referred to the "one-to-many" one-way services used for the distribution of audio and video while telecommunication has meant a "one-to-one" two way service, such as telephony and data transmission. With the growth of the Internet these distinctions have become less pronounced. People are able to receive broadcasts on TV sets, but engage in telecommunication with their PCs connected to the Internet. The convergence of these technologies implies providing two-way communication in the services that have remained one-way for a long time. It is expected that in coming times, TV sets will no longer be restricted to receive-only services, but will also support two-way interactive services. Two-way communication in a conventional broadcasting system entails the implementation of return channels, such as from TV sets back to a TV station. The return channels may be carried by wire connections, by terrestrial radio channels, or via satellite channels. The digital video broadcasting through satellite using return channel via satellite is known as digital video broadcasting, return channel via satellite (DVB-RCS). The DVB-RCS is a system that permits two-way communication between the satellite interactive terminals (SITs) installed at customer's sites. DVB-RCS systems are based on VSAT technologies (two-way interactive data networks) that can serve up to several hundred thousand users using a distributed gateway providing integrated services. VSATs (very small interactive terminals) are a much easier way to provide interactive broadband communications over satellite compared to existing terrestrial access networks (based on dial-up modems, leased lines, and cable modems). The natural multicasting characteristics of the satellite, the wireless access and the fixed station connectivity are some of the major advantages of DVB-RCS. In a nutshell, DVB-RCS is a satellite-based access technology that allows users' high-speed access to the Internet and its value added services. The DVB-RCS system supports communication channels that operate in two directions: a forward channel from the hub station to many terminals, and a return channel from each terminal to the hub station. As with any satellite based communication system, DVB-RCS requires at least three stations, two on the Earth and a repeater station on the satellite as shown in Figure 5.3. In the space segment, the satellite is shown as are the transmission paths through the atmosphere. The ground segment shows how the Earth stations communicate via the satellite, and how the user terminals interface with the terrestrial networks and the satellite system. A typical user terminal in a digital satellite communication system comprises an antenna system (the outdoor unit or ODU), the receiver/transmitter unit (indoor unit or IDU), and the peripherals such as a multimedia personal computer or wireless device.

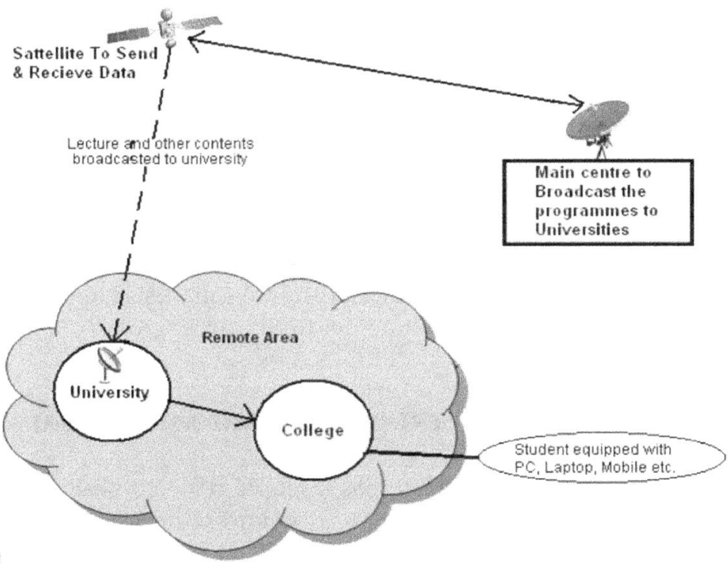

Figure 5.3. Mechanism of EDUSAT.

Edusat is a technology network comprising three main attributes as noted following:

1. Uplink stations in selected nationals and state locations (to act as teaching end)

2. Downlink stations or facilities in various educational institutions(as learning ends)
3. The satellite

EDUSAT world's first satellite meant only for educational purposes is being used. Training by teleconferencing overcomes the problem of transmission loss since participants are watching, listening, and interacting with the primary resource persons. CIET, a constitute unit of NCERT, has been using this technology of teleconferencing over a decades to give training/ orientation to teachers and teacher educators. Other institutions like IGNOU, Vigyan Prasar, Sarva Shiksha Abhiyan (SSA), Rehabilitation Council of India (RCI), and National Trust are regularly using tele-training methodology for implementation of their all India level schemes and projects.

CIET, NCERT has been utilizing satellite technologies for about three decades. It has gained a wide range of experience in designing and organizing programs using such technologies. The EDUSAT configuration has allowed CIET, NCERT to develop a network of institutions, together constituting a national network. This network facilitates an on demand two-way communication between institutions.

The school sector is to get a National channel along with necessary uplinks and down-links. CIET (NCERT) has taken an initiative in this regard and entered into a MOU (memorandum of understanding) with ISRO for this purpose. A Ku-band sub/mini hub has been installed at the CIET along with 100 terminals for installations at different locations in all the states and UTs. The proposed school network could be used by various agencies for undertaking training programs directly with the target groups, as opposed to the current approach of training master trainers and key resource persons, and then reaching out to the target groups.

NATURE AND CONCEPT OF LEARNING WITH EDUSAT

As mentioned earlier, the satellite has multiple regional beams covering different parts of India; five Ku-band transponders with spot beams covering Northern, North-Eastern, Eastern, Southern and Western regions of the country, a Ku-band transponder with its footprint covering the Indian mainland region, and six C-band transponders with their footprints covering the entire country. This EDUSAT network provides satellite based tele-education facilities to students and teachers of the engineering colleges across the country.

While ISRO provides the space segment for EDUSAT System and demonstrate the efficacy of the satellite system for interactive distance education, content generation is the responsibility of the user agencies. ISRO provides technical and managerial support in the replication of EDUSAT ground systems to manufacturers and service providers. End users are expected to provide funds for this. All educational institutions having satellite interactive terminals (SITs) or receive only terminals (ROTs) can now receive educational programs from EDUSAT, the first Indian satellite built exclusively for serving the educational sector, and can interact and ask questions through audio-video conferencing, text mode, or through telephone.

Curriculum-based education is being imparted via the satellite by the University Grants Commission (UGC) through the Consortium for Educational Communication (CEC). The infrastructure of EDUSAT is being utilized by Indira Gandhi National Open University (IGNOU) for curriculum-based education, teachers' training, professional educational courses, and for conducting teleconferencing sessions for software content generation.

National Council for Educational Research and Training (NCERT) also conducts inter-active orientation/training programs of teachers and teachers' educators. The Department of Science and Technology (DST) utilizes EDUSAT network for group discussion, lectures, demonstrations, video-shows, training and capacity building programs.

After getting freedom, India has got revolution in the educational sector. It can be seen that there is substantial increase in the number of educational institutions/organizations at primary level, secondary level, and higher levels. The numbers of students are also increased in the same proportion. But one thing is lacked, such as the lack of enough infrastructure in the rural areas and unavailability of qualified and trained teachers.

EDUSAT network is responsible to provide satellite based education and learning facilities to the students and faculties of the engineering colleges around the country. ISRO is providing the space division for EDUSAT systems and demonstrating the effectiveness of the satellite system for interactive learning and education. Syllabus based education is being communicated via satellite by University Grants Commission (UGC) through the Consortium for Educational Communication (CEC).

The launch of EDUSAT has helped a lot in providing quality education and learning through audio and video programs to students studying in remote areas. The students have improved from the programs delivered through the satellite. They are getting more and more quality learning and education. The are getting a better understanding of the course content, better understanding of the subject matter, improving attendance for viewing programs which are displayed through the educational satellite. The teacher's involvement is also very important during the broadcast as a facilitator and conduct of pre- and post-broadcast activity.

HOW EDUSAT WORKS FOR TEACHING AND LEARNING?

In this model, there is a main broadcast centre to broadcast the lectures and other contents in text, audio, video, and other multimedia format. The main centre broadcasts the content to the satellite, and the satellite is responsible for sending all content to the registered universities. Universities then have a web-based application to consume the content and, from the websites, the colleges can access the contents.

The live lectures are received at classrooms of the colleges. Two types of classrooms are there: interactive classrooms and non-interactive classrooms. The 1.2 meter wide antenna has been installed on top of each college. In the interactive sessions, the students can interact with the professor/lecturer or subject expert through a voice link by means of satellite. The students can hear the question and the reply of the subject expert for the question live in all classrooms. They can also experience videoconferencing with the experts.

EDUSAT NETWORKS AND THEIR APPLICATIONS

EDUSAT has enormous capacity for providing a variety of options for broadcast/telecast/interactive modes and online communication networks at the national, regional, and state levels.

Telecast

Like INSAT series of satellites, EDUSAT is being used for broadcasting audio and video programs: one-way audio and one-way video (1A and 1V). These are receive only terminals (ROTs). Audio-video signals are sent by hub/sub-hub/ uplink located at the national, regional, or state level and are received at the learning centres equipped with downlink facilities or through local cable-operated networks. However, no talk-back facility is available in this mode. Therefore, ROTs are useful for transmitting information-based programs and replicate good lectures at several locations for learners and empowerment of the society on issues such as law, health care, human rights, disaster management, consumer protection, entrepreneurship, and the like.

Interactive Network I

Interactivity is the key element of the EDUSAT network. In two-way audio and one-way video (2A and 1V) also, the audio-video signals are transmitted through EDUSAT hub/sub-hub/ uplink and received at the tele-learning centres equipped with downlink facilities or through local cable operated networks. The centres equipped with a talk back facility can interact through the EDUSAT network. This defined a milestone in the way education could be delivered.

Interactive Network II

In two-way audio and two-way video (2A and 2V), both the audio and the video signals are sent and received by the hub/sub-hub/ uplink at the national, regional, or state level. This system is particularly useful for demonstration of experiments, microscopic as well as macroscopic processes, and situations which need visual support. The learners can interact with experts to clarify their doubts. In this system, both the uplink and the downlink centres have studio facilities. The learning centres also have EDUSAT-based connectivity. The main limitation of the system stems from the fact that not many learning centres can be linked simultaneously.

A major strength of EDUSAT is that it can provide connectivity to all schools, irrespective of their location, and help create a nation-wide distributed classroom-like situation, where teachers and students can see and interact with an expert, wherever he/she may be situated. For this to happen, an essential pre-requisite with availability of appropriate technology, that is, the institutions under reference must possess or be equipped with necessary e-gadgets to receive and transmit information. This marks a paradigm shift in the quality of teaching-learning; the expertise of the best resource person available in the country is extended to all.

To be precise, EDUSAT is a vehicle for ensuring the same quality of education to all recipients. In a pluralistic society endowed with cultural diversity, EDUSAT is intended to offset the impact of heterogeneity on inequality in educational opportunities, outcomes, and success. For example, about 6,000 primary school teachers in 22 states from rural areas could interact through EDUSAT with national-level experts in training workshops organized by the National Council for Educational Research and Training (NCERT) on implementation of Curriculum Frame Work, 2005. Similarly, the distance learners residing in the remotest areas of the country got opportunity to resolve their difficulties when they assembled at District headquarters, where EDUSAT network had been installed.

Two-Way Data Transmission

EDUSAT also provides computer connectivity between hub/sub-hub/ uplink. This system can be used for the transfer of data to and from the central, regional, and state level centers located in schools, colleges, district institutes of educational research and training (DIETs), or block resource centers (BRCs). This ensures a minimum of e-mail connectivity to interact as well as two-way audio-visual transmission (Figure 5.3). Among various other advanced options, at the school level the EDUSAT is being used to strengthen and up-scale the virtual classroom initiatives.

REACH OF EDUSAT NETWORK IN INDIA

The network of EDUSAT has been successfully reached in all over India. It can be easily seen through the Figure 5.4 as given below:

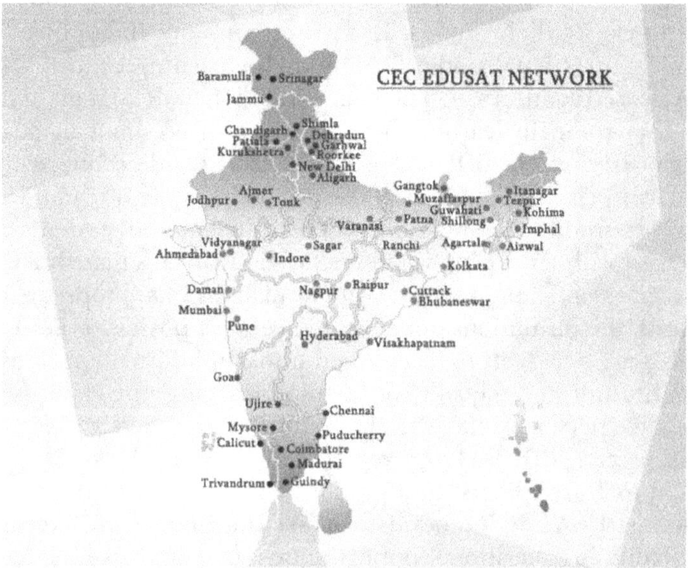

Source: http://cec.nic.in/EDUSAT/Pages/edusatnetwork.aspx

Figure 5.4. CEC EDUSAT network.

REMARKABLE NETWORKS OF EDUSAT

One of the innovative networks on EDUSAT is the network for "blind schools." Blind People's Association, Ahmedabad is a leading organization promoting education, training, employment, and rehabilitation for blind persons. Considering the specific needs of blind people, an altogether different kind of broadcast network configuration delivering live audio and data, which is read by blind person through its printed impression (Braille), was set up.

Another special network in Ext C-band connecting 50 engineering institutes across the country has been established to impart teaching by distinguished professors and faculty from the top 21 universities in the U.S. who would visit India to conduct eight-week courses in various subjects in engineering. This network is now shared by IIT-Bombay network with an additional 30 end users.

Apart from this network for IIM, Bangalore has been connecting with its other center in Chennai; an extended C-band network connecting all the five centers of the National Council of Science Museums for promoting scientific temperament among students and the general public; a network for Mahabharatha Sansthan for online transmission of digitized manuscripts from remote areas through mobile terminals to a centralized center for archival so as to preserve them; two networks in Kerala for imparting education and awareness to parents and teachers of mentally challenged children schools; and a network in Tamilnadu and Pondicherry connecting centers of Aravind Virtual Academy for providing eye-care, among others, are a few of the special networks that have been set up/under implementation under EDUSAT Utilization Program.

TRAINING AND DEVELOPMENTAL COMMUNICATIONS CHANNEL (TDCC)

A total of 8 Ext. C-band channels—6 on INSAT-3B and 2 on EDUSAT—are being used for Training, Development and Communication Channel (TDCC), a service that has been operational since 1995. It provides a 1-way video and 2-way audio system of interactive education. The teaching-end includes a studio and an uplink facility for transmitting live or pre-recorded lectures. The participants at the classrooms located nationwide receive lectures through simple dish antennas (DRS) and have a facility to interact with lecturers using telephone lines.

Several state governments and universities are using the TDCC system extensively for distance education, rural development, women and child development, Panchayati raj, health, agriculture, forestry, and more. The teaching-ends are now available at Gujarat, Madhya Pradesh, Orissa, Karnataka, and Goa. The DRS network consists of more than 5000 classrooms spread over the country.

ADVANTAGES OF LEARNING THROUGH EDUSAT

Branded as Sky Teacher, India's first thematic satellite dedicated exclusively for educational services is designed to provide a variety of telecommunication and television broadcasting services. Research on the various approaches to use satellite-based education in bettering lives of the underprivileged is hoped to bridge the much talked about digital divide. Most importantly, the new and unique education from the sky will be an eye opener for other developing countries in Asia as it facilitates sharing of information and knowledge, and paves the way for universalization of education. The sky tutor is slated to empower the poor and illiterate through education. It is in this perspective that EDUSAT assumes significance. Never in the history of humanity have the floodgates of technology been brought within the reach of the poor and impoverished. EDUSAT is slated to provide mind boggling services like radio broadcast, TV broadcast, on-line education through Internet, computer connectivity and data broadcasting, talk back channel, audio-video interaction, voice chat on Internet, asymmetric Internet through TVRO, and video conferencing. This experience will bring this part of the world on par with developed countries and help countries in Asia to reap benefits of better connectivity. It will also be used for interactive satellite based distance education system in India. EDUSAT, which is armed with ICT capabilities, is configured to provide access to digital interactive classrooms and multimedia multicentric systems with provision for multiple regional beams reaching the length and breadth of this country.

Satellites serving as a significant tool of educational technology as a tutor will be demonstrated by the launch of EDUSAT. Today there is widespread dissatisfaction with our educational system among educators, parents, and policymakers. Efforts to reform and restructure education have met with low success rate as the role of social context of learning has been marginalized. Community's vision of learning needs to be integrated into goals of education. Further, the digital divide has alienated the poor and impoverished people from reaping benefits of technology and its application. One can hope that, based on the research experience of EDUSAT, the current programs and plans should be suitably modified and updated to reflect the hopes and aspirations of the new generation. EDUSAT has the capability to provide ICT linked educational infrastructure to deprived village schools and facilitate the state governments to accomplish the task of education for all. The ICT based education will promote distance education and infuse quality in conventional system of education. The satellite has given impetus for e-learning, enabling students to access quality content materials in the multimedia form consisting of graphics, video, and well-designed texts. The State of Karnataka has already shown the way by launching the first ever e-learning site on January 8, 2005 by the Vishweshwariah Technological University in partnership with ISRO for the benefit of students of engineering colleges.

The President of India, A. P. J. Abdul Kalam, predicts that EDUSAT will be a boon to students as they are destined to receive quality education. The President, who is also an eminent scientist, states that "EDUSAT is useful for schools, colleges, higher level of education and non-formal education, EDUSAT, when fully operational will have 30 up links and about 5,000 remote terminals per up link. Expected to provide 150,000 ground terminals at full capacity, EDUSAT is not merely a Receive Only Terminal system; it works on an IP protocol and brings both-way interactivity and collaboration. EDUSAT coupled with broadband through fiber, and Wireless Broadband, will form a heterogeneous network for providing quality education. For example, students at Samastipur in Bihar could receive a mathematics teacher at Bhimavaram in Andhra Pradesh, in real time. Hence good teachers teaching anywhere, in any language can be heard, seen and interacted with through this delivery system."

EDUSAT program was implemented in various states in India for improving the quality of education, which is given below:

In Haryana

EDUSAT was launched in Haryana with a 3.8 meter antenna for uplink at Panchkula. The teachers take the class from the studio at Panchkula, which is transmitted to the EDUSAT satellite. This is then further transmitted by EDUSAT to entire state of Haryana. These lectures are received by 9000 Primary Schools, 1250 Secondary Schools, and 92 Government-aided Colleges through satellite interactive terminals. Initially live lectures were provided, which was further enhanced to record as well. Apart from prescribed courses several various other course-like training for engineering entrance exams and soft skills development courses were also provided. Moreover, a test was also conducted periodically to evaluate the progress of students. To propitiate interests among teachers, coordinators and students' prizes like "Best Questions Asked by Student" & "Best Teacher/Coordinator" are given.

Impact in Haryana

1. Better performance of students in exams
2. Timely coverage of syllabus
3. More interests and involvement of students
4. An increase in the attendance status of students
5. Uniform standard of teaching to all the students both urban and rural
6. High class and reputed teaching staff took the classes

In Gujarat

EDUSAT is extensively used in Gujarat to provide educations to masses. A total of 22,000 primary schools were linked to the satellite to improve the education. The Chief Minister of Gujarat is using EDUSAT as a channel to interact with 40,000 teachers once every month. This mode of education was so popular among the students that ISRO has to increase the bandwidth by six times, as per the request from the Gujarat. A network for blind people's association was formed using this satellite covering 10 schools. EDUSAT aims to provide the following functions in Gujarat:

1. A uniform primary education to all the rural schools
2. Provide training to teachers about the latest teaching technologies
3. Providing training to health care staff especially nursing
4. Increase the interests of students in studies
5. Helping the blind students by making specialized lectures for them

In Karnataka

EDUSAT is used by most in Karnataka. Here, a separate e-learning center is established in Visvesvaraya Technological University (VTU) where all the 120 engineering colleges are linked up via EDUSAT [19]. Here the engineering students have the benefit of interacting with the best resource person for their subject. More than 1000 lectures have been completed. web-based e-learning has prepared the course for 12 full semester subjects. For the primary education too, EDUSAT, with the help of a scheme named "Sarva Siksha Abhiyan," has covered 885 primary schools.

In Kerala

Kerala was the first state which made use of EDUSAT in 2004. A dedicated EDUSAT lab was set up and introduced the concept of virtual university. After being associated with Kerala University, live interactive sessions have started with students to impart quality education.

In Punjab

Punjab is one state which is most efficiently utilizing the satellite. A studio is built to facilitate the smooth working of the e-learning activity. A special grievance section is working to regularly note the evaluation process. A special program for the students giving engineering entrance examination is prepared, which is helping the students who are unable to pay heavy fees to private organizations. Recently 2,960 schools of Punjab were linked to EDUSAT to get the service of live interactive lectures. A special study material for all the lectures were prepared to have a better understanding of the lectures.

In Madhya Pradesh

This was the most advanced use of EDUSAT. Here EDUSAT was introduced by the forest department in January of 2008. This was done to provide training to the forest officials to increase efficiency of forest officers, employees, and dwellers through online training and discussion. 52 satellite interactive terminals (SITs) have been set up for 27,000 forest employees and forest communities.

Selvakkani (2011), in his research study, found that EDUSAT in schools enhances students' abilities to visualize. Programs are capable of increasing attendance, learning interest, vocabulary, questioning tendency, acting, and analyzing abilities. It also enhances the quality of learning and provides quality instruction through video programs. It increases gain in knowledge and understanding of the content, improvement in attendance and holding attention, and interest in viewing programs. The teacher involvement during the broadcast as facilitator and conduct of pre- and post-broadcast activity is noteworthy.

To assess the success of EDUSAT network in terms of the academic achievement of primary school children (Classes III and IV), Dash (2007) compared the academic achievements of children of ROT schools with those of their counterparts of non-ROT schools. The study was conducted in seven EDUSAT network Blocks. The analysis of data indicated that EDUSAT transmission was making steady progress toward improvement of academic achievement of children and creation of an academic environment in schools. However, the study revealed that there was a need to employ strategic planning and effective implementation for the desired impact of EDUSAT-supported education on the overall quality of primary/ elementary education.

To achieve the target of universalization of elementary education, the Indian Parliament passed the Right to Education bill, which provides for free and compulsory education to all children in the age group of 6–14 years. To support these efforts toward quality education, the MHRD, GoI decided to use the capabilities of satellite based teaching-learning. Accordingly, an educational satellite, EDUSAT, was launched to provide an interface between face to face and open flexible learning. The Rajiv Gandhi Project for EDUSAT-supported Elementary Education was launched to strengthen elementary education in four educationally less developed states. Initially, the project focused mainly on the Sidhi district in M.P., which is predominantly inhabited by tribal people who have remained on the margins of development, and for 700 schools, DIETs and BRCs were connected. For the achievement of project objectives, multi-pronged strategy to identify hard spots, develop e-content, beam programs at pre-decided schedules, and train school teachers from within the district in presentation skills was adopted. Within a year of the launch of the program, EDUSAT supported education helped to increase attendance of students in schools and their retention for more time, apart from empowering teachers in teaching hard spots and motivating them to make their teaching more effective using innovative methods and aids.

LIMITATIONS OF EFFECTIVE UTILIZATION OF EDUSAT

EDUSAT was in operation for six years from September 2004 to September 2010. Fifty-seven percent of the satellite capacity of the EDUSAT was idling as late as the fifth year of its operation. The bigger states with higher illiteracy such as Uttar Pradesh and Bihar did not have an EDUSAT network even in the fifth year of operation of the satellite. In fact Uttar Pradesh, which had an illiterate population of more than 90 million, did not have any network as of June 2013. None of the states or Union Territories could achieve envisaged 1,200 interactive satellite based educational terminals meant for colleges and universities. Large states having substantial illiterate population such as Uttar Pradesh, Bihar, Maharashtra, Tamil Nadu, Odisha, Jharkhand, and Assam, did not have satellite based network. They were till operating with receiver only educational terminals meant for schools only. These states were operating on a far less effective level. The objective of reaching quality education to the primary schools in the bigger states was not achieved even as late as the fifth year of operation of the satellite. Thus, the objective of reaching quality primary, higher, technical, and professional education to the unreached poor masses of the country remained unachieved.

It was observed in audit that EDUSAT failed to effectively achieve its objectives due to deficiencies in planning for the network connectivity, content generation, and failure to have a robust management structure. There were deficiencies in actual implementation of the program such as delay in establishment of ground network, idling of network connectivity, disparities in the allocation and idling of satellite bandwidth, inadequate content generation, and deficiencies in monitoring and evaluation. Their placement strategy for the existing satellite was also deficient, resulting in idling of operational networks. Thus, the objectives of implementation of EDUSAT could not be met fully even at the end of its life.

NEEDS FOR EFFECTIVE USE OF EDUSAT

At the current pace of developments, we may not be able to see the real fruit of educational development in terms of increasing access with quality. We may spend huge amount of money in purchasing hardware and technology, but without any pedagogic thought and planning, all these investments are a waste. Is it possible for us to integrate EDUSAT into our existing educational infrastructure? The current development is like part of the distance education scenario of the country, whereas the satellite can effectively cater to all the sectors of education. Also, conventional school, college, and university can use the EDUSAT to deliver online education as a support to their classroom teaching. The system allows us to think beyond audio and video, and we should develop learning resources in multimedia, animation, and simulation formats.

The technology also needs improvement to allow access from anywhere (not necessarily thorough SIT or ROT), especially as the technology is based on HTTP. If this can be done, the government of India can focus on setting up ROTs only in the rural, hilly, and remote areas which do not have access to the Internet (of course, we have to think of electric power supply, and for that matter solar energy could be tapped). This will also bridge the digital divide and improve the Internet penetration in the country. The next important issue is developing digital content as national resource for all levels of education. As we all realize that interaction is important for learning, EDUSAT can be used for supporting this interaction on the basis of the need of the learner or the need of the subject/discipline. Teachers need to be trained on the new technology, especially how best they can make use of the EDUSAT for helping the students to learn better. There is a long way to go beyond lecturing to the television camera. If we continue doing this, there is every danger of going back to the face-to-face teaching implemented through distance education technology. We need to remember that distance education follows the rigor of developing learning materials (in print, audio, video, and now multimedia) in a team mode taking help of best experts in content, media and learning design.

MEASURES TO EXPAND THE QUALITY OF EDUCATION WITH EDUSAT

Improving the quality of education and training is a critical issue, particularly at a time of educational expansion. EDUSAT can enhance the quality of education in several ways: by increasing learner motivation and engagement, by facilitating the acquisition of basic skills, and by enhancing teacher training. EDUSAT have also transformational tools which, when used appropriately, can promote the shift to a learner-centered environment.

Motivating to Learn

EDUSAT technologies such as videos, television, and multimedia computer software that combine text, sound, and colorful moving images can be used to provide challenging and authentic content that will engage the student in the learning process. Interactive radio likewise makes use of sound effects, songs, dramatizations, comic skits, and other performance conventions to compel the students to listen and become involved in the lessons being delivered. More so than any other type of ICT, networked computers with Internet connectivity can increase learner motivation as it combines the media richness and interactivity of other ICTs with the opportunity to connect with real people and to participate in real world events.

Facilitating the Acquisition of Basic Skills

The transmission of basic skills and concepts that are the foundation of higher order thinking skills and creativity can be facilitated by ICTs through drill and practice. Educational television programs such as Sesame Street use repetition and reinforcement to teach the alphabet, numbers, colors, shapes, and other basic concepts. Most of the early uses of computers were for computer-based learning that focused on mastery of skills and content through repetition and reinforcement.

Enhancing Teacher Training

ICTs have also been used to improve access to and the quality of teacher training. Courses include "Computers in the Information Society," "Education Reform," and "Future Society and Education." Online tutorials are also offered, with some courses requiring occasional face-to-face meetings. At Indira Gandhi National Open University, satellite-based one-way video- and two-way audio-conferencing was held in 1996, supplemented by print-materials and recorded video, to train 910 primary school teachers and facilitators from 20 district training institutes in Karnataka State. The teachers interacted with remote lecturers by telephone and fax.

CONCLUSION

Consequently, it can be said that EDUSAT is helping a lot in improving the quality and quantity of education. The use of this satellite is not only useful for elementary or primary education but also for higher and technical education. As per students, live classes are very effective to get study-related doubts clarified. As per teachers, digital classes are expected to benefit new teachers as well as classes which are unmanned by teachers. As per higher education ministry officials, there is a lack of innovative measures in polytechnics when compared to the engineering colleges. Moreover, the standard of teaching in polytechnics needs improvement as well. Hence, regular and adequate training needs to be provided to teachers.

The EDUSAT program provides the facility to students to access live lectures in digital class-rooms. It is expected to benefit rural students of government first-grade colleges, polytechnics, and engineering colleges. The program aims to supplement the efforts of teachers for better learning. EDUSAT will strengthen education efforts by augmenting curriculum based teaching, providing effective teachers' training, and community participation. Networks based on EDUSAT consist of either receive only (one way communication) terminals or interactive (two way communication).

EDUSAT has been playing an important role to enhance the literacy rates among remotest areas. Hence this satellite can be called as a ray of hope for eradicating illiteracy in all over India. The efforts of government are quite effective, but need more serious endeavor to overcome disparities in demography and education in all over India.

REFERENCES

Chaudhary, S., & Garg, S. (2010). On using satellite-based networks for capacity building and education for all: A case study of Rajiv Gandhi project for EduSat-supported elementary education. *Educational Research and Reviews, 5*(4), 158–168. Retrieved from http://www.academicjournals.org/ERR

EDUSAT: A Satellite Dedicated to Education in India. (2007). Retrieved from http://teachknowlogist.blogspot.in/2007/02/edusat-satellite-dedicated-to-education.html

EDUSAT—the Indian satellite for education. (2004). *Current Science, 87*(8), 1034. Retrieved from http://www.iisc.ernet.in/currsci/oct252004/1034.pdf

Garg, M., & Jindal, M. K. (2009). Edusat-e-learning through satellite—Reaching the unreached. *International Journal pf Recent Trends in Engineering, 1*(2). Retrieved from http://www.academypublisher.com/ijrte/vol01/no02/ijrte0102149151.pdf

Pallai, P. (2013). Education and satellite communication (EDUSAT) in India. *Journal of Education & Research for Sustainable Development, 1*(1). Retrieved from http://www.jersd.org/papers/Education%20and%20Satellite%20Communication%20%28EDUSAT%29%20in%20India.pdf

Pallai, P. (2013). Use of educational satellite in teacher education. *Techno LEARN: An International Journal of Educational Technology, 3*(1). Retrieved from http://www.ndpublisher.in/admin/issues/tlv3n1b.pdf

Selvakkani, P. V. (2011). Edusat—A revolutionary project in Indian education. Retrieved from http://ksmaniamseminar.files.wordpress.com/2011/03/p-vaijayanthi-selvakani.doc

Sharma, R. (n.d.). Satellite-based distance education in Indiamore. *Online Journal of Space Communication: An International Electronic Journal.* Retrieved from http://spacejournal.ohio.edu/issue12/sharma.html

SECTION II

THE INFLUENCE OF SOCIAL MEDIA ON SELF-IDENTITY-EFFICACY-REGULATION

CHAPTER 6

SELF-EFFICACY AND ROLE OF TECHNOLOGY TO SUPPORT UNIVERSITY-TO-WORK TRANSITION

Maria Antonietta Impedovo

ABSTRACT

This chapter investigates self-efficacy and the role of technology in supporting the university-to-work transition in order to better understand their potential in promoting adult people's integration in the world of work. It reports and discusses in-depth interviews addressing university students (between 25–30 years old) from Eastern European countries (Romania, Armenia, Estonia, Georgia, and Croatia) and Italy, who are in transition from university to work. The interviews focus on educational and vocational guidance received by the formal education system of their countries and the role of technology in effective job search. Though the sample is limited and the conclusions cannot be generalized, the findings suggest that the transition between university and work is influenced by personal perspective and self-efficacy. The benefits of the Internet in job search are widely confirmed by all participants, stressing the importance to grow their own personal social networking.

E-Learning and Social Media:
Education and Citizenship for the Digital 21st Century, pp. 121–141

INTRODUCTION

The work involves most of our daily life, defining who we are and it "serves as a major source of personal identity and self-evaluation" (Bandura, Barbaranelli, Caprara, & Pastorelli, 2001, p. 187). During the high school years, students make crucial career decisions that will inevitably influence their career aspirations, plans, and goals (McWhirter, Rasheed, & Crothers, 2000). Important also are the phases of transition (such as university-to-work or changing job positions) that activate and emphasize personal resources and skills, influencing the trajectory of life (Zittoun, 2012).

Transition is an important, however a neglected, area of attention for educators and trainers in schools and in employing organizations (Hays & Clements, 2012). In particular, the knowledge and the skills that are necessary during the transition are very often neglected. With this in mind, this chapter focuses on Self-efficacy as a cross-boundary competence (Akkerman & Bakker, 2011), which can facilitate and lead to a positive transition between educational and work systems. More specifically, it investigates self-efficacy nurtured by technology in the university students involved in the university-to-work transition.

The first part of the chapter provides an overview of educational and vocational guidance during the school-to-work transition. Implications for identity are considered and discussed. The chapter then explores the notion of self-efficacy and the use of technology in university-to-work transition. The empirical part reports in-depth interviews addressing university student (aged 25–30) from Eastern European countries (Armenia, Croatia, Estonia, Georgia, and Romania) and Italy, who were in the phase of university-to-work transition. The questions primarily focus on educational and vocational guidance received by the interviewees in their formal education system, and about the role of technology in active search for work. The chapter concludes with a reflection of the role of self-efficacy and technology in promoting university-to-work transition.

TRANSITIONS AND EDUCATIONAL AND VOCATIONAL GUIDANCE

Transition is a process that requires human transformations and changing in relationship with the environment, emphasizing the dynamic process of "being-in-change" (Zittoun, 2014). In fact, a range of terms that elucidate transition includes evolution, progression, advancement, conversion, adaptation, passage, and journey. Generally the transition is conceived in three phases: separation, transition, and re-incorporation (Taylor, Millwater, & Nash, 2007) or anticipation, adjustment, and achievement (Wendlandt &

Rochlen, 2008). Handy (1995) uses an "S" curve to describe life transitions. One of the life's biggest challenges is to know when to make changes and move to another "S" curve.

Here we focus in the university-to-work transition. This challenging moment in students' life calls into questions of models, values, and beliefs: a successful transition is a precursor of promising career development (Pinquart, Juang, & Silbereisen, 2003). According to Hays and Clements (2012), we consider that transition is not a clearly delineated stage between two separate states (in our case, university and work), but an overlapping phase. Both universities and organizations may affect and contribute to smoothing the transition process, enhancing the learning that might take place during it.

Various actions and programs are taking part by European and national institutions to guide students (generally, at the end of higher school and university) to support educational-to-work transition and to gather new skills. This is in line to pursue global competitiveness and seeks the political goal of creating a more inclusive society (Cedefop, 2011). The credit system for vocational educational training is an example of programs that enable the transparency and adaptability of skills across the boundaries of countries and different jobs. Great emphasis is also on developing soft skills (e.g., communication, social integration, collaboration, etc.), as established by the program Erasmus Plus, with a focus on non-formal activities. Entrepreneurship is also considered another key skill for a better transition from educational system to work for youth (for example, one action is the European Program Erasmus Entrepreneurs). EU Skills Panorama (a website presenting quantitative and qualitative information on short- and medium-term skills needs, skills supply and skills mismatches) describes entrepreneurial attitude as an attribute that goes further than required for business activity, to include an "active and reactive spirit" and a "mindset" that supports everyone in society, also providing a foundation for entrepreneurs to establish a social or commercial activity. All these actions are generally addressed to youth from 18 to 30 years old. Indeed, this age group refers to a period where training is crucial to develop "competent knowledge workers for the knowledge era" (Chan, Ma, & Law, 2007, p. 2).

Despite these international programs, a key role for educational and vocational guidance is played by local educational institutions. Indeed, high schools and universities create pathways of educational and vocational guidance. In educational guidance, the role of the school as a system of activities (Engeström, 1987) composed of artifacts, people, community, rules, division of labor, and objects in communication with other contexts and realities (family, professional training, and non-formal and informal contexts) clearly emerges. The school must be the first break in developing useful and updated skills, preparing learners for the needs and challenges of the forthcoming competitive world. In the same time, it is during the higher school and university years that students should learn how to develop their vocational identity, defined as the realization of an increasingly stable conceptualization of one's own vocational interests, talents, and goals (Holland, Daiger, & Power, 1980). The educational and vocational guidance could then be the add-on between individual expression and the demands of social and economic growth, bridging the structural gap between education and work.

In the forthcoming text, we will examine closer the university-to-work transition and implications on personal identity.

Transition and Identity

The university-to-work transition can be viewed as a form of learning (Taylor et al., 2007), resulting from continuous hybridization between the personal identity and external environment. For this reason, in the next section, we explore self-efficacy as a transversal skill to support young people in the university-to-work transition.

According to Zittoun (2012) transition entails: (1) identity alterations; (2) learning process and definition of new skills; (3) the construction of meaning. These are three types of changes that are interrelated and mutually dependent.

From the educational community of the university, the student crosses toward a new work community that is totally different in aims, role, and structure. This process of learning starts the passage from the acquisition of expertise to the activation of knowledge to "become" an expert: learning, in fact, is strictly connected to identity (Brown & Campione 1990; Lave & Wenger, 1991). Switching between university and work communities gives the student and future worker the opportunity to try and test new identity stances and positions (Hermans & Kempen, 1993): "transitions of identity require experiencing possible new positions, not yet fully inhabited, and perform as-if one was already there" (Hviid & Zittoun, 2008, p. 126). Moreover, the contradictions and contaminations between individuals, communities, and organizations favor mutual changes and reciprocal enrichment, emerging newness, creativity, and new understanding (Wenger, 2000; Zittoun & Cerchia, 2013).

Indeed, according to Wenger (2011), the 21st century will be the century of identity: the new source of value creation depends on the engagement of people's identity in their work. He suggests to transfigure from the dimension of curriculum to identity within communities of practices, a space where challenges, passions, or interests are shared. This process of "geographical landscape," as Wenger states, consists of four dimensions:

(1) established connectivity (e.g., togetherness and separation, virtual and real presence); (2) active medium (socio-informational computing, semantic web); (3) modes of engagement (self-expression, mass collaboration, and thin connections); (4) reconfiguring geographies (multi-membership, dynamic boundaries). Finding our identity in this landscape of practices is the main challenge.

Wenger (1998) indicates three different modes of identification as: (1) engagement, understood as an active involvement of individuals in concrete and reciprocal processes of negotiation of meaning; (2) imagination, meant as the creation of images of the world and the generation of new relations in time and space which affect the self; (3) alignment, defined as the coordination of energy, actions, and practices. All these elements can be integrated into broader structures and contribute to broader enterprises. Furthermore, according to Wenger (2011), competence implies "knowledgeability," which is a set of socially defined attributes and personal experiences. This "knowledgeability" becomes a modulation of identification, practice, and identity in social learning spaces. The ability, then, is no longer something embedded in one individual, but "a situated domain of expertise found in inter-psychological processes of how individuals act within social practice" (Billet, 2001, p. 3).

In the next section, we explore self-efficacy as a transversal skill to support university students in the university-to-work transition. Then, we explore the role of technology in this process.

SELF-EFFICACY AS A SKILL FOR TRANSITION

The reality of work is not easy to understand for students at the exit of the formal education system. The university-to-work transition is particularly relevant at identity level: the world of education is almost closed and the projection to the work becomes "urgent"; stressed by family, peer, and social expectations. To better handler this process, in our opinion, the skill of self-efficacy could be a transversal skill to facilitate the transition between university and work community.

Bandura (1997) defined self-efficacy as an individual's "judgments about his or her capabilities to organize and execute courses of action required to attain designated performances" (Bandura, 1986, p. 391). People with the same intelligence and specific abilities, but with a higher sense of self-efficacy, are more motivated to achieve goals. He identifies four main sources of information for the construction of self-efficacy: (1) direct behavioral experience: people who have shown themselves to possess cognitive and behavioural ability have the resources to succeed even in new and complex situations; (2) vicarious experiences and modelling: through a comparison with the performance achieved by other models of success; (3) verbal persuasion: people who have been incurred are committed in the realization of their goals; (4) physiological and emotional: how people judge their strength and vulnerability, that could be negatively or positively oriented. These sources of self-efficacy "continually and reciprocally interact to affect performance judgements which, in turn, influence human action" (Lent & Hackett, 1987, p. 348).

Bandura (1997) also stresses the role of the locus of control: people with an internal locus of control believe that their rewards in life are guided by their own decisions and efforts; people with an external locus of control think that rewards or outcomes are determined by either luck or others with more power than them. In the first case, if they do not succeed, they believe it is due to their own lack of effort; in the second case, if they do not succeed, they believe it is due to forces outside of their control. Personal efficacy, in his view, is a dynamic aspect of the self-system that interacts complexly with the environment, with capabilities, performance and motivational, and self-regulatory mechanisms.

Bandura's self-efficacy theory has been gaining empirical attention in the career literature "as both a mediator and outcome measure of career-related behaviours" (Mau, 2000). The self-efficacy theory has been adopted in many specific domains of vocational behavior, such as career decision making (Luzzo, 1995), vocational identity (Munson & Savickas, 1998), career exploratory behavior (Blustein, 1989), and career decision-making difficulty (Osipow & Gati, 1998). Research with adults confirms that beliefs of personal efficacy play a highly influential role in occupational development and pursuits.

Lent, Brown, and Hackett (1994) developed the social cognitive career theory (SCCT) based on Bandura's model. SCCT hypothesizes that personal, contextual, and social cognitive factors influence the development of career interests, selection of career goals, and career behaviors. Betz and Hackett (1981) introduced the concept of career decision-making self-efficacy. This notion indicates individuals' degree of confidence that they can successfully engage in tasks associated with making a career choice and with commitment to a career.

The concept of self-efficacy has several related concepts like, for instance, the notion of empowerment. This latter includes other features as autonomy and motivation, implying an economic and empowering relationship. According to Perkins and Zimmerman (1995), basic components of the construct are participation with others to achieve goals, efforts to gain access to resources, and some critical understanding of the socio-political environment.

Even the contextual dimension (family, economic conditions, etc.) is extensively studied in relation to self-efficacy and the dimension of work.

For example, Ali, McWhirter, and Chronister (2005) explore self-efficacy and vocational outcome expectations for adolescents of lower socioeconomic status, observing that "personal and contextual variables do not determine an individual's career interests and goal activities but set the stage for the experiences that influence the career development process" (p. 42).

The next section discusses the role of technology in effective job search and possible use of technology to support self-efficacy.

SELF-EFFICACY AND TECHNOLOGY

Technology has created new patters of communication and new ways of looking at work and employment. Technology is a key tool in searching job position: there is a capillary sharing of job posting or shared information about specific characteristics of a particular position. According to Stevenson (2008), "for workers, the Internet may reduce the cost of acquiring information about jobs both by impacting how workers learn about job openings and how they respond to openings" (p. 2).

The relationship between technology and self-efficacy can be seen as biunivocal: the capacity of a better use of technology depends on self-efficacy and, at the same time, the improvement of self-efficacy depends on the use of technologies. Different studies can be found in the literature on the first relation: for example, some studies focus on technological self-efficacy, considered as the belief in one's ability and skills to successfully perform a technologically sophisticated new task (McDonald & Siegall, 1992; Huffman, Whetten & Huffman, 2013), other studies focus on computer self-efficacy (Broos & Roe, 2006; Kher, Downey, & Monk, 2013).

Less common are the studies relating to the improvement of the self-efficacy relying on technological proficiency. We can consider that some online environments may become spaces of "meta-reflection" (Azevedo, 2007). For example, in the field of educational and vocational guidance, the best-practice Cascaid (https://www.cascaid.co.uk/) from the United Kingdom seems to be interesting. This platform offers personalized careers information and guidance solutions based on innovative technology. This project is also taken up in Italy with the project "S.OR.PRENDO" (http://www.sorprendo.it/), a database with detailed descriptions of 438 occupational profiles. In particular, this software combines the features of individual job profiles with the interests of each user. The usefulness of these software consists of their feature of expanding knowledge about the world of work and professions, identifying lists of profiles consistent with their interests in real-time, and reflecting on their expectations with respect to future profession and build career paths.

Online social networks can have an active role in facilitating the transition: widely used by teenagers, this is a challenging area of exploration around self-efficacy (Krämer & Winter, 2008). In fact, online social networking appears to have a positive influence on youth. For example, youth maintain their social capital through the management of online relationships (Regan & Steeves, 2010), and social networks can encourage students to share interests and personal and professional aspirations (Anderson, 2009). In the same time, online communities spread out on online social networks (like Facebook) for professional development (Pachler, Ranieri, Manca, & Cook, 2012).

The following section presents the results of the exploratory study carried out in the context of the Erasmus Plus program.

EXPLORATORY STUDY: UNIVERSITY STUDENT IN TRANSITION

Objectives of the Study

The study aimed at investigating self-efficacy and the role of technology to support the university-to-work transition through a series of interviews addressing a group of young adults in Europe. In particular, we focused on the following questions:

- What educational and vocational guidance have young people received in their country?
- How do young people in transition between work and school use technology for active search of job?
- How could self-efficacy, especially when supported by technology, help the transition between school and work?

The Participants

The study involved ten participants (three boys and seven girls) from Romania, Estonia, Georgia, Armenia, Croatia, and Italy. All participants were in the transitional period between and overlapping university study and a graduate's entry into the professional workforce. Their ages range from 25 to 30 years. All of them were involved in Erasmus Plus activities and were invited to participate in the interview via e-mail. The selection of the countries was based on their medium-high level of unemployment. For example, as indicated by OECD (2012), more than one out of five 15–29 year-old youths in Italy is neither in education nor employed, and the labour market for young graduates has become more difficult over the past decade.

Data Collection

Semi-structured interviews have been carried out with the aim of gathering information about university students' subjective experiences of their transition. The interviews were conducted via Skype and lasted in average 30 minutes. We opted for this type of interview because it allowed the interviewees to freely talk about their own experiences providing examples and episodes. Both the interviewee and the interviewer were engaged in a sense-making process that turned the interview into an active process (Bruner, 1990). The interviewer used the mirroring technique (Rogers, Stevens, Gendlin, Shlien, & Van Dusen, 1967) with no judgment or valuation. The interview (in Appendix) was based on 11 questions: 6 questions on vocational education and transition university/work and 5 questions on role of technology for active job's search.

Data Analysis

Data analysis was carried out in three steps: (1) interviews were recorded and transcribed; (2) the texts of the interviews were read and analyzed by two independent researchers, to familiarize with the content of the interviews and to collapse the parts of the text expressing similar ideas; (3) the researchers listed all the sections of the interviews where university students' self-efficacy emerged.

Self-efficacy of participants was assessed indirectly through the analysis of the answers. The categories that have been considered were: internal or external locus of control; positive or negative attitude. At this purpose, the qualitative discourse analysis was used (Schiffrin, Tannen, & Hamilton, 2001).

The main results of the analysis of the interviews are reported and discussed in the next paragraphs.

FINDINGS

Provided that each respondent is not representative of the reality of his/her own country and that this research has an exploratory aim, we present the results emerged from the semi-structured interviews. It may be noted that not everyone has answered all the questions and with the same accuracy.

Guidance and Transition as a Sense-Making Process

Generally speaking, not all respondents seem to be familiar with technical terminology (e.g., vocational orientation, guidance, etc.) Nevertheless, they seem to consider vocational orientation and guidance as important elements for local development, recognizing the added value they could bring to policy and strategy guidance, if well implemented. The educational and vocational guidance is related mainly with formal education (schools, universities, public institutions). The role of a non-government agency (NGO) becomes the only support in the absence of educational and vocational guidance provided by institution, in a framework of non-formal learning. All programs and national actions evocated by the respondents are about university choice (transition to higher school, to university, or to professional field) and not specifically related to the university-to-work transition. Some excerpts are reported below (E1).

E1. Extracts of interviews about educational and vocational guidance

Croatian boy: Good technical education in high schools. Programs for adult education called People Schools

Croatian girl: Free career guidance and vocational education for students at Croatian Employment Services

Estonia girl: Educational and vocational guidance is present in country because that was made by profession Tax department

Georgia girl: Vocational education and orientation is a new field. Needs to be further developed

Armenia girl: It is considered important to find proper job in the country. I have not received any career orientation from the University. There have been private orientation courses provided by some NGOs.

Romanian boy: It is considered very useful for young people to find a workplace

Italian boy: Focus on university choice

Specifically, during the handling of transaction phase, the interviewed expresses the need of an additional support. This delicate moment is made more difficult by the economic situation and unemployment levels of local country. Landmarks become the skills acquired through the university and teachers or/and relatives (see next page, E2).

E2. Extracts of interviews about handling the transition

Croatian boy: It is hard enough to find employment. High unemployment rates among youth in Croatia where country is on third place in the European Union after Greece and Spain.

Estonia girl: There is not institution to help in the transition

Georgia girl: University provided enough skills to be employed

Armenia girl: The only helpers are for us teachers and parents, and myself

Romanian boy: Feeling that working choices could be better

Italian boy: University as the best public institutions as facilitators of transitions, together with public institution like region.

About the skills useful to find a job, the respondents put attention to technical (mainly, ITC and languages), communication, and creative skills. The skills described are generic and cut across all sectors. Only the Italian boy proposes specifically skills focused to his field of interest (E3):

E3. Extracts of interviews about skill to find a job

Croatian boy: Technical skills like languages, computer skills, driving license

Estonia girl: Good IT skills. English and Russian languages

Georgia girl: Flexible to find a job, having a critical and creative mind, be purposeful and self-determined, committed and responsible person

Armenia girl: Language and computer knowledge, creativity, team working

Romanian boy: No idea

Italian boy: Scientific field, like improve mathematical knowledge, both theoretical and applied, consider learning programming languages at a good level.

About an advice to give to a peer, they express various strategies: activation of personal network; strategies to adapt to the local context; skill to improve or update and emigration. All assume an attitude of problem solving for the issue "work," aware of the various options and the different strategies (E4).

E4: Extracts of interviews about advice to a peer for job searching

Croatian boy: Find jobs in other countries. Youth in Croatia I think are quite informed and the problem is not in them

Estonia girl: Personal network

Georgia girl: Follow up the job vacancies published on the internet spaces. If possible start as an internships

Georgia girl: Personal network and study on related field.

Georgia girl: Improve English because it is the working language of number organizations of Georgia

Armenia girls: Learn the language and be creative.

Romanian boy: IT

Italian boy: Get ready to accept offers from closely related areas

We can consider the transition as a process of learning: the change leads to acquire new information on local and international context (i.e. economic trends), to seek information and advice on job search (activating personal network or peer support), find strategies and update the skills required by the market. This learning process will continue throughout all the working life, shaped by the work practices in which individuals participate (Billet, 2001).

Cultural differences between the university students interviewed are difficult to grasp. However, following Oettingen (1997), we can say that "the social transactions are considered to be mediators of cultural effects on self-appraisals" (p. 157). Indeed, during the university-to-work transition, personal, social, and cultural aspects are blended.

New Technology as a Tool to Bridge the Gap Toward The Work

The technology is recognized as a crucial tool in active job search, since it is embedded in daily life. The Internet and computers have a central role in young people's strategy to find a job, both to search for jobs (national job-seekers site) and to learn strategies for job selection (YouTube advice). Some excerpts are reported on the next page (E5).

E5: Extracts of interviews about the role of technology for active job's search

Croatian boy: Internet connection, YouTube advice's on job applications to find advice and send applications.

Estonia girl: Using computer is the main element to find a job. We have sites on the Internet where you can find big list of jobs.

Croatian girl: There are some web-sites and Facebook groups where employers offer vacancies. However, I have never paid attention.

Georgia girl: Computer is the only tool for me to find a job.

Georgia girl: Media technologies and in general the Internet; use of cell-phone. I use the Internet very often for my job search on daily basis.

Armenian girl: Today most job seekers try to find work via online advertisements, less often via printed media. I myself found it on job-seekers' site. I can surely say that computer technologies are the most used means of job searching.

Romanian boy: No use of technology for finding actual job but useful to registration to a portal for jobs.

Italian boy: I use Internet for activities web-searcher.

Almost all participants declared that they quite often use online tools for learning and educational needs, using some international learning platform like Courera or Moocs (Massive Open Online Course—a course of study made available over the Internet without charge to a very large number of people) (E6).

E6: Extracts of interviews about the use of online tools for learning

Croatian boy: I take MOOC's at Courera and EdX. I think it is very interesting for things you cannot find in general education.

Estonia girl: Language courses.

Georgia girl: E-learning courses of the Soliya.

Georgia girl: I have once attended the session delivered via Skype from The USA. The training was on Human rights.

Armenian girl: Yes, several of them. I'd like to mention just one organized by American Embassy in Armenia: it was an online training course-webinar with representatives of Armenia, Georgia and Azerbaijan.

Romanian boy: No. But I would like doing it.

Italian boy: Yes, Coursera lectures and "Laboratori dal Basso (regional initiative) training".

In describing through a metaphor their relationship with technology, the respondents provided different and creative answers. The use of technology is depicted with connotations of a human relationship, sometimes felt as an intrusive experience (E7).

E7: Metaphor of the relationship with technology

Croatian boy: Mistrustful but find it useful for a lot of stuff in my life. Still, mistrustful.

Estonia girl: Unfortunately use it half a day.

Croatian boy: Love at the first sight.

Georgia girl: Confident user.

Georgia girl: In good relationship.

Armenian girl: It is like a language. If you don't speak it, you can't communicate in 21st century.

Romanian boy: Love.

Italian boy: A good lady, I feel engaged with it.

From the interviews, we can say that the use of the Internet for job's search is highly spread out among all the participants involved in the study, in line with the literature (Stevenson, 2008). For example, as we have seen, a girl from Georgia refers to the Internet as "the *only* tool for me to find a job." Technology means having access to relevant cultural practices and objects, favoring processes of inclusion and equity. Technological devices have a central role as "cultural resources" (Cook, Pachler, & Bachmair, 2013) through which one can learn about the social structures and cultural practices of the society, enabling active participation in the community and a better quality of life.

Elements involved in the relationship with new technology are: not trust of technology (*I have never paid attention)*; absence of the Internet in some contexts (*Unfortunately I use it half a day*); or because embedded in the inclusive term "Internet" (*I use Internet for web-searching activities)*. From the small sample of interviews, it does not emerge a specific vision about the role of online social networks.

At the same time, the need of a continuous use of the Internet, also through mobile devices, clearly appears. In fact, there is a recurring reference to the connection and the need to cultivate personal social network. One *leitmotif* is "staying connected." According to Tomai et al. (2010, p. 265), "these types of networks literally create 'bridges,' which give people, who might not have had the possibility to encounter one another in their daily lives, the opportunity to become acquainted," providing the chance to improve their life.

In general, we can state that technology can support the process of transitions between different communities, facilitating the connection between virtual and real presence, allowing learners to be an active medium in the search of information, and supporting dynamic hybridizations between contexts.

Self-Efficacy as a Personal and Transversal Resource

In this section, we attempt to analyze how self-efficacy takes shape looking at the personal experiences of the respondents. Four main categories have been considered for the analysis: "internal or external locus of control" and "passive or active attitude." From the cross-reading of interviews, we can note a relation between self-efficacy, job search, and the use of technology.

In the question about finding a job, we can observe different nuances about internal or external locus of control. Some respondent expresses a more external locus of control to find a job related to the context (e.g., "*hard, with no assistance from aside*"), while others a more internal locus of control related to the personal features (e.g., "*It was not easy to find it, but I did it*") (see E10).

E10. Extracts of interviews about find a job

Croatian boy: Taking in consideration social context
Croatian girls: Hard, with no assistance from aside
Estonia girl: Reiterating the need to offer more vocational training
Georgia girl: Finding my job was not really hard
Armenia girl: For me there was nothing so hard to handle. It was not easy to find it, but I did it
Romanian boy: Do not know
Italian boy: Be a curious person
Italian boy: Working where I could find a job

The personal perspective towards the internal capacities and external resources influences the managing of the transition process. Indeed Youths who are ready to make meaning from the differing experiences are more able to find resources and new opportunities, increasing their adaptation to the situation. For example, the Croatian boy has a broad vision of the world of work; he is able to give concrete advice anchored to a broad understanding of the political context of his country. His self-efficacy and active attitude clearly emerges from his use of active verbs and first-person pronouns (I will not recommend/I will recommend/I think etc.).

}On the other hand, attitudes of passiveness may be linked to lack of information, which generates a circle of inactivity. The Croatian girl, for example, considers that the best strategy for finding a job is having relatives in a position of power. The building blocks of such meaning is fuelled by collective images, which lead to forms of dialogic imagination (Markovà, 2013), which is in this case negatively oriented. Here some extracts are reported (E11).

E11: Extracts of interviews

Croatian girls: To find a job it is useful have connections and relatives

Croatian girls: Have a family member on the important position

At the same time the Croatian boy uses technologies (e.g., Youtube or MOOC) in a critical and instrumental way. Indeed, developing self-efficacy also implies for individuals being involved in a sense-making process: "the aggregate of all the psychological facts that arise in our consciousness as the result of the word" (Vygotsky, 1987, pp. 275–276). Moreover, the Croatian girl appears to be a passive user of technology, talking about generic uses of the Internet for job search. Even the guy from Romania shows the same attitude in many of the responses, answering "*I do not know*" about useful skills in his country. He expresses also a generic way of "*love*" for the Internet, without any further specification.

Considering the prospective of Bandura (1997), we can state that having a higher sense of self-efficacy can help the subject handle moments of change, such the phase of the university-to-work transaction. Especially in context of stressful life transitions, general beliefs of efficacy may serve as a personal resource or vulnerability factor: "People with a high sense of perceived efficacy tend to interpret demands and problems more as challenges than as threats or subjectively uncontrollable events" (Jerusalem & Mittag, 1995, p. 178).

At the same time, a greater confidence in their own abilities can bring a more creative use of technology, customizing the role of technology to personal needs and objectives.

CONCLUSION

In the present chapter we aimed to investigate the notion of self-efficacy and the role of technology in the university-to-work transition. The study was limited to a few listening "voices" (Bakhtin, 1961/1986). It was conducted in an exploratory perspective. To draw general conclusions, more evidence can be collected on how technology can positively influence and support self-efficacy.

From interviews the emotional dimension of the university-to-work transaction does not emerge (also due to the more impersonal use of Skype compared to a face to face interview).

Designing and delivering programs aimed at preparing students and supporting them through the transition process may have important implications for learners' effective approach to transition and dealing with it. Students can learn how to handle the transition between university and work, activating internal and external resources. Cultivating self-efficacy makes the youth most confident in projecting themselves into the future, especially "who may have particularly difficult circumstances to overcome or barriers to surmount" (Hackett, 1997, p. 253).

The technology could become a tool to support the self-efficacy through forms of social support, for example in online groups to share difficulties, frustrations, and action strategies and get advice about the difficulty of transition. For example, specific virtual communities, through dialogue and exchange, could help renegotiate direct behavioral experiences; receive vicarious experiences and modelling; verbal persuasion from others or help in interpretations of psychological and emotional states, all main sources of information for the construction of self-efficacy (Bandura, 1997).

In conclusion, both school and technology can become a space for a transitional frame in the educational system.

ACKNOWLEDGMENTS

I thank the editors and anonymous review for the support and for the comments that have contributed to improve the chapter.

APPENDIX

Interview

University-to-Work Transition:

1. What type of educational and vocational guidance did you receive from educational institutions in your country?

2. In your opinion, to what extent educational and vocational guidance is useful to find job in your country?
3. Were there bodies/institutions/educational services that have helped you in the university-to-work transition in your country?
4. How have you handled the university -to-work transition?
5. What skills do you believe are the most useful to find work in your country?
6. What would you recommend to one peer in order to find employment in your country?

Role of Technology in University-to-Work Transition

1. What was the most important technology that facilitates your entry into the world of work in your country?
2. What type of technology do you use for job search?
3. How do you use technology for job search?
4. Have you ever attended online activities to supplement your training? If yes, what kind?
5. Which metaphor better describes your relationship with technology?

REFERENCES

Ali, S. R., McWhirter, E. H., & Chronister, K. M. (2005). Self-efficacy and vocational outcome expectations for adolescents of lower socioeconomic status: A pilot study. *Journal of Career Assessment, 13*(1), 40–58.

Akkerman, S. F., & Bakker, A. (2011). Boundary crossing and boundary objects. *Review of Educational Research, 81*(2).

Anderson, T. (2009). Social networking. In S. Mishra (Ed.). *Stride Handbook 8—E-learning*. New Delhi, India: Indira Gandhi National Open University.

Azevedo, R. (2007). Understanding the complex nature of self-regulatory processes in learning with computer-based learning environments: An introduction. *Metacognition and Learning, 2*, 57–65.

Bakhtin, M. M. (1986). *Speech genres and other late essays*. Austin, TX: University of Texas Press. (Original work published 1961)

Bandura, A. (1986). *Social foundations of thought and action: A social cognitive theory*. Englewood, NJ: Prentice-Hall.

Bandura, A. (1997). *Self-efficacy: The exercise of control*. New York, NY: Freeman.

Bandura, A., Barbaranelli, C., Caprara, G. V., & Pastorelli, C. (2001). Self-efficacy beliefs as shapers of children's aspirations and career trajectories. *Child Development, 72*(1), 187–206.

Betz, N. E., & Hackett, G. (1981). The relationship of career-related self-efficacy expectations to perceived career options in college women and men. *Journal of Counseling Psychology, 28*, 399–410.

Billett, S. (2001). Learning throughout working life: Interdependencies at work. *Studies in Continuing Education, 23*(1), 19–35.

Blustein, D. L. (1989). The role of goal instability and career self-efficacy in the career exploration process. *Journal of Vocational Behavior, 35*, 194–203.

Broos, A., & Roe, K. (2006). The digital divide in the playstation generation: Self-efficacy, locus of control, and ICT adoption among adolescents. *Poetics, 34*, 306–317.

Brown, A. L., & Campione, J. C. (1990). Communities of learning or a content by any other name. In D. Kuhn (Ed.), *Contribution to human development* (pp. 108–126). New York, NY: Oxford University Press.

Bruner, J. (1990). *Acts of meaning*. Cambridge, MA: Harvard University Press.

Cedefop. (2011). *Lifelong guidance across Europe: Reviewing policy progress and future prospects*. Luxembourg: Publications Office of the European Union.

Chan, C., Ma. R, & Law, N. (2007). *Teachers' understanding of knowledge building in an emerging community*. Paper presented at the Summer Institute, University of Toronto. Retrieved from http://ikit.org/SummerInstitute2007/Highlights/SI2007_papers/51_Chan.pdf

Cook, J., Pachler, N., & Bachmair, B. (2013) Using social network sites and mobile technology to scaffold equity of access to cultural resources. In G. Trentin & M. Repetto (Eds.), *Using network and mobile technology to bridge formal and informal learning* (pp. 31–56). Sawston, Cambridge, England: Woodhead.

Engeström, Y. (1987). *Learning by expanding: An activity-theoretical approach to develomental research*. Helsiki, Finland: Orienta-Konsultit.

Hackett, G. (1997). Self-efficacy in career choice and development. In A. Bandura (Ed.), *Self-efficacy in changing societies* (pp. 232–258). New York, NY: Cambridge University Press.

Hays, J., & Clements, M. (2012, June 20–22). *Transition: bridging the gap between study and work*. Paper presented at the 9th International Conference on Cooperative Education and Work-Integrated Learning, Where East meets West and Theory meets Practice, Istanbul, Turkey.

Handy, C. (1995). *The Empty Raincoat. Making Sense of the Future*. Australia: Random House.

Hermans, H., & Kempen, H. (1993). *The dialogical self*. Toronto, Canada: Academic Press.

Holland, J. L., Daiger, D. C., & Power, P. G. (1980). *My vocational situation*. Palo Alto, CA: Consulting Psychologists Press.

Huffman, A. H., Whetten, J., & Huffman, W. H. (2013). Using technology in higher education: the influence of gender roles on technology self-efficacy. *Computers in Human Behavior, 29*(4), 1779–1786.

Hviid, P., & Zittoun, T. (2008). Transitions in the process of education. *European Journal of Psychology of Education, XXIII* (2), 121–130.

Jerusalem, M., & Mittag, W. (1995). Self-efficacy in stressful life transitions. In A. Bandura (Ed.), *Self-efficacy in changing societies* (pp. 177–201). New York, NY: Cambridge University Press.

Kher, H. V., Downey, J. P., & Monk, E. (2013). A longitudinal examination of computer Self-efficacy change trajectories during training. *Computers in Human Behavior, 29*(4), 1816–1824.

Krämer, N. C., & Winter, S. (2008). Impression management 2.0: The relationship of self-esteem, extraversion, self-efficacy, and self-presentation within social networking sites. *Journal of Media Psychology: Theories, Methods, and Applications, 20*(3), 106–116.

Lave, J., & Wenger, E. (1991). *Situated learning: Legitimate peripheral participation.* Cambridge, UK: Cambridge University Press.

Lent, R. W., Brown, S. D., & Hackett, G. (1994). Toward a unifying social cognitive theory of career, and academic interest, choice and performance. *Journal of Vocational Behavior, 45*, 79–122.

Lent, R., & Hackett, G. (1987). Career self-efficacy: Empirical status and future directions. *Journal of Vocational Behavior 30*, 347–382.

Luzzo, D. A. (1995). The relative contributions of self-efficacy and locus of control to the prediction of career maturity. *Journal of College Student Development, 36*, 61–66.

Marková, I. (2013, October). *From the prohibition of thought to dialogical imagination.* Neuchâtel, Switzerland: University of Neuchatel.

Mau, W. C. (2000). Cultural differences in career decision-making styles and self-efficacy. *Journal of Vocational Behavior 57*, 365–378.

McDonald, T., & Siegall, M. (1992). The effects of technological Self-efficacy and job focus on job performance, attitudes, and withdrawal behaviors. *The Journal of Psychology, 126*, 465–475.

Munson, W. W., & Savickas, M. L. (1998). Relation between leisure and career development of college students. *Journal of Vocational Behavior, 53*, 243–253.

McWhirter, E. H., Rasheed, S., & Crothers, M. (2000). The effects of high school career education on social cognitive variables. *Journal of Counseling Psychology, 47*, 330–341.

OECD. (2012). *Education at a Glance 2012: OECD Indicators*. Paris, France: Author.

Oettingen, G. (1997). Cross-cultural perspectives on self-efficacy beliefs. In A. Bandura (Ed.), *Self-efficacy in changing societies* (pp. 149–176). New York, NY: Cambridge Press.

Osipow, S. H., & Gati, I. (1998). Construct and concurrent validity of the career decision-making difficulties questionnaire. *Journal of Career Assessment, 6*, 347–364.

Pachler, N., Ranieri, M., Manca, S., & Cook, J. (Eds.). (2012). Editorial: Social networking and mobile learning. *British Journal of Educational Technology, 43*(5), 707–710.

Perkins, D. D., & Zimmerman, M. A. (1995). Empowerment theory, research, and application. *American Journal of Community Psychology, 23*(5).

Pinquart, M., Juang, L. P., & Silbereisen, R. K. (2003). Self-efficacy and successful school-to-work transition: A longitudinal study. *Journal of Vocational Behavior, 63*, 329–346.

Regan, P., & Steeves, V. (2010). Kids R Us: Online social networking and the potential for empowerment. *Surveillance & Society, 8*(2), 151–165.

Rogers, C. R., Stevens, B., Gendlin, E. T., Shlien, J. M., & Van Dusen, W. (1967). *Person to person: The problem of being human: A new trend in psychology.* Lafayette, CA: Real People Press.

Schiffrin, D., Tannen, D., & Hamilton, H. E. (Eds.). (2001). T*he handbook of discourse analysis.* Hoboken, NJ: Blackwell.

Stevenson, B. (2008). The Internet and Job Search, National Bureau of Economic Research Inc, NBER Working Papers: 13886.

Taylor, P., Millwater, J., & Nash., R. (2007, July). *Talking about transitions: the value of a conceptual approach.* Enhancing higher education, theory and scholarship. Proceedings of the 30th HERDSA Annual Conference, Adelaide, Australia, 8–11.

Tomai, M., Rosa, V., Mebane, M. E., D'Acunti, A., Benedetti, M., & Francescato, D. (2010). Virtual communities in schools as tools to promote social capital with high schools students. *Computers & Education, 54*(1), 265–274.

Vygotsky, L. S. (1987). Problems of general psychology (including the volume Thinking and speech). In *The collected works of L. S. Vygotsky* (Vol. 1, pp. 39–285). New York, NY: Plenum Press.

Wendlandt, N. M., & Rochlen, A. B. (2008). Addressing the college to work transition: Implications for university counselors. *Journal of Career Development, 35*(2), 151–165.

Wenger, E. (1998). Communities of practice: Learning, meaning, and identity. Cambridge, UK: Cambridge University Press.

Wenger, E. (2000). Communities of practice and social learning systems. Organization, 7(2), 225–246.

Wenger, E. (2011, May). *Knowledgeability in landscapes of practice: From curriculum to identity.* Second International Seminar on Education Labour, Università degli Studi Roma Tre.

Zittoun, T. (2012). Une psychologie des transitions : des ruptures aux ressources [A psychology of transitions: Breaks to resources]. In P. Curchod, P. A. Doudin, & L. Lafortune (Eds.), *Les transitions à l'école* [Transitions to school] (pp. 261–279). Québec: Presses de l'Université du Québec.

Zittoun, T. (2014). Transitions as dynamic processes—A commentary. *Learning, Culture and Social Interaction, 3*(3), 232–236. doi:10.1016/j.lcsi.2014.02.010

Zittoun, T., & Cerchia, F. (2013). Imagination as expansion of experience. *Integrative Psychological and Behavioral Science, 47*(3), 305–324.

CHAPTER 7

BUILDING A PRESENCE IN THE ONLINE SPACE

An Opportunity and a Challenge for 21st Century Students

Mónica Aresta, Luís Pedro, and Carlos Santos

ABSTRACT

In the new global and connected world, the study and comprehension about how identity is built and materialized in online environments is one of great importance. As producers of online content, individuals now have the chance and the stage to develop and manifest an identity able to reflect the personal, professional, and academic dimensions of their lives. Introducing a conceptual framework and a model developed to analyze the construction of the self in online environments, this chapter presents the main results of a case study developed at the University of Aveiro (Portugal) focused on the online presence built in social online spaces (Facebook and Twitter) and in an institutionally supported online platform (SAPO Campus). Data was collected through the application of questionnaires, direct observation, and in-depth interviews made to 13 students from a master's degree course (convenience sample). Observation included the analysis of all messages

E-Learning and Social Media:
Education and Citizenship for the Digital 21st Century, pp. 143–166

published by the participants on the three online spaces (n = 3692). This chapter addresses and discusses issues related with the construction and management of identity in online environments, and its contribution in the development of more valuable, labor-market valued, and well-prepared learners.

INTRODUCTION

The democratization of the online space and the multiplicity of tools and services made available on it fostered the development of numerous forms of interaction and communication between its users and in several activities (Buckingham, 2008a; Downes, 2005; Greenhow, Robelia, & Hughes, 2009).

In educational contexts, social software tools such as blogs, wikis, photo and video sharing tools, and social networks are being adopted in order to support the teaching-learning process. The use of technology is leading to changes in the traditional patterns of behavior and interaction between students and the institutions (Collis & Moonen, 2011), altering some of long-established dynamics of collaboration and cooperation. Used by individuals within and outside education institutions (Clark, Logan, Luckin, Mee, & Oliver, 2009; Franklin & Harmelen, 2007; Trinder, Guiller, Margaryan, Littlejohn, & Nicol, 2008), these tools are playing an important role in the promotion of communication and interaction, creating new and easy ways to create and share content, and fostering the development of collaborative content curation.

Learning with and through media, individuals can also develop competencies and skills as well as a personal awareness of their own identity (Aresta, Santos, Pedro, & Moreira, 2013a; Buckingham, 2008b). Introducing online identity as a concept that encompasses digital representation, privacy, and reputation, this chapter will discuss the main results of a study focused on the analysis of the online presence built in formal and informal online spaces. By focusing on the importance of building, sharing and managing an online identity over the web, it will also reflect on its contribution in the development of more valuable and well-prepared learners.

DIGITAL LITERACIES IN THE 21ST CENTURY

The integration of social software tools in educational contexts brought deep changes in the way knowledge is processed and negotiated. More than just knowing how to use technology, the adoption of social software tools and underlying principles demands for changes in the way individuals access and interpret information, and how they relate and select different content and information sources with a critical perspective. Beyond technology expertise and mastery of tools and applications, it becomes important to develop an awareness regarding the importance and the consequences of creating and sharing content over the network, that is, regarding the development of digital literacies.

Literacies in the Digital Society

Over the years, there have been several attempts to expand the concept of literacy beyond its initial meaning, which is the ability to perform reading and writing operations.

Nowadays, technology is simultaneously a mediator—as a way to access, create and share information—and a facilitator—diminishing geographical and social barriers and establishing more flexible and immediate communication channels. Expressions as computer and information literacy (Guth & Helm, 2010; Shapiro & Huges, 1999, as cited in Bawden, 2008), participation literacy (Giger, 2006, as cited in Guth & Helm, 2010) and digital literacy (Gilster, 1997, as cited in Goodfellow, 2011; Martin, 2008; Guth & Helm, 2010) have been used in different contexts in order to describe and circumscribe the different sets of skills and competencies needed to be an expert in specific areas of knowledge and work (Guth & Helm, 2010).

Perceived as the ability to understand and use information presented through computers in multiple formats and from multiple sources (Gilster, 1997, as cited in Goodfellow, 2011; Martin, 2008), digital literacy is often understood as an umbrella concept that encompasses the different ways technology is integrated and used in the lives of individuals and institutions. In this line of thought, digital literacy may include: (1) socially situated practices supported by competencies, strategies and attitudes that encourage and support the individuals' ability to present and understand ideas and concepts, using different digital tools (O'Brien & Scharber, 2008, as cited in McLoughlin, 2011); (2) the abilities that allow individuals to live, learn, and work in the digital society, and that can address or go beyond specific knowledge fields (Joint Information Systems Committee, 2012); (3) the creative use of technologies, including the development of knowledge and new digital tools, and the use of tools in order to meet personal and professional needs (Bawden, 2008; Martin, 2008); and (4) the knowledge needed to manage public and private digital spaces, allowing the construction of an identity able to reveal the individuals' life path and profile, thus integrating the academic and professional dimensions of their lives (Costa & Torres, 2011).

When thinking about digital literacy as a concept that goes beyond the use of tools and technologies, one must also think about how technology changed the way individuals communicate, see, and place themselves in the world, that is, about technology as a cultural experience (Buckingham, 2008a). By using technology and tools in their everyday lives and embedded in real-life contexts, individuals are creating spaces and scenarios where they can interact and communicate with other people and communities. And by connecting themselves to other users and communities, they are using technology as a way to manifest their thoughts, opinions, and preferences in the online space.

Nowadays, critical thinking and digital citizenship are considered key skills in an economic and socially global society, a society where learners are expected to be able to solve problems, finish projects, and transmit, in a creative way, their abilities and skills. Beyond the mastery of tools and applications, it is expected—among others—that learners are able to practice safe, legal, and responsible use of information and technology and reveal a positive attitude toward using technology to support collaboration, learning, and productivity. It is also expected that learners are able to reveal creativeness and innovation in their communication and collaboration processes, as well as to use technology in order to gather, evaluate, and use information (International Society for Technology in Education, 2007).

Taking this into consideration, the next section will address the importance of having an online identity as a way for individuals to build a presence and a reputation in the digital world. As it will also focus on the main challenges of building an identity in digital environments, issues related with the persistence and visibility of information published by individuals and its importance for the construction of a reputation will also be addressed.

ONLINE SPACE, SCENARIO FOR PARTICIPATION AND IDENTITY CONSTRUCTION

The development of competencies and skills related with digital literacy can be found in the individuals' creative use of digital tools, when looking for the development of social and cognitive competences (McLoughlin, 2011). As active producers of online content, individuals have now the means to build and share an identity able to encompass both the personal and professional/academic dimensions of their lives. More than a curriculum vitae, the online presence of individuals—identifiable through participation and interaction—can reveal to the wide community the sum of their experiences, skills, and abilities to communicate, interact, and share online.

In a context where technology allows learners the acquisition and development of competencies and skills that reflect their learning needs, the online space emerges as an environment favorable to participation and interaction, a space where individuals can build an identity able to reflect and translate their capabilities, skills, and interests. When it is almost impossible to remain outside the digital world and, therefore, difficult to avoid the production of an online presence (Costa & Torres, 2011; Mislove, Viswanath, Gummadi, & Druschel, 2010; Warburton, 2009), the construction of a presence over the web enables the construction of an identity and a reputation on the network, recognizable through: (1) the publication of content (Coiro, Knobel, Lankshear, & Leu, 2008; Zhao, Grasmuck, & Martin, 2008; Greenhow & Robelia, 2009; Greenhow et al., 2009; Costa & Torres, 2011); (2) the creation of profiles (boyd, 2008; Greenhow & Robelia, 2009); and in (3) the typology of participation (Fraser, 2009).

From Analogic to Digital: Building Identity in Digital Environments

In the physical world, individuals use their bodies as a mean to share information regarding their own identity and the way they position themselves in relation to the world. Gestures, verbal and non-verbal expressions, posture, and even clothing are contextual elements that allow the expression of the individuals' identity. According to the feedback received through the interaction with others, individuals may or may not adjust their behavior, working on their social identity in order to obtain the reaction they expect or desire, a process that Goffman (1959) called "impression management". In "The presentation of the self in everyday life," Goffman discusses the performative dimension of identity formation, emphasizing the idea that individuals act like actors, playing different roles in different times to different people, changing or adjusting their behavior in order to influence the perception of others.

The architecture that supports online environments, however, does not include the feedback and contextualization mechanisms that individuals are used to in the physical world (boyd, 2002). In fact, as the emergence of the Internet and online environments changed the traditional conditions of production of identity (Zhao et al., 2008), it has also brought up questions related to how individuals should look at their own online presence. Online, individuals resort to tools in order to create a digital representation of their presence: avatars, profile pages, social networks profiles, nicknames, written word (boyd, 2002; Buckingham, 2008a; Greenhow & Robelia, 2009; Peachey & Childs, 2011) are used by individuals as a way to represent themselves online. By establishing interaction with other individuals and communities, individuals are also producing a vast amount of information able to reveal aspects and dimensions of their identity and that, once archived, can be easily recovered. Inadequately transposed to the digital environment, actions and behaviors characteristic of the offline world can lead to the decontextualized exposition of the individuals, thus being necessary in the development of a consciousness regarding the similarities and differences between the physical and the digital world.

While in the physical world, information and behaviors are somehow confined to the time and place where they were produced, online content, however, can be easily searched, retrieved, processed, rearranged, and reproduced in ways almost impossible to control. Among the main differences between the representation of individuals in physical and online environments, boyd (2008b) enhances: (1) the persistence of information (non-recorded speech is transient, online text can be stored forever); (2) the content's searchability (information can be searched and identified through search engines); (3) the content's replicability (electronic media ease the replication and transformation, by others, of content created by the individual, aka as remix); and (4) the existence of invisible audiences (it is almost impossible to identify and control how and by whom content is accessed and interpreted).

The Representation of the Self in Digital Environments

Creating an Online Presence

When individuals share content over the web, they are also building an online presence able to encompass the different dimensions of their lives, a presence that arches over many spaces. Understood as a *continuum* (Warburton, García, Attwell, & University King's College, 2010), online identity emerges as a concept that includes the information published by and related to the individual in digital environments. Either related to data (the information that validates the identity of the user in digital systems) or content (the information published by the user in order to establish interaction with the online environment), online identity enables individuals to build a presence and a reputation on the network.

Often emerging as a result of a process of self-reflection, the individual's profile on social networking sites or sharing content services may also reflect the way he/she wishes to present himself/herself to the community:

> Creating a profile is an act of impression management, requiring teens to consider who might see their profiles and how they might be interpreted. The desire to be seen in a positive or accurate light compels teens to carefully craft their profiles. (boyd, 2008b, p. 130)

In this scenario, the construction of online identity emerges as a social, self-reflexive, and performative process (Greenhow & Robelia, 2009), based on the intrinsic characteristics of the individuals and how they react and internalize the experience in which they engage (boyd, 2002). By providing an environment where users can freely explore different roles or identities, without the risk of social rejection or physical consequences (Suler, 2004, as cited in Peachey & Childs, 2011), the online space seems to emerge as an environment where the construction and reconstruction of "self" occurs independently of space and time.

Addressing the network as a space for participation and sharing, Kurhila (2006) and boyd (2008) introduce a typology for classifying users according to their degree of involvement with and within the online space.

To Kurhila (2006), online space users can be classified as expert users, social users, and *lurkers*. Expert users take a proactive approach when using online tools and interacting in the network, using social software in order to support learning and to access information in a more direct and faster way. As for social users, this typology includes the ones who adopt technology in order to participate and keep up with what is happening inside social networks and environments, taking advantage of the communicative and interactive potential of tools and services. *Lurkers* are described as users who recur to the online space just for searching information, remaining as observers and rarely evolving to participants.

To boyd (2008), social networks are spaces where users can build an identity and reputation. Nevertheless, boyd (2008) points out potential reasons for individuals (teenagers) choice about not to become involved with the digital environments: not having access to Internet access, having access only in public spaces where social networks are conditioned or prohibited or having Internet access prohibited by parents (named marginalized teens); and people who decide not to get involved in social networks for reasons related to security and privacy, or for reasons related with moral or social questions (conscientious objectors).

As the result of a social and negotiated process, online presence must also consider more structured or formal dimensions that, although not being fully controlled by individuals, are assumed as part of their identity. Josie Fraser (2009), reflecting on how users interact, move, and build their presence in online environments, classifies the users' online presence as personal, professional, and organizational. To Fraser, personal use includes the use of social media as a way to interact and share information with friends and family, while professional use can be seen in the adoption of networks, networking sites, or blogs as spaces for addressing and referring to professional or academic achievements, presenting portfolios. As for the organizational dimension, it involves the adoption of tools or platforms on behalf of the users' employer or in the line of their professional tasks: managing blogs, creating social networks profiles in order to disseminate institutional information, and creating an institutional online profile.

Managing Privacy

By enabling the construction of an identity that overcomes the geographical, temporal, and social barriers existing in the physical world, the Internet also creates a space where the individual's presence is constantly accessible and exposed to various threats and vulnerabilities. Because online content remains searchable and retrievable for a long time, individuals may resort to strategies in order to create barriers to the automatic aggregation of information by search engines. Among others, the adoption of different usernames or e-mail accounts when registering to different online platforms (boyd, 2002), or even the separation of contexts—by presenting different information or content to different people in different contexts (boyd, 2002; Childs, 2011; Coiro et al., 2008; Costa & Torres, 2011; Stankovic, 2009; Warburton et al., 2010)—are being used as strategies to avoid the collision between the individual's different online presences:

> By maintaining multiple accounts, users associate context locally. In other words, rather than adjusting one's presentation according to the current situation or population, one can maintain an account that represents a specific face and present oneself through that. (boyd, 2002, p. 42)

Building a Reputation

The separation between different contexts, however, could be a difficult solution to maintain over time. As individuals start to interact and build relationships with other users and spaces, they may feel uncomfortable or face difficulties in maintaining that separation: as they increasingly involve themselves with the online world, they may feel the desire to build a more solid and stable identity, leaving their *visitor* role—using the network as a tool, in order to solve specific tasks such as booking flights, communicating with distant relatives, and becoming *residents*—individuals whose identity extends to the online world (White, 2008).

Thus the risks and benefits of having an online identity should be considered during the process of managing the presence in digital environments:

> Hence, digital identity management is important, as it can impact on our activity both face-to-face and online. In a digitally connected world, educators have a two-fold role when it comes to address the issues cyberspace poses on their practice: on the one hand they need to mentor their students to be digitally savvy, which is far more complex a task than teaching them to create accounts in social networks or help them create a blog, for instance. On the other hand, they need to do what they preach in order to model behavior, i.e., establish a reputable digital identity which students can look up to and follow as example. (Costa & Torres, 2011, p. 927)

ONLINE IDENTITY IN AN HIGHER EDUCATION SCENARIO

Background

As the creative, participatory, and social features of the Internet changed the way individuals and institutions look at issues related with identity, education, practice, and knowledge, there is also the need to look at the individuals' and institutions' online identity as a characteristic of great importance. No longer able to ignore the changes brought by the Internet and social media to the social and educational context, institutions are now facing the challenge to recognize the digital dimension of identity construction. Educational institutions have now the chance to offer their student digital environments and communities where they can build and explore their own identity as persons and as learners.

The SAPO Campus Project

Developed at the University of Aveiro (Portugal), SAPO Campus is an integrated Web 2.0 services platform based on user-generated content production and aggregation for use in education institutions and organizations. As a social platform, SAPO Campus offers its users a technological infrastructure able to support the development of communication, sharing and collaboration competencies. Addressing online presence as a concept that includes "multiple presences and different services that may have similar goals" (Santos, 2009, p. 42), SAPO Campus includes blogs, wikis, and photo and video sharing services that allow each user (lecturers, students, staff) the creation of an individual and personal presence able to reflect his/her path as individual and learner.

Offering its users the space to enhance, in an institutional environment, their digital presence and reputation, SAPO Campus has a space where users can assemble and manage information (through a feed aggregator). All content—published under a Creative Commons license—is visible not only to the academia members, but to all the web community from outside the university, thereby allowing the expansion and visibility of the user's presence. Moreover, users can still access and work on their SAPO Campus space after leaving university, adding information, sharing content, and developing their online presence along their personal and professional lives. More about the SAPO Campus project can be found at http://campus.ua.sapo.pt.

Research Approach

Having a main purpose to analyze how a group of students build, manage, and perceive the presence built in digital environments, a case study was developed at the University of Aveiro (Portugal). Data was collected through questionnaires, observation and in-depth interviews made to students from the Multimedia Communication Master's Degree course. From the universe of 58 students, aged from 21 to 50, 38 male and 20 female, it was chosen a sample of 13 SAPO Campus' users (ages between 21 and 40, 7 male, 5 female, convenience sample). The group included both students and working-students, and students with different levels of use of the online space (occasional users, regular users, frequent users), thereby enriching and improving the depth of the analysis.

The in-depth interviews, made to the 13 students, were conducted in order to understand how participants perceived their online self (i.e., how they saw and described their online behavior), and how they managed their privacy and reputation in formal and social online environments. During the interviews, participants were also asked to think and talk about the personal, social, and professional impact of the identity they were building in online environments.

The case study also included the gathering and analysis of the content published by the participants in three different online spaces: two social networks, Facebook and Twitter; and in SAPO Campus, the institutionally supported Web 2.0 platform provided by the participants' Higher Education Institution. Observation of the participants' online presence occurred during a period of nine months (an academic year), and all collected messages were classified according to its context and format. Context categories were established based on the works of Fraser (2008) and Kurhila (2006) and were organized in: (1) personal content (reference to family or friends, emotions, or state of mind, revealing opinion regarding sensitive issues); (2) social content (related with films or music, trivial content, content that do not reveal the individual's opinions or preferences); (3) academic content (related with the academic activity of the participants); (4) professional content (content that addressed the individual's competencies and skills); and (5) organizational content (content related to the individual's organization or employer, and publishing content on behalf of the individual's organization or employer). Three thousand six hundred and ninety two messages were analyzed: 1,249 Facebook posts, 2,096 Twitter messages and 347 SAPO Campus posts.

Discussion of Results

The analysis of data collected through direct observation showed that participants approached and used the institutionally supported platform and the informal online environments in a distinctive way, building different kids of online presences.

Encouraged by their lecturers to use SAPO Campus as a space for dissemination and sharing of their master degree work (information reported by participants during interviews), students built, in the institutionally supported platform, a presence based mostly in academic content. Sixty-six percent of the content posted by participants on this platform was coded as *academic*, that is, related to the research activities and course work, mostly text messages (blog posts).

On Facebook, the participants' online presence is mainly social (82% of published content was coded as "social"), as well as on Twitter, where 81% of the content published by the participants was added to the "social" category. Nevertheless, on Twitter 10% of content was related with the academic activities of participants.

Table 7.1. Content Published by Students

Online Space	*Content*	*Format*				*Total*
		Text Message	*Link*	*Audio/Video*	*Photo*	
SAPO Campus	Personal	0	0	0	0	0
	Social	6	1	3	108	118
	Academic	105	54	21	49	229
	Professional	0	0	0	0	0
	Organizational	0	0	0	0	0
Facebook	Personal	54	5	3	31	93
	Social	74	185	674	86	1,019
	Academic	4	41	7	0	52
	Professional	4	43	7	11	65
	Organizational	0	15	3	2	20
Twitter	Personal	40	10	0	12	62
	Social	598	748	272	88	1,076
	Academic	68	120	5	9	202
	Professional	26	27	3	2	58
	Organizational	6	59	3	0	68

Source: Content published by participants in SAPO Campus, Facebook and Twitter

Identity in SAPO Campus

During the interviews, participants were asked to talk about the presence they were building in the institutionally supported platform. When addressing this issue, participants characterized their SAPO Campus' online presence as being based on academic content. As lecturers gave instructions to use the platform to share their work and concerns (stated by five participants), most of the published content was related with their master's degree thesis, namely the publication of interim reports.

On SAPO Campus all content, once published, is immediately available to everyone. Questioned about the advantages and disadvantages of this situation, participants pointed out as main advantages the possibility of having immediate feedback (from lecturers and colleges), the possibility to interact with other audiences or communities, and the wider and faster dissemination of their works and reports. Regarding disadvantages, two participants considered the risk of copying or appropriation of their work by others as the main disadvantages of using the open institutionally supported platform.

When asked if the institutional dimension of the platform had influenced the kind and structure of their publications, participants mentioned to have adopted, in SAPO Campus, a more careful and structured discourse. To the participants, the institutional and formal dimension of the platform led to the creation of a sense of responsibility regarding the published content, as what they would publish would be linked to the Institution's own online presence. As content published in SAPO Campus would be associated with the university's image, there was the need and the carefulness to publish content that would not affect the reputation and credibility of the institution. Questioned about the importance of building an online presence associated with their education institution and about the impact of that same presence in the university's image and identity, nine participants pointed out that, by using the institutionally supported platform, they were establishing a connection between their online identity and the Institution's online identity, therefore receiving some of its credibility and reputation. Regarding the disadvantages, one participant mentioned copyright and authoring issues as a possible reason for not using the platform. According to this participant, content published in the SAPO Campus platform could be considered as property of the university, a fact that could condition the platform's adoption by students.

Managing Identity in Digital Environments: The Online Identity Analysis Model

During the interviews, participants were asked to reflect and talk about the presence they were building in the online space, describing how they managed contents and connections and reflecting about the potential or real impact of their digital presence.

The treatment and analysis of the interviews' transcripts revealed the existence of three major areas around which participants described and characterized their online presence: the information and content they shared in order to represent themselves in the digital world; the mechanisms and strategies adopted in order to control and manage their digital *persona*; and the academic, professional and social impact of the presence they were building in both formal and informal online environments.

The information was then crossed with data collected through direct observation leading to the conception of the Online Identity Analysis Model (Aresta, Pedro, Santos, & Moreira, 2013b), a model that can be adopted by individuals and institutions in order to analyze the presence they are building online, presented in Table 7.2.

Table 7.2. The Online Identity Analysis Model

Thematic Category: Digital Representation [DR]		
Subcategory	*Subject of Analysis*	*Indicators*
Identification Elements [DR/IE]	Username	Choosing real name, pseudonym, nickname as digital name
	Profile picture	Selecting a self-portrait, avatar, group photo, or landscape image as a way of representation
Additional Information [DR/AI]	Biographical information	Sharing information about name, birthdate, place of birth, nationality
	Contact information	Sharing information about postal address, e-mail
	Personal information	Sharing information related to interests, preferences, personal motto
	Relation with the community	Sharing information that establishes a connection with the community
	Connection to other online spaces	Sharing information that establishes the connection with other online spaces where the individual builds his/her presence
Content [DR/C]	Topics	Selecting topics according to the characteristics of the online space (personal, social, professional)
		Selecting topics according to the user's preferences, disregarding the online space where it is published
	Structure of the discourse	Adjusting the discourse (i.e. grammatical structure, vocabulary) according to the online space where content is published
		Non-adjusting the discourse (i.e., grammatical structure, vocabulary) according to the online space where content is published

(Table continues on next page)

Table 7.4. (Continued)

Subcategory	Subject of Analysis	Indicators
Thematic Category: Digital Representation [DR]		
Content [DR/C]	Content typology	Selecting and sharing content (personal, social, professional) according or adjusted to the online space where it is published
		Sharing content (personal, social, professional) disregarding the online space where it is published
	Content format	Selecting and sharing content (text messages, videos, links, audio files) according to the online space
		Sharing content (text, messages, video, links, audio files) disregarding the online space
Thematic Category: Privacy Management [PM]		
Registration process [PM/RP]	Registration e-mail or username	Using different usernames or e-mail accounts when registering in different online spaces
		Using the same username or e-mail account when registering in different online spaces
Contacts management [PM/CM]	Contact network (friends, followers)	Adding or segregating contacts according to the online space where the individual builds his/her presence
		Creating and managing groups
		Adding contacts disregarding the online space where the individual builds his/her presence
Contexts management [PM/CtxM]	Content published between spaces	Enabling automatic synchronization of content across platforms, establishing connection between different spaces
		Republishing content on platforms different from where it was initially published (e.g. sharing a blog posts on social networks)
Thematic Category: Reputation [R]		
Demonstration of skills, competences or abilities [R/DSC]	Published content	Sharing content with the intention of showing or demonstrating the existence of general or specific skills (e.g., sharing videos, posts, artworks, reports produced in formal or informal contexts)

(Table continues on next page)

Table 7.4. (Continued)

Thematic Category: Reputation [R]		
Subcategory	*Subject of Analysis*	*Indicators*
Visibility and exposure [R/VE]	Reproduced content (between platforms or online spaces)	Sharing content in platforms others than the ones where it was initially produced, therefore increase visibility and exposure of produced content
	Interaction with peers or experts	Addressing and interacting with peers and/or experts, showing interest, sharing opinions and revealing interests in specifics fields of knowledge
Reputation Scaffolding [R/RS]	Reference/mention/connection to the institutional online identity	Reproducing content published by the institution
		Sharing information that evidences the connection between the person's online identity and the institution online identity (e.g., sharing information about roles or job positions)

Source: Arest et al. (2013b).

Digital Representation [DR]

Online, individuals represent themselves through data and information. Name, date of birth, photo, e-mail, interests, and preferences are shared in order to create a representation of the self, either real (that is, reflecting the true characteristics of the individual) or fictional (by the creation of personas, several identities or recurring to anonymity). In order to reveal to others the role they play in society, individuals may also add information regarding their job, groups or associations they belong to, family connections. They can also add information regarding their presence in other online spaces, therefore revealing a more detailed profile.

In the online identity analysis model, *digital representation*—that is, the sum of the information and content shared by the individual in order to create its online identity—is organized into three subcategories: identification elements, additional information, and content.

Identification elements include the name and photo chosen by individuals as a way to represent themselves: real name or nickname, a portrait picture, a landscape picture, an avatar, a photo with family or friends.

Additional information is a sub-category related with the information individuals chooses to share in order to contextualize their presence in the online spaces where they build their identity. Usually in the "about me" or "profile" sections, they can include *biographical information* (full name, date of birth, place of birth); *contact information* (postal or e-mail, telephone number); *personal information* (information related with the individuals interests, such as favorite music, favorite TV shows); *relation with the community* (school attended by individuals or the sports club to which they belong); and *connection to other online spaces* (sharing a personal page web address on Facebook profile section, sharing a personal or professional blog address on Twitter profile.

During the interviews, participants mentioned to adopt different behaviors when publishing content on institutionally supported platforms and on informal online environments. Taking this into account, in the online identity analysis model, *content* encompasses all the publications posted by individuals in their online spaces, and that can vary according to the formal or informal characteristics of the online space, or be published independently of those same characteristics. Content can be analyzed according to the *topics*/themes addressed, the *structure of the discourse*, *content typology* and *content format*. According to the individuals' approach to online presence issues, they can select and publish content according to the formal or informal characteristics of the platform (as it has happened with some of the study's participants in the SAPO Campus platform) or publish content disregarding the social constraints of the online space. They may also choose to adopt different kind of discourses in formal and informal environments, adopting a more structured and grammatically accurate speech in formal online spaces and more colloquial speech in informal spaces. Finally, individuals may choose to publish different kind of content in formal and informal online spaces, sharing content according or disregarding the online space where it is published (*content typology* and *content format*).

Privacy Management [PM]

When publishing content online, individuals are at the same time producing a vast amount of information able to reveal certain aspects of their identity. By building a presence in online environments, they trust their data and information to systems that they do not control. Online, published data lingers. Between the persistence of data, decontextualization, the perpetual beta stage of programs and applications, individuals cannot control who sees their data and how it is interpreted. Once published online, information is stored and accessible, and can be used to trace and construct an individual's profile.

In order to surround the permeability of online environments and to gain a certain control of the kind of information that is associated with their identity, individuals may recur to anonymity or, instead, create and manage different e-mail accounts to be used in different platforms and online systems and therefore avoid the automatic aggregation of information (boyd, 2002). They may also decide to present, in digital environments, a *faceted identity* (boyd, 2002), revealing to different publics different parts of their identity.

In the online identity analysis model, *privacy management*—that is, the mechanisms and strategies adopted by individuals in order to control and manage their digital presence—is organized into three subcategories: registration process, contacts management, and contexts management.

Registration process focuses on the possibility that individuals have to use different e-mail accounts or usernames when registering in different online spaces, thus bypassing the automatic aggregation of their information. They may, instead, choose to build a unique or more representative online identity and adopt the same username and/or e-mail account in most of or in all their online spaces.

As the identity of individuals is built not only from the information they publish on the internet but is also composed by links and connections established with other users or communities, *contacts management* addresses the way contacts are associated by users to their online spaces. As mentioned before, this process may include the segregation or aggregation of contacts according to the online space or the association of contacts disregarding the formal or informal characteristics of the platform. It may also include the creation and management of groups (possible on Facebook and Google+).

When building their online presence, individuals may choose to build a presence that reveals the different dimensions of their identity or, instead, to maintain a certain degree of separation between their online environments. *Contexts management,* therefore, is related with the information that individuals provide in their online spaces and that may or may not establish a connection between the different spaces or platforms where they build their identity. Either by enabling the automatic synchronization between platforms (thus allowing the publication of content between different online spaces) or by republishing content on platforms different from those where it was initially produced, individuals may opt to work on an identity that encompasses different dimensions of their lives. Or they may, instead, choose to keep those dimensions apart.

Reputation [R]

By interacting with online communities, establishing new connections, and sharing content across multiple platforms, individuals are also expanding their area of influence and possibly setting the foundations for building a strong and credible online identity. Through the identity they are building online, individuals may reveal to a wider audience the existence of competencies and skills (either personal, social, or professional) able to show what they are capable of, what defines them as a member of a group or organization. During the interviews, five participants mentioned to use their online presence as a way to reveal their expertise and knowledge. In order to achieve it, they shared in both formal and informal online environments information about their academic work and professional interests, often sharing on informal online networks links to the work published in the institutional platform.

In the online identity analysis model, *reputation*—the actual or potential impact of the online identity built by the individual—is approached from the individuals' point of view, that is, from the intentions behind the construction of an online presence, and it is articulated between the *demonstration of skills, competencies or abilities*, the *visibility and exposure* of the online presence and the *reputation scaffolding* of the individuals' online identity.

The *demonstration of skills, competencies or abilities* focuses on how individuals use their online identity as a way to reveal to their contacts and to a wider audience abilities or skills acquired or developed in formal, informal or non-formal contexts. In this scenario, individuals may share works or essays they have produced online, they can build portfolios, reveal creative or scientific writing skills, revealing what they are able to do and achieve.

In order to increase the *visibility and exposure* of their online identity, individuals may opt to *reproduce content* across platforms, replicating content originally published in other spaces, namely between formal and informal environments. By doing so, they are disseminating content they have produced or accessed, increasing the chances of it being seen by colleagues, friends or even experts in their fields of interests. In order to build a reputation, individuals may also opt to share content and *interact with peers or experts*, revealing their own interests, knowledge or expertise in general or specific areas.

When working to or being a member of an organization or institution, individuals may choose to connect their online identity with the one of the institution or organization. Either by mentioning the institution they are attending (e.g., in the profile page), by sharing content on behalf of the institution or even by sharing information about roles or job positions, individuals engage in a process of *reputation scaffolding*, a scenario where their online presence is connected with the presence of the institution, in order to benefit from its reputation and credibility.

Graphical Representation of the Online Identity Analysis Model

The preceding section presented the online identity analysis model, describing each one of its three dimensions: digital representation, privacy management, and reputation. Although each dimension has an importance of its own, that does not mean that they should be considered as separate entities or elements when analyzing the identity built in online environments. As it is possible to see in Figure 7.1, each one of the three dimensions is connected with the others. The way individuals choose to represent themselves (digital representation) can be influenced by adopted privacy settings: an individual who wishes to keep a separation between professional and personal context probably would not reveal his or her professional e-mail account or mention a professional blog or website in the profile section of a social network space. As another example of permeability of these dimensions, privacy management strategies can be changed in order to increase the visibility of the individuals' identity and, therefore, make his/her identity more visible to experts and/or the community.

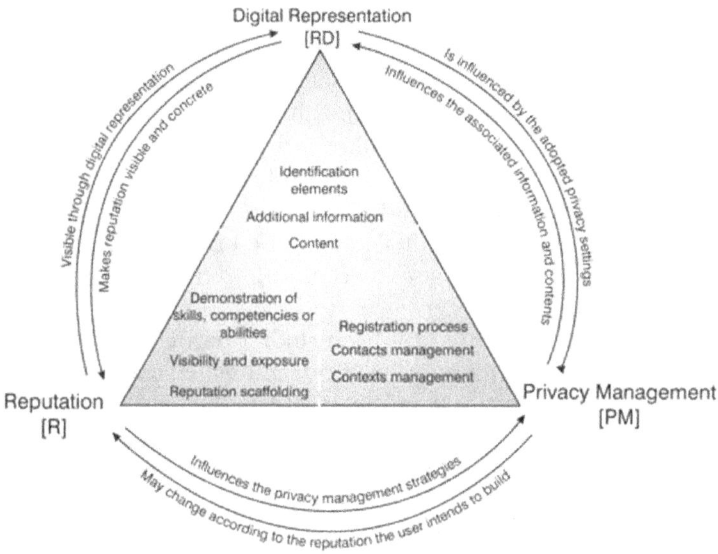

Figure 7.1. Dimensions of the Online Identity Analysis Model.

CONCLUSIONS

The work and reflections presented in this chapter are the result of a research project developed in order to understand, analyze, and characterize the processes behind the construction of an online identity. Moreover, the study aimed to understand the importance of building an identity in online environments as a way to manifest competencies and skills.

This final section will present two online identity profiles that have emerged from the application of the online identity analysis model. It will also present some thoughts and concerns regarding the importance of having an online presence, either by individuals or by institutions.

The Context-Driven and User-Driven Online Identity Profiles

In a scenario where the contextualization of data and information is becoming increasingly important, the study presented in this chapter may contribute to understanding why and how students build their presence in both formal and informal online environments. Through the application of the online identity analysis model to the information provided by the 13 participants and collected through direct observation and the interviews, we were able to identify two kinds of profiles: context-driven and user-driven online identity profiles.

Context-driven online identity profiles included participants who managed and distributed information according to the digital environment they were working in, revealing to have special attentiveness when choosing content to be added to their online presence. Either choosing not to reveal too much about themselves online and therefore not using the network as a way to reveal their skills and abilities (five participants) or by sharing information about their academic and professional interests and using the online space as a way to build a professional profile and reputation (five participants), these individuals mentioned to have special attention to context, distributing information according to the digital environment they were working in.

User-drive online identity profiles included participants who claimed to be building an online identity free from contextual constraints, publish content disregarding the audience or the formality or informality of the online environment.

Throughout the study, it was also possible to see that the institutional character of the formal platform may influence the type of publications: as an example, in the study described in this chapter the association between the participants and the institution's online identity led to a sense of responsibility regarding published content. Participants in the study were also revealed to appreciate the sense of security provided by institutional technologies, as well as the possibility of constructing an identity associated with their education institution. It is also possible to assume that students are aware that, by publishing content on the network, they are also building an identity available to almost everyone. They are also aware of the relevance and importance of building a solid and authentic identity and reputation.

Online Identity: Why Is It That Important?

Nowadays, skills such as innovation and creativity, multidisciplinary collaboration and cooperation, digital literacies, communication skills, the ability to build and manage identity in online environments, and even proactivity are considered as core competencies for new working realities contexts (Fernandez-Sanz et al., 2010). Hence, when offering the conditions to build not only their academic curriculum, but also their personal identity and profile, educational institutions should consider their students as promoters of their own quality, presenting students not as standard products but as singular entities, with the competencies adjusted to the market needs (Aresta et al., 2013a).

The Internet is now seen as an alternative space for the construction of identity, and the web emerges as a space where the *self* can be built, edited, deleted, and transformed according to the individual's intentions (Turkle, 2011). Therefore, the conscience and perception about the positive and negative implications of having an online identity should not be devalued either by individuals or by institutions. It is important that both students and institutions become aware of the relevance of building a digital identity, and the role digital identity plays in a global society that expects learners to be able to share and transmit, in a creative a distinctive way, their skills and competencies.

The study presented in this chapter pretends to contribute to a more clear understanding of the processes of building an identity in online environments, as well as to understand the importance—for individuals and institutions—of having an online presence.

ACKNOWLEDGMENTS

The authors would like to thank Labs.sapo/ua and the SAPO Campus team for all the support to this investigation. This work was supported by the Foundation for Science and Technology (Fundação para a Ciência e Tecnologia—FCT, Portugal, ref. SFRH/BD/70474/2010).

REFERENCES

Aresta, M., Santos, C. Pedro, L., & Moreira, A. (2013a). Building up digital identity in higher education. In S. Warburton, & S. Hatzipanagos (Eds.), Digital *Identity and social media* (pp. 176–191). London, UK: IG GLobal. doi: 10.4018/978-1-4666-1915-9.ch013

Aresta, M., Pedro, L., Santos, C., & Moreira, A. (2013b). Online identity analysis model: Analysing the construction of the self in digital environments. *International Journal of Knowledge Society Research, 4*(3), 89–102. doi:10.4018/ijksr.2013070108

Bawden, D. (2008). Origins and concepts of digital literacy. In C. Lankshear & M. Knobel (Ed.), *Digital literacies, concepts, policies and practices* (pp. 17–32). New York, NY: Peter Lang.

boyd, d. (2002). *Faceted id/entity: Managing representation in a digital world* (Unpublished master's thesis). Massachusetts Institute of Technology, Massachusetts.

boyd, d. (2008). Why youth ♥ social network sites: The role of networked publics in teenage social life. In D. Buckingham (Ed.), *Youth, identity, and digital media* (pp. 119–142). Cambridge, MA: MIT Press.

Buckingham, D. (2008a). Defining digital literacy- What do young people need to know about digital media? In C. Lankshear, & M. Knobel (Eds.), *Digital literacies: Concepts, policies and practices* (pp. 73–91). New York, NY: Peter Lang.

Buckingham, D. (2008b). Introducing identity. In D. Buckingham (Ed.), *Youth, identity, and digital media* (pp. 1–24). Cambridge, MA: MIT Press.

Childs, M. (2011). Identity: A primer. In A. Peachey, & M. Childs (Eds.), *Reinventing ourselves: Contemporary concepts on identity in virtual worlds* (pp. 13–32). New York, NY: Springer.

Clark, W., Logan, K., Luckin, R., Mee, A., & Oliver, M. (2009). Beyond web 2.0: Mapping the technology landscapes of young learners. *Journal of Computer Assisted Learning, 25*(1), 56–69. doi:10.1111/j.1365-2729.2008.00305.x

Coiro, J., Knobel, M., Lankshear C., & Leu, D. (2008). Central issues in new literacies and new literacies research. In J. Coiro, M. Knobel, C. Lankshear, & D. Leu (Eds.), *Handbook of research on new literacies* (pp. 1–21). New York, NY: Lawrence Erlbaum.

Collis, B., & Moonen, J. (2011). Flexibility in higher education: Revisiting expectations. *Scientific Journal of Media Literacy, 37*(9), 15–24.

Costa, C., & Torres, R. (2011). To be or not to be, the importance of digital identity in the networked society. *Educação, Formação e Tecnologia* (extra number), 47–53.

Downes, S. (2005, October). E-Learning 2.0. *eLearn Magazine.* Retrieved from http://elearnmag.acm.org/featured.cfm?aid=1104968

Fernandez-Sanz, L., Gutierrez de Mesa, J. A., Hilera, J. R., LaCuesta, R., Palacios, G., & Cuadrado, J. J. (2010). New challenge for teachers: dealing with soft skills in multinational environments. In *Proceedings of World Conference on Educational Multimedia, Hypermedia and Telecommunications 2010* (pp. 2680–2684). Chesapeake, VA.

Franklin, T., & Harmelen, M. (2007). Web 2.0 for content learning and teaching in higher education. Retrieved from http://www.jisc.ac.uk/media/documents/programmes/digitalrepositories/web2-content-learning-and-teaching.pdf

Fraser, J. (2009, June). Personal – professional – organisational: Three basic online identities [Web log post]. Retrieved from http://fraser.typepad.com/socialtech/2009/07/personal-professional-organisational-three-basic-online-identities.html

Giger, P. (2006). Participation literacy (Licenciate thesis, Blekinge Institute of Technology), Karlskrona, Sweden. Academic thesis published in Web 2-0 format. Retrieved December 26, 2010, from http://www.participationliteracy.com

Gilster, P. (1997). *Digital literacy.* New York, NY: John Wiley & Sons.

Goodfellow, R. (2011). Literacy, literacies, and the digital in higher education. *Teaching in Higher Education, 16*(1), 131–144.

Goffman, E. (1959). *The presentation of self in everyday life.* London, UK: Allen Lane, The Penguin Press.

Greenhow, C., & Robelia, B. (2009). Informal learning and identity formation in online social networks. *Learning, Media and Technology, 34*(2), 119–140.

Greenhow, C., Robelia, B., & Hughes, J. (2009). Learning, teaching, and scholarship in a digital age. *Educational Researcher, 38*(4), 246–259.

Guth, S., & Helm, F. (Eds.). (2010). *Tellecolaboration 2.0—Language, literacies and intercultural learning in the 21st century.* Bern, Switzerland: Peter Lang AG, International Academic Publishers.

Hobbs, R. (2010). *Digital and media literacy: A plan of action* (White Paper). Washington, DC: The Aspen Institution.

ISTE–International Society for Technology in Education. (2007). NETS for students 2007. Retrieved from http://www.iste.org/standards/nets-for-students/nets-for-students-standards-2007

Kurhila, J. (2006). "Unauthorized" Use of social software to support formal higher education. In T. Reeves & S. Yamashita (Eds.), *Proceedings of the World Conference on E-Learning in Corporate, Government, Healthcare, and Higher Education 2006* (pp. 2602–2607). Chesapeake, VA.

Manca, S., & Ranieri, M. (2013a). *Identity, credibility, and trust in social networking sites: Old issues, new mechanisms, and current challenges for privacy and security.* In L. Caviglione, M. Coccoli, & A. Merlo. (Eds.), Social network engineering for secure web data and services (pp. 5–31). Hershey, PA: IGI Global.

Manca S., & Ranieri M. (2013b). Is it a tool suitable for learning? A critical review of the literature on Facebook as a technology enhanced learning environment. *Journal of Computer Assisted Learning,* 1–18.

Martin, A. (2008) Digital literacy and the digital society. In C. Lankshear & M. Knobel (Eds.), Digital literacies: Concepts, policies and practices (pp. 151–176). Oxford, UK: Peter Lang.

McCarthy, J. (2010). Blended learning environments: Using social networking sites to enhance the first year experience. *Australasian Journal of Educational Technology, 26,* 729–740.

McLoughlin, C. (2011). What ICT-related skills and capabilities should be considered central to the definition of digital literacy?. In T. Bastiaens & M. Ebner (Eds.), *Proceedings of World Conference on Educational Multimedia, Hypermedia and Telecommunications 2011* (pp. 471–475). Chesapeake, VA.

Mislove, A., Viswanath, B., Gummadi, K., & Druschel, P. (2010). *You are who you know: Inferring user profiles in online social networks.* Proceedings of the third ACM international conference on Web search and data mining (pp. 251–260). San Diego, California, USA.

O'Brien, D., & Schaber, C. (2008). Digital literacies go to school: Potholes and possibilities. *Journal of Adolescent & Adult Literacy, 52*(1), 66–68.

Peachey, A., & Childs, M. (2011). Virtual worlds and identity. In A. Peachey & M. Childs (Ed.), *Reinventing ourselves: Contemporary concepts on identity in virtual worlds* (pp. 1–12). London, UK: Springer.

Santos, C. (2009). *SAPO Campus—Plataforma Integrada de Serviços Web 2.0 para Educação.* Proceedings da VI Conferência Internacional de TIC na Educação: Challenges 2009 (pp. 34–48). Universidade do Minho, Braga.

Shapiro, J. & Hughes, S. K. (1999). Information technology as a liberal art. *Educause Review, 31*(2).

Stankovic, M. (2009). *Faceted online presence—A semantic web approach* (Unpublished master's degree thesis), Université Paris-Sud XI, Orsay, France.

Trinder, K., Guiller, J., Margaryan, A., Littlejohn, A., & Nicol, D. (2008). Learning from digital natives: Bridging formal and informal learning. *The Higher Education Academy. Research Project Report, Final Report.*

Turkle, S. (2011). *Alone together—Why we expect more from technology and less from each other.* New York, NY: Basic Books

Warburton, S. (2009, April). Out of control? Managing our digital reputations. Retrieved from http://www.slideshare.net/stevenw/out-of-control-managing-our-digital-reputations?from=share_email_logout2

Warburton, S., García, M., Attwell, G., & University King's College. (2010). Digital identity matters. In *Rhizome Project.* Retrieved from http://digitaldisruptions.org/rhizome/wp-content/uploads/2010/06/rhiz08_DigitalIdentityMatters.pdf

White, D. (2008, July 23). Not "natives" & "immigrants" but "visitors" & "residents" [Web log post]. Retrieved from http://tallblog.conted.ox.ac.uk/index.php/2008/07/23/not-natives-immigrants-but-visitors-residents/

Zhao, S. Grasmuck, S., & Martin, J. (2008). Identity construction on Facebook: Digital empowerment in anchored relationships. *Computers in Human Behavior, 24*(5), 1816–1836.

CHAPTER 8

INFORMATION LITERACY AND WEB 2.0 TECHNOLOGIES TO SUPPORT LEARNERS IN DEVELOPMENTAL COURSES

Katura M. Lesane and Kennesha Bracely

ABSTRACT

Current research indicates that many students who enroll in developmental courses never complete their requirements or experience college-level coursework (Bailey, Jeong, & Cho, 2008; Hodara, Jaggars, & Karp, 2012; Roska, Jenkins, Jaggers, Zeidenberg, & Cho, 2009). There is a need for instructional practices that prepare these students for a global workforce that demands independent critical thinkers. Instruction is needed that develops sound educational practices that improves the academic achievement of these learners while encouraging their independence and self-efficacy. One of the most profound and current ways to prepare learners is through the use of technology. The marriage of information literacy, Web 2.0 technologies, and developmental courses supports the education, evolution, and empowerment of learners. A course redesign of developmental courses, to include student learning outcomes (SLOs) and instructional practices that use information

E-Learning and Social Media:
Education and Citizenship for the Digital 21st Century, pp. 167–182

literacy and Web 2.0 technologies, will change the way students create, think, communicate, collaborate, and achieve while aiding them in attaining 21st century skills and being prepared for credit-bearing courses.

The goal of any education program should be to educate, to evolve, and to empower its learners. To educate and to evolve learners is to provide them with relevant knowledge to compete in a global society that is forever changing. These learners must have their finger on the pulse of their field and be able to do more than duplicate, but create and transform their field of study. Additionally, a sound program empowers learners, making them feel capable of competing in a global society where critical thinking, problem solving, and technology are ever-present requirements. The education, evolution, and empowerment of learners in not limited to the advantaged, but should be available to learners of all socio-economic and academic backgrounds. Information literacy and Web 2.0 technologies are two viable instructional options for instructors to educate, evolve, and empower learners, particularly those in development courses who need additional support during the learning process.

A NEED FOR ALTERNATIVE TEACHING AND LEARNING PRACTICES

In 1995, all public two-year institutions and 81% of public four-year institutions offered remedial reading, writing, or mathematics courses (National Center for Educational Statistics, 1995). A 2002 study conducted by the Academic Senate for California Community Colleges notes that American faculty believes that freshman students are ill-prepared for college level learning. The concern includes basic skills in mathematics, writing, text comprehension, critical thinking, and analysis. The Stanford University (2006) Bridge Project notes that many students entering college are ill-prepared for the rigors of their college courses. Kutner, Greenberg, and Baer (2005) provide research that shows declining skills in college students' ability to problem solve, to write, and to think critically. This becomes even more challenging for under-represented and economically disadvantaged students, many of whom are placed in developmental programs or who never matriculate.

This body of research speaks to a need for a change in the way teaching and learning is conducted in the college classroom. There is a need for instructional practices that prepare this group of learners for college success and for a global workforce; adjustments in instruction are needed that improve academic achievement. There is a need for education programs to recognize these challenges, to set a course of action to address the challenges, to implement the plan, and to assess the plan for effectiveness. Faculties must be cognizant of the fact that their classes contain students who have deficiencies. Their classrooms contain students for whom lecture is an outdated and ineffective mode of instructional delivery when used in isolation. Their classrooms contain students who need scaffolding and support to garner understanding and to build deeper understanding of content and skills. Their classrooms contain students who need visual and auditory cues to aid in making meaning of content. Their classrooms contain students who need to relate content to their experiences and to the real world. A commitment is needed from college administrators to ensure that their faculty is not only knowledgeable about the most effective, research-based ways to address these learners, but that there is also ongoing assessment of instructional practices occurring in the college classroom.

In addition to having a clear understanding of the type of students inhabiting the college classroom, college administrators and instructors must also understand the type of skills necessary for students' success in today's workforce. Wagner (2008) notes that 21st century skills are those learners will need to be successful in today's workforce. They include but are not limited to collaboration, critical thinking, problem solving, effective communication skills, and the ability to access and to analyze information. Access to 21st century skills can be attained with a focus on information literacy instruction for developmental learners. "Information literacy forms the basis for lifelong learning. It is common to all disciplines, to all learning environments, and to all levels of education. It enables learners to master content and extend their investigations, become more self-directed, and assume greater control over their own learning" (Association of College and Research Libraries, 2000, p. 2). In addition, the use of Web 2.0 technologies is an effective means to address the deficiencies of students in developmental courses while providing them with instruction that supports acquisition of 21st century skills. "Web 2.0 technologies share characteristics that accommodate support for autonomy, competence, and relatedness, which promotes student engagement" (Park, 2013, p. 50). The connection between information literacy and Web 2.0 technologies helps to prepare learners to think critically and to gain the level of autonomy necessary to effectively operate in their courses and in today's workforce.

Wagner's (2008) research on 21st century skills provides a direct link to the benefits of information literacy and Web 2.0 technologies by aiding learners as they access, process, and use information. It is proposed that information literacy and Web 2.0 technologies strengthen collaboration, critical thinking, problem solving, and effective communication skills for learners in college developmental courses. These tools also aid in learners' ability to access and to analyze information—necessary 21st century skills in a technology-driven world where information is forever changing and new information created. Using these tools provide instructors with viable instructional options for effectively educating and preparing learners in developmental courses.

THE 21ST CENTURY DEVELOPMENTAL LEARNER IN HIGHER EDUCATION

Developmental education (DE) and remedial instruction are terms that are often used interchangeably for students who enter postsecondary education underprepared for college-level instruction. Developmental education is defined by the National Association of Developmental Education as

> a comprehensive process which focuses on the intellectual, social and emotional growth and development of all learners. Developmental education includes, but is not limited to tutoring, personal and career counseling, academic advisement and coursework. Developmental education is a field of practice and research with a theoretical foundation in developmental psychology and learning theory. It promotes the cognitive and affective growth of all learners, at all levels of the learning continuum. It is sensitive and responsive to the individual differences and special needs among learners (Casazza, 1999, p. 3)

Remedial instruction is defined in a joint statement by the Charles A. Dana Center, Complete College America, Education Commission the States, and Jobs for the Future as

> required instruction and support for students who are assessed by their institution of choice as being academically underprepared for postsecondary education. The intent of remedial education is to educate students in the skills that are required to successfully complete gateway courses and enter and complete a program of study. (Glossary of Terms, 2012)

The demographics of students having to take at least one or more remedial courses has evolved into a more diverse picture over time. This diverse picture includes: 28 to 40% of all first-time undergraduates, high school students who were functioning below other students in their age or grade level, those who may have earned a GED, students who deliberately chose easier senior year courses which caused them to miss opportunities for more rigorous college preparatory coursework, nontraditional adults who have been out of high school for some time and are returning to college, returning veterans, and new immigrants needing basic skills before attempting college-level work (Bautsch, 2013; Osterholt & Barratt, 2012). This picture not only shows the range of students who enter college with academic inadequacies, but there continues to be an academic achievement gap that exists among low-income minority students entering college. According to research, low income Hispanic and African-American students are more likely to need remediation than their wealthier, white peers. Forty-one percent of Hispanic students and 42% of African American students require remediation, compared to 31% of Caucasian students (Bautsch, 2013, p. 2). This diverse picture of students needing remediation calls for pedagogical, paradigmatic shifts that mirror 21st century skills.

The Digital Natives

Twenty-first century educators must be prepared to address the needs of the diverse learners as described in the work of Bautsch (2013), Osterholt and Barratt (2012), and other researchers. Prensky (2001) notes that today's students have changed, and are no longer the people our education system was originally designed to teach. "Our students have changed radically. Today's students are no longer the people our educational system was originally designed to teach" (Prensky, 2001, p. 1). In an attempt to provide the rich and engaging learning experiences, we will have to consider how to address academic deficits from an angle that speaks directly to the 21st century DE student In an attempt to provide rich and engaging learning experiences, we will have to consider how to address academic deficits from an angle that speaks directly to the 21st century student enrolled in developmental education courses. For the purposes of this research, the focus is on the most continuous generational uprising of digital natives, a term coined by Marc Prensky. According to research, digital natives are those born after 1990 who have "spent their entire lives surrounded by and using computers, videogames, digital music players, video cams, cell phones, and all the other toys and tools of the digital age" (Prensky, 2001, p. 1). Prensky (2001) paints a descriptive picture of the communication disconnects that often occur due to generational gaps that can potentially hinder the student learning environment. He writes,

> Digital Natives are used to receiving information really fast. They like to parallel, process, and multitask. They prefer their graphics before their text rather than the opposite. They prefer random access (life hypertext). They function best when networked. They thrive on instant gratification and frequent rewards. They prefer games to "serious" work. Digital Immigrant accents can be seen in such things as turning to the Internet for information second rather than first, or in reading a manual for a program rather than assuming that the program itself will teach us to use it. Digital Immigrants typically have very little appreciation for these new skills that the Natives have acquired and perfected through years of interaction and practice.

> These skills are almost totally foreign to the immigrants who themselves learned—and so choose to teach—slowly, step-by-step, one thing at a time, individually, and above all, seriously. (Prensky, 2001, p. 2)

The native/immigrant comparison provided by Prensky (2001) helps us to understand the impact that this cultural and linguistic divide can have on student learning when the student (digital native) and the educator (digital immigrant) do not speak the same language. Technology greatly enhances instructional environments, and there should be a balance in the approach to redesigning developmental education course curricula to include both traditional methods of teaching and technology.

It appears that there has been no empirical data to support the claims of Prensky (2001). The native/immigrant analogy provided by Prensky does gives us an understanding, although limited, of the impact that this cultural and linguistic divide can have on student learning when the student and the educator do not speak the same language. Although it is agreed that the use of technology greatly enhances instructional environment, it should not be assumed that students' use of technology in their everyday lives equates to them having high level skills in the use of technology as it relates to studying, or use of sophisticated technology software. There should be a balance in the approach to redesigning DE course curricula to include both traditional methods of teaching and technology.

Culture, age, gender, and socioeconomic status all play a role in the accessibility and skill levels that students have as it relates to the use of technology. Therefore, one has to be careful to not assume that the digital native theory is universal, and that all students fit the mold of what is has been considered "digital natives," "net generation," or "millenials." Although a high percentage of students own technology "a significant portion of students have lower skills than might be expected of digital natives" (Bennett, Maton, & Kervin, 2008, p. 778). Also, students are more accustomed to "living" technology as opposed to "learning" technology. The knowledge and skills that are obtained through the use of technology for daily communication and social purposes (living technology) do not necessarily transfer to the technological knowledge and skills needed for intellectual and studying purposes (learning technology) (Kennedy, Judd, Churchward, Gray, & Krause, 2008). Several studies have suggested that "students may come to universities with some digital skills, but the use of digital media for studying might be quite different and the transfer of these skills is not automatic" (as citied in Gros, Garica, & Escofet, 2012, p. 192).

The goal here is not to sensationalize the need for a radical change for the use of technology, as the use and skills of students are much more complex than what has been introduced in the digital native theory. "Young people have extensive access to technology, but the use of technology to support learning is very heterogeneous. There are some who engage in a wide range of technology-based activities, including content creation and self-publishing, while others never participate in those activities" (Gros, Garicia, & Escofet, 2012, p. 193).

It is being proposed that by providing technology-enriched learning environment, students' digital and academic competencies will be enhanced. As previously mentioned, Perensky (2001) states, "Our students have changed radically. Today's students are no longer the people our educational system was designed to teach" (p. 1). This is true, but not in the simplistic form that has been presented through the digital native theory. There is a need for fresh perspectives on how technology can be utilized to enhance learning environments.

DEVELOPMENTAL COURSE REDESIGN

Redesigning the curricula of developmental education courses should utilize an approach that reduces the stigma associated with taking developmental courses. Research suggests that "students coming to college need to believe they are taking college-level courses consistent with their goals. If they do not, they are likely to become discouraged and drop out" (Brothen & Wambach, 2012, p. 37). Therefore, the redesign of developmental education courses should include the rigor expected in college level coursework, precise identification of student academic deficits, student engagement and relativity within coursework instruction, and the supportive instruction necessary for DE students to meet the challenges of the coursework. This redesign will also require instructional practices that go beyond the didactic lecture seen in most college level courses. There is a significant body of research that states that lecturing alone is not an effective instructional method for student learning. According to research conducted by the National Center for Academic Transformation (NCAT),

> The lecture method treats all students as if they were the same, as if they bring to the course the same academic preparation, the same learning style, the same motivation to learn, the same interest in the subject, and the same ability to learn. The lecture format simply cannot accommodate the broad range of differences among students. Lecture-based courses are notoriously ineffective in engaging students: they neither encourage active participation, nor offer students an opportunity to learn collaboratively from one another, nor provide adequate tutoring assistance. (Twigg, 2005, p. 21)

Twigg's (2005) focus on active participation and engagement are direct connections to research on information and Web 2.0 technology's ability to reach learners taking developmental courses by promoting active learning and promoting student engagement and self-directed learning. It is being proposed that there be a pedagogical, paradigmatic shift toward an innovative redesign of DE curricula by incorporating the use of information literacy and Web 2.0 applications for 21st century DE students. This shift includes establishing student learning outcomes (SLOs) that promote engagement and critical thinking in DE course curricula and establishing lessons that are engaging and relative in a digital age, to digital natives.

INFORMATION LITERACY AND THE DEVELOPMENTAL LEARNER

Higher education prepares students to be life-long learners. The knowledge, skills, and application of knowledge and skills to the real world (Constructivism) is a primary goal of post-secondary education. There is a move from simply knowing and remembering to applying and to transforming. These goals do not change because of students' presence in developmental courses. Students who enter college with deficiencies in reading, math, or critical thinking will also face a workforce that has high expectations for its employees. The focus should be placed on developing instructional practices that provide learners with the tools necessary to be successful, to enter college-level, credit-bearing courses, and to matriculate.

In their study, Arum and Roska (2011) point out that in students' first two years of college, their critical thinking, reasoning, and writing skills show marginal gains. This is even more challenging for students who enter college with academic weaknesses. One of the primary concerns for students taking remedial courses is their ability to think critically and to process information beyond basic levels of Bloom's Taxonomy (knowledge and understanding). Information literary is a vehicle for expanding students' ability to think critically while using higher levels of Bloom's Taxonomy (application, analysis, synthesis, and evaluation). According to Mackey and Jacobson (2004), "Information literacy (IL) is an essential skills set that prepares students for critical thinking in college, the workplace, and everyday life" (p. 201). With critical thinking being a primary concern for students in developmental courses, information literacy is a viable tool for leading these learners to success and to being competitive in college and beyond.

In defining information literacy, the American Library Association (1989) states that it is "a set of abilities requiring individuals to recognize when information is needed and have the ability to locate, evaluate, and use effectively the needed information" (p. 1). These students access knowledge and understand through research, writing, and communication while advancing these activities through ongoing practice" (Mackey & Jacobson,

2004, p. 202). Both the American Library Association's (1989) definition and the definition offered by Mackey and Jacobson (2004) takes learners from basic levels of recognizing and locating to evaluating and using (application) information. These are also the skills noted by Wagner (2008) when discussing 21st century skills and Twigg (2005) when discussing the need for active participation and engagement for learners' success.

With an understanding of the benefits of information literacy to learners in developmental courses, the question for school leaders and educators becomes how to introduce and effectively use information literacy in the classroom. The Society of College, National University Library's (SCONUL, 2011) Seven Pillars model provides a prescription for information literacy use to include:

- Recognizing when one needs information
- Accessing and distinguishing between sources that help meet the need for information
- Developing search strategies to accesses needed information
- Locating needed information
- Analyzing, comparing, and evaluating the information found
- Organizing the information found to effectively apply it to a given setting
- Synthesizing the knowledge found, transforming it by applying new knowledge

These pillars can easily be written as student learning outcomes (SLOs) for skills to attain in developmental courses. An analysis of the pillars demonstrates a move from basic levels of Bloom's Taxonomy to higher levels where learners must apply, analyze, synthesize, and evaluate. Not only do these pillars provide students in development courses with acquisition to 21st century skills, but they encourage these learners' to move from basic thinking to critical thinking skills.

WEB 2.0 TECHNOLOGIES AND THE DEVELOPMENTAL LEARNER

Like information literacy, use of Web 2.0 technologies benefits developmental learner's acquisition of knowledge and skills to be successful in college and beyond. Technology is everywhere, and if educators are going to be prepared to address digital natives or the web generation, technology must be present in the classroom. "Web 2.0 is a collection of technologies that create a participatory, common space where multimedia can be shared, discussed, and manipulated with little or no digital programming sophistication" (Caverly, Nicholson, Battle, & Atkins, 2008, p. 34). Web 2.0 technologies take learning from passive to active. There is not so much of a focus on what is found but how that knowledge is applied—what new information is created. According to Hicks and Graber (2009), there are five characteristics of Web 2.0 technologies. In their 2009 work, the authors explain these five components.

> The participatory and open nature of Web 2.0 gives us the capability to collaborate with new knowledge and to create empowering connections and community between people. It allows us to creatively use and reuse material in novel ways because there is not one centralized power controlling the web. Finally, and most importantly, Web 2.0 changes us from passive to active information consumers, allowing our online voice to be part of the conversation. (p. 623)

Web 2.0 technologies allow educators to gain improved knowledge of what the technology has to offer, enhance skills and use of the technology, and foster new ways of working with the technology (Godwin, 2007). Benefits to using Web 2.0 technologies with developmental learners are many. Students in developmental courses, as noted in research, need support in the learning process. Web 2.0 technologies support active learning (Godwin, 2009). According to research, when students are actively involved, they use higher order thinking including analysis, synthesis, and evaluation (Chernay, 2008). Active learning is important as a means of support for learners with deficiencies; thus, Web 2.0 technologies are viable tools for learners in developmental courses. It should also be noted that many Web 2.0 technologies address multiple intelligences that tend to support learning for those who struggle with writing and with processing information in order to think critically. Visual and auditory learners as well as linguistic, intrapersonal, and interpersonal learners are all supported through the use of Web 2.0 technologies. Also, Web 2.0 technologies encourage reflective learning which is a higher order thinking process and one that should be addressed with developing learners. Providing these students with time to think about their thinking (metacognition) through technology supports critical thinking. These learners need support, but as part of the support process, effective instructors are aware of the zone of proximal development for each learner. This means encouraging independence. As noted by Knobel and Wilber (2009), Web 2.0 allows learners to take control of the learning process. These learners become independent thinkers—necessary in a work force that encourages employees to be innovative, forward-thinking, and to work with very little guidance. These researchers also suggest that when planning, educators should focus less on teacher delivery of content and more on "designing collaborative projects that tap into cross-curricular content, abstract concepts, and learning in meaningful ways (Knobel & Wilber, 2009, p. 24). This suggestion supports active learning, multiple intelligences, reflective learning, and student independence as learners. Furthermore, information literacy and Web 2.0 technologies fit hand-in-hand. Information literacy encourages acquisition of knowledge and how best to obtain needed information. Web 2.0 technologies encourages application, synthesis, and evaluation of learning by using the information found. Combining these practices provides the developmental learner with opportunities to move from basic thinking to higher-order critical thinking skills.

Not all research supports the use of Web 2.0 technologies in the higher education classroom or in developmental courses. A case study conducted by Zelnick (2013) on professor perceptions of Web 2.0 technologies found no relationship between faculty members' perception of developmental programs affecting technology integration or course effectiveness. In a case study that reviewed Web 2.0 technologies with students, Waycott and Kennedy (2009) found that "while technologies such as mobile phones, digital cameras, and social networking sites may be prominent in students' social spaces, harnessing these tools for use in students' learning spaces may not be straightforward or unproblematic. It appears that the blending of social and formal spaces for learning may not always be desired or welcomed by students" (p. 1093). Thus, there is a need to evaluate both teacher and student perceptions of Web 2.0 technologies, understanding that this is not a fix-all for all students and that there are barriers and challenges for use of this technology in learning environments.

Information Literacy and Web 2.0 in the English Classroom

It is critical for instructors to understand the nexus between information literacy and Web 2.0 technologies. Being able to apply these in the developmental education course room will work to meet the needs of learners and prepare them for credit-bearing courses. Jo An and Williams (2010) conducted a case study revealing that the use of Web 2.0 technologies in teaching improved communication and collaboration, knowledge creation and retention, and improved technology skills. Most freshman year course schedules include general education courses with mathematics and English as subjects. This design is not accidental. These courses provide a foundation to enhance learners' basic skills in order to meet the demands of courses in their major of choice. Students in developmental courses lack the skills necessary for success in these courses. However, these courses provide instructors with opportunities to implement information literacy and Web 2.0 technologies as a means to address learner deficiencies. In any English class, effective writing practices are a part of course objectives. Effective writing skills or communication is not only an aspect of Wagner's (2008) 21st century skills, but a component of information literacy. Writing instruction plays a critical role in the attainment of information literacy (Norgaard, Arp, & Woodard, 2004). Traditionally, writing application has come in the form of formal papers. "The research paper places its focus on format and final product, on sources and citations instead of intellectual process" (Norgaard, Arp, & Woodard, 2004, p. 222). While students' writing capabilities are important, 21st century skills extend beyond the ability to write a sentence or simply to provide an organized interpretation of a given topic as found in research. Twenty-first century skills deconstruct the research paper by including both information literacy and Web 2.0 technologies. For example, the traditional English instructor or digital immigrant may attempt to engage the developmental learner by teaching the writing process and having the learner complete a five paragraph research paper on a given topic. The 21st century English professor in touch with digital natives uses information literacy and writing in innovative ways. The focus is not simply writing a paper. The processes of acquiring and accessing information, analyzing, comparing, and evaluating the information, and creating new products with the information not only addresses 21st century skills but empowers learners in preparation for credit-bearing courses and for today's workforce.

R.A.F.T. in the Developmental English Classroom

A specific example may include the professor who uses the R.A.F.T.S. writing strategy to incorporate research skills, writing skills, critical thinking skills, information literacy, and Web 2.0 technologies in a college English course. This strategy encourages learners to process information and to critically attack the information as opposed to simply restating what is found in research. Instructors of students in developmental courses, by using R.A.F.T.S., will help them write for different audiences. Learners write in ways that require them to think from various perspectives when using R.A.F.T.S. (Santa & Havens, 1995). The following are components of the strategy:

- Role: What is the writer's role—reporter, principal, project manager, eyewitness, or something else? This is where research and information literacy become relevant to the learner.
- Audience: Who will be reading the submission—the editor, the parents, the client, the public, or someone else? Like the role, audience helps learners with accessing and distinguishing between sources that help meet the need for information.

- Format: What is the best way to present this writing (web. 2.0 technologies)—a blog, a presentation (Prezi), a visual collage (Glogster), an audio-visual presentation (YouTube), or another medium? Format is when Web 2.0 technologies are important for learners as they aid in presenting work in the most useable design.
- Topic: Who or what is the subject of this writing: a whistleblower in a company, a need for differentiated instruction in the classroom, an understanding of a specific industry for a business venture, a report of police abuse, or something else? Specific research skills and information literacy are important to the learner in this step of R.A.F.T.S.
- Strong verb: What higher order thinking verb can be used to demonstrate what the writer will accomplish—assess, propose, illustrate, argue, or some other strong verb? Critical thinking is stressed by use of strong verbs in the assignment expectations.

In a 21st century English class, R.A.F.T.S. can be used in the following manner to address research, writing, and critical thinking learning outcomes while addressing information and Web 2.0 technologies:

> You are the warden (role) of a prison in a major city in the United States. You are being pressured by staff (audience) to implement new safety practices (topic) after a recent prison uprising by inmates. You must create a presentation (optional format using Web 2.0 technology) that proposes (strong verb —synthesis from Bloom's Taxonomy) a plan for safety. Appropriate research is a necessary component of your plan.

The example above includes information literacy as defined by the American Library Association (1989). Learners must recognize what information to use, locate the necessary information, evaluate what they find, and use the information in ways that support their argument or proposal. In addition to addressing information literacy, the example above supports the use of Web 2.0 technologies by encouraging creativity, choice, higher-order thinking, critical thinking, appropriate use of information, and by mimicking real world tasks that may be addressed in the workforce. Information literacy is "the kind of literacy which the twenty-first-century citizen requires: recognizing appropriate information, collaborating, synthesizing and adapting it wisely and ethically" (Godwin, 2009, p. 267). These are the types of skills and the type of higher order and transformative thinking that we must teach learners in developmental courses. Learners do more than find information and repurpose it in a paper. They access the information and construct the information in new, creative ways that demonstrate learning in practical situations.

CONCLUSION

Information literacy and Web 2.0 technologies work hand-in-hand. They form a bond that assists instructors in better preparing the digital natives who inhabit the classroom. A learner with 21st century skills must be affluent with both information literacy and technology to be competitive in today's workforce. This is especially necessary for students in developmental courses who need instruction that supports real world application of knowledge and active learning while addressing their diverse needs through multiple intelligences. This is not to say that the use of information literacy and Web 2.0 technologies are the answer to all of the problems associated with today's developmental learners. However, by updating student learning outcomes (SLOs) and by developing instructional practices to reflect use of information literacy and Web 2.0 technologies, instructors of students in developmental courses can move learners' from basic skills to higher order thinking skills and prepare them for credit-bearing courses and beyond.

REFERENCES

Academic Senate of California Community Colleges. (2002). *Academic literacy: A statement of competencies expected of students entering California's public colleges and universities and economic stability*. Retrieved from http://senate.universityofcalifornia.edu/reports/acadlit.pdf

American Library Association. (1989). *Presidential committee on information literacy: Final report.* Chicago, IL: American Library Association.

Arum, R., & Roska, J. (2011). *Academically adrift: Limited learning on college campuses*. Chicago, IL: University of Chicago Press.

Association of College and Research Libraries. (2000). Information literacy competency standards for higher education. Chicago, IL: Author. Retrieved from http://www.ala.org/ala/mgrps/divs/acrl/standards/standards.pdf

Bailey, T., Jeong, D., & Cho, S. (2008). *Referral, enrollment, and completion in development education sequences in community colleges.* New York, NY: Community College Research Center, Columbia University.

Bautsch, B. (2013). Reforming remedial education. Retrieved from http://www.ncsl.org/research/education/improving-college-completion-reforming-remedial.aspx

Bennett, S., Maton, K., & Kervin, L. (2008). The 'digital natives' debate: A critical review of the evidence. *British Journal of Educational Technology, 39*(5), 775–786.

Brothen, T. & Wambach, C. A. (2012). Refocusing developmental education. *Journal of Developmental Education, 36*(2), 34–39.

Casazza, M. E. (1999). Who we are and where did we come from? *Journal of Developmental Education, 23*(1), 1–7.

Caverly, D., Nicholson, S., Battle, J., & Atkins, C. (2008). Techtalk: Web 2.0, blogs, and developmental education. *Journal of Developmental Education, 32*(1), 34–35.

Charles A. Dana Center, Complete College America, Education Commission the States, and Jobs for the Future. (2012). *Core principles for transforming remedial education: A joint statement.* Boston, MA: Jobs for the Future.

Chernay, I. D. (2008). The effects of active learning on students' memories for course content. *Active Learning in Higher Education, 9*(2), 152.

Godwin, P. (2007). Information literacy meets web 2.0: How the new tools affect our own training and our teaching. *New Review of Information Networking, 12*(2), 101–112.

Godwin, P. (2009). Information literacy and web 2.0: Is it just hype? *Electronic Library and Information Systems, 43*(3), 264–274.

Gros, B., Garcia, I., & Escofet, A. (2012). Beyond the net generation debate: A comparison of digital learners in face-to-face and virtual universities. *International Review of Research in Open and Distance Learning, 13*(4), 190–210.

Hicks, A., & Graber, A. (2009). Shifting paradigms: teaching, learning and Web 2.0. *Reference Services Review, 38*(4), 621–633.

Hodara, M., Jaggars, S., & Karp, M. (2012). *Improving developmental education assessment and placement: Lessons from community colleges across the country.* New York, NY: Community College Research Center, Columbia University.

Jo-An, Y., & Williams, K. (2010). Teaching with web 2.0 technologies: Benefits, barriers, and lessons learned. *International Journal of Instructional Technology and Distance Learning, 7*(3). Retrieved from http://www.itdl.org/Journal/Mar_10/article04.htm

Kennedy, G., Judd, T. S., Churchward, A., Gray, K., & Krause, K. L. (2008). First year students' experiences with technology: Are they really digital natives? *Australasian Journal of Educational Technology, 24*(1), 108–122.

Knobel, M., & Wilber, D. (2009). Let's talk 2.0. *Educational Leadership, 66*(6), 20–24.

Kutner, M., Greenberg, E., & Baer, J. (2005). *National Assessment of Adult Literacy (NAAL): A first look at the literacy of America's adults in the 21st century.* Washington, DC: National Center for Educational Statistics.

Mackey, T., & Jacobson, T. (2004). Integrating information literacy in lower- and upper-level courses: Developing scalable models for higher education. *The Journal of General Education, 53*(3–4), 200–224.

National Center for Educational Statistics. (1995). *Digest of Educational Statistics, 1995.* Washington, DC: U.S. Department of Education.

Norgaard, R., Arp, L., & Woodard, B. (2004). Writing information literacy in the classroom: Pedagogical enactments and implications. *Reference & User Services Quarterly, 43*(3), 220–226.

Osterholt, D. A., & Barratt, K. (2012). Ideas for practice: A collaborative look to the classroom. *Journal of Developmental Education, 36*(2), 22–27.

Park, S. (2013). The potential of web 2.0 tools to promote reading engagement in a general education course. *Techtrends: Linking Research & Practice to Improve Learning, 57*(2), 46–53.

Prensky, M. (2001). Digital natives, digital immigrants. *On the Horizon, 9*(5), 1–6.

Roska, J., Jenkins, D., Jaggars, S., Zeidenberg, M., & Cho, S. (2009). *Strategies for promoting gatekeeper course success amount students needing remediation: Research report for the Virginia Community College System*. New York, NY: Community College Research Center, Columbia University.

Santa, C., & Havens, L. (1995). *Creating independence through student-owned strategies: Project CRISS*. Dubuque, IA: Kendall Hunt.

SCONUL Advisory Committee on information literacy. (2011). *Seven pillars of information Literacy: Core model for higher education*. Retrieved from http://www.sconul.ac.uk/sites/default/files/documents/coremodel.pdf

Stanford University. (2006). *The bridge project*. Retrieved from http://www.stanford.edu/group/bridgeproject/

Twigg, C. A. (2005). *Increasing success for underserved students: Redesigning introductory courses*. Retrieved from http://www.thencat.org/Monographs/IncSuccess.pdf

Wagner, T. (2008). *The global achievement gap*. New York, NY: Basic Books.

Waycott, J., & Kennedy, G. (2009). Mobile and web 2.0 technologies in undergraduate science: Situating learning in everyday experience. In *Same places, different spaces. Proceedings ascilite Auckland 2009*. Retrieved from http://www.ascilite.org.au/conferences/auckland09/procs/waycott.pdf

Zelnick, S. A. (2013). The perception of web 2.0 technologies on teaching and learning in higher education: A case study. *Creative Education, 4*(7A2), 53–93.

CHAPTER 9

SOCIAL MEDIA AND SELF-REGULATION

The Need for Strategies to Achieve High Quality Learning

Gisella Paoletti

ABSTRACT

The new social media holds many promises: it allows us to follow the latest news and to be informed on what our friends are doing and planning. However, it also makes us feel that we have to be always connected and forced to interrupt work and study to check our text messages, a Facebook feed, or a post. By dividing our attention on more than one media, we may believe we are multitasking and are processing multiple sources of information simultaneously, without significant cognitive costs. We are not always aware of the cost of task-switching and, even when we do, we are unable to disconnect. In this chapter we are going to describe the results of a data collection on the use of social media in academic contexts. The investigation was conducted with university students who were asked, through interviews and questionnaires, whether and how the connection with Facebook and instant messaging

E-Learning and Social Media:
Education and Citizenship for the Digital 21st Century, pp. 183–197

interfered with the execution of their *primary* tasks (listen to the lesson, study) and what they do to reduce this interference: to prevent it and to recover focus and concentration. As we will see, the problem is perceived by many researchers as well as by students, and is related above all to listening in class and, to a lesser degree, to studying.

INTRODUCTION

Multitasking usually describes the phenomena of divided attention between simultaneous activities or rapid switching between two or more tasks. The term media multitasking has been mainly used to describe the behaviors that takes place in many educational environments when students use multiple digital technologies, including laptops, tablets, and smart phones, for on-task and off-task purposes that supplement learning or social interaction. Multitasking and media multitasking are not recent phenomena, including those that take place in school and in the academic environments analyzed herein. However, today's scenario is highly affected by the constant presence of technological devices and social media that allow us—or even force us—to be connected at all times.

The diffusion of social media has many positive results as well as unexpected and problematic consequences. Social media allows an easy and constant access to up-to-date information about the latest events and our own personal social network. At the same time, there is a need to be constantly available and ready to answer those who contact us. Frequently receiving texts or news feeds does interrupt work or study. We may believe that shifting from one device to another does not imply great mental fatigue, because we are not aware of the effort that task-switching actually requires. Furthermore, even when we are aware of the problem, we are still unable to disconnect or keep our mobile phone off while studying or listening to a lecture. Checking if we have received a text or an update on our mobile makes us frequently distracted and consequently we do not always follow a teacher's lesson.

We might wonder if usage of more than one media during lectures or while studying represents a problem, and in which contexts and conditions. Studies on multitasking show that we cannot easily perform more than one task at a time. A constant and focused attention is required for a successful learning process. Exceptions are represented by routine tasks or tasks which do not make demands on the same processing or representational apparatus (Feng, Schwemmer, Gershman, & Cohen, 2014).

In this chapter we will summarize the main view points regarding the effects of media multitasking. We will start from the concerns expressed by mass media, and then we will summarize some of the results of the research that we carried out which studied the effects of processing and learning.

The Alarm of Mass-Media

Media Multitasking is not ignored by mass-media. Relevance has been given to the delays in the diffusion of communication technologies. At the same time, concerns in regards to the explosion of digital media have been put forth. Paper and online newspapers have expressed apprehension for the massive usage of a variety of media among very young people. “Generation M2: Media in the Lives of 8- to 18-Year-Olds,” a survey conducted by the Kaiser Family Foundation, showed that almost a third of those surveyed said that when they were doing homework, “most of the time” they were also watching TV, text messaging, or listening to music (Rideout, Foehr, & Roberts, 2010).

Another aspect of the problem which has been underlined is that this phenomenon seems almost impossible to limit. Young people acknowledge that they cannot study without a digital device and that they cannot avoid text messaging, checking their Facebook feeds (Kessler, 2011), or task-switching from one device to another (Marci, 2012), convinced that it will not affect the learning process (Clayson & Haley, 2012). Even during a short 15 minute observation period, while aware that they were being observed, participants were capable of maintaining one-task behavior only for a short time, averaging less than 6 minutes on each task before switching to another (Rosen, Carrier, & Cheever, 2013).

Evidences of the Negative Aspects of Multitasking

There is little doubt that engagement in simultaneous tasks, in most cases, slows down the process and may reduce the quality of learning and the amount of information learned (Arrington & Logan, 2004; Monsell, 2003; Paoletti, 2010).

When there are two or more tasks, such as reading and listening, that simultaneously require the same processing or representational apparatus (multiplexing), a simultaneous performance of these two tasks will be impossible (Feng et al., 2014). Therefore, fast task-switching becomes necessary, by quickly moving from one task to another.

The cost of task-switching in terms of time, effort, and effectiveness may be high. *Time* is a key factor, because task switching delays and complicates the whole process (Cades, Werner, Trafton, Boehm-Davis, & Monk, 2008). By switching from a first task to a second one (and viceversa), the learner has to activate the mental procedures and rules needed to perform the different tasks. Another problem is posed by the fact that even though the learner is not fully aware of it, the learner moves many times the focus of attention among different tasks (Brasel & Gips, 2011; Pool, Koolstra, & van der Voort, 2003).

Along with time, media multitasking can take a toll on the quality of mental processing. The learner should pay attention in order to process the important information. This implies one ignores the distracting elements and concentrate on relevant information, which is difficult to perform when one is dividing attention among different sources of information (Forster & Lavie, 2013).

Finally, the quantity of learning has to be taken into account. Students claim that when they do multitask with different media, they cannot perform all the assigned tasks (Junco & Cotton, 2011). Moreover, they report lower grades and lower class performance (Clayson & Haley, 2013). Finally, their capacity to memorize is impaired (Hembrook & Gay, 2003; Pool et al., 2003).

Evidences on Positive Aspects

Other researchers have highlighted positive points of view considering the access to information from multiple media. Access to one's own devices can encourage multitasking, but it does not necessarily have negative effects. BYOD (bring your own device) is a frequently used term in the field of educational research. BYOD is considered the solution to the lack of public funding for technological innovation (Avvisati, Hennessy, Kozma, & Vincent-Lancrin, 2013). It is also seen as a tool which connects formal and informal environments such as home, school, and the workplace. As Tim Panagos wrote: "By acknowledging that smartphones, tablets, and laptops are a factual component in the lives of every human being and by embracing openly and actively the exploratory use of these tools for both education and entertainment, we are opening the door that leads to the heart of the 21st century experience for our students" (Panagos, 2013, p. 3).

In a research published in 2013, Park indentified some interesting elements of self-regulation among a group of students who had been given a tablet for one year. Interviews and observation of the subjects yielded interesting results. The students reported an increased control over the learning process. They felt that they had more control over the learning environment as well as an increased acquisition of new strategies for self-control and organization (Park, 2013).

Prohibition to carry smartphones or other devices into class or to use them while studying appears less effective. It eliminates the external source of distraction, but may activate internal sources of distraction such as task-unrelated-thinking and mind wandering and various forms of anxiety (Levinson, Smallwood, & Davidson, 2012; Risko, Anderson, Sarwal, Engelhardt, & Kingstone, 2012) which compromise the processing of information. Research found that the students who were used to checking in with their virtual social world, through text messaging and social media, every 15 minutes or less were highly anxious when they couldn't check in. Studies suggest that students start multitasking in the belief that this will have a positive effect on their general performance. In reality, they did not achieve what they had expected, but obtained a favorable feedback that satisfied their emotional and social needs (Wang & Tchernev, 2012).

Some variables may mediate the less positive effect of media multitasking. Research proves that, with practice, multitasking can become easier and facilitate task performance (Spelke, Hirst, & Neisser, 1976; Strobach, Liepelt, Pashler, Frensch, & Schubert, 2013). Initially, it may be hard to perform two tasks simultaneously, but in time at least one of the two tasks can be performed automatically, reducing the attention needed for the second one. For instance, a research carried out by Spelke and colleagues revealed that two subjects were able to read short stories while taking dictation of a list of words. After some weeks of practice, they were able to write words, discover connections among the dictated words, categorize them for meaning, all while reading for comprehension at normal speed (Spelke et al., 1976).

Another element which could reduce the negative impact of multitasking is the time dedicated to elaborating information and to studying. Some studies reveal that if the time dedicated to reading to understand the material and to studying is not limited, and if the process is under the control of the student, then the results will be more favorable (Cauchard, Cane, & Weger, 2012; Pool et al., 2003). Extra time may be needed, but the end results and performance can be satisfactory.

The Aim of This Investigation

Starting from the assumption that, in our technological world, media multitasking is already a part of our daily lives and that there are both positive and negative aspects in the use of personal devices in learning and academic settings, we conducted a survey to investigate the behaviors, opinions, and beliefs of a group of Italian undergraduated students. Interviews and questionnaires were issued to investigate the interference of common devices and social media like Facebook and text messaging on the performance of their primary tasks, such as following a lesson and studying. Moreover, we investigated their ways to prevent or limit the negative effects of interference on concentration.

The research shows an outline of their media usage. The situation in Italy is peculiar because on one hand there is a scarcity of digital media at school and on the other there is an extremely high diffusion of digital devices, smartphones in particular (Kemp, 2014). Consequently, young people in particular should have familiarity and mastery of these devices. But which representation do they have of the consequences of their use? And do they know how to use them in order to minimize the negative effects?

Our initial hypothesis was that a constant use of multiple devices does not necessarily have a negative effect on processing and understanding. This is based on the fact that self-regulating strategies can be used to limit distraction and stimulate an effective use of digital devices. In accordance with the approach described by Park (2013), we tried to introduce new elements that could clarify how digital devices are being used in the educational environment.

METHOD

Participants

Participants in the research were students who live in a city in Northern Italy.

At a pilot stage, in which we performed individual interviews based on ten subjects, students of various ages and academic levels were involved.

Subsequently, another group of one hundred young adults participated in the investigation by answering a questionnaire. These were undergraduate students who studied Psychology, Maths, and Education at a University in the North-East. Their average age was 22 years old with a high grade point average (average grade 25,6/30). These students studied on an average of 2 to 3 hours per day (national data shows that they tend to spend almost 7 hours a day online). They reported to spend an average of 3 weeks to prepare for an exam.

These 100 students were selected for the research on the basis of age homogeneity and for the completeness of their answers. All were volunteers.

Measurements and Procedure

The research was based on interviews and questionnaires.

We based our interviews on the existing literature of related research fields. We took into account the following elements: suggestions from studies on media multitasking (Clayson & Haley, 2013; Kirschner & Karpinski, 2010; Junco & Cotton, 2011), the motivational conflict between school and study (Hofer et al., 2010), and the strategies of self-regulation (Mccann & Garcia, 1999).

In a preliminary phase, we carried out individual interviews with seven subjects. Participants have been asked to collaborate to the investigation by commenting on the series of questions on the use of media in class and during studying.

They were asked to think aloud while elaborating each question and answer. Their verbal expressions have been transcribed and analyzed. On the base of their comments and remarks, the list has been revised and transformed into a questionnaire and submitted to a second group (three subjects) for a verification. Questions which resulted poorly comprehensible have been revised. The answers of the 10 subjects have been used to build alternatives using closed answers questions.

The questionnaire consisted of four blocks of questions. The first block (with open answers) was aimed at collecting information on age, study field, and the academic performance of the students. A second block (with closed answers) inquired about their daily media diet, asking which was the most used device, which were simultaneously used and for which purposes, and whether they were used during lessons and study. The third group of questions investigated the type of motivation for study (if related to the interest in the topics, to family expectations, to job expectations), and also the possible conflict between study and leisure time.

Finally, the last block of questions (with both open and closed answers) investigated the self-consciousness of the possible effects of multitasking in listening and studying, and the use of attention calibration and strategies in order to keep distraction under control.

The overall questionnaire consisted of forty closed answer questions and fourteen open answer questions. Most of the closed answer questions came with a list of options among which students could choose one of more than one. It was also allowed to add further information and additional options (e.g., Question n. 8: Which is the device you mostly use? Answers: mobile phone/tv/gaming console/Mp3/Other...). The remaining closed answer questions proposed a Likert scale. Open answer questions were aimed at collecting information on students' characteristics and strategies.

RESULTS

Here we will focus mainly on the responses to the questionnaire. We will refer to interviews only to offer some explanations and interpretations of the students' behavior.

The answers to the questionnaire show a profile of a student/user of the network. Over a half of the students who answered the questionnaire declared to be motivated and interested in their studies. They said that studying is pleasant and interesting and that they consider it very important for their future, identifying themselves with the "ideal/model" student who prefers to stay at home, and either does not accept invitations or completes his or her assignments before going out.

The student/user states that she/he is online many times a day (she/he is not always online). She/he says that the mobile phone (more than the computer) is used to write and receive text messages and Facebook feeds, rarely to play games.

E-mails are rare, both those received (an average of 6) and those sent (an average of 1). Text messaging is much more frequent: 20–30 incoming/outgoing daily messages with peaks of 150.

Text messages are written/read with WhatsApp (70 students out of 100 use this application), with the mobile phone (68 out of 100), and with Facebook (42 out of 100).

K., one of the students interviewed, said "*Frequently people do not have money enough to make calls, therefore you wait for an answer on Facebook or on Whatsapp because you do not have to pay.*"

Students were asked about the purposes of using Facebook. The main purposes were looking at main and recent news (N = 82 out of 100) and newsgroups (N = 40 out of 100). (K: *When I open Facebook I look at the main and recent news and at the groups which is very important to me and send messages*).

Our sample has confirmed the tendency toward multitasking. Out of the 100 students who answered the questionnaire, 95 confirmed using more than one media simultaneously. In 85% of cases the mobile phone was used, together with the computer, TV, or both. Furthermore, the mobile phone (the most commonly used device) was employed to perform different tasks: write and receive texts messages, go on Facebook, or listen to music.

The learners recognized to use mobile phones, tablets, and other devices while studying and during lectures. The framework which emerged from our study revealed that when the learner is about to study, he/she switches off the TV and the computer or tablet and closes the windows that he/she does not need (Facebook or e-mail). Finally, he/she may use the computer to take notes or to review the slides of the teacher. On the contrary, the mobile phone is never switched off (only five students did it), but sometimes it is put on vibrate mode. While attending the lectures, those students who have a tablet turn it off or close the irrelevant windows. Most of the students (88 students out of 100) turn off the ringtone of the phone.

Defence, Productive, and Distracting Behaviors

As stated by Park (2013), we hypothesized that the processing of information and comprehension is not necessarily negatively affected by the coexistence of different stimuli and devices. The quality of the process depends on the activities undertaken.

To prove our hypothesis we identified three different categories or levels of behavior, which were more or less strategic and functional as related to the comprehension/learning process. These categories have been employed to classify the behaviors and strategies described by the students when asked to tell what they do with their personal devices when they study or listen to a lecture.

The first category describes the behaviors of students who, while studying, switch off the computer, close the unnecessary windows, switch off the TV, move to a more quieter room, or listen to music to avoid distracting sounds. These are preventive behaviors meant to put up a *defense* against distractions. Some of these behaviors can be put in place even while listening to a lesson.

The second category describes the behavior of students who multitask in order to support their study: they use the computer to take notes, view slides made by their teachers, and look for information and explanations. These behaviors can be considered *coherent* with the lecture/study (and therefore productive/germane) because the use of one source can support the processing of the other (Ayres & Sweller, 2005; Mayer, 2005).

The third category describes potentially distracting behaviors, such as keeping windows open, keeping the mobile with silent ring options, but not off, and answering calls immediately.

Each student could mention more than one action, describing the manner in which he/she organized his or her studio environment or followed the lessons.

In Figure 9.1 we show the distribution and prevalence of the behaviors and strategies used while studying and during lectures.

As shown, while studying (and much less during lectures) strategies of prevention prevail. These imply switching off the devices or distancing from them (see first column: defence). Defense actions that are put in place during the study are three times (218 vs. 70) the actions of defense put in place during a lesson.

Productive/coherent behaviors (carrying out researches, studying slides, listening to music) are more frequent while studying (98 possible actions are mentioned for studying vs. 16 possible actions for listening). On the other hand, distracting behaviors (mobile on vibration or on other silencing options) appear to be more frequent during lectures (97 vs. 70).

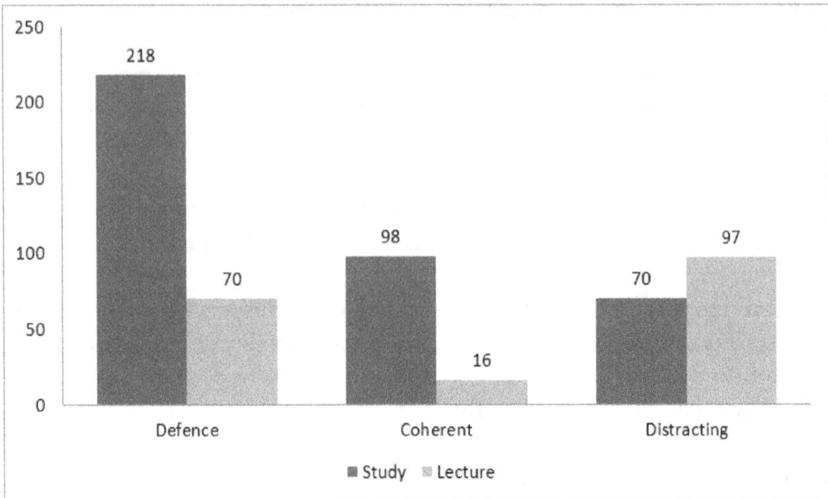

Figure 9.1. Behaviors and strategies while studying and during listening to lectures.

Another block of questions focused in particular on the students' opinions on the effects of messaging. It reveals the students' beliefs in respect to a possible adverse effect of text messaging on preparation, time, and methods for studying and in following a lesson.

Students' evaluations of the effects of messaging reveal that only 38 out of 100 students think that text messaging may have a negative effect on their final results. However, it seems that text messaging will have a stronger adverse effect on time (56/100) and on the methods of study (51/100). Finally, less than a half of the students (44 out of 100) think that text messaging may have an adverse effect on understanding and processing of the information supplied during the lesson.

It is worth noting that about nearly 3/4 (73 out of 100) of the students said that they preferred to eliminate the sources of distraction instead of relying on their capability to oppose external stimuli. However, only a few switched off their mobile phone (only 5 students out of 100) while all the others turned them on silent or vibration mode.

The answers to the questionnaires issued revealed that the students who admitted to immediately answering phone calls are just a few (6 out of 100). We had asked this question in the questionnaire because during the previous interviews the topic had been treated for a long while. The interviews gave more than one explanation of this phenomena, also demonstrating that this is a hot topic. There are some students who plan a time for studying and a time for socializing (T., during the interview, said: *I take a break at the end of a chapter... I give myself a prize if I study for one hour without looking at my mobile phone*). What may be feared is a sequence of calls and answers (D. said during the interview: *if you have your mobile phone at hand and basically we all have ... it's the most distracting thing, particularly if you answer ... because that is the worst mistake that you can make ... the basis is avoid answering*). Frequently, before resuming studying, a break is needed as well as a distancing from the source of distraction (V., during the interview, said*: I take a break and then I restart studying*).

CONCLUSIONS

The purpose of our research was to gather information about the average behavior of a group of undergraduate students who were asked whether and how the connection with Facebook and instant messaging interfered with the execution of their *primary* tasks (listen to the lesson, study) and what they do to reduce this interference: to prevent it and to recover focus and concentration.

A dependence on social media—such as Facebook—and online games was not detected. Students affirm using them only occasionally and for short periods of time (a statement confirmed by Phan & Chaparro, 2013). The interference among different tasks, when it takes place, is mostly due to text messaging, which is done among peers using any available media and in any place, at home or during lectures. They do this in the belief that it really does not constitute a serious disturbance and that it does not affect understanding or disrupt attention.

As we have seen, students thought that text messaging had an effect on the time dedicated to studying, but not on exam preparation nor on the attention given during lectures. They claimed that they stopped using their mobile phones when they had to study and that they spend only a few seconds to read and answer text messages, and that this pause did not affect their concentration.

First we can notice that the research on multitasking confirms the students' statements that text messaging has an effect on time, but not on preparation in certain conditions. Pashler and collegues, for example, have demonstrated that the most important element when performing more than one task is to keep under control the pace of presentation (Pashler, Kang, & Renita, 2013). When the learner controls the pace at which educational materials are provided, the interference between the two tasks should not adversely affect the learning process. In other words, it is possible to read/listen to stories while having brief conversations (akin to an instant messaging conversation).This might not be an effective method (Rosen, 2008) because of the breaks in concentration and the increase in the time needed. However, engagement in two simultaneous tasks is possible and may not affect the good results or the favorable results of the learning process.

However, this possibility (engagement in two different tasks with a minimal or nihil adverse effect on understanding/learning) takes place only when studying is interrupted by brief conversations, not while listening to a lesson. In fact, the very same research (Pashler et al., 2013) questions the possibility of productive listening while text messaging in a class. In class the learner does not control the pace/time of the presentation, cannot interrupt the process, listen, or read again. What has taken place parallel to the conversation is lost, probably not understood nor learned.

There are other factors and conditions that determine the effects of multitasking during lectures and while studying. For instance, the effectiveness of communication depends, for the most part, on a quantitative element —the number of text messages sent and received. A research carried out by Rosen and collegues and published in 2011 showed that performance worsens if eight texts are sent and received during a lesson, while this does not happen if there are only four texts (Rosen, Lim, Carrier, & Cheever, 2011). Unfortunately, we do not know how many messages were written/received by our students during the study session and during the lessons. This is one of the limitations of our research and of our questionnaire, which should be revised and integrated.

Furthermore, much depends on the timing of the answer. Research shows that when the answer is immediate, the performance is not as good as when the student waits for a break in the lesson. Also, the length and complexity of the text sent and received has to be considered. It is obvious that a brief answer does not have the same effect as a complex conversation (Cades et al., 2008). In our research, only six students recognize that they respond immediately to a message, and they believe that this takes only a few seconds. However, the previous interviews reveal that this behavior may be more widespread than acknowledged by the students.

Along with texting, which we classified among the distracting behaviors, our questionnaire examined the spread of behaviors of defense (from distractions) and those coherent with the task. As we have seen, multitasking is not always distracting. In fact, even if demanding and time consuming, the processing of two sources of information may support learning and understanding (Ayres & Sweller, 2005; Mayer, 2005). The usage of more than one media stimulates elaborations and the integration between sources of information, in particular while studying. In fact, these positive and integrative behaviors seem to be most common during the study, which is under the responsibility of the student. Or perhaps listening to the lecture is for them so unpleasant that they can not resist the consultation of the phone. Studying is important for these students, but it does not cover all their interests and needs. Therefore, a connection with the outside world contributes to their well-being, to help them relax and to make lessons and studying more bearable.

Implications for Citizenship for the 21st Century

The most recognized and evident obstacle to the introduction and diffusion of the new technologies at school is the shortage of equipment. As shown by recent surveys carried out by Ocse, this is a real problem in many countries. This is certainly the case of Italy, where an inadequate number of computers in schools and classrooms is reported (Avvisati et al., 2013).

At home the situation is different due to the frequent presence of Internet connections and of computers and smartphones, particularly in families with an adolescent or young child. This can be considered good news because it reveals a new element on the usage of one's own device at school. Once condemned and banned, this behavior is about to become the solution to the problems of the technological deficiency in our country.

On one hand, the use of BYOD can be considered a solution to the problems of underfunding, on the other there may be some positive effects in the constant use of the same device in different contexts. At the same time, the usage of the same device for different purposes and in different contexts may have unpredictable and problematic consequences, because it can activate behaviors which are not effective.

A solution appears to be a familiarization with a positive use of these devices. It takes time to learn how to use a new device properly and appropriately. The process of trial and error can be backed up with a metacognitive training on the conditions that make multitasking productive or distracting.

We are increasingly dependent on new technologies to acquire knowledge, skills, and competencies. Technology is evolving rapidly, the required knowledge is increasingly sophisticated and requires constant updates. To keep pace with the times and fully comply with the requirement of the new century, we need to go beyond mere technology and promote a competent and productive use of the new tools.

Let us conclude by noting that the ideal student is always depicted as one who is always studying and resists temptations. Maybe this image is not entirely correct. It is equally important to be able to enjoy some rest and relaxation without being bothered by thoughts about study and work. At the same time, a student should be able to enjoy the time dedicated to study without feeling anxious every time he or she does not immediately answer a text message.

REFERENCES

Arrington, C. M., & Logan, G. D. (2004). The cost of a voluntary task switch. *Psychological Science, 15*, 610–615.

Avvisati, F., Hennessy S., Kozma, R., & Vincent-Lancrin S. (2013). Review of the Italian Strategy for Digital Schools. Retrieved from http://www.oecd-ilibrary.org/education/review-of-the-italian-strategy-for-digital-schools_5k487ntdbr44-en

Ayres, P., & Sweller, J. (2005). The split attention principle in multimedia learning. In R. Mayer (Ed.), *The Cambridge handbook of multimedia learning* (pp. 135–145), Cambridge, UK: Cambridge University Press.

Brasel, S., & Gips, J. (2011). Media multitasking behavior: concurrent television and computer usage. *Cyberpsichology, Behavior and Social Networking, 14*, 527–534.

Cades, D. M., Werner, N., Trafton, J. G., Boehm-Davis, D. A., & Monk, C. A. (2008). Dealing with interruptions can be complex, but does interruption complexity matter: a mental resources approach to quantifying disruptions. *Proceedings of the Human Factors and Ergonomics Society 52nd Annual Meeting*. Sage.

Cauchard, F., Cane, J., & Weger, U. (2012). Influence of background speech and music in interrupted reading: an eye-tracking study. *Applied Cognitive Psychology, 26*, 381–390.

Clayson, D., & Haley, D. (2013). An introduction to multitasking and texting prevalence and impact on grades and GPA in marketing classes. *Journal of Marketing Education, 35*(1), 26–40.

Feng, S. F., Schwemmer, M., Gershman, S. J., & Cohen, J. D. (2014). Multitasking versus multiplexing: Toward a normative account of limitations in the simultaneous execution of control-demanding behaviors. *Cognitive, Affective, & Behavioral Neuroscience, 14*(1), 129–146.

Forster, S., & Lavie N. (2013). Distracted by your mind? Individual differences in distractibility predict mind wandering. *Journal of Experimental Psychology: Learning, Memory, and Cognition, 40(*1), 251–260.

Hembrook, H., & Gay G. (2003). The laptop and the lecture: the effects of multitasking in learning environments, *Journal of Computing in Higher Education, 15*, 46–64.

Hofer, M., Schmid, S., Fries, S., Kilian, B. & Kuhnle, C. (2010). Reciprocal relationships between value orientation and motivational interference during studying and leisure. *British Journal of Educational Psychology, 80*, 623–645.

Junco, R., & Cotton, S. (2011). Perceived academic effects of instant messaging use. *Computers and Education. 58*(1), 365–374.

Kemp, S. (2014). Internet consumption around the world. Retrieved from http://wearesocial.sg/category/news/

Kessler, S. (2011). 38% of college students can't go 10 minutes without tech [STATS]. *Mashable Tech.* Retrieved from http://mashable.com/2011/05/31/college-tech-device-stats/

Kirschner, P. A., & Karpinski, A. C. (2010). Facebook and academic performance *Computers in Human Behavior, 26*(6),1237–1245.

Levinson, D., Smallwood, J., & Davidson, R. (2012). The persistence of thought: evidence for a role of working memory in the maintenance of task-unrelated thinking. *Psychological Science, 23*, 375–380.

Mccann, E., & Garcia, T. (1999). Maintaining motivation and regulating emotion: measuring individual differences in academic volitional strategies. *Learning and Individual Differences, 11*(3), 259–279.

Marci, C. (2012). A (biometric) day in the life: Engaging across media. *Paper presented at Re: Think 2012,* New York, NY.

Mayer, R. (2005). *Cambridge handbook of multimedia learning*. Cambridge, UK: Cambridge University Press.

Monsell, S. (2003). Task switching. *Trends in Cognitive Sciences, 7,* 134–140.

Panagos, T. (2013).The future of education: BYOD in the classroom. *Wired.* Retrieved from http://insights.wired.com/profiles/blogs/the-future-of-education-embracing-byod-in-the-classroom

Paoletti, G. (2010). Social software and Multitasking? A virus or a resourse? *Form@are)* Social software e Multitasking: un Virus o una Risorsa? *Form@re.* Retrieved from http://formare.erickson.it/wordpress/?p=4184

Park, S. (2013). The process of adapting to mobile tablet devices by switching between productive and distractive multitasking. *Selected Papers of Internet Research, 14.* 0. Retrieved from http://spir.aoir.org/index.php/spir/article/view/809

Pashler, H., Kang, S., & Renita Y. I. (2013). Does multitasking impair studying? Depends on timing. *Applied Cognitive Psychology, 27*(5), 593–599.

Phan, M., & Chaparro, B. (2013). Understanding how and why people play Facebook games, *Usability News*. Retrieved from http://usabilitynews.org/understanding-how-and-why-people-play-facebook-games

Pool, M., Koolstra, C., & van der Voort, T. (2003). Distraction effects of background soap operas on homework performance. *Educational Psychology, 23,* 361-380.

Rideout, V., Foehr, U., & Roberts, D. (2010). GENERATION M2 Media in the Lives of 8- to 18-Year-Olds. *A Kaiser Family Foundation Study*. Retrieved from http://files.eric.ed.gov/fulltext/ED527859.pdf

Risko, E., Anderson, N., Sarwal, A., Engelhardt, M., & Kingstone, A. (2012). Everyday attention: variation in mind wandering and memory in a lecture. *Applied Cognitive Psychology, 26,* 234–242.

Rosen, C. (2008): The myth of multitasking. *The New Atlantis, 20*(1), 105–110.

Rosen, L., Carrier, L., & Cheever, N. (2013). Facebook and texting made me do it: media induced task-switching while studying. *Computers in Human Behavior, 29,* 984–958.

Rosen, L. D., Lim, A. F., Carrier, L. M., & Cheever, N. A. (2011). An empirical examination of the educational impact of text message-induced task switching in the classroom: Educational implications and strategies to enhance learning. *Psicología Educativa, 17*(2), 163–177.

Spelke, E., Hirst, W., & Neisser, U. (1976). Skills of divided attention. *Cognition, 4,* 215–230.

Strobach, T., Liepelt, R., Pashler, H., Frensch, P. A., & Schubert T. (2013). Effects of extensive dual-task practice on processing stages in simultaneous choice tasks. *Attention, Perception, & Psychophysics, 75*(5), 900–920.

Wang, Z., & Tchernev, J. (2012). The "Mith" of media multitasking: reciprocal dynamics of media multitasking, personal needs, and gratifications. *Journal of Communication. 62,* 493–513.

CHAPTER 10

USING THE VOICE OF TEEN YOUTUBE USERS FOR WEB 2.0 TECHNOLOGY-ENHANCED CLASSROOM TEACHING

Sun Hee Jang, Yang Yang, and John Williamson

ABSTRACT

Since Web 2.0 was launched, it has become ubiquitous and it is possible to observe teenagers' active involvement in a wide range of Web 2.0 sites. In the literature, (1) features of Web 2.0 and (2) characteristics of teenagers' learning styles particularly influenced by technology are often discussed to understand this social phenomenon. This chapter argues that the two aspects, (1) and (2), are inadequate for designing a Web 2.0 technology-enhanced learning environment which incorporates the authentic experiences of teenagers who have been actively participating in Web 2.0 sites such as YouTube. This chapter discusses data collected from a heterogeneous group of seven active teen YouTube users based on six common aspects of (1) and (2) identified in the literature. The findings have significant implications for Web 2.0 technology-enhanced classroom teaching as it prepares the newer Web generation for their futures. The chapter concludes by suggesting that educators

E-Learning and Social Media:
Education and Citizenship for the Digital 21st Century, pp. 199–220

need to adopt the six dimensions of accessibility, participation, connectivity, recognition and feedback, entertainment, and independency—as a checklist when they consider adopting a Web 2.0 tool or application in their teaching.

INTRODUCTION

It is commonly accepted that teenagers spend a considerable amount of their time on the Internet for information consumption, content creation, and social networking. An omnipresent use of technology in their daily life has suggested that 8 to 18 year olds in the U.S. spent over seven hours per day on average interacting with digital media, which has been a significant increase from 2004 to 2009 (Rideout, Foehr, & Roberts, 2010). A recent study conducted in 25 countries also revealed that over 60% of mid-teenagers used the Internet on a daily basis for a significant amount of time (Livingstone, Kirwil, Ponte, & Staksrud, 2013). Furthermore, a large number of teenagers create content online and are involved in different activities such as creating a blog or website and sharing many different types of their own created content with others online (Alvermann, 2008; Black, 2007).

There are a number of studies presenting young users' enthusiastic participation in content creation and social networking in online spaces. According to the exploration of the much-cited Pew Internet survey, 64% of online teenagers, ages from 12 to 17, have participated in one or more among a wide range of content-creating activities on the Internet, and 55% of youths, of the same age range in the United States, use an online social networking site (Lenhart & Madden, 2007). Correspondingly, in more recent years, a study carried out in the U.K. showed that 49% of those aged 8 to 17 who use the Internet have set up their own profile on a social networking site (Ofcom, 2008). Since these studies were conducted, the number of online teen users has rapidly increased and the range of ages has been expanding continually (Kupiainen, 2013).

In recent years, due to the fast development of the broadband service and web technologies, the use of the Internet and web technology has become more practicable and pervasive in teenagers' lives. It has largely taken place on the assumption that the advent of the second generation of web technology, commonly known as Web 2.0, has boosted teen participation in various online activities, which in turn results in a growing phenomenon of youth engagement with newly developed tools and applications associated with Web 2.0 (Fahser-Herro & Stienkuehler, 2009; Ito et al., 2010 Kupiainen, 2013). Taking into consideration the enthusiasm, passion, and willingness that young people are widely presenting in popular online spaces, education researchers have begun to document the educational values from teen experiences of being involved in the web spaces.

As seen in the teenagers' growing engagement with online activities in various Web 2.0 environments, especially outside schooling, educators have concluded that pedagogy needs to consider adopting Web 2.0 tools to prepare teenagers to be active multimodal authors and participants in such a digital world (Jenkins, 2006). The promise underlying the conclusion that "today, the ability to navigate social networks, play games, or participate in online conversations affects the way young people present themselves to the world. There's an informal learning that takes place as they interact with digital media, which gives way to certain skills, competencies, and literacies" (Jenkins, 2008, para. 4). On the other hand, there is a distinctive new generation of students in possession of sophisticated technology skills with learning preferences for which education is not equipped to support, and this has excited much recent attention (Kennedy et al., 2007). Thus, it is important to understand how the younger generation uses the relatively new web technologies and what they expect of the new technologies being used in the classroom for their learning, otherwise teachers are unlikely to change the situation where the classroom teaching is disconnected from engaging with the new generation of students and their culture (Berk, 2009).

In the literature, three main factors for effective teaching practice have been commonly pointed out when educators consider adopting Web 2.0 in classroom teaching and learning. These are (1) the availability of Web 2.0 making best use of its identified advantages and benefits of Web 2.0 applications; (2) the characteristics of a new Web generation and learning styles; and (3) the students' experiences of being involved in various activities on Web 2.0 technologies, outside mainstream schooling/in daily life. The first two aspects increasingly have been well documented at different education levels in different study areas, but the latter relating to students' authentic learning experiences of being involved in a Web 2.0 environment has not been fully considered (Bennett, 2012; Bennett, Maton, & Kervin, 2008). Thus, there has not been much reported about the ways teenagers socialize, create, and share multimedia contents in Web 2.0 settings, particularly YouTube, albeit the increase of their participation is clearly known.

In this chapter, a group of seven YouTube users, all under 18 years of age, provide their authentic experience of participating in various activities on YouTube, supporting YouTube as one of the most popular Web 2.0 applications. The seven YouTube users come from countries including the United States, Norway, Slovenia, and Singapore. This was a small qualitative study involving interviews with an opportunity sample of teen users who had uploaded a considerable amount of video onto YouTube. While there has been research investigating youth participation on YouTube, few studies taking the three factors above into consideration have focused on teen "active" YouTube users for an in-depth analysis of their participation. As a result, the three factors above are closely intertwined and therefore are discussed insofar as they relate to what classroom teachers may consider in an attempt to incorporate Web 2.0 applications in teaching to enhance students' learning.

It is anticipated that this study, while limited in scope, provides some implications for teaching practice in relation to the features of Web 2.0 that attract teenagers and how the features of Web 2.0 and teenagers' experiences of Web 2.0 gained outside the school can be of benefit to their learning in school.

AIMS OF THE STUDY

The attention from educators has resulted in a question of how a Web 2.0 tool should be used in the classroom setting. This study aims to address the question of what classroom teachers may need to consider when they attempt to adopt a Web 2.0 tool in their classroom.

The chapter applies the findings of a small empirical research study to design a pedagogical approach, by employing a Web 2.0 tool as an instructional technology to utilise students' experience gained *outside* school to contribute to their learning *in* school.

LITERATURE REVIEW

Web 2.0

The term Web 2.0 was originally coined by O'Reilly (2005) as a turning point for the development of Web technology, to define Web 2.0 as "seductively simple, invoking the now-familiar rhetoric of computer software versions" (Allen, 2009, p. 1). In contrast to Web 1.0 designed sites, a number of Web 2.0 tools and applications have offered significantly different opportunities and practices to their users, which results in a widespread participation in contemporary global discourse in return. Considering the new direction of web technology, the social phenomenon emerging from Web 2.0, Kidd (2012) notes that Web 2.0 itself is "the growth of users, the increased interconnected interactivity of new Internet tools and the affordability and availability of broadband 'always-on' Internet connections" (p. 53).

THE USE OF GENERATION LABELS

A number of scholars have used different labels to distinguish children or young people, who are technologically literate and engaged, from other generations. These labels include "digital natives," "Net Generation," "electronic generation," "Generation C," "Generation M," "Google YouTube-eyed generation," "the Google generation," "YouTube Google-eyed generation," and many others. These terms are commonly defined by birth year with the use of technology in terms of frequency, brand, or type. Table 10.1 presents a summary of these terms.

Table 10.1. The Use of Generation Labels

Term	*Birth Year*	*Definition*
Digital Natives (Prensky, 2001)	Born since 1980s	Digital natives are innately confident in using new technologies as they are born and have grown up in the era of technology.
Electronic Generation (Buckingham, 2002)	Linked to the age group of Net Generation	The term electronic generation appears in a discussion about the impact of new media on children's lives and its results in changes in childhood and the media environment.
Generation C (content) (Trendwatching.com, 2005)	No age range defined	Generation C refers to the people who create and share content on the Internet.
Generation M (media) (Roberts, Foehr & Rideout, 2005)	Between the early 1980s and late 1990s	Since a study named *Generation M: Media in the Lives of 8-18 Year-Olds* conducted from October, 2003 to March, 2004 by the Kaiser Family Foundation, the term Generation M is used to address "media-savvy, multitasking" young people (Vie, 2008)
Homo Zappiens (Veen & Vrakking, 2006)	Linked to the age group of Net Generation	Homo Zappiens was coined to represent a set of common behaviors and attitudes of a generation born with technology devices and tools.
Net Generation (Tapscott, 2009)	Born from 1977 to 1997	The Net Generation are the boomers' children who have grown up immersed in digital technology.
The Google generation (Rowlands, Nicholas, Williams, Huntington, Fieldhouse, Gunter, Withney, Jamali, Dobrowolski, & Tenopir, 2008).	Born after 1993	Google generation refers to the most Web literate. The Google generation refers to children and young people growing up in a world driven by the Internet. Thus, they search information about anything on the Internet.
YouTube Google-eyed generation (Duffy, 2008) Google-eyed YouTube generation (Ashraf, 2009)	Emphasized on students at higher education, but no specific age group defined	YouTube Google-eyed generation and Google-eyed YouTube generation were used to discuss students who demand Web 2.0 environments like YouTube or Google for their learning.

In the literature, although the term "digital natives" is most commonly used and adopted by others, it has caused considerable controversy and criticism by others (Bennett, 2012; Bennett, Maton, & Kervin, 2008; Berk, 2009; Jenkins; 2007). Based on findings from studies conducted in several universities in Australia, a group of education researchers argue that the label "digital natives" presents Prensky's "weak empirical and theoretical foundations" (Bennett, Maton, & Kervin, 2008, p. 777). The term seems inappropriate to characterize young people in general as there is a great variety in their technology use, and diversity in their skills, knowledge, and interests in technology (Ashraf, 2009; Berk, 2009; Jenkins, 2007; Selwyn, 2009). Whereas, Palfrey, and Gasser (2008) claim in their book entitled *The First Generation of Digital Natives* that the term "generation" is overly simplified in describing today's young people and instead suggest the word "population" in use to describe those young people who are heavily engaged with technology in daily life. Nevertheless, it is not deniable that Prensky's claim about "digital natives" has alerted educators to realize the fundamental gap between non-digital teaching approaches and digital learning styles as well as the hidden tension between challenges in formal teaching and changes in informal learning.

According to the age group set for these generation labels organized in Table 10.1, the shared characteristics and learning styles among them can be applied to teenagers. The commonly held assumption is that these generations could not be isolated from technology in that they are born or grown up with technology as part of their life experiences (Duffy, 2008). Thus, the impact of the technology on their daily life has significantly changed their learning styles making them fundamentally different from previous generations, and this needs to be taken into account when proceeding into research areas where these new web generations apply (Berk, 2009; Hawkins & Oblinger, 2006).

TEENAGERS AND WEB 2.0

There is a claim that teenagers have their distinguishing characteristics of learning from previous generations and their implications for education while Web 2.0 has its distinctive features and services different from Web 1.0. Table 10.2 presents a comparison of characteristics of the new generation and Web 2.0 specifically for instructional use:

Common features that either Web 2.0 has developed with its unique functions for users' usage or the new web generation has identified and amplified in learning practices brought about by the use of Web 2.0 and its applications. The review of sharing features provides theoretical evidence of what have been found as the affordances of Web 2.0 as well as what characteristics and learning styles have been identified as the new web generation in terms of the consideration pedagogical implications for incorporating Web 2.0 into instructional learning environments. The understanding of common features shared by the literature also provides a basis for the inclusion of empirical learners' experiences of which activities on Web 2.0 technology outside schooling contribute to their learning (see Figure 10.1).

Table 10.2. A Comparison of Characteristics of the New Generation and Web 2.0 Specifically For Instructional Use

Features	*Teenagers (A Newer Web Generation)*	*Web 2.0*
Accessibility	Expectations on ease or free access to information at any time (Abram & Luther, 2004; Berk, 2009, Hawkins & Oblinger, 2006). Efficient web searching (Rowlands et al., 2007).	Easy and multi-data access (Ashraf, 2009; Murugesan, 2007). Easy access to knowledge generation (O'Reilly, 2005).
Connectivity	Social in nature (Veen & Vrakking, 2006). A high priority on social relationships in both online and offline (Berk, 2008; Junco & Mastrodicasa, 2007; Strauss & Howe, 2006). Need to feel constantly connected to the Internet (Rowlands et al., 2008).	Peer-social interaction in a flattened hierarchy (Pauwels & Hellriegel, 2009). Broaden local and global connectivity (Crook, 2008). Interest-based social connection (O'Reilly, 2005).
Entertainment	Highly engaged with entertainment-oriented activities (Rowlands et al., 2008). Prefer to learn in entertaining ways (Ivanova & Ivanova, 2009). Mixing play and work: Play is work and work is seen as achievement, winning, and beating others (Berk, 2009).	Playful places (Selwyn, 2008). Can be a tool for entertainment.
Independency	Independent learning style (Prensky, 2006; 2008). Forming their own world and lifestyle in their own ways (Alsop, 2008).	Support independent leaning through first-person learning experience (Ashef, 2008).
Participatory	Seeking the opportunity to express their opinions and ideas (Berk, 2009). Prefer They prefer to work in teams rather than alone. (Berk, 2009).	Civic participatory (O'Reilly, 2005). Multiple ways of participation (O'Reilly, 2005).
Recognition/ Feedback	The pursue of recognition for their efforts and achievements (Berk, 2009).	Rich/efficient responsive user interface (Murugesan, 2007). Provide experiences of having attention (Ashef, 2009).

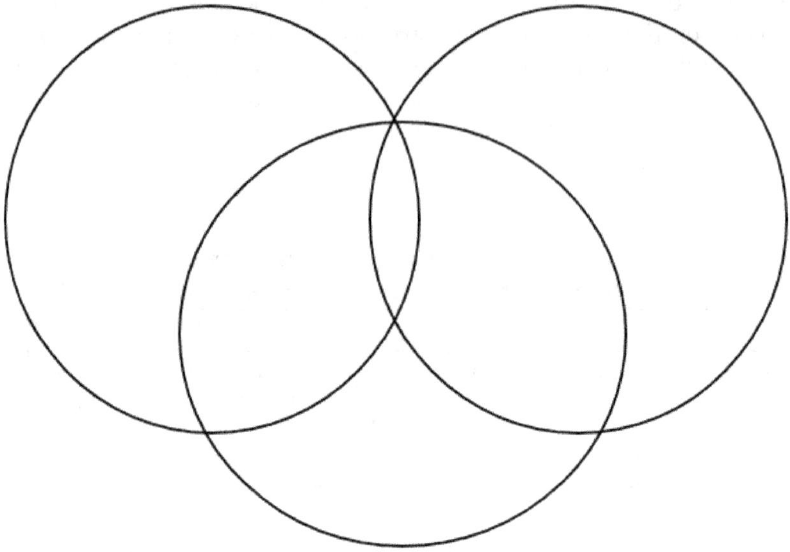

Figure 10.1. An integration of three factors: Web 2.0, new Web generation and the generation's experiences outside schooling.

SAMPLE

In order to achieve the research aim and to explore students' experience gained *outside* school which might contribute to their learning *in* school, a multiple-case study of a selection of YouTube teenagers who were actively engaged in related online activities was conducted. The sample selection rationale was based upon the fact that it is not possible to randomly sample all the population of teenagers on YouTube since social engagement on YouTube is very much dynamic, with numerous teenagers joining as new users every day. Theoretical sampling, based on a grounded theory approach (Corbin & Strauss, 1998) was used to select participants in the present study. The criterion of relevance was that the participants should be active, engaged participants of YouTube and that they have their own personal channels as well as a wealth of ongoing video products uploaded to maintain their regular social participation. It is reported more than 1 billion unique users visit YouTube each month, 100 hours of video are uploaded to YouTube every minute (YouTube, 2014). Therefore, those who are teenagers with their own channels and video products are active social participants on YouTube and, most importantly, were willing to participate in the present study are only the smallest tip of the user iceberg. The sampling process was continued until the criterion of "theoretical saturation" was satisfied (Strauss & Corbin, 1998). This chapter reports seven cases as examples of thin "slices of data" from the present study to address the research question. While these seven cases were selected from youth aged between 11–17 years from different countries, the aim was to understand the "societal significance" of these multi-cases and not to provide a "statistical significance" and to generalize from them, but help understand this phenomena. The details of the three female and four male youth are shown in Table 10.3.

Table 10.3 Participants' Descriptive Statistics

Participant	*Gender*	*Age in 2011*	*Joined Date*	*Nationality*
Adam	M	11	Oct. 26, 2008	Slovenia
Brandon	M	11	Sept. 28, 2006	United States
Byrd	F	14	Nov. 25, 2009	United States
Celena	F	16	Feb. 2, 2010	Singapore
Earth	F	14	May 22, 2007	United States
Frasilia	M	14	Jan. 21, 2009	Norway
Key	M	17	June 14, 2008	United States

All of the participants had an ongoing active participation in video creation and sharing social activities on a well-known site of Web 2.0, YouTube, for more than three years. Most of them became YouTube members before turning 13 years of age and it simply required them to join YouTube by opening a free e-mail account. Although YouTube is officially designed for people aged over 13 with parental supervision or over 18 without it, children and teenagers increasingly are becoming YouTube account holders. An easier access from mobile devices to YouTube has also boosted their involvement in YouTube (YouTube, 2014).

DATA COLLECTION

Each participant was recruited by a YouTube video specifically designed for this study as an online ethnographic research methods process through an uploaded video on YouTube, which matched with established criteria. The interviews were subsequently carried out online after permission was granted by the University's Ethics Committee to use their online materials for research purposes. This chapter reports data collected from interviews which were scheduled to fit participants' availability.

Most participants chose asynchronous communication tools: for example, Adam from Slovenia, Bryd (United States), Celena (Singapore), and Earth (United States) were interviewed using instant messaging (IM), an internal communication function supported by YouTube; Henry and Key (United States) were interviewed by e-mail; Brandon (United States) was interviewed by a video; and Frasilia (Norway) chose Skype to answer interview questions synchronously.

DATA ANALYSIS

All the data were analyzed utilizing constructivist grounded theory (Charmaz, 2003, 2006) which involved an inductive data analysis approach to themantic analysis (Grbich, 2007; Sarantakos, 2005; Strauss & Corbin, 1998). With respect to the grounded theory, interview data were organized as themes without the intent of providing formal codes and themes. The generated themes were further systematically summarized by revisiting the main ideas situated in the participants' responses. As the final step of coding processes, relationships between themes, complexity, and associations emerging from a set of the themes were taken into consideration to address the aim of the study (Sliverman, 2005). Thus, only dominant themes were included in the findings section below, and the participants seem to concern more than other issues in relation to the research aim.

FINDINGS

The participants reported that they are participating in YouTube not only because of the web brand or YouTube's popularity, but also the opportunities that YouTube offered them. Although they started on YouTube with different personal interests, reasons, and purposes at a different time, they reported that YouTube offered valuable learning opportunities and meaningful social interaction experiences to a higher, deeper degree of involvement. The following findings are based on the six themes identified in Table 10.2.

TECHNOLOGICAL ACCESSIBILITY

Several participants reported that they access YouTube on a daily or regular basis, although they do not often make and upload videos on YouTube. With easy access to YouTube from their mobile phone, they are able to check their message inbox on YouTube, views of their uploaded videos, new subscribers, or others' new videos especially uploaded by their favorite YouTube users, even at school. Most participants are able to access the YouTube site from their school or school computer; they also able to use their own mobile device to access web resources. Adam summarized how they achieved accessibility: "Well we have free Wi-Fi in school so I can access YouTube over my phone but sometimes I can do it over the schools PCs" (Adam—11 years)."

The interview data suggested that technological accessibility provides opportunity for the participants to be exposed to new technologies and to be highly motivated to learn and use diverse technology tools and devices, multimedia resources, and Web 2.0 applications such as YouTube. All participants reported that they did not know how to make and upload videos on the Internet before they became YouTube members. Although interest, knowledge, and skills in technology varied from one participant to another, all of them had to learn about making videos and uploading them through the accessibility of different multimedia devices such as smartphones, computers, laptops, tablets, and camera devices. The following interview excerpts exemplify this: "I usually use Facebook, Twitter, Skype, and YouTube to communicate with my friends online [rather than other methods]"(Frasilia—14 years) and "You find inspirations from other videos. You've always watching videos which is the best part out of it. You are always creating, editing, talking on ... Twitter and Facebook, social media ... I am always creating, editing, talking online" (Brandon—11 years).

Of particular interest was that learning had taken place through the technological accessibility. Key had uploaded more than 300 videos on a weekly basis since he joined YouTube in 2007, but he goes on YouTube every day: "I spend a lot of time on the site and checking out everything is has to offer. I check it every day for comments and new videos from others to learn new things." It is not only text-based learning, but also audio-visualized information, such as video clips that teenagers use for their learning. In addition, the study found a high volume of Google search engine use for information seeking from the participants. Since Google started providing YouTube videos as part, especially on the first page, of search results, and since people uploaded How-to-style videos of any topic on YouTube, participants have found that it is relatively easy to find and learn things from YouTube videos. In Adam's case: "It was 2006 when I first found YouTube. When I had some problems on my PC, I googled the problem and that's how I found a video on YouTube. I went YouTube and it was just epic, so I stayed." At that time Adam from Slovenia was only six years old. As shown in Table 10.1, most participants joined and became part of web culture before they turned 9 or 10.

Connectivity and Participation

The interview participants reported that on YouTube the subscriber plays an important role for them to keep up their video sharing activity, suggesting a sense of connectivity, which in turn, sustains their participatory learning, as exemplified in the following quote: "I have a lot of people making videos on the YouTube community who I have met through YouTube ... I do communicate with them by text and email. I contact people on YouTube even though I haven't met them face to face" (Brandon—11 years).

This suggests that the video creator provides a video as the pivotal communication mechanism on YouTube which potentially turns into the foundation of social networking between the video creator and the audience, while the subscriber initiates a form of social networking by returning a positive recognition of the video content to the video creator. Although participants have developed close social relationships with only a small number of subscribers, the meaning of subscriber unquestionably refers to a positive return on their performance in video production.

Although YouTube is not technically counted in the group of social networking sites, it clearly has a strong social networking phenomenon. Participants in this study, for example, Brandon, Key, Frasilia, and Celena, asserted that they usually upload a video once a week, fortnight, or month. Common repeated reasons were that weekly-based video posting helped them get their audience on-side and build their own social network. For Frasilia, interest-based social connection might expand to his future career: "I want to be a movie director or video maker because I really enjoy making videos. I make videos on YouTube because I want to get into the film industry, it is easy for me to contact people involved in that field."

While participants were geographically separated, they reported that YouTube had been a community bringing people together to share their different interests. Brandon described the function YouTube served:

> All sorts of different communities come together. We all come together to be one thing. We all share our talents to the world, so people can see. That's what YouTuber is made for. Talents we made and found are shared on YouTube ... I really think YouTube has brought a lot of people together. It makes people more aware of stuff. YouTubers in the community are really awesome. Not one, two, three, four, five people are doing things. More people create things, doing things what people like. Making music, meeting each other. You know people usually wouldn't be together. This is really what YouTube is about as a community. I think everyone's interest in building a community, but nobody is the same. Community is really big part of YouTube. That's true. (Brandon—11 years)

The findings suggested that social connections were built among YouTube users through shared videos, which did not foreground the personal factors such as social class, demographic background, and geographic boundary.

Entertainment: A Fun Way of Learning Things

Most participants search and watch videos related to their interests or video categories for which they make videos. They engaged with YouTube as an entertainment-oriented practice, which further made them obsessive with YouTube. When asked why they enjoyed the experience of involving with YouTube, one participated commented: "I have learned a lot of stuff, since I became a YouTube user, YouTube is my No. 1 entertainment on the Internet" (Adam—11 years).

Participants from this study also reported enjoyment and a sense of satisfaction with YouTube. Being able to share their products to the wider audience was the most significant aspect for them. Being listened to and then subscribed to by an external anonymous audience indicates that they enjoyed the opportunities that YouTube provided and their relevant practices. For example, one participant reported: "Whenever I have a bad day, I read comments saying how people enjoy watching my videos, which makes me really happy. Knowing over 3000 people watching my video and subscribing to me is really really grateful" (Celena).

Another important finding suggested that those who upload how-to or tutorial videos were those who watch videos to gather ideas, gain knowledge on a chosen topic, and to improve their video making and editing skills for their next videos. For example:

> Usually for my tech. videos I learn how to use the things by myself. There are some instances, especially with windows movie maker that I have learned by watching YouTube videos though. This has helped me make my videos better and more professional over the years which have helped my channel grow. YouTube can also help with basic online skills since there is such a large community and many video makers.

This implies a learning ecology system on YouTube as video creators learn from videos made by others and, in turn, to teach others through videos. Participants, especially from non-native English speaking countries such as Norway and Slovenia, search and watch videos to look for words to use or to improve their expression in English in their next videos. "I could actually think of what to say before I say it, so it gets better. But I often notice on post-production on a video, that I could have used some other words some places in a video" (Frasilia).

Independency: Web 2.0 Technology-Enhanced Independent Learning Behavior

Participants reported that they have independently learned effective video making and editing techniques and strategies deployed by others through watching others' videos, and they have applied these techniques and strategies to their video making and editing practices. As a result, the ease of access to use various online resources and tools serves teenagers also as a way to learn independently. When asked to articulate the most important independent learning experience they felt using YouTube, one participant reported:

> It is kind of a swimming pool thing. You have to throw yourself in. Because you never gonna learn from somebody. You go so quickly once you have learnt it by yourself. Like what is subscribe thing? You just click it and learn how it works. You've actually cannot show YouTube to someone. You actually kinda pushed in. like you push people in the pool. To teach how to swim, the teacher pushes us.

Instead of looking for someone else, learning happened through self-exploration and by self-engagement. The findings also suggested that learning-by-necessity or in-time learning are the keys for the participants to be active learners rather than passive recipients. Being able to be independent learners also developed their understanding of the ways they prepare themselves for their future career paths. This was confirmed by one of the participants, commenting that:

> YouTube has made me find out what I want to do in my life and the future. I want to make videos on YouTube, and also become a director. That is probably my biggest dream, and because of YouTube, I have seen and found out that there are a lot of directors that get big through YouTube. They start off with making films for YouTube, in which they actually have a budget on, and then people get to know who they are. YouTube has made me realize that I want to do that as well.

Content-Based Attention, Recognition and Feedback

On YouTube, the subscriber plays an important role for teenagers to keep up their video sharing activity. Henry reported that "I like YouTube. I love YouTube. I upload videos and check how many views I have got." Participants also expressed that YouTube provided the opportunity that allowed their voice to be heard. This is evidenced by one of the participants who reported that: "Basically, I joined YouTube because I wanted my voice heard. I wanted to have a place where I can sing and get some feedback. And I found YouTube was the only place for me" (Earth).

In their reports, there is a significant difference in the meaning of the term "subscriber," ranging from someone with whom the participants already have contact to others whom the participants do not know at all. Participants reported that having family, relatives, and friends as their YouTube subscribers means care, support, and encouragement which they have whether or not they make videos, whereas having people whom they never met before, especially from outside their countries, subscribe to them means that their videos are evaluated, and gives them an oportunity to receive positive feedback based on the video content and quality, which in turn enhances their confidence in making and sharing videos with a wider audience. The following quotes illustrate how the anonymous audience is important to them: "It is always exciting to go a little bit outside my comfort-zone, and see what happens ;) Putting videos on YouTube is about really putting yourself out there" (Frasilia) and "The guy actually came up and he subscribed my videos. So I was like this guy is subscribing my video, so I probably make a lesson for this" (Key).

It can be understood that the relationship between the video creator and the unknown subscriber is based on interest shared between them through videos. Most importantly, their self-improving skills through their learning experiences were increased. The following comment demonstrates this:

> I feel like I have awesome attention personally. It's great. I have got thousands of views on my videos ... it's all depends on what people like. That's how you learn what kind of videos people like to watch from you.... It is a thing to help you learn what people like and what people don't like.... To be a successful person in anything even in the film making industry, you have to learn what people like what people don't.

Most participants also reported that it was the supportive and encouraging comments from the wider audience that made them to be engaged on YouTube. They expressed that they are highly motivated and encouraged to post videos when the number of their subscribers grow.

> I make them to see how people respond to them. I do post videos to wait for people to commend on them ... when someone watches my video and say "Thank you!", that is touching! It really is, because the thought of that actually someone out there, in this big world, has actually seen my videos is so cool! Talking to someone who I've never met, but wants to support me is also so COOL! (Frasilia)

There are always some negative comments on YouTube. However, most participants reported that they are motivated by the positive comments to learn and to improve their videos rather than giving up when confronted with the negative comments. Participants reported that, for example: "The emotional support from certain people always can get me away from the negatives that people talk about on my videos about me" (Key) and "You might get motivation you need to keep on building. People should not give up because their video only gets 20 or 30 views. Eventually people will find you" (Frasilia).

DISCUSSION

In this chapter, there are some important findings reported that suggest YouTube is the core Web 2.0 technology utilised by many in the younger generation. It explores their experiences in learning outside school and suggests six themes which proposes a view of the implementation of Web 2.0 technology in a school' learning and teaching. The themes are: (1) accessibility, (2) connectivity, (3) entertainment, (4) independency, (5) participation, and (6) recognition and feedback. There is a fundamental difference between formal learning spaces and Web 2.0 environments such as YouTube from a spatial perspective. Undoubtedly the opportunities and experiences teenagers have through their engagement within their virtual spaces can be significantly different from physical spaces.

The data suggest a continuation of current trends in the school sector will mean more student disengagement and, perhaps, a tipping point will be reached where students are not challenged or engaged by traditional curricula or pedagogy. Notwithstanding the use of emerging new technologies in schools, there is little focus upon the transformation of students' learning experiences gained outside classroom and how it may be brought into mainstream school education. Participants in this study clearly reported their outside-school experience of being involved in YouTube as demonstrating quality learning, which needs to be brought into classroom teaching and explored for its learning implications (Bennett, 2012; Berk, 2009).

Educators will have questions as to how a Web 2.0 enhanced learning environment may be achieved in a traditional classroom considering the fundamental differences in structure and setting. The data suggest the need to understand that the classroom setting does not necessarily need to change or be replaced with a Web space, and of course, it is not recommended to take the entire YouTube site into classroom teaching and learning. Educators will need to identify what Web 2.0 environment is appropriate and available for them and students at their school; for example, it might be a photo sharing site (Davies, 2006), an online fiction site (Black, 2007), or an online game domain (Gee & Hayes, 2011). Any of these could potentially trigger a technologically-based effective learning environment and maximise learning outcomes. The data suggests teen YouTube users do not expect their teachers to 'hang out' with them in the same virtual domain, especially outside schooling. Participants did, however, agree that their teachers need to understand the reasons why they like YouTube, and particularly what YouTube offers them as users.

Educators may adopt the six themes in Table 10.2 as a simple checklist to ensure an effective instructional link with an enhanced Web 2.0 learning environment. In doing so, the checklist must not be seen as being simply binary and prescriptive, but they must use it as appropriate in their contexts. The six themes shown in Table 10.2 can be considered as a sequence so that accessibility needs to be considered as an important starting point of creating a Web 2.0 learning environment. The meaning of accessibility here in this study includes (1) access to information including content shared by their teachers as well as themselves both in-school and outside-school time and (2) access to content generation and sharing. In these stages, educators need to encourage the students to be active in using, creating, and sharing materials and to explain the importance of sharing materials as a holistic learning process. The data show the participant teenagers independently used various online resources, and they were often confronted with the problems of information overloaded on the Internet and a heavy reliance on a speed of collecting information (Berk, 2009; Prensky, 2006). Educators need to provide sufficient supervision and explicit direction to enhance students' research processes and skills of information gathering and to develop their critical skill in evaluating their findings.

The study also suggests that when learners use information, educators need to ensure that the information utilized is also part of their content generation activity; and when learners contribute to content generation and sharing, they need to realize that their contribution matters for them and others (Jenkins, Clinton, Purushotma, Robison, & Weigel, 2006), regardless of the quality of content and the quantity of sharing. If these two types of access are provided in conjunction with the self-directed learning-by-necessity (Carr et al., 2007, as cited in Selwyn, 2007) to learners, it leads to active participation which creates self-directed linkage between learners and between content. In the participatory process as reported in this study, it was important that educators allow the learners to participate impartially between "new to experienced, novice to expert, unskilled to highly skilled, minorly interested to addicted, and everything in-between" (Gee, 2007a, p. 20). This impartial participation ultimately may result in creating interest-based or content-based online communities and, consequently, boost intellectual convergence (O'Reilly, 2005; Jenkins, 2006).

Recognition and feedback contribute to a richer and more fruitful learning process, and they need to be visible in the classroom. They can be defined in numerous ways; for instance, recognition includes acknowledgement of students' work and their learning attitudes such as sharing knowledge, ideas, and skills. Feedback from teachers and peers is not necessarily in textual format but may be in more audio and visual-based interaction that they may be more familiar with if possible. In addition, it is important that learners are able to receive both positive and negative feedback from others. The data confirm that participants learn and engage in problem solving when they are given both positive and negative feedback on their work. They reported they seek improvement when they are emotionally supported and cognitively stimulated. More specifically, the study suggests that educators play an important role during the feedback stage of learning, as learners need to be guided on how to provide both companionable and critical feedback to others concerning their work in order to help them improve their learning as well as to encourage them to continue being an active learner. When learners experience accessibility, participation, connectivity, and recognition and feedback of the new technological milieu in which they validate with their own ideas emerging from their self-motivation, a valuable social learning aspect for education could be extended beyond classroom boundaries and the constraints of the current school system. As Gee (2004) argued, "people learn best when their learning is part of a highly motivated engagement with social practices which they value" (p. 70), the Web 2.0 enhanced learning environment can offer a meaningful 'participatory culture' (Jenkins et al., 2006) and provides a distinctive learning ecology and context.

While bounded by limited classroom space and the provision of education services, the data suggests the Web 2.0 enhanced learning environment allows access to the unlimited virtual spaces. This conclusion has a major implication for educators and their need to enhance their understanding of what learning means in this new environment.

CONCLUSION

This chapter has discussed three key aspects for creating a Web 2.0 learning environment in a formal learning setting. These are (1) affordances of Web 2.0; (2) the characteristics of teenagers and their learning styles; and (3) teenagers' experiences of being involved in YouTube from sociocultural and technological perspectives. Six themes—accessibility, participation, connectivity, recognition and feedback, entertainment, and independency —identified from both (1) and (2) were examined to understand how a group of seven teen YouTube users participate in utilizing information, creating and sharing their own generated contents and building social relationships with a wider audience. This chapter has summarized findings from interview data and provided evidence of learning practices in their active involvement in YouTube. It has further suggested that when educators consider providing a Web 2.0 enhanced learning environment to their students, they might adopt the six themes as a checklist in sequence as these themes are closely interrelated to each other.

Although the minority of teenagers are actively participating in sharing their own generated contents on YouTube and many other Web 2.0 sites and the majority of teenagers are simply consuming online information and watching videos on YouTube, the small portion of teenagers on YouTube might be achieving the aim of 21st century learning, that is, to be active in linguistic and cultural diversity in private, public, and work places (New London Group, 1996), and to be an active author who is able to create meanings with different resources for different social purposes (Gee, 2007 b).

REFERENCES

Abram, S., & Luther, J. (2004). Born with the chip: The next generation will profoundly impact both library service and the culture within the profession. *Library Journal, 129*, 34–37.

Allen, M. (2009). Tim O'Reilly and Web 2.0: The economics of memetic liberty and control. *Communication, Politics & Culture, 42*(2), 6.

Alsop, R. (2008). *The trophy kids grow up: How the millennial generation is shaking up the the workplace*. San Francisco, CA: Jossey-Bass.

Alvermann, D. E. (2008). Why bother theorizing adolescents' online literacies for classroom practice and research? *Journal of Adolescent & Adult Literacy, 52*(1), 8–19. doi:10.1598/jaal.52.1.2

Ashraf, B. (2009). Teaching the Google-eyed YouTube generation. *Education + Training, 51*(5/6), 343–352. doi:10.1108/00400910910987165

Bennett, S. (2012). Digital natives. In Z. Yan (Ed.), *Encyclopedia of cyber behavior*. Hershey PA: IGI Global.

Bennett, S., Maton, K., & Kervin, L. (2008). The "digital natives" debate: A critical review of the evidence. *British Journal of Educational Technology, 39*(5), 775–786.

Berk, R. A. (2009). Teaching strategies for the net generation. *Transformative Dialogues: Teaching & Learning Journal, 3*(2), 1–24.

Black, R. W. (2007). Fanfiction writing and the construction of space. *E-Learning, 4*(4), 384. doi:10.2304/elea.2007.4.4.384

Buckingham, D. (2002). The electronic generation? Children and new media. *The Handbook of New Media*, 77–89.

Charmaz, K. (2003). Grounded theory: Objectivist and constructivist methods. In N. K. Denzin & Y. S. Lincoln (Eds.), Strategies of qualitative inquiry (2nd ed.) (pp. 249–291). Thousand Oaks, CA: Sage.

Charmaz, K. (2006). *Constructing grounded theory: A practical guide through qualitative analysis.* London, UK: SAGE.

Crook, C. (2008). *Web 2.0 technologies for learning: The current landscape-opportunities, challenges and tensions.* Manchester, UK: Manchester Metropolitan University.

Davies, J. (2006). Affinities and beyond! Developing ways of seeing in online spaces. *E-Learning and Digital Media, 3*(2), 217–234.

Duffy, P. (2008). Engaging the YouTube Google-eyed generation: Strategies for using web 2.0 in teaching and learning. *The Electronic Journal of e-Learning, 6*(2), 119–130.

Fahser-Herro, D., & Stienkuehler, C. (2009). Web 2.0 literacy and secondary teacher education. *Journal of Computing in Teacher Education, 26*(2), 55–62.

Gee, J. P. (2004). *Situated language and learning: a critique of traditional schooling*. New York, NY: London, UK: Routledge.

Gee, J. P. (2007a). *Social linguistics and literacies: Ideology in discourses*. New York, NY: Routledge.

Gee, J. P. (2007b). Affinity Spaces: from age of mythology to today's schools. Retrieved from http://www.jamespaulgee.com/sites/default/files/pub/AffinitySpaces.pdf

Gee, J. P., & Hayes, E. (2011). Nurturing affinity spaces and game-based learning. *Cadernos de Letras* (UFRJ), 28.

Grbich, C. (2007). *Qualitative data analysis: An introduction.* London, UK: SAGE.

Hawkins, B., & Oblinger, D. (2006, July/August). The myth about the digital divide. *EDUCAUSE Review, 41*(4), 12–13. Retrieved from http://www.educause.edu/ir/library/pdf/erm0647.pdf

Ito, M., Baumer, S., Bittanti, M., Boyd, D., Cody, R., Herr-Stephenson, R., ... & Tripp, L. (2010). Hanging out, messing around, and geeking out: Kids living and learning with new media. Chicago, IL: The John D. and Catherine T. MacArthur Foundation Series on Digital Media and Learning.

Ivanova, A., & Ivanova, G. (2009, June). Net-generation learning style: a challenge for higher education. In *Proceedings of the International Conference on Computer Systems and Technologies and Workshop for PhD Students in Computing* (p. 72). ACM.

Jenkins, H. (2006). *Convergence culture: Where old and new media collide*. New York, NY: New York University Press.

Jenkins, H. (2007). Reconsidering digital immigrants. Retrieved from http://www.henryjenkins.org/2007/12/reconsidering_digital_immigran.html

Jenkins, H. (2008). The participation gap. Retrieved from http://www.nea.org/home/15468.htm

Jenkins, H., Clinton, K., Purushotma, R., Robison, A. J., & Weigel, M. (2006). *Confronting the challenges of participatory culture: Media education for the 21st century.* Chicago, IL: MacArthur Foundation.

Junco, R., & Mastrodicasa, J. (2007). *Connecting to the net.generation: What higher education professionals need to know about today's students.* Washington, DC: Student Affairs Administrators in Higher Education (NASPA).

Kennedy, G., Dalgarno, B., Gray, K., Judd, T., Waycott, J., Bennett, S., & Churchward, A. (2007). The net generation are not big users of Web 2.0 technologies: Preliminary findings. ICT: Providing choices for learners and learning. *Proceedings ascilite Singapore*, 517-525.

Kidd, W. (2012). Utilising podcasts for learning and teaching: a review and ways forward for e-Learning cultures. *Management in Education, 26*(2), 52–57. doi:10.1177/0892020612438031

Kupiainen, R. (2013). *Media and digital literacies in secondary school.* New York, NY: Peter Lang.

Lenhart, A., & Madden, M. (2007). Teens, privacy, and online social networks: How teens manage their online identities and personal information in the age of MySpace? Pew Internet and American Life Project. Retrieved from http://www.pewinternet.org/PPF/r/211/report_display.asp

Livingstone, S., Kirwil, L., Ponte, C., & Staksrud, E. (2013). Risks and safety on the internet: The perspective of European children. Retrieved from www.eukidsonline.net website: http://www2.lse.ac.uk/media@lse/research/EUKidsOnline/EU%20Kids%20II%20(2009-11)/EUKidsOnlineIIReports/D4FullFindings.pdf

Murugesan, S. (2007). Understanding Web 2.0. *IT Professional, 9*(4), 34–41.

New London Group. (1996). A pedagogy of multiliteracies: Designing social futures. *Harvard Educational Review, 66*(1), 60–92.

Ofcom. (2008). Social networking: a quantitative and qualitative research report into attitudes, behaviours and use. Retrieved from http://news.bbc.co.uk/2/shared/bsp/hi/pdfs/02_04_08_ofcom.pdf

O'Reilly, T. (2005). What Is Web 2.0 design patterns and business models for the next generation of software. Retrieved from http://www.oreillynet.com/pub/a/oreilly/tim/news/2005/09/30/what-is-web-20.html

Palfrey, J., & Gasser, U. (2008). *Born digital: Understanding the first generation of digital natives*. New York, NY: Basic Books.

Pauwels, L., & Hellriegel, P. (2009). Strategic and tactical uses of Internet design and infrastructure: The case of YouTube. *Journal of Visual Literacy, 28*(1), 51–69.

Prensky, M. (2001). Digital natives, digital immigrants Part 1. *On the Horizon, 9*(5), 1–6.

Prensky, M. (2006). *—Don't bother me mom—I'm learning*. St. Paul, MN: Paragon House

Prensky, M. (2008). Backup Education?: Too many teachers see education as preparing kids for the past, not the future. *Educational Technology, 48*(1), 1–3.

Rideout, V. J., Foehr, U. G., & Roberts, D. F. (2010). Generation M2: media in the lives of 8-to 18-year olds. A Kaiser Family Foundation Study. Retrieved from http://kaiserfamilyfoundation.files.wordpress.com/2013/01/generation-m-media-in-the-lives-of-8-18-year-olds-report.pdf

Roberts, D. F., Foehr, U. G., & Rideout, V. J. (2005). *Generation M: Media in the lives of 8-18 year-olds.* Oakland, CA: Henry J. Kaiser Family Foundation.

Rowlands, I., Nicholas, D., Williams, P., Huntington, P., Fieldhouse, M., Gunter, B., . . . Tenopir, C. (2008). The Google generation: the information behaviour of the researcher of the future. *Aslib Proceedings, 60*(4), 290–310. doi:10.1108/00012530810887953

Sarantakos, S. (2005). *Social research* (2nd ed.). Melbourne, AU: Macmillan Education Australia.

Selwyn, N. (2007, October). Web 2.0 applications as alternative environments for informal learning-a critical review. In *Paper for CERI-KERIS International Expert Meeting on ICT and Educational Performance* (pp. 16–17).

Selwyn, N. (2008). *Education 2.0? Designing the web for teaching and learning: A commentary by the technology enhanced learning phase of the teaching and learning research programme*. Teaching and Learning Research Programme, Institute of Education, University of London.

Selwyn, N. (2009). The digital native–myth and reality. *New Information Perspectives, 61*(4), 364–379.

Silverman, D. (2005). *Doing qualitative research: A practical handbook.* Los Angeles, CA: SAGE.

Strauss, A., & Corbin, J. (1998). *Basics of qualitative research: Techniques and procedures for developing grounded theory* (2nd ed.). Thousand Oaks, CA: SAGE.

Strauss, W., & Howe, N. (2006). *Millennials and the pop culture: Strategies for a new generation of consumers in music, movies, television, the Internet, and video games.* Great Falls, VA: LifeCourse Associates.

Tapscott, D. (2009). *Grown up digital: How the net generation is changing your world.* New York, NY: McGraw-Hill Professional.

trendwatching.com. (2004). "Generation C". Retrieved from http://www.trendwatching.com/trends/GENERATION_C.htm

Veen, W., & Vrakking, B. (2006). Homo Zappiens: Growing up in a digital age. Bel Air, CA: Network Continuum.

Vie, S. (2008). Digital Divide 2.0: "Generation M" and online social networking sites in the composition classroom. *Computers and Composition, 25*(1), 9–23. doi:10.1016/j.compcom.2007.09.004

YouTube. (2014). YouTube. Retrieved from http://www.youtube.com/yt/press/statistics.html

SECTION III

FOSTERING CITIZENSHIP AND SOCIAL JUSTICE ACROSS SOCIAL MEDIA PLATFORMS

CHAPTER 11

RECOGNITION OF THE SOCIAL DIFFERENT-SOCIAL JUSTICE FOR LEARNING WITHIN AN INDIVIDUALIZED, MOBILE, CONVERGENT MASS COMMUNICATION

Ben Bachmair

ABSTRACT

The following discussion applies a widened concept of social justice to the dramatic changing of mass communication with the intention to explain some features of formal learning as an individualized social risk. With reference to cultural sociology and social semiotics the detraditionalization of formal learning and of mass communication is considered as a general delimitation. User generated context are an outcome of this delimitation. The intention is to adapt *social justice* to education in this process of delimitation. The chapter proposes that for education to concentrate on the new mass medial cultural resources of learners as essential in their social stratification of milieus, which influences also social inequality. In concordance with contribution to the post-PISA discussion three areas of social justices for school

E-Learning and Social Media:
Education and Citizenship for the Digital 21st Century, pp. 223–248

education are considered: institutional prerequisites of justice; agency and life orientation as focus of social justice and the communicative intention to recognize the culturally different. Examples of school projects attempt to explain these three areas of social justice in the light of a blurred mass communication and for the practices of learning in schools.

LEARNING AS INDIVIDUALIZED SOCIAL RISK

The leading idea of the argumentation is to understand learning as a social risk in formal learning of schools. Of course in the educational theory the interrelation of social variable and learning is a well know problem (see Goldthorpe & Bukodi, 2013 for the United Kingdom; Bertelsmann Stiftung, Institute für Schulentwicklungsforschung, 2012 for Germany; OECD, 2010, 2012). The following chapter is not interested to give a summary of this discussion. Instead it tries to analyze what happens with the social frame and social prerequisites of and for learning if the societal features of what is social about are changing or have already changed. This chapter concentrates on the changed mass communication with the media convergent Internet, with ubiquitous and mobile accessed Internet and its multimodal representation. YouTube and Facebook are visible artefacts of this structure. The pivot of this changing is individualization. Individualization is a result among others of consumption as leading feature of the industrial societies. Consumption is based on individual decisions and individual appropriation within a standardised offering. Amazon makes this visible.

Following the socio-cultural explanation of these processes this chapter argues within the framework of Ulrich Beck's Risk Society (Beck, 1986; Beck, Bonss, & Lau 2003; Beck & Grande, 2010) that individualization determines the interrelation of structures and agency (see Giddens, 1984) in the way that structural conditions of individual activities fall into the responsibility of the actor. Beck tags this development as reflexive modernization (see Beck, Giddens, & Lash, 1994). For these circumstances Beck uses the image of the *Nichtversicherbarkeit des Sozialen* (uninsurability of the social). In this line of the societal development by the individualization of structures and agency it was of high relevance for education that the way of experiencing the world is determined by the mode of personal perception. Personal perception constitutes what is socially real. Just by me the real exists. Real is because it is formed in my experience in the view of my small personal world: the world in my sense (see Bachmair, 2009; Schulze, 1992).

For learning and in the perspective of the social semiotics Gunther Kress concretized this for learning by seeing all learning as meaning making which is characterized by provisionality. The feature of provisionality is entangled with the semiotic resources of multimodality (Kress, 2010) with a large variety of semiotic objects, which appears as Internet arrangement of still and moving images, typed text, sound etc. Such "arrangements" "make" "meanings material" (Kress 2010, p. 145) in an ambiguous way. Kress (2010, p. 24) calls it "social and semiotic blurring" with the "dissolution, abolition, disappearance of frames and boundaries."

This interrelated societal, personal and semiotic changing marks the actual process of detraditionalization which enhances also the detraditionalization of education. This chapter tries to give some educational answers to the social and semiotic blurring in which more and more informal learning happens but formal learning in schools is still essential. Although the institution of the school is not longer successful to reach all young people. PISA results inform that around a 5th of the age group of the 15th is not really able to use competently reading and writing as its cultural resource.

On the other hand since generations the educational debate puts in the foreground to address learners in schools as persons with their specific and individual subjectivity, biography and social context. But within the actual process of cultural changing learning is getting an individualized social activity with its risk on the shoulders of each learner. This means that a learner has to deal with the amalgamation of societal, cultural, social structures, his or her agency and the social practices of learning. If he or she put his or her attention to the informal learning mediated, for example, by social sites of the Internet he or she receives the seek gratification in her or his social milieu but gets no reward in the assessment of the formal learning in school. It is her or his risk; an individualized risk like any other kind of investment.

LANDMARKS FOR EDUCATION IN THE PROCESS OF DELIMITATION

Of course education is in a passive role and has to react to learning as individualized social risk within a kind of diffuse complex structures, agency and practices (see Pachler, Bachmair, & Cook, 2010). How education can and should react to this development? Is it the right way to enhance new forms of flexible knowledge production in the sense of school as part of a creative industry but with a relevant portion of losers: boys, migrants, low income families, so the results of PISA research? A trend is to segregate, in the sense of out dropping NEETs, such week learners who are not able to deal with the personal burden of learning as their own risk. The headline of this chapter tries to show an alternative and education way. Educational landmark on this way is to see learning as substantial feature of personal development which is possible by learning as personal appropriation of cultural products.

Learning as personal development by appropriation of cultural products requires the recognition of the social different. For education this seems a more or less obvious argument. But in the dynamic of cultural delimitation we have to face that what is social emerges in flexible and individually constructed contexts as amalgamation of social sites, peer groups, school, wikis, video platforms, families in flux, perpetual assessment, success and failure, cultural poverty and virtual overabundance. For institutionalized learning could be helpful the landmark: social justice for learning which is aware of the individualized, mobile, convergent mass communication. Of course the idea of social justice stems from the enlightenment and seems rather inadequate to the actual delimitation by individualization and frameless cultural resources. But in this argumentative line of social justice one practical pivot could and should be the appropriation and application of the cultural resources of the individualized, mobile, convergent mass communication. This could be writing with multimodal cultural resources, for example, in its extreme form, by copy and paste. But also learner generated contexts are relevant. Such contexts like the cases below include videos from several sources, graphic forms downloaded from Internet, smartphones, tablets with their content and applications.

The following cases of school projects have the task to concretize the educational interpretation of the category *social justice*. They stem from the author's field research on innovative use of mobile devices for learning in school contexts. These studies intended to integrate learning as personal development, situated learning and learner generated contexts, to connect formal and informal learning with teacher guided learning in schools by means of digital mobile devices. These categories were operationalized by a taxonomy for planning and evaluation of innovative and technology enhanced learning (Bachmair, 2011; Bachmair, Pachler, & Cook, 2011). The field studies in the London school for special educational needs (Bachmair & Peters, 2014) and in the Grammar school example on context awareness "Awareness path" (Bachmair, 2014) were part of the European project "we-learn-it" (see http://we.learn.it/). One example about learner generated contexts was part of European Grundtvig project "mymobile" (Bachmair & Pachler, 2012). The example of the workshop on creative writing is reported and considered in the perspective of learners' self-representation (Bachmair, 2012). These cases serve to exemplify the educational view on social justice and its three perspectives of institution, agency and lifestyle, also of process of recognition of the different in the process of developing personality and identity.

EDUCATIONAL VIEWS ON SOCIAL JUSTICE

In the German post-PISA discussion the powerful endowment Bertelsmannstiftung (Bertelsmann Stiftung, 2012) was engaged to find a new access to evaluate the school system under the headline of justice of opportunities (*Chancengerechtigkeit*) (for a wider discussion see Dietrich, Martin, & Thieme, 2013).

This corresponds with the question about social inequality which is discussed in the United States among others by Carter and Reardon (2014). The German debate driven by the Bertelsmann Endowment focuses on three types of theories about social justice: institutional prerequisites of justice/agency and life orientation as focus of social justice/recognition of the different as another focus of social justice.

Institutional, Scholastic Prerequisites for Social Justice

John Rawls (1971) asked about rules for social institutions, in our case, the school, and their implications for basic right of freedom for everybody. This implies the fair chance to access positions and to get special support which avoids inequality.

Looking for the institutional prerequisites of social justice the school of the following example provides what is possible. The school, a school for special educational needs, offers one specialized teacher and two teaching assistants for a group of nine boys and girls. The curriculum is explicitly oriented to the profile of the learning group with and their special educational needs. The teacher is fully aware about the attributing function of "special educational needs." Further, actual digital devices are available: PC, electronic whiteboard, three tablets are in classroom. Food is provided. Also it is up to the parents to look for schools which offer an inclusion orientation.

In this institutional perspective of social justice the school fulfils all requirements which are defined by the Bertelsmann-endowment (Bertelsmann Stiftung, 2012):

- Social and systemic integration (p. 27);
- "Permeability" in addition to the selection function of school (p. 28);
- Capacity building by enhancing all potentials of students and to avoid systemic biases to promote preselected competences (p. 29);
- Adequate certificates in respect of internal and external requirements of the school system which link to life options (p. 29).

Agency and Life Orientation of Social Justice

In addition to the institutional prerequisites the teacher works intensively on an agency and life orientations of his teaching. Agency and life orientation of social justice is a second feature of social justice which was introduced by Amartya Sen (1999) to the discussion about social justice.

For Sen social justice should not only be guaranteed by institutional implications and prerequisites but also by the people's way of living and their agency. Justice means to be capable to decide on the personal way of living and the personal life course. In this perspective our school for special educational needs asks from which family and which social background their pupils come from. The teaching team is aware of the advantages and disadvantages for learning which comes among others from their social conditions. But does the school react to the students everyday life and the cultural resources of everyday life? Of course tablets as siblings of the computer for working are in school but not smartphones as tools of everyday life, entertainment, small talk conversation and informal learning. Like in all school also in this school for special educational needs mobile phones or smartphones are strictly forbidden. Additionally and in the orientation to agency and to living it is to ask if the width of informal learning should not be assimilated into school. In respect of informal learning a school has to consider mobiles in the context of an Internet based mass communication, for example, from YouTube.

The teacher in the school for educational needs is aware of these deficits in life orientation. He tries to widen the perfect educational support of the school as institution to the cultural resources of the students' everyday life. The institutional requirements for social justice in the sense of John Rawls is optimal fulfilled by small learner groups, teacher with teaching assistants, also with tablets and electronic white board. But for the life orientation of social justice the teacher emphasized the multimodal form of representation for the school. This meant to see writing not only as based on typed or handwritten characters but also as collage, bricolage of characters, images and sound. *Copy and paste* is seen as a part of writing. This means also to open writing of reports and essays to the manifold forms of narration (see Figure 11.1). Therefore the teacher introduced multimodal writing of narration to the learning groups which worked on the issue "animals in war." One way of writing was that students copied images from the Internet into their exercise book to express their ideas what is war about (Bachmair & Peters, 2014).

In his personal workspace (see Figure 11.4) Jermaine developed his writing style in the form of creating a comic strip (Figure 11.1). Figure left above shows his hand written story, which is in the same multimodal manner like the stories of the other students.

TV and Smartphone as Personal Resource of Everyday Life

On his personal smartphone the teacher shows the story of *Lizzy, the Elephant*, a BBC podcast and he refers explicitly to the related BBC website. Leading question for this lesson was how *working* animals can be involved

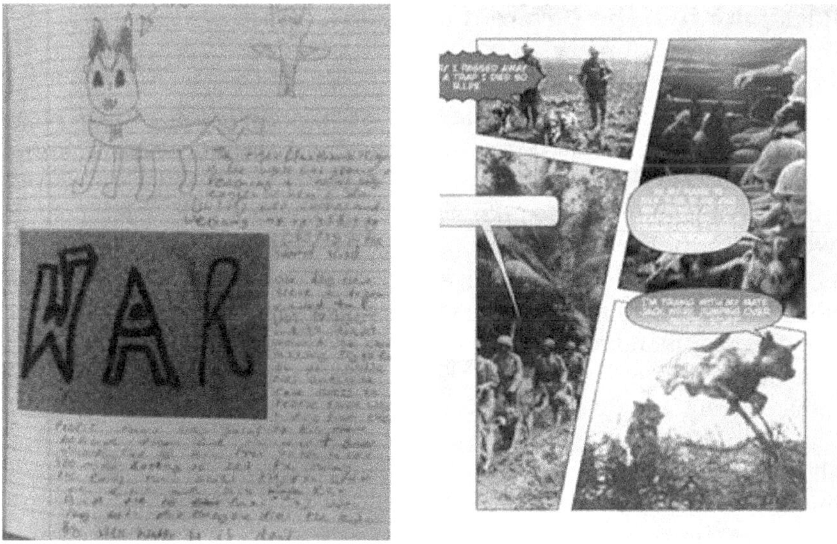

Figure 11.1. Jermaine's story in his exercise book: "tiger."

in wars? Teacher presented the story of *Lizzy the Elephant* as his personal learning experience which he got as podcast from the BCC website. *Lizzy* was used by a scrap metal dealer to transport scrap metal for recycling toward the war effort when all horses were commandeered. By showing the podcast to the pupils on his personal smartphone the teacher made visible that he learned during watching television in his spare time and with his personal mobile device (Figure 11.2). Afterwards three groups with three students worked together at one common table. They write on their table with a wipe-clean marker pen. The group's tablet is available on the desk.

Figure 11.2. In a circle around tablet and his mobile teacher tells the story of *Lizzy, the Elephant.*

Recognition of the Different as Essential Part of the Formation of Identity

As third perspective about social justice Bertelsmann Endowment refers to Axel Honneth (2007) who put the communicative aspect of social justice in the foreground. Honneth argues in a long historical conceptual arch from the beginning of the industrial society, which emphasized freedom as autonomy of merchants to set up contracts. Pedagogy will immediately agree that autonomy emerges in interpretative, communicative interactions but of course not in the form of conversations like these of contracts. For interaction and communication Honneth states that “human beings depend on the supportive experience of mutual recognition to secure their individual autonomy” (p. 6). This argument leads to basics of the modern formation of subjectivity or, with other terms, to the formation of personality and the identity of a citizen. A leading and indispensable feature of modern personality in a democratic society is the process to recognize the different.

I would like to extend this idea also to formal learning. On the surface of formal learning the process of recognition seems in contrast to the school’s task to support equality and to work in homogenous groups of learners. But in the interpretation of the Enlightenment, and learning personal development, the key name with respect to education is Jean Jacques Rousseau. For personal development recognition is an essential feature which emphasizes the different as part of identity. Teaching implies therefore communicative forms of recognition which blows up the narrow frame of assessment.

Recognizing Family Story and Leisure Time Activities in a Grammar School: Awareness Path

At this point of argumentation all children or young people are at-risk learners not only low achievers like the students in a school for special educational needs. In the irreversible trend of delimitation school meets extremely different learners’ personalities. All of them depend of adequate recognition for their learning and development. The following example of a British Grammar School shows that the family stories of the students are rather diverse. And it is taken for granted that these stories are excluded from learning. An alternative provided a half day workshop within a lesson about war and peace. The workshop was designed in the way that, for example, family story or leisure time activities as part of the students’ life should lead to a communicative recognition in the form of becoming aware of the own family story or of leisure time activities.

The lessons on war and peace was based on an anti-war film and students' video production. In addition and during an half day workshop the school chaplain organized an *awareness path*. Aim of this *awareness path* was to integrate the students life, experiences and resources outside of the school into their video production. The "awareness path" started with a fine-art-performances at the local war memorial on a churchyard. The second station of the *awareness path* was a coffee shop with an informal discussion about the fine-art performance. The third station took place in a theatre lounge with the presentation of what the students had prepared for the performance but not shown. The *awareness path* ended in school with writing a very short poem, a cinquain. At the beginning of the *awareness path* at the local war memorial just the facilitators not the students presented their prepared material. But students approached and came in discussion with the school pastor. It was a form of recognizing the teachers endeavours. The next step of recognition used the informal discussion in a coffee shop about what was going on. The participants learned from each other and their referential fame to evaluate what had happened. Afterwards students were ready to display their own view on war and peace. They expressed their views by using their cultural resources. Their resources were their prefabricated media, for example, a family photo or a video on a smartphone which they displayed and explained to the other students and to the facilitators. Students used their personal mobile devices but also a photo on paper or written text on paper. These contributions opened a wide field of war and peace-related contexts from family to sports, from entertainment to poetry. The examples also showed the wide range of expertise of the students.

Extract from the report (Bachmair, 2014):

> In the lounge of the Oval Theatre, further discussions took place of the already raised issues and presentation of what students have prepared for the live art performance
>
> On the way from St. Mark's churchyard and war memorial, via the coffee shop to school, a local theatre is situated. In its lounge with sofas and armchairs the group sat around a table. In the background a rehearsal ran. On this third site of the morning, the group starts with a general discussion, among others, about conscientious objectors. Facilitators also contributed to this discussion as well as students. The positive and informal climate of the coffee shop supports the discussion. Everybody's contribution is appreciated and widely acknowledged. One strand of the discussion is on football and war.

The main issue of this third morning session and site is the students' contribution to the live art performance. Students display, explain and discuss their media material, which they have prepared but did not show in the live art performance in the churchyard.

Students' Expression of Their Expertise and Widening the Context of War Issues to Include Sports, Family History, Poetic Texts and Entertainment

One might assume that students needed the churchyard and the coffee shop as a kind of warming-up to rely on their own media material. In the theatre lounge the situation is prepared to introduce their personal media expertise. Probably this expertise is rather far away from the school's mainstream concepts of war and belongs to contexts which usually don't match school, for example, family history, app for using the mobile phone as gun, gun sports, and so forth.

Family History and Algerian Liberation War

Seymour presents a printed photo of his grandfather who fought and was pursued in the Algerian liberation war. Seymour is definitely an expert in his family story but also in the history of the Algeria history during the time of his grandfather, for example, involvement of Algerians as French combatants in Germany in World War II. With his family photos, Seymour opened the context of family history and to an unusually unknown war.

Poetic Text

Darrin reads a possibly self-produced text from the display of his Smartphone and explains it. He presents his poetic expertise and refers to one of the objectives of the project. At the end of the morning, back in school each of the students composes his cinquain, a poem which consists of five lines.

Franklyn's Poem and the Discussion About Grace

With the mobile in his hand Franklyn speaks about his poem which opens a discussion to which the chaplain contributes a longer theological explanation among others about grace. Grace is the central issue of the religious strand of the project. In this context, one of the facilitators asks the chaplain to explain grace as the leading religious input to the event. The chaplain focuses his explanation with the gesture of forming a cross with his hands.

Tomas's Poetic Text

Tomas's contribution is a well formed poetic text accompanied by figures which he illustrated in his exercise book.

Neal's Photos/Video of a Gun Sport Site

Neal show his contribution, photos or videos of gun sport, which he discusses with the group (Figure 11.3).

Figure 11.3. Neal talks about gun sport. He recorded an example on his mobile device.

The Gunner App on the Smartphone: Expertise and Context of Entertainment

Students were deliberately invited to bring war-related material from entertainment to the live art event. It should or could be media material which they use themselves. Just at the end of third session outside of school Tomas introduced the gunner app to a baffled and laughing group. The app transforms the mobile into a hand gun. Two other students, who had the same app on their mobiles, displayed themselves as gunners at the entrance to the school. This leads to a short discussion of whether this app can be used inside school.

THE DYNAMIC OF DELIMITATION, PROVISIONALITY AND CONTEXTS

Societies are always in transition which can be interpreted as detraditionalization. Detraditionalization produces always losers and winners, gains and losses. The interrelation of the determinants of social justice for learning, such as institutional features, agency and life orientation, recognition of the different, is changing, actively or just by happening in the complex processes of transformation. One stream of these processes in the field of culture is the individualized, mobile, convergent mass communication, which is concrete and visible with smartphones, Facebook, YouTube and so on. Of course visible but more or less hidden to educational awareness is multimodality of representation and meaning making (Kress, 2010); it is also part of the cultural transformation. Without multimodality the actually running convergence of distinct media like TV with Internet would not possible. The case of Jermaine above and his multimodal writing in his exercise book is a case of this convergence which is result of individualized use of Internet. This multimodal writing is still rather unusual for school. Nevertheless Jermain's teacher tries explicitly to assimilate features of the actual mass communication with his lessons although these features are transgressing the school's long tradition of writing. Instead of the concept of transgressing parts of cultural sociology uses the term of delimitation to describe these forms and similar developments of detraditionalization (Beck, Bonss, & Lau, 2003; Beck & Lau, 2004). One leading argument is that the actual process of societal and cultural transformation does not only updates institutions and processes. Like already written in the introduction the changes of societal structures, personal agency, and cultural practices together with their interrelationship it getting increasingly unpredictable (Beck, Giddens, & Lash, 1994) and provisional (Kress, 2010). The assumption is that this happens by delimitation and in the process of boundary blurring. One of the phenomena visible to schools is migration. Schools in inner-city areas especially may have high percentages of students who are migrants—some naturalized, some not, some with permission to stay only a short time, some with citizenship but with parents who do not have permission to work, some accepted as asylum seekers, some without official status, and so on. As already stated another form of delimitation are the young people who are not in education, employment, or training (NEETs).

In the context of detraditionalization, cultural resources get rid of their binding definition and get optional in respect of flexible contexts. Not the least because of the manifold Internet-convergent mobile devices that are changing mass communication. The emergence of new institutions such as Google contributed to the dynamic of delimitation. Detraditionalization in the form of delimitation results also from multimodality and provisionality of meaning-making in new mass communication. Social semiotics has explored multimodality:

> Modes are semiotic resources which allow the simultaneous realisation of discourses and types of (inter)action. Designs then use these resources, combining semiotic modes, and selecting from the options which they make available according to the interests of a particular communication situation. (Kress & van Leeuwen, 2001, p. 21)

The new "arrangements" to which mobiles and the Internet or apps belong to make meaning "material" (Kress, 2010). These arrangements are multimodally constructed as photograph, sound, printed characters, mise-en-scène, and so on. Mobile devices fit with this multimodality by virtue of the variety of applications they support: from the typed characters of a text message to videos amalgamated with characters. Mobile devices do not just fit with multimodality; they promote multimodality in a highly individualized way.

In this line of argumentation, education can focus on the affordance of specific modes of representation (Kress, 2008), such as written text with characters in a printed book or several modes of representation created with mobile apps and residing in the mobile device and close to the Internet. In addition, education can question the affordances of specific modes of representation linked to specific competencies. The ubiquity of mobile devices goes beyond individualization and offers a specific orientation. Kress (2010) describes this orientation as "multimodal orchestrations ... of meaning": "The world arranged by me: the world arranged for me." But mobile, individualized, multimodal arrangements of meaning provide provisional contexts and work in provisional contexts. We know this phenomenon as user-generated contexts. User-generated contexts enhance the "social and semiotic blurring: the dissolution, abolition, disappearance of frames and boundaries" (p. 24).

I would like to add, they make the "social and semiotic blurring" to a element of everyday life and the life course. Provisional contexts are on the way do become taken for granted.

Examples of Learning in and by Generated, Provisional Contexts

A closer look on the examples Jermaine's multimodal writing in his exercise book (see above) stems from a his specific access to his sites of the Internet, to sites which relates to the issues war/soldier/animals and a specific software, the app Halftone 2. With Halftone 2 he produces his comic strips in school. All together they are part of Jermaine's writing context.

The example above about the recognition of students' resources for discussion on war in a Grammar school depicts the combination of the resources within a situation during the *awareness path*. These resources belong to different contexts and, together, they set up a fragile and non-repeatable contexts. A photo of the Algerian Grandfather together with a video of gun sport together with a gunner app on smartphone enhanced a common discussion in which the pastor's reflection about war and grace was adequate and coherent. This is the beginning of understanding each other and his specific contribution to the issue war and peace. It lays also the ground to become aware of the singular context of learning as interpretation. With other words, context awareness is emerging.

Writing on the Own Body in a Special Course for NEETs Which Enhances Context Awareness

The following example turns the school into the object of a photo investigation by students with their mobile phones/smartphones. It was the starter task of a new course aimed at students previously not in education, employment or training (NEETs). Beginning with an investigation of the new school the students were invited to add to their photos of the college site their preferred images from outside of college. The presentation of the photos depicts the contexts inside and outside the college. Here context awareness is an issue for both students and teachers.

The initial 2-day course began with an investigation of the college through the students' personal mobile phone. Students worked in groups. After the investigation, the teacher gave an introduction to the presentation software Prezi in the computer lab of the college. The students subsequently worked on a Prezi presentation of their photo investigation of the college. At the end of the second day the student groups were asked to present their results to the class. The teacher invited them to bring in other material from outside of the school, for example, from the Internet or from at home. While working on the Prezi presentation, the students selected one image, a photo taken during the investigation of the school or brought in from outside of the school. This image was printed on a t-shirt, which made visible aspects a student's personal identity in the new group of students inside of the school. The second reason was to make visible the context in which the students stood in relation to the new college environment. Third, the intention was for specific resources in the students' contexts to become visible, especially for the teacher.

On a first view the variety of t-shirts signaled individuality; a second viewing, however, shows a variety of contexts, resources in contexts and accesses to contexts. The resources presented and the routes of access to the selected contexts are relevant, because they are part of individual students' self-presentation as part of their learning habitus.

Some t-shirt images originate from the investigation of the college. They are a result of the students' perspective of the college. The photos appear as still lifes, which convey an important message for these students, namely to see the college from the perspective of a young artist. The images are not about teaching, learning or assessment but convey interests around media design. Furthermore, these four images give the impression of the students as people with a professional-orientation, not as beginners but as experts. The bearer of the t-shirt invites themselves to be addressed professionally not as unmotivated young person or as an outsider.

The other implicit contexts in evidence, not depicted here, also carry messages about context relationships, which are of high relevance to the teacher, mainly: as media experts we are interested in media design. The students do not need extrinsic motivation, but professional equipment with reference to Internet design, to social media within a professional context of fine arts and design. They expect, of course on a low level of awareness, a context for design and communication with media practitioners and it is important for students not to be patronized. Their t-shirts problematized the following themes:

- entertainment media: one t-shirt displays the faces of the two protagonists of a manga cartoon for young people, *L vs. Kira*. The girl who chose this image portrays herself as a media specialist. In so doing she refers to the media design focus of her course but with clear reference to media and design styles outside of school.
- Internet and social media: one student presents himself as a dancer on a photo which he had downloaded from his Facebook site. A girl wears the well-designed characters MEHR on her t-shirt, another a stylish and also well-designed combination of faces and characters. One boy chose a photo of a fashion model. Perfection in the use of the Internet and a world of design are the messages here.
- at home, family and peers: one t-shirt features photos with friends having a good time; the style is that of a photo album. The girl who wore this image on her t-shirt was probably looking for a familiar context with peers within the college context.
- national origin: one young man featured his national color on his t-shirt; perhaps it carried the meaning of being politically aware as a migrant.

Tablets for Investigation and for Games in the School for Special Education Needs

During the *animals in war*-workshop the teacher facilitated that students opened contexts by showing his media sources, for example, the BBC podcast about *Lizy, the Elephant* (see above). Another contexts was opened by the students during an excursion to a memorial for animals in war. Students combined their three available tablets of the school as well for investigating the memorial with their entertaining during the picnic break in front of the memorial. But also during the break some student play on a tablet. Look deeper the students' use of the tables is adapted to two context, the leisure time contexts of games with the game software on the tablet and, the second context, the demands of lecture and excursion in the school context. The same cultural resource is used but different application on the tablets—taking photos of the memorial or playing a digital game—link the students' activities to different contexts and their specificities.

A Personal, Protective Workspace in the School for Special Education Needs

When producing his story about animals in war for his exercise book (see above) Jermaine needed a protective space which he organized by himself by listening, partly by watching music videos. Jermaine accessed the video platform *Vimeo*. The teacher is familiar and cooperative with Jermaine's desire for a protective space. Music from mass communication and entertainment is a usual form of separating from the here-and-now environment. Generally spoken, the here-and-now situation is widened by a user generated video-context. Target oriented working, writing as narrative, is integrated part of a user generated context by means of tablet and video platform in the Internet. In his communication with Jermaine, the teacher calls this "Jermaine's workspace." Alternatively to this protective workspace by means of tablet and user generated Internet context in the classroom a noise protected area with chair and table is made available for a student.

The visible part of the *workspace* is set up by the tablet, which is connected to the Internet (Figure 11.4). Jermaine does not use an ear set which is why the music sound is audible to the class but not as loud that it is disturbing. In this *workspace* Jermaine writes his rather complex story about animals in war (see Figure 11.1).

In such a self-generated *workspace*, Jermaine searches for his own graphic tools to write his story about animals in war in addition to his handwritten story in his exercise book. He used the app Halftone 2 for his comic strip (see above)

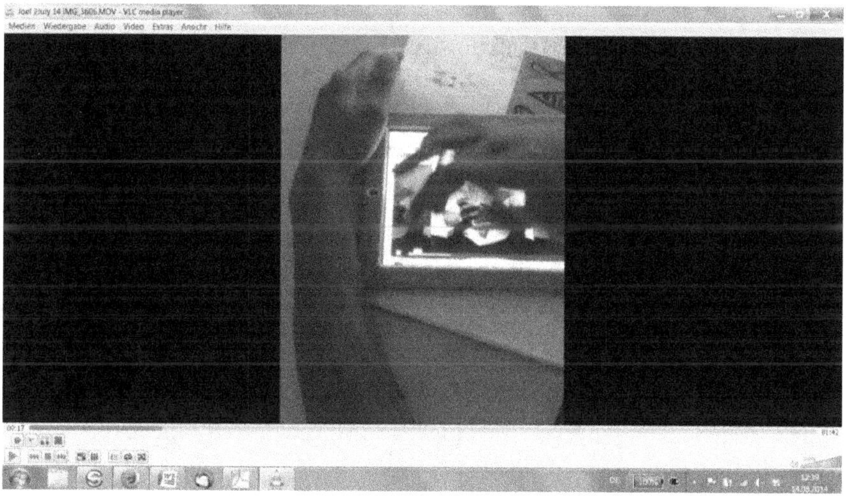

Figure 11.4. Jermaine's personal work space in which he use videos as background for writing.

CULTURAL RESOURCES FOR LEARNING, AGAIN THE EDUCATIONAL TASK OF RECOGNITION

Above the concept of cultural resources was used which needs an explanatory link to already well known concepts and research result for the sociology like these from Pierre Bourdieu (2006, p. 106) about cultural capital and its incorporation as habitus and the different language codes in school which reproduce social segmentation in, better, by schools (see Bernstein, 1987). In this chapter the concept of *cultural capital* is widened to *cultural resources* and its function for socialization and learning. In the sense of Bourdieu all cultural resources are always contributing to a "system of social differences" (p. 181). In this argumentative line recent research describes the social stratification of our society as socio-cultural milieus which are dependents of different socio-economic status and values (see Sinus, 2014; Sinus Sociovision, 2007). Living in specific socio-cultural milieus produces specific life styles and forms of habitus with values and attitudes toward learning. The group of at-risk-learners are of high relevance for considering the sustainability of m-learning (see Pachler, Bachmair, & Cook, 2010, pp. 249–272; Rummler, 2012) especially in the socio-cultural milieus of the social *hedonists (sensation orientated)* and *consum materialists*.

Lifestyle Habitus

The new socio-culturally oriented stratification of mileus gives an impact to a reinterpretation of what relevant resources are about, for example, traditional formal education and training or digital native competences or resources which are not acknowledged at school. Living within socio-cultural milieus leads to new milieus specific forms of habitus. One can say it leads to a lifestyle habitus which correlates with its specific cultural resources. School and its traditionally typical resources, from the book and its text format to teacher guided instruction, can now coincide or being acceptable, but also being in conflict, and so forth, with typical cultural resources of specific milieus. Forms of lifestyle habitus are compatible with or repel to each other, intensively or more or less, and so forth, which depends of the lifestyles.

The continuous empirical research of the private German company Sinus Sociovision/Sinus provides data on the social stratification of socio-cultural milieus with reference to everyday life. The Sinus milieus depict different modes of habitus, which include also the description of the agency of students from different socio-cultural milieus.

As an example which hits NEETs the basic orientation of the *hedonistic-subcultural milieu* (BC3, escapists) in the migration context (Sinus Sociovision, 2007, p. 65) can be described as follows:

- Against the background of the social exclusion experienced (self image of being a "Kanak") on the one hand the dream of a rich life in Germany with "easy money," luxury, prestige; on the other hand resignation and a defiant 'underdog' mentality: being unemployed, without chances, discouraged;
- (partly aggressive) distance to the mainstream of society together with not being adjusted, for example, in the outfit, in behavior and language, conflicts with authority and authorities (parents, teachers, supervisor, police); on one hand disapproval of demands for integration and achievement, and on the other hand the desire for success, appreciation, a higher income and a better job;
- orientation toward the "here and now," hardly any long-term and future planning, uncontrolled spending of money, financial problems, often no perspective for the future, insecurity, being passive.

The Precarious Consumers' main mechanism of participation is consumption. For them consumption, for example, the purchase of often expensive items, compensates for the lack of access to other cultural resources. Due to lack of financial strength and a high rate of unemployment, the uncontrolled purchase of goods promises closer proximity to mainstream society. But for Precarious Consumers' consumption itself is already risky. They seek safety in society and try to get closer to the mainstream of society, for example, through their taste in clothing and music by seeking well-known brands, music groups and song titles to avoid uncertainty. The main reason for buying fashionable and well-known brands comes from the hope to be acknowledged by others. The risk for them lies not in failing this acknowledgement but in ending up in an even weaker position in society particularly by running into worse financial difficulties.

Male Precarious Consumers aged 14 to 24 mention the following things as being important in lives: having many friends, family and partnership, financial independence, being successful in their job, being able to afford something, having a safe future, being or looking attractive. Most of them see themselves as open to new things, say that they live in a healthy environment, have a good job/education, have holidays, live in a nice home or apartment, are sportive and active, eat healthily. Just a few think having much leisure time, hanging around from time to time, having a lot of fun and action and having a good all-round education are important issue in life.

Learning Resources for Precarious Consumers, an Example of Self-Representation and Writing in a School Context

In a German school of the lowest level of the German school hierarchy boys aged 13 with a migrant background and living in the milieu of the precarious consumers were invited to a voluntary workshop. During this workshop the boys produces posters from material which they found on the Internet or by use of their mobile devices in their everyday life. Additionally, they were offered a short workshop on how to write and perform a rap lyric. This curricular design, for the basic workshop on creative writing, had the intention to introduce the boys' own "cultural resources" from their youth culture and everyday life into school but also to elaborate the use of these resources. One curricular intention was to get from simple copy and paste images and deleting them to arrange the copied images on a poster which makes visibly relevant personal narration of the students. As additional developmental step was planned to widen the resources for self expression from Internet images to traditional writing of a Rap lyric. But recognition of the precarious consumers resources was the basic of the educational endeavor.

As already mentioned above Bernstein (1987: Bernstein & Henderson, 1973) investigated in the 1950s to 1970s, the verbal resources and the symbolic forms of lower class students which were not recognized by schools as elaborated enough for formal expressions in school. From an educational and a curricular point of view there are two essential tasks. First, the facilitator for the workshop had to recognize the cultural resources brought in by the boys as being adequate and functioning material for self-expression.

This was a real challenge because students wrote by copy and paste images from the Internet which they deleted after a short time. The second task was to integrate the boys in a process of development so that their input has relevance for the school curriculum. Thus the goal is to lead the boys from their naïve articulation of resources, for example, copy and paste to a position where these resources are seen as necessary and relevant, for example for getting an apprenticeship. At the beginning of the workshop the boys copied and pasted material from the Internet; for example strange male bodies like a video of an extremely fat dancer, deformed babies or an old man with the head of a baby. They did not store these images. In summary, the boys are viewed as having engaged in a kind of "consumptive appropriation" of cultural resources; this was achieved by archiving, selecting, evaluating, transforming into printable images and compiling the image for their personal poster. A closer look onto the poster made clear that the boys used the Internet images to depict a personal narration. The poster with the images of babies can be read as associations about me as a baby, me as a baby monster, me entangled, and so forth.

Figure 11.5. Photos stem from the teacher's mobile portfolio.

The images above (Figure 11.5) stem from a mobile portfolio of a teacher, who summarized the process of the workshop by images. One advantage of a mobile teacher portfolio is to use images as resources for the teacher's reflection. Further it is interesting to compare the teacher's m-portfolio with the m-portfolio of the students (see Figure 11.6).

Figure 11.6. Photos stem from the students' mobile portfolio.

With respect to the way the rap workshop worked, and the resulting m-portfolio, the boys took photos that thematically emphasized the color blue. Blue is a featured design element of the local underground. Consequently, such a color theme is of relevance for the boys, but of course not on a high level of reflection. However, it can be seen as a link to find an intersection with the boys' creative expression. As expected, the boys used their mobiles to represent themselves. During the workshop the teacher paid particular attention to the emergent writing process and the products of writing, the text of rap lyrics, and so on. However, this was not at the foreground of the students' interest. Instead the students took photos from the technical set up of the sound studio (see below). This technical set up can therefore be viewed as one of their resources of interest; this is of course not an unknown motivation but it was now a visible one. The sound studio portrayals appear without people and students in them, just the mixing desk, speakers, keyboards, and so forth. The teacher's portfolio above was concentrated on the target oriented performance of a student in the studio. This shows a striking difference in the evaluation or interpretation by the participants; the teacher's view focussed on the studio-student.

The summary of the teacher's portfolio shows a written short text of a Rap lyric which students composed during the workshop. But this was just a kind of a gesture to recognize the students' writing. But the teacher did not considered these texts in respect to the poetic tradition. Just later and in a general discussion of the outcomes of the project teacher discovered parallels between one Rap lyric about roses and girls and the poem of Goethe also about roses and a girl, which is central for the German poetry canon. The handwritten text is divided in two section and section starts about fighting to impress girls, which is expectable for precarious consumers. This gives a specific drive to the teacher's perception of the second part of the text (Figure 11.7).

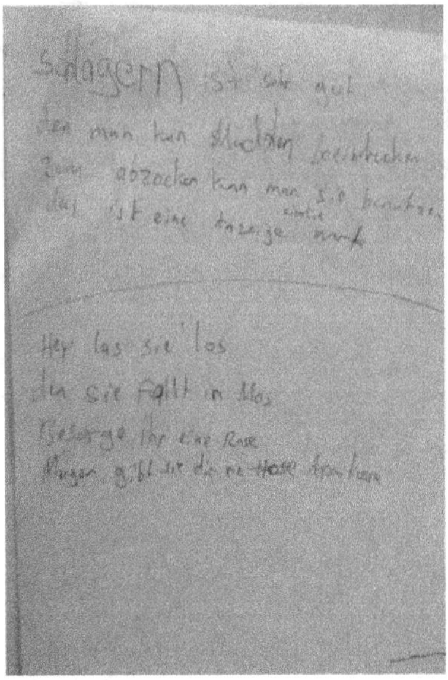

Figure 11.7. The Rap lyric.

Recognizing Cultural Resources for Composition as Multimodal Bricolage

The above presented examples display a variety of representational modes from images to short written lyrics to photos and images on the interface t-shirt. This form of writing remains on simple forms of awareness. But they can also be read as narration, even if, at a first glance, they do not meet the established ideas of literacy for narration. The conceptual frame of "deference" is useful for helping us widen our expectations about the cultural resources that children and young people use for self-expression and narration. In the dynamic of individualization, keeping cultural resources standardized is also not easy. The concept of deference promoted by Rymes (2011), which focuses on embracing mass-mediated youth cultural practices, is helpful to make educators aware of the individualization of cultural resources for literacy. Formal learning institutions should recognize the variety of cultural resources that include visual and graphic forms. A deference approach supports the assimilation of resources of the international youth culture, seeing learners as naive experts of their everyday life.

A second helpful perspective is that of Jocson (2012), who views text production as narrative bricolage. She valorizes the text production of young people from non-dominant racial and ethnic backgrounds, recognizing that their literacy is changing and that the separation of the world of learning in school from everyday life is dissolving in a "proliferation of spaces" (p. 298). Young people traverse spaces and use different interfaces for their communication. Further, they copy and paste prefabricated material to produce "assemblages" that contain their stories and narratives.

CONCLUSION: EDUCATIONAL AIMS FOR SOCIAL JUSTICE

These arguments support the concept to assimilate the width of contexts and their multimodal representation as cultural resources into formal learning. The triple folded concept of social justice: institutional prerequisites, agency and lifestyle, recognition of the different in the development of personality and identity—suggests to deal, for example, with new contexts, with user generated context as cultural resources for formal learning. School and its protagonists should deal or have to deal with the width of social culturally defined habitus form also for formal learning. Therefore formal education should especially react educationally to the "losers" of the existing school system, should react to the NEETs, the young people who are not in education, employment or training. Core idea is to recognize the learners' cultural resources although they dissent the scholastic definition of resources for learning. One feature element of such a definition is sustainability of using cultural resources which tries to follow the book and its written text. I am sure that the book is still of relevance but it is just one cultural resource in an individualized, mobile, convergent mass communication. Of course school, that means formal learning, and the new forms of mass communication have not to be seen as cultural companions or as exclusive counterparts. With educational intentions an assimilation is on the agenda. It has to be taken into account what kind of educational pursuits are followed. In this chapter the core idea is to understand learning as personal development which succeeds in the learner's process of appropriation and expression of cultural product. In this process cultural products become personal resources. Of course formal learning is a processes of appropriation which is not exterritorial to the provisional user-generated contexts, their multimodal representation of the individualized, mobile, convergent mass communication.

Further it is to consider that our society produces new form of social differences which led to an individualization also of learning as a social risk, which depends of the appropriated habitus for learning within the new social segmentation of socio-cultural milieus and their specific cultural resources. School and formal learning has to become aware of these diverse and also contradictory cultural resources. The key argument for become aware is the intention to follow pivots of social justice under the conditions of individualization, mobility, multimodality, convergence.

Recognition of the width of habitus modes for learning and writing is one of the educational results. That means to recognize among others cultural resources for writing from non-institutionalized and provisional learning contexts in school. But in addition and as answer to the provisionality of divers user-generated context the awareness in and for contexts should get on the school's curricular agenda. The curricular portfolio idea is helpful if it follows the recognition of the diverse cultural resources also for such portfolios.

REFERENCES

Bachmair, B. (2009). *Medienwissen für Pädagogen. Medienbildung in riskanten Erlebniswelten*. Wiesbaden: VS Verlag für Sozialwissenschaften.

Bachmair, B. (2011): Sechs didaktische Eckpunkte zur Planung und Analyse des Unterrichts mit dem Handys. In K. Friedrich, B. Bachmair, & M. Risch (Ed.), *Mobiles Lernen mit dem Handy. Herausforderungen und Chancen für den Unterricht* (pp. 7–11). Weinheim, Basel: Beltz Verlag.

Bachmair, B. (2012). Kulturressourcen für Selbstrepräsentation jugendlicher Migranten im Kontext der Schule. In A. Kriwak & G. Pallaver (Hrsg.): Medien und Minderheiten, Innsbruck: innsbruck university press. pp 173–198.

Bachmair, B. (2014). *Awareness path from war memorial to school*. Project: Re-interpretation of war and peace: a personal learning journey using mobile devices. Report on the Third Project Session, 9th May 2014: "Language and Media Warstorm" at Archbishop Tenison's school, KS 5, Project "We Went to War".

Bachmair, B., Pachler, N., & Cook, J. (2011). Parameters and focal points for planning and evaluation of mobile learning. Retrieved from http://www.londonmobilelearning.net/downloads/Parameter_flyer.pdf

Bachmair, B., Pachler, N. (2012). Training scenario number 1: Bridging informal and formal education through mobile images. Integration of learners at a distance to formal education. In K. Friedrich, M. Ranieri, N. Pachler, P. de Theux (Eds.), The *"my mobile" handbook: Guidelines and scenarios for mobile learning in adult education*. Retrieved from http://mymobile-project.eu/IMG/pdf/Handbook_web.pdf

Bachmair, B., & Peters, J. (2014). *Report workshop animals in war*. Project at Lansdowne School, London, Lambeth, School for Special Educational Needs.

Beck, U. (1986). *Risikogesellschaft. Auf dem Weg in eine andere Moderne*. Frankfurt: Suhrkamp

Beck, U., Bonss, W., & Lau, C. (2003). The theory of reflexive modernization: Problematic, hypotheses and research programme. *Theory, Culture & Society*, *20*(2), 1–33.

Beck, U., & Grande, E. (2010). Varieties of second varieties of second modernity: the cosmopolitan turn in social and political theory and research. *The British Journal of Sociology*, *61*(3), 409–443.

Beck, U., & Lau, C. (Eds.). (2004). *Entgrenzung und Entscheidung: Was ist neu an der Theorie reflexiver Modernisierung?* Frankfurt: Suhrkamp

Beck, U., Giddens, A., & Lash, S. (1994). *Reflexive modernization: Politics, tradition and aesthetics in the modern social order*. Cambridge, UK: Polity Press.

Bernstein, B. (1987). *Elaborated and restricted codes: An overview, 1958–1986* (Occasional papers No. 2). Amsterdam: Amsterdam University, Centre for Race & Ethnic Studies.

Bernstein, B., & Henderson, D. (1973). Social class differences in the relevance of language to socialization. In B. Bernstein (Ed.), *Class, codes and control* (Vol. 2, pp. 24–47). Applied Studies towards a Sociology of Languages. London and Boston: Routledge & Kegan Paul.

Bertelsmann Stiftung, Institute für Schulentwicklung. (Eds.). (2012). *Chancenspiegel. Zur Chancengerechtigkeit und Leistungsfähigkeit der deutschen Schulsysteme*. Gütersloh: Verlag Bertelsmann Stiftung.

Bourdieu, P. (2006). The forms of capital. In H. Lauder, P. Brown, J.-A. Dillabough, & A. H. Halsey (Eds.), *Education, Globalization, and Social Change* (pp. 105–118). Oxford: Oxford University Press. (Reprint of the text in J. G. Richardson. (Ed.). (1986). *Handbook of theory and research for the sociology of education*. Westport, CT: Greenwood Publishing Group.

Carter, P. L., & Reardon, S. F. (2014). *Inequality matters*. William T. Grant Foundation (http://wtgrantfoundation.org). Retrieved October 30, 2014, from https://www.dropbox.com/s/s2yrq0288llo6it/Inequality%20Matters.pdf?dl=0

Dietrich, F., Martin, H., & Thieme, N. (Eds.) (2013). *Bildungsgerechtigkeit jenseits von Chancengleichheit. Theoretische und empirische Ergänzungen und Alternativen zu ‚PISA'*. Wiesbaden: Springer Fachmedien.

Giddens, A. (1984). *The constitution of society: Outline of the theory of structuration*. Berkley and Los Angeles, CA: University of California Press.

Goldthorpe, J. H., & Bukodi, E. (2013). Institutional change and social class inequalities in educational attainment: the British experiences since 1945. In D. Dreißner (Ed.), *Chancen bilden. Wege zu einer gerechteren Bildung - ein internationaler Erfahrungsaustausch* (pp. 101–110). Wiesbaden: Springer.

Honneth, A. (2007). Gerechtigkeit und kommunikative Freiheit. Überlegungen im Anschluss an Hegel. *EUROZINE*. Retrieved October 30, 2014, from http://www.eurozine.com/articles/2007-01-17-honneth-de.html

Jocson, K. M. (2012), Youth media as narrative assemblage: examining new literacies at an urban high school. *Pedagogies: an International Journal*, 7(4), 298–316.

Kress, G. (2008). "Literacy" in a multimodal environment of communication. In J. Flood, S. B. Heath, & D. Lapp (Eds.), *Handbook of research on teaching literacy through the communicative and visual Art* (Vol. II, pp. 91–100). New York and London: Lawrence Erlbaum.

Kress, G. (2010). *Multimodality. A social semiotic approach to contemporary communication*. London and New York: Routledge.

Kress, G., & van Leeuwen, T. (2001). *Multimodal discourses. The modes and media of contemporary communication*. London, UK: Arnold.

OECD. (2010). *PISA 2009 results: Overcoming social background—Equity in learning opportunities and outcomes* (Vol. II). Retrieved from http://dx.doi.org/10.1787/9789264091504-en and Retrieved October 30, 2014, from http://www.oecd.org/pisa/pisaproducts/48852584.pdf

OECD. (2012). *Equity and quality in education: Supporting disadvantaged students and schools*. Retrieved from http://dx.doi.org/10.1787/9789264130852-en and Retrieved October 30, 2014, from http://www.oecd.org/edu/school/50293148.pdf

Pachler, N., Bachmair, B., & Cook, J. (2010). *Mobile learning: Structures, agency, practices*. New York, NY: Springer.

Rawls, J. (1971). *A theory of justice*. Cambridge, MA: Belknap Press of Harvard University Press

Rummler, K. (2012). *Medienbildungschancen von Risikolernern. Eine Analyse der Nutzung mobiler und vernetzter Technologien männlicher jugendlicher Risikolerner und die in den Nutzungsmustern angelegten Chancen für Medienbildung* (Dissertation). Kassel: Universität Kassel.

Rymes, B. (2011). Deference, denial, and beyond: A repertoire approach to mass media and schooling. *Review of Research in Education, 35*(1), 208–238. Retrieved October 30, 2014, from http://rre.sagepub.com/content/35/1/208

Schulze, G. (1992). *Die Erlebnisgesellschaft. Kultursoziologie der Gegenwart*. Frankfurt a.M., Campus, 2. Auflage.

Sen, A. (1999). *Development of freedom*. Oxford and New York: Oxford University Press.

Sinus Sociovision. (2007). *Die Milieus der Menschen mit Migrationshintergrund in Deutschland. Eine qualitative Untersuchung von Sinus Sociovision*. Heidelberg: Auszug aus dem Forschungsbericht'. Sinus Sociovision GmbH. Ezanvillestraße 59 / D-69118 Heidelberg. Postfach 251265 / D-69080 Heidelberg

Sinus Markt-und Sozialforschung, Heidelberg (2014). *Sinus-Milieus in Germany. Social Status and Basic Orientation*. Retrieved November 3, 2014, from http://www.sinus-institut.de/de/infobereich-fuer-studierende.html

CHAPTER 12

UNLOCKING THE POTENTIAL OF SOCIAL MEDIA FOR PARTICIPATION, CONTENT CREATION, AND E-ENGAGEMENT

Students' Perspectives and Empowerment

Maria Ranieri, Alessia Rosa, and Stefania Manca

ABSTRACT

In recent years, interest in the potential of social media and social networking sites for young people's participation in public spaces has gained momentum. These media have been seen as adequate to support the development of participatory culture. However, some studies have questioned their participatory power and demonstrated that online participatory culture is still in an early stage. This chapter reports on a study involving 163 Italian youths with the aim of presenting the development of an instrument to evaluate

E-Learning and Social Media:
Education and Citizenship for the Digital 21st Century, pp. 249–274

participatory attitudes of teens (ePAAA, Assessing Adolescents' Attitudes towards e-Participation) and advance in our knowledge of how young people are appropriating social media. In the first part, the theoretical background is illustrated focusing on the different forms of participation and content creation, the notion of civic engagement and the role of social media. In the second part, the characteristics of the assessment tool are described and the results of its administration are discussed, while considering its implications for education and citizenship. Indeed, since there are no deterministic links between social media usage and active engagement, the main conclusion of the chapter is that education, especially media education, should play a major role in supporting adolescents' civic engagement and empowerment.

INTRODUCTION

Over recent years, there has been an increasing emphasis on the potential of the Internet as a means for improving young people's participation in digital public spaces (Jenkins, Clinton, Purushotma, Robison, & Weigel, 2009). The Internet has been recognized as a technology enabling participatory attitude, facilitating content creation and supporting civic engagement. The rise of Web 2.0 tools and social network sites has also been viewed as a driver for young people's participation: from discussing in a web forum to creating content in a wiki, from sharing useful resources to using information in every field of life—education, politics, economy, and society. Indeed, new digital media are offering young people opportunities to undertake participative roles with positive implications on the development of their abilities (empowerment): at the individual level (development of competences, exposure to different points of view), at the community level (the richness of different points of view and sharing of information), and at the social level (civic involvement and democratic participation).

However, some studies have questioned the enthusiasm in the participatory power of the Internet. Hargittai and Walejko (2008) found that, despite new opportunities to engage in such distribution of content, relatively few people are taking advantage of these recent developments. Therefore, though the Internet might seem to have great potential, research on online participatory culture is still at the beginning.

The aim of this study is to add a "piece of evidence" about the issues of online participation, content creation, and civic engagement through the development of an instrument that was pilot tested with 163 Italian students. In particular, it intends to provide a conceptual framework to explore adolescents' perceptions of the participatory potential of the Internet, particularly social media and social networking sites.

It begins with a theoretical introduction focusing on the different forms of participation and content creation, the notion of civic engagement and the role of social media. It then presents a methodological approach to investigate adolescents' participatory attitudes and the results of the pilot testing. It concludes with a discussion on the implications of findings for education and citizenship, and some considerations for future research.

THEORETICAL BACKGROUND

Learning Through Participation and Content Creation in the Social Media Landscape

The widespread diffusion of social media tools, as strictly derived from the advent of the so-called Web 2.0, has deeply influenced reflection on the theoretical models and paradigms that better incorporate these new participatory practices. From the premises of situated learning, to the more socially oriented streams of constructivism, up to the connectivist approach, social media have been emphasized as means through which to encourage participation within learning contexts. They are perceived and proposed as able to deeply transform teaching and learning practices as more social, open and collaboration oriented (e.g., Siemens & Weller, 2011).

According to situated learning theory (Brown, Collins, & Duguid, 1989), learning is located in contexts and relationships and is mediated by artefacts such as technology and language. Relying on real-life problems and on informal and non-institutional contexts, the role of peer groups and of social movement activities is seen as fundamental in socializing younger generations into civic, political, and cultural identities. From this perspective, the design of learning environments where students may improve their skills of participation proves to be of high value. At the same time, in educational contexts the social constructivist model has greatly emphasized the role of collaborative knowledge building as the process of shared-meaning making within learning communities (Stahl, Koschmann, & Suthers, 2006). Collaboration refers to much more than individual learning in groups, since it refers to the practices of meaning making that occur in contexts of joint activities. Finally, the connectivist view of knowledge as articulated connections, through which to create a network of relationships or intellectual patterns across disciplines, further explores the concepts of situated learning as it sees knowledge as being located both in people, groups, and networks (Siemens, 2005). From this perspective, knowledge resides especially in the social networks that individuals, together with the artefacts and the technological tools used to collaborate and communicate with each other, constantly build and shape.

Social media and social network sites incorporate these broad concepts in so far as knowledge building processes are embodied as decentralized, accessible and co-constructed among users. They exploit the connections among people and tools through features that promote individual users, interconnections, and sharing of user-generated content. Integrating social media in learning and teaching environments seems to promote new forms of critical inquiry, communication, collaboration, identity formation, and knowledge development (Gao, Luo, & Zhang, 2012; Greenhow & Burton, 2011; Greenhow & Robelia, 2009a, 2009b), which may be further exploited in informal learning environments. As reported in the next section, informal participation practices such as civic engagement may especially benefit from the provision of social media tools.

By exploring in more detail the nature of different ways of participation and content creation on the Internet, we can identify a continuum that goes from lighter and less engaging forms of social aggregation such as that of crowds (Haythornthwaite, 2011) to more defined and engaging aggregations such as communities of practice (Wenger, 1998). The former are based on contributions submitted by unrelated individuals, that require little learning or training for submission, with minimal commitment to belonging and continuing with future contributions. In the latter, participants are required to learn and be apprentices before contributing, as well as being committed to belonging, staying, and continued contribution.

An intermediate form of network is provided by the concept of networks of practices (Brown & Duguid, 2000). The term "network" implies a set of individuals who are connected through social relationships, whether they be strong or weak, whereas the term "practice" represents the substrate that connects individuals in their networks. What distinguishes a network of practice from other networks is that the primary reason for the emergence of relationships is that individuals interact through information exchange in order to perform their work, asking for and sharing knowledge with each other, and it needs not necessarily be restricted to include those within one occupation or functional discipline. In electronic networks of practice, individuals may never get to know one another or meet face-to-face, and they generally coordinate through means such as electronic mailing lists or social media sites.

Another concept, which is related to the different forms of participation and content creation, is social capital. Defined as "the aggregate of the actual or potential resources which are linked to possession of a durable network of more or less institutionalized relationships of mutual acquaintance or recognition" (Bourdieu, 1986, p. 248), social capital has a positive role within groups and communities of individuals in so far as it facilitates coordination and cooperation for mutual benefit. Individual benefits come from the exchange of resources, which can take the form of useful information, personal relationships, or the capacity to create and manage groups (Putnam, 2000). These benefits are mainly constituted by the nature of network ties, either strong or weak (Haythornthwaite, 2002). Whereas, for instance, communities of practice are mainly made by strong ties, crowds advocate the crucial presence of weak ties.

In the study of social media and social network sites the notion of social capital has been adopted to denote the use of technologies to expand, enhance, and accelerate an individual's social network with an increase in available information, opportunities, and benefits from this wide and heterogeneous network. In particular, boyd and Ellison (2007) underlined that social network sites are typically used by individuals to maintain offline social relationships rather than to try to meet new people online. In this perspective, social network sites are mainly seen as tools supporting existing social relationships and, therefore, enabling the maintenance of social capital (Ellison, Steinfield, & Lampe, 2007). However, Facebook for instance also includes features that allow people to create new connections, whose nature may be better described through the construct of "latent ties," defined by Haythornthwaite (2005) as connections that are "technically possible but not yet activated socially" (p. 137). The information included in an individual's Facebook profile may motivate users to activate latent ties, transforming them into the weak ties linked to bridging social capital outcomes. Although research suggests that the practice of using Facebook to maintain existing social relationships is more common than that of using it to create new connections with strangers, there is also some evidence that "users may use the site to convert latent into weak ties" (Ellison, Steinfield, & Lampe, 2011, p. 877). This may be of particular interest in the study of Facebook groups, where it is highly likely that most members are technically linked but not yet socially connected (Ranieri, Manca, & Fini, 2012).

In relation to social media and social network sites, experiences of use reported in several research studies show how these sites facilitate collaboration and coordination through a number of embodied features such as: non-hierarchical structures, that allow ownership at different levels; tools to co-produce content asynchronously; automatic publishing capabilities; and the ability to adapt the layout or functionality of the site (Greenhow & Li, 2013). At the same time, social media tools allow different degrees of participation and the construction of forms of social capital that may greatly vary according to the purpose of the project or activity and to the pedagogical model in use. As can be seen in the next section, forms of participatory culture such as civic engagement may benefit greatly from these socio-technical devices in informal contexts of learning.

Civic Engagement and Social Media

The expressions e-engagement, engagement 2.0 (Pettingill, 2008), community engagement, and civic engagement (Greenhow & Li, 2013) indicate new forms of civic participation and active citizenship, including political and electoral activities, campaigning, petitioning lawmakers, and voting, enabled by the use of social media and inspired by the principles of the "participatory culture" (Jenkins et al., 2009). According to Jenkins and colleagues (2009),

> the participatory culture is a culture with relatively low barriers to artistic expression and civic engagement, strong support for creating and sharing creations, and some type of informal mentorship whereby experienced participants pass along knowledge to novices. In a participatory culture, members also believe their contributions matter and feel some degree of social connection with one another. (p. 11)

Due to their distinctive features, such as being "people centric," "interactive," "social," and "adaptive," social media seem to provide opportunities to support the development of a participatory culture, since they enable users to create and share products and projects, participate in communities of interest, take part in discussions, promote and exchange ideas, compare different points of view, participate in social, political, and cultural groups, and virtual or hybrid (online and offline) communities or networks.

The emergence of civic engagement is particularly concerning with the younger generation (Rheingold, 2008). Indeed, young people are increasingly seen as far and distant from the traditional models of civic participation, with negative consequences for active citizenship and democratic practice (Levine, 2007). Overall, there is a gradual decline today in the participation of citizens in public debate, which is accompanied by a pervasive sense of mistrust in public institutions and political life. Social media seem to offer an opportunity to face decline of participation enabling the development of a new model of citizenship (Bennett, Maton, & Kervin, 2008). Networked activism includes both personal and collective values, with a shift from the idea of a cultural and common public sphere to the concept of active participation in networked and open public sphere in daily life (Burgess, Foth, & Klaebe, 2006). From this perspective, a number of scholars have tried to explore and analyze the relationship between users' participation in social media, particularly young people and their civic engagement (e.g., Eikenberry, 2012; Hull & Stornaiuolo, 2010; Kassem, 2013; Östman, 2012; Robelia, Greenhow, & Burton, 2011; Theocharis, 2012; Valenzuela, Park, & Kee, 2009). For example, Valenzuela and colleagues (2009) found positive relationships between the intensity of general Facebook use among college students and their reported level of civic engagement and political participation. They argued that increased participation in online Facebook groups helps to build trusting relationships among members and potentially increased levels of civic engagement offline over time. With a focus on the role of Facebook use in non-formal civic learning in an Egyptian secondary school, Kassem (2013) reported that the use of Facebook was crucial to students' civic learning by blurring the differences in civic learning outcomes between general and technical secondary school students. Similarly, in a study on the implications of user generated content (UGC) involvement in democratic engagement among young people, Östman (2012) found that UGC involvement predicts offline as well as online political participation, and suggested that the expressive, performative, and collaborative features of UGC involvement can promote political participation. Theocharis (2012) analyzed the role of old and new online platforms in student protests against the increase in the tuition fee cap in the United Kingdom and concluded that they demonstrated the potential of new media for political mobilisation, while stressing the need to better understand the role of digital tools in political activism.

Moreover, exploring civic engagement in a formal learning environment, Hull & Stornaiuolo (2010) conducted a content analysis of adolescents' contributions within an international social network bridging middle and high school students to develop local and global citizenship and found an increased level of community engagement. Robelia and colleagues (2011) examined the impact of a social networking application on students' adoption of environmentally responsible behavior and found that participation in a community of like-minded users spurred many participants to learn more about climate change and do more to limit its impact.

Overall, these studies suggest that social media may facilitate young people's civic engagement. As observed by Greenhow and Li (2013),

> Features unique to SNSs may foster norms of reciprocity and trust as users feel more inclined to express their ideas in spaces with prominent personal profiling; join causes they learn about through their "friend" networks; keep updated via user-centred news feeds; and increase their knowledge of other members' civic, political, or electoral activities, influencing their own participation. (p. 133)

However, there are also negative aspects, or at least controversial issues, that need to be taken into account. For example, according to Friesen and Lowe (2012) the commercial nature of Facebook would limit the opportunities to express disagreement, since the relational model that underpins the Facebook architecture is based on the implicit concept of conviviality and "Like." This culture of agreement, which reflects the same logic informing television in the 1960s, would encourage compliance and conformity with respect to dominant positions, reducing the potential for critical thinking. In addition, as pointed out by Selwyn (2011) and Banaji and Buckingham (2013), not all of the opportunities offered by social media automatically transform into individual and social benefits. For instance, Byrne (2007) examined community life in BlackPlanet, a social network site that features user-driven discussion forums on topics ranging from entertainment to race-related issues, and found that while participants were deeply committed to ongoing discussions about black community issues, none of these discussions moved beyond a discursive level of civic engagement. More recently, in a survey on civic engagement in the digital age, Smith (2013) found that social networks are playing an increasingly important role on the political level in the United States, where a third of the population is involved in media activism. However, the majority of those who take part in engaged activities have a good level of cultural and socio-economic background. Furthermore, as underlined by Jenkins and colleagues (2009), the development of a participatory culture requires socio-technical and communication skills as well as media awareness and critical thinking. Not all these competences can be taken for granted in people who have not yet reached a sufficient cognitive and emotional maturity and in social groups at risk of exclusion. From this perspective, Hargittai and Walejko (2008), in a study on participatory and creative uses of digital media, found that, despite the new opportunities for production and sharing offered by social media, there are few people who actually produce and distribute content. The main trend is to consume information rather than to produce it. Similar data are consistent with results from other surveys on young people's digital competence (Bennett & Maton, 2010; Bennett, Maton, & Kervin, 2008; Calvani, Fini, Ranieri, & Picci, 2012; Hargittai, 2010; Li & Ranieri, 2010), which demonstrate that, though young people have high familiarity with information and communication technology, they have lower levels of cognitive, social, and ethical abilities in the use of technology.

HOW TO INVESTIGATE ADOLESCENTS' ATTITUDES TOWARD ONLINE PARTICIPATION

There are several types of research design that may be usefully adopted to explore adolescents' attitudes toward online participation, content creation, and e-engagement. With no claim to be exhaustive, in the following an overview of these approaches and their related research tools are provided. They include, to different degrees, the active participation of youths in the investigation of their digital habits and attitudes and may be differently combined together, thus intertwining tools and methods originating from separate approaches.

One of these approaches is based on online ethnography (also called virtual ethnography), which adapts methods to the study of the communities and cultures created through computer-mediated social interaction (Crichton & Kinash, 2003; Rheingold, 2008; Schuck, Aubusson, & Kearney, 2010). Earl and Schussman (2008), for instance, have explored, through after analysis grids, the proliferation of online petitions, in which cultural contestation and engagement are made visible. Their approach involves the researchers participating in various Web 2.0 spaces and interacting with other users to understand what is happening. Due to the presence of researchers in the observatory context, this approach results strictly related to ethical sensitivities, as pointed out by the Association of Internet Researchers (AoIR) ethics working committee (Ess & AoIR, 2002). Ethical issues range from confidentiality and anonymity to more serious concerns about the consequences of encouraging adolescents to engage with adults entering their environment covertly.

Virtual ethnography is often associated with the action research approach. In the Youth Internet Radio Network experience, established at Queensland University of Technology to engage young people in creative forms of cultural production through online networks, researchers have observed and analyzed how students participate in these networks and how they are affected by this kind of interaction (Notley & Tacchi, 2005).

Other approaches are based on the observation and intervention in offline contexts such as schools and learning centres. In this case, youths are pre-emptively informed and their participation is generally voluntary and confidential. The researcher collects stories from the group of subjects involved in the research that provide meaningful insights into how youths use several online tools to engage and make positive changes in their communities. These stories can be used in the initial phase of analysis of the context or as a means of understanding the data collected through surveys and questionnaires (Raynes-Goldie & Walker, 2008). This type of tool aims at collecting data about students or youths' self-assessment and evaluation of their digital experiences, such as their engagement in a specific social community or their perceived ability to react in various ways to a hypothetical scenario. For example, Jugert and colleagues (2013) measured civic engagement with seven items adapted from Lyons (2008). They assessed both participation in the past 12 months and future intentions to participate through the following actions: to link news, music, or video with a social or political content to their contacts; to discuss societal or political contents on the net; to participate in an online-based petition; to protest or boycott; to connect to a group in an online social network dealing with social or political issues; and to visit a website of a political or civic organization.

Though these methods are adequate for deep analysis of young people's media practices, either they require long-term observation or they focus on Internet usages rather than on attitudes and values. This brought us to reflect on alternative methodological tools, such as the tool presented in the following.

A TOOL FOR ASSESSING ADOLESCENTS' ATTITUDES

Background of the Tool and Research Questions

The tool and the results of its testing that are presented here derive from a one-year (2011–2012) project on media literacy education and digital citizenship funded by the Italian Ministry of Education that involved a network of schools in Tuscany (Italy). The aim of the project was to develop students' socio-technical, communicative, and cognitive skills to promote citizenship and youth engagement. About 800 students from primary to secondary schools were engaged with a range of media education activities that have been described and discussed in Bruni (2013) and Ranieri and Bruni (2013).

In this chapter, we will focus on a specific section of the project that consisted of the development and testing of the tool, ePAAA (Assessing Adolescents' Attitudes towards e-Participation), to assess teens' attitudes toward online participation and civic engagement. The tool was developed and tested with a sample of 163 students of first and second grades in a secondary school in Cecina (Livorno, Italy). Participants were from lower to lower middle class backgrounds, which is a target that has received less attention in the specialized literature.

It is worth clarifying that the purpose that guided the study was not to rate young people's skills, rather to explore adolescents' perceptions of the participatory potential of the Internet for community building, content creation, and civic participation. Briefly, we can summarise our research interests through the following questions:

Q1. How to assess young people's attitudes toward the potential of the Internet for online participation and civic engagement?

Q2. How do adolescents perceive the role of the Internet for self-expression, content creation, and networking in the public sphere?

Operationalization of Constructs and Development of Indicators

The first step to develop the assessment tool was the operationalization of the concept of online participation. For this purpose, we identified four levels of online engagement by referring to notions such as public versus private, active versus passive involvement, and strong ties vs. weak ties, which are widely documented in the literature on social media, learning and civic participation (see above).

Level 1. Crowd

The first level refers to the idea of a crowd intended as "a 'lightweight' collaborative structure" (Haythornthwaite, 2011) where people are widely interconnected by weak ties: indeed, crowd sourced projects do not require knowing others and working with them directly as a prerequisite for participation (e.g., OpenStreetMap, a collaborative project started by Steve Coast in the U.K. in 2004 with the aim of creating a free editable map of the world, http://www.openstreetmap.org). In addition, crowds are very often public spaces and their members may be more or less active depending on their interests, time and resources.

Level 2. Network

The second level is inspired by the concept of network of practices (Brown & Duguid, 2000) intended as an intermediate entity between social structures requiring strong involvement and continued contribution on one hand, and entities where individuals contribute in a completely unrelated way on the other hand. In these networks, ties could be either strong or weak and the level of involvement ranges from passive to active. What is relevant is the availability to share information and contacts to develop and maintain social capital (see boyd & Ellison, 2007). Moreover, like social networking sites, networks can be seen as semi-public spaces with different levels of privacy settings.

Level 3. Community

The third level is related to the notion of virtual communities defined by Rheingold (1993) as "social aggregations that emerge from the [Internet] when enough people carry on those public discussions long enough with sufficient human feeling to form webs of personal relationships in cyberspace" (p. 5). They are characterized by commons interests, public discussions, conviviality, and interaction. Unlike crowds and networks, communities are based on stronger ties and they are not necessarily public, which means that participation in communities may require some kinds of affiliation or approval by the community manager.

Level 4. Collaborative Groups

The fourth level is linked to studies on collaborative knowledge building (Stahl, Koschmann, & Suthers, 2006) where collaborative groups are intended as small groups of people (5–7 members) working on the achievement of the same goal through strong interactions and social negotiation enhanced by computer-mediated communication. These groups may be seen as heavyweight collaborative structures (Haythornthwaite, 2011), with strong affiliation and membership, and as private spaces where members contribute for a certain period to the finalization of a task.

After in-depth discussion within the research group, three indicators were identified for each level for an overall number of 12 indicators, referring to personal attitudes or behavior toward the others in terms of responsibility, openness, trust, and engagement. Each indicator, in turn, was explored in relationship to a specific value-based situation with civic and ethical implications. More specifically, these situations were chosen taking into consideration the literature on online communities and civic engagement, as well as real events that researchers experienced in their activities as media educators at school. Table 12.1 provides an overall picture of indicators and situations.

INSTRUMENT DEVELOPMENT

Once indicators had been defined, the assessment tool was developed. It is structured into two sections. The first section includes multiple choice questions (15 items) on socio-demographic data and Internet usage. The questions around Internet usage were included to better contextualize the overall data collected and to stimulate students to reflect on their own Internet activities before answering the questions included in the second section.

The second section is more strictly related to the focus of the study aiming at developing a participatory assessment tool to investigate teens' participatory attitudes. Questions were elaborated according to an adapted version of the storytelling technique applied to research. This method was originally developed by Marradi (2005) and then revised by Trinchero and Tordini (2011) to explore people's values. It relies on the assumption that personal values and attitudes play a crucial role in guiding people to take decisions in key situations where the subject is not asked to describe their views, but to take a stand on a certain issue choosing from a limited number of options. The situations are thought of as everyday scenarios rather than ideal events. Stories are indeed used as interviewing tools aimed at exploring the position of respondents on the four levels of online engagement identified above (crowd, network, community, and collaborative group).

Table 12.1. Conceptual Representation and Indicators of Participation and Civic Engagement

Level	*Indicators*	*Value-Based Situations*
Crowd level	Being willing to share personal views/opinions/ratings	Engaging with socio-political issues
	Being interested in considering and trusting in views/opinions/ratings by others	Engaging with taking informed decisions
	Making public the access to self-produced contents	Engaging with supporting open culture
Network level	Being willing to share resources within his/her own social network	Engaging with sharing information as public good
	Sharing his/her personal contacts	Engaging with sharing social capital
	Connecting people and resources	Engaging with developing open knowledge
Community level	Being a member of a community	Engaging with environmental campaigns
	Engaging with mentoring	Engaging with supporting open culture
	Respecting rules and others	Engaging with respecting others
Collaborative level	Being willing to work with others to achieve a common goal	Engaging with managing social events
	Taking responsibilities and roles	Engaging with communication as a cooperative process
	Contributing to the work group in an active way	Engaging with developing open knowledge

Each item is made up of two different parts. In the first part, a short story is reported that is typically based on a situation entailing a controversial choice, while in the second part, a direct question is asked requesting respondents to express their positions about the story. For each level, three stories are proposed for an overall number of 12 items. Table 12.2 shows some examples of items (one example for each level of participation investigated).

Table 12.2. Examples of Items

Level 1: Crowd

Example: During a festival of independent cinema, Isabella convinces Andrea and Luca to watch a movie directed by an African Director about the wars for the control diamond extraction. Surprisingly the film excited them. The movie is scheduled in a small cinema which, however, has an interesting website where people can rate the films and evaluate them. Luca is determined to provide and disseminate his positive feedback, since the film is barely advertised and shown in few cinemas, so others will be intrigued or maybe they're going to see it. Andrea instead thinks it's just a waste of time because no one will read or trust his judgment. According to you which is right?

> Andrea
>
> Luca

Level 2: Network

Example: While writing a science essay, Simona has managed to create a collection of websites on the topic and has decided to publish it on the blog of Luca who collects and shares digital learning resources.

From your point of view,

> Simona is right because this could be of help to some other students.
>
> Simona is wrong because the sites she identified are public, so everyone can seek them for themselves rather than using things done by others.

Level 3: Community

Example: Jonathan is very skilled in understanding how software and computer applications work, so he decides to create and share online a list of the best freeware video-editing programs and produces a number of useful tutorials.

In your opinion,

> Jonathan is very generous and is right to share his ability with other people
>
> Jonathan is just an egocentric person.... Actually, if he has a skill, he should keep it to himself!

Level 4: Collaborative (groups)

Example: Beatrice, Luca, Simone, Roberto and Maria are great fans of Lady Gaga and decide to develop together a Wikipedia page. For this purpose, they plan for different roles and responsibilities with some of them presenting her biography, others searching for images and others for music. In their view, this is the only way to achieve the goal in a complete manner.

In your opinion,

> The final result will hardly be satisfactory as someone will work more and some less: since there is no grade, there will be different levels of contribution.
>
> Only by working together the final result will be satisfactory since there is so much material. Satisfaction is given by the result and the accuracy of the work.

To increase the reliability of the tool, the stories were analyzed by a panel of experts who provided their feedback on each item. Moreover, to verify that the situations described in the stories were adequate to the target, the instrument was administered and discussed with a small group of teenagers (23 students) randomly selected from a sample of secondary school students in Northern Italy. The input received from experts and teenagers led to an iterative process of reviewing that ended with the production of the final version of the tool.

Data gathered through the administration of the stories were calculated by giving 1 score for each answer indicating active participatory attitudes and 0 score for each answer indicating poor participatory attitudes. For each participatory level, the percentage of respondents showing positive or negative attitudes was calculated in relation to each indicator.

To better understand the value and meaning of the quantitative data, two of the seven classes involved in the study were randomly selected (corresponding to 30% of the sample) for interviews through a focus group. The focus group aimed at deepening understanding about teens' views on information searching (e.g. What types of content do you search for?), creation and sharing (e.g., What types of content do you create or share online?), and e-engagement (e.g., Do you engage with active practices of supporting others or producing contents?). At the same time, the focus group helped to improve the tool and identify further areas to be investigated.

RESULTS

Participants' Characteristics and Internet Usage

Participants were quite balanced in terms of gender, including 70 males (43%) and 93 females (57%) (Table 12.3). On the contrary, the age varied significantly with 6 (4%) participants over 20 years old, 94 (58%) aged between 14 and 16 years, and 63 (38%) between 17 and 19 years. This variety is mainly due to the high number of students who failed their exams.

With regard to parent education, their educational background is rather low with very few parents having an academic degree (40 parents out of 323), while most of them have a middle school diploma (135 parents out of 323) or a secondary school diploma (151 parents out of 323). Table 12.3 summarizes the main characteristics of the sample.

Results relating to Internet usage (Table 12.4) show that the most common activities were using social networks (M = 4.27; SD = 1.06), listening to music (M = 4.21; SD = 0.88), and chatting online (M = 4.18; SD = 1.04). On the other hand, participants declared they spent less time

Table 12.3. Socio-Demographic Characteristics

Characteristics	*No.*	*%*
Gender		
Male	70	43%
Female	93	57%
Students' Age		
14–16	94	58%
17–19	63	38%
20	6	4%
Mother's Education		
Middle school	66	41%
Secondary school	74	45%
University	23	14%
Father's Education		
Middle school	85	52%
Secondary school	61	37%
University	17	10%

shopping online (M = 1.81; SD = 0.99), reading and sending e-mails (M = 2.9; SD = 1.1), playing online games (M = 2.55; SD = 1.18), and posting personal contents (M = 2.67; SD = 1.1).

Table 12.4. Internet Usage (N = 163)

Variation of Use	*M*	*SD*
Searching for information	3.18	0.93
Reading and sending e-mail	2.90	1.10
Using social networks	4.27	1.06
Chatting online	4.18	1.04
Watching online videos	3.82	0.95
Listening to music	4.21	0.88
Downloading files	3.38	1.12
Posting personal contents	2.67	1.10
Playing online games	2.55	1.18
Shopping online	1.81	0.99

Scale: 1 = never, 2 = rarely, 3 = sometimes, 4=often, 5=very often

Participatory Attitudes

On the whole, respondents revealed active participatory attitudes toward the use of the Internet (Table 12.5): for each level they mostly opted for active participatory behavior. However, it seems that they preferred to share and be in a network rather than engage with collaborative work within small groups. More specifically, on a crowd level (level 1) respondents showed a positive attitude toward being willing to share personal views (75.46%) and trusting views/opinions/ratings from others (74.85%), while they were less willing to publish their self-productions (55.21 %).

Table 12.5. Participatory Attitudes

Participatory Attitudes	
Level 1 Crowd	
Being willing to share personal views/opinions/ratings	75.46%
Being interested in considering and trusting views/opinions/ ratings by others	74.85%
Making public the access to self-produced contents	55.21%
Level 2 Network	
Being willing to share resources within his/her own social network	70.55%
Sharing his/her personal contacts	92.64%
Connecting people and resources	70.55%
Level 3 Community	
Being a member of a community	84.05%
Engaging with mentoring	88.96%
Respecting rules and others	70.55%
Level 4 Collaborative Group	
Being willing to work with others to achieve a common goal	47.24%
Taking responsibilities and roles	79.75%
Contributing to the work group in an active way	74.23%

Moving to the network level (level 2), they appeared to be very willing to share their personal contacts (92.64%), while they were slightly less open to sharing resources within their network (70.55%) and connecting people and resources (70.55%).

In terms of approaches to community (level 3), respondents showed positive attitudes to engaging with mentoring (88.96%) and being part of a community (84.05%), and slightly less positive attitudes toward respecting rules and others (70.55%).

Finally, looking at participation in collaborative groups (level 4), while participants showed positive attitudes toward taking responsibilities and roles (79.75%) and contributing to group work, they resulted not being very willing to work with others in order to achieve a common goal (47.24%).

Participation, Content Creation, and E-Engagement

When exploring what type of information teens search for and share, there emerged through the focus group a clear distinction between content searched to achieve school related tasks and content sought for personal interest and pleasure. In the first case, participants declared to mainly use textual content from Wikipedia and through general search engines, and then very often "copy and paste." In the second case, both searching strategies and sources vary from images and pictures, to videos, music, and songs. Females are inclined to limit themselves to searching for songs and their translations, while males tend to share music and create media products such as a web radio supported by regional bodies. During the focus group, teens involved in the web radio project underlined the motivations that inspired the initiative: they wanted to promote non-mainstream music produced by small local bands through alternative broadcast channels.

As far as videos are concerned, teens mainly search for videos that are not available on media mainstream such as TV, but they are not used to participating in public commenting through blogs or other social media platforms. They clearly prefer to access information rather than engage with discussions in the networked public sphere.

Social networking sites are very often used to organise social events or to get information of some kind. Respondents mainly create private events such as birthday parties by inviting friends through private groups in Facebook. They do not create public events, but share public content created by others, though only when referred to local initiatives. For instance, some teens observed in very pragmatic terms that national events may not be of interest for their contacts. Therefore, it would be useless to circulate them among friends. Again they appeared to be more inclined to echo local rather than national events and to spread contents generated by others.

Overall, respondents seem rather indifferent or even suspicious toward participation in social or humanitarian events, because of scepticism on their impact. Basically, teens do not believe that their engagement might have any positive consequences. And yet a few of them argued that the use of social network sites may help to let a larger audience know certain aspects of reality, and this is a strength of these networks. Some of the awareness campaigns mentioned during the focus group were those against the abandoning of dogs, support for medical research and associations to contrast violence against women. In particular, the women's campaign was repeatedly named during the discussion reflecting a national trend which characterizes the Italian situation where in recent years violence against women has increased and women's movements have launched several initiatives promoted mainly through the web.

Teens also use social network sites to share their artworks in order to get hints and improve their productions. In this case, they are open to exchange views and opinions not only with peers who they know, but also with strangers. Some of the respondents also declared they use social media as a commercial tool in order to sell their own products and advertise the commercial initiatives of their friends (painted T-shirts and bracelets).

DISCUSSION AND IMPLICATIONS FOR CITIZENSHIP

To sum up the results, the respondents revealed a participatory approach to the Internet, particularly in the sense of sharing contacts (networking) as well as being engaged in both weak and strong ties (crowd and community). At the same time, participation as a personal active contribution seems to be less common when referred to the Internet potential: teens are, indeed, less enthusiastic about posting personal contents, sharing self-productions and engaging in collaborative work. In other words, when ePAAA stories were related to open culture values linked to sharing social capital and contacts, there emerged a clear option for positive attitude toward participation. On the contrary, when stories refer to open culture values related to content production and sharing, participants were less sensitive toward open practices of content sharing. Moreover, participants declared their positive attitudes toward helping other people through mentoring and sustaining behavior, but showed lower levels of awareness of the relevance of respecting rules and others.

These results are roughly confirmed by participants' comments and observations during the focus group. Indeed, teens are willing to share content such as news about social events, but merely when the spread of that news may have an impact on a local level. A sort of pragmatism seems to arise in use of the Internet, a pragmatism that guides teens' choices and daily practices of sharing. This is also the case when they stated they shared their artworks to get feedback for improvements. But this is only one side of the coin. When asked about a more politically engaged use of the Internet, such as using it for social campaigns, online petitions and so on, respondents answered they were not confident in their power to influence reality by using social media and digital tools. They basically distrust their self-efficacy and the efficacy of digital activism as well.

Though the results of our research present several limitations, mainly due to the sample, which is small, and not representative, they reflect some of the main trends emerging in current literature, though with some differences as discussed below.

Tackling the issue of participation and content creation, other studies (e.g., Hargittai & Walejko, 2008) reported that, though great emphasis is put on the specific features of social media and their potential for content generation and distribution, young people prefer to consume information —and sometimes in a very uncritical way—rather than create it. Overall, this is in line with our results. However, from our study, things seem to be slightly more complicated. In particular, looking at participants' comments during the focus group, an interesting difference takes shape between in and out of school practices of using content. In one case, students naïvely admitted to "cutting and pasting" content, when using the Internet for school related tasks, while in the other case they underlined sharing their artworks and creations. Briefly, in school students mainly replicate content, while out of school they create it. One might speculate that school expectations influence students' attitudes toward the use of the Internet. An implicit pedagogy based on the assumption that learning at school is a quite traditional practice with no place for creativity seems to affect students' perceptions of Internet usage at or for school. After all, some studies have shown that there could be several tensions between creativity and formal education: for instance, Beghetto (2007) found that teachers prefer standardised answers rather than unique ones, partly because they associate creativity with non-conformity and disruptive behavior that can threaten teachers' authority and their control of the classroom. Therefore, it is not surprising that students associate the creative use of the Internet to out of school activities. At the same time, this brings us to the consideration that, though the affordances of the media are fundamental in enabling certain activities rather than others, the social representation of institutions such as schools could be more influential in determining individuals' media practices and perceptions. More attention should be paid to this theme in future research on the topic.

Another issue concerns civic participation and engagement. As a first approximation, students showed a general awareness of the social value of sharing information and being part of a community. However, their interest in supporting civic uses of the Internet was low. No matter how we interpret this result, it is too early to draw any conclusions. Indeed, while a number of studies have explored the relationship between young people, social media, and civic engagement, we have to recognize that results on this aspect are still contrasting. For example, Livingstone, Bober, and Helsper (2005) found that interactive and creative uses of the Internet are encouraged by the very experience of using the Internet, but that visiting civic websites depends primarily on demographic factors (with older, middle-class girls being most likely to visit these sites). On the other hand, Kassem (2013) stated that the use of Facebook with its features of exposing people to different expertise and resources was crucial for the improvement of students' civic informal learning in the particularly sensitive context of Egypt after the Arab Spring.

Although we cannot draw a unique conclusion, we may nevertheless recommend not disarticulating the relationship between technology and society when exploring young people's media practices. In particular, we agree with Buckingham and Martinez-Rodriguez (2013) when they claim that

> While some see media and technology as a primary cause of the decline of "social capital' and of civic participation, others look to the internet in particular as a means of creating new forms of "networked citizenship" [*particularly referring to young people*].... Yet there is a need to move beyond these polarized arguments. The media are not solely responsible for the apparent decline in democracy; but neither are they likely to save it. (p. 10)

In this situation, a pivotal role may be played by education, particularly media literacy education, although education can achieve its results only in the long run. As well known, media literacy education aims at developing both critical understanding and active participation. In particular, it promotes young people's capacities to interpret and make informed judgments as consumers of media as well as their abilities as producers of media to become more powerful participants in society. This calls for a stronger commitment by educational institutions toward the implementation of new media literacy education projects.

CONCLUSION AND NEXT STEPS

While the debate on the potential of social media for active participation and civic engagement is still open, there are several research areas that deserve the attention of the education community. A better understanding of certain issues may help to overcome the dichotomous positions that often characterize the current discussion.

First, though there are several studies on social media and, more in general, Internet usages, research on users' attitudes toward online participation and values is relatively less common. Besides ethnographical approaches based on observation, specific instruments to assess those dimensions in wider contexts are still rare. In this chapter, we have presented a tool characterized by the use of stories that ask people to take a decision by opting between two different choices. Each choice entails agreement or disagreement with a range of values that can be brought back, at different levels, to the open participatory culture of sharing and offering. The tool was object of discussion among experts and administered in a pilot test to a sample of adolescents. However, it still needs improvements, both in terms of validation and content. Indeed, as emerged during the focus group, the relationship between teens and social media is more complicated than certain linear representations of their behavior and, though we were distant from linear representations, some stories require improvement.

Second, if things prove to be more complex, rather than opting for simplistic representations, more attention should be paid to teens' voices. As recommended by boyd (2014) in her latest book on the life of networked teens "my hope is that you will suspend your assumptions about youth in an effort to understand the social lives of networked teens. By and large, the kids are all right. But they want to be understood" (p. xi). In other words, very often adults—from researchers to teachers and parents—limit themselves to judging adolescents' media practices without taking into account their points of view. Therefore, the new generation appears in one way or another depending on the theoretical assumptions of the adults commenting on or interpreting them. If we want to support adolescents' empowerment, something must change even in the way we research them. boyd's recommendation on teens' listening should guide our research in this field.

And again, if things are complex, education, particularly media literacy education, may play a crucial role in empowering young people by influencing the way they perceive their own role as citizens in the new media landscape. According to Hobbs (2010), media literacy education refers to five main abilities that would be necessary for an individual's full participation in our media-saturated lives. They include the capacity to make responsible choices and access pertinent information, being able to analyze messages and evaluate their credibility, the ability to create content using new digital tools, the capacity to reflect on one's own conduct and communication behavior by applying social responsibility and ethical principles, and the ability to take social action by working individually and collaboratively to share knowledge and solve problems and participating as a member of a community. To make media literacy education support empowerment and citizenship, major investments in the field are needed to enable individuals to face the new ethical and societal challenges that social media are raising in the multiple contexts of contemporary daily life.

REFERENCES

Banaji, S., & Buckingham, D. (2013). *The civic web: Young people, the Internet and civic participation*. Cambridge, MA: MIT Press.

Beghetto, R. A. (2007). Does creativity have a place in classroom discussion? Prospective teachers' response preferences. *Thinking Skills and Creativity*, *2*(1), 1–9.

Bennett, S., & Maton, K. (2010). Beyond the "digital natives" debate: Towards a more nuanced understanding of students' technology experiences. *Journal of Computer Assisted Learning*, *26*(5), 321–331.

Bennett, S., Maton, K., & Kervin, L. (2008). The "digital natives" debate. A critical review of the evidence. *British Journal of Educational Technology*, *39*(6), 775–786.

Bourdieu, P. (1986). The forms of capital. In J. Richardson (Ed.), *Handbook of theory and research for the sociology of education* (pp. 241–258). New York, NY: Greenwood.

boyd, D. (2014). *It's complicated: The social lives of networked teens*. New Haven and London: Yale University Press.

boyd, D., & Ellison, N. B. (2007). Social network sites: Definition, history, and scholarship. *Journal of Computer-Mediated Communication*, *13*(1), 210–230.

Brown, J. S., Collins, A., & Duguid, P. (1989). Situated cognition and the culture of learning. *Educational Researcher*, *18*(1), 32–42.

Brown, J. S., & Duguid, P. (2000). *The social life of information*. Boston, MA: Harvard Business School Press.

Bruni, I. (2013). "Oltre lo Specchio dei Desideri". Percorsi di new media literacies nella scuola media [New media literacies paths in secondary school]. *TD – Tecnologie Didattiche*, *21*(1), 46–51.

Buckingham, D., & Martínez-Rodríguez, J. B. (2013). Interactive youth: New citizenship between social networks and school settings. *Comunicar*, XX, *40*, 10–13.

Burgess, J., Foth, M., & Klaebe, H. (2006). Everyday creativity as civic engagement: A cultural citizenship view of new media. In *Proceedings of Communications Policy & Research Forum*, 1–15.

Byrne, D. N. (2007). Public discourse, community concerns, and civic engagement: Exploring 35raditions on BlackPlanet.com. *Journal of Computer-Mediated Communication*, *13*(1), 319–340.

Calvani, A., Fini, A., Ranieri, M., & Picci, P. (2012). Are young generations in secondary school digitally competent? A study on Italian teenagers. *Computers & Education*, *58*(2), 797–807.

Crichton, S., & Kinash, S. (2003). Virtual ethnography: Interactive interviewing online as method. *Canadian Journal of Learning and Technology*, *29*(2), 1–5.

Earl, J., & Schussman, A. (2008). Contesting cultural control: Youth culture and online petitioning. In L. W. Bennett (Ed.), *Civic life online. Learning how digital media can engage youth* (pp. 71–96). Cambridge, MA: The MIT Press.

Eikenberry, A. M. (2012). Social networking, learning, and civic engagement: New relationships between professors and students, public administrators and citizens. *Journal of Public Affairs Education*, *18*(3), 449–466.

Ellison, N. B., Steinfield, C., & Lampe, C. (2007). The benefits of Facebook "friends": Social capital and college students' use of online social network sites. *Journal of Computer-Mediated Communication*, *12*(4), 1143–1168.

Ellison, N. B., Steinfield, C., & Lampe, C. (2011). Connection strategies: Social capital implications of facebook-enabled communication practices. *New Media & Society, 13*(6), 873–892.

Friesen, N., & Lowe, S. (2012). The questionable promise of social media for education: Connective learning and the commercial imperative. *Journal of Computer Assisted Learning, 28*(3), 183–194.

Gao, F., Luo, T., & Zhang, K. (2012). Tweeting for learning: A critical analysis of research on microblogging in education published in 2008–2011. *British Journal of Educational Technology, 43*(5), 783–801.

Greenhow, C., & Burton, L. (2011). Help from my "friends": Social capital in the social network sites of low-income students. *Journal of Educational Computing Research, 45*(2), 223–245.

Greenhow, C., & Li, J. (2013). Like, comment, share: Collaboration and civic engagement within social network sites. In C. Mouza, & N. Lavigne (Eds.), *Emerging technologies for the classroom: A learning sciences perspective* (pp. 127–141), Dordrecht, NL: Springer.

Greenhow, C., & Robelia, E. (2009a). Old communication, new literacies: Social network sites as social learning resources. *Journal of Computer-Mediated Communication, 14*(4), 1130–1161.

Greenhow, C., & Robelia, E. (2009b). Informal learning and identity formation in online social networks. *Learning, Media and Technology, 34*(2), 119–140.

Hargittai, E. (2010). Digital na(t)ives? Variation in Internet skills and uses among members of the net generation. *Sociological Inquiry, 80*(1), 92–113.

Hargittai, E., & Walejko, G. (2008). The participation divide: Content creation and sharing in the digital age. *Information, Communication & Society, 11*(2), 239–256.

Haythornthwaite, C. (2002). Strong, weak and latent ties and the impact of new media. *The Information Society, 18*(5), 385–401.

Haythornthwaite, C. (2005). Social networks and Internet connectivity effects. *Information, Communication & Society, 8*(2), 125–147.

Haythornthwaite, C. (2011). Learning networks, crowds and communities. In *Proceedings of the 1st International Conference on Learning Analytics and Knowledge (LAK '11)*(pp. 18–22), New York, NY: ACM Press.

Hobbs, R. (2010). *Digital and media literacy: A plan of action* (White Paper Recommendations of the Knight Commission on the Information Needs of Communities in a Democracy). Washington DC: Aspen Institute. Retrieved from http://www.knightcomm.org/digital-and-media-literacy

Hull, G. A., & Stornaiuolo, A. (2010). Literate arts in a global world: Reframing social networking as cosmopolitan practice. *Journal of Adolescent and Adult Literacy, 54*(2), 85–97.

Jenkins, H., Clinton, K., Purushotma, R., Robison, A., & Weigel, M. (2009). *Confronting the challenges of participatory culture: Media education for the 21st century*. Chicago, IL: The MacArthur Foundation.

Jugert, P., Eckstein, K., Noack, P., Kuhn, A., & Benbow, A. (2013). Offline and online civic engagement among adolescents and young adults from three ethnic groups. *Journal of Youth and Adolescence, 42*(1), 123–135.

Kassem, M. M. (2013). Facebook as a nation-wide civic education classroom listening to the voices of egyptian secondary school students. *Journal of Emerging Trends in Educational Research and Policy Studies (JETERAPS)*, *4*(5), 771–785.

Levine, P. (2007). *The future of democracy: Developing the next generation of American citizens*. Medford, MA: Tufts University Press.

Li, Y., & Ranieri, M. (2010). Are "digital natives" really digitally competent? A study on Chinese teenagers. *British Journal of Educational Technology*, *41*(6), 1029–1042.

Livingstone, S., Bober, M., & Helsper, E. J. (2005). Active participation or just more information? Young people's take-up of opportunities to act and interact on the Internet. *Information, Communication & Society*, *8*(3), 287–314.

Lyons, E. (2008). *Political trust and political participation amongst young people from ethnic minorities in the NIS and EU: A social psychological investigation*. Queen's University Belfast, NI: Final Report.

Marradi, A. (2005). *Raccontar storie* [Telling stories]. Roma, IT: Carocci.

Notley, T. M., & Tacchi, J. A. (2005). Online youth networks: Researching the experiences of 'peripheral' young people in using new media tools for creative participation and representation. *3CMedia: Journal of Community, Citizen's and Third Sector Media and Communication*, *1*(1), 73–81.

Östman, J. (2012). Information, expression, participation: How involvement in user-generated content relates to democratic engagement among young people. *New Media & Society*, *14*(6), 1004–1021.

Pettingill, L. (2008). Engagement 2.0? How the new digital media can invigorate civic engagement. *Gnovis*, *VIII*(III), 155–161.

Putnam, R. D. (2000). *Bowling alone: The collapse and revival of American community*. New York, NY: Simon and Schuster.

Ranieri, M., & Bruni, I. (2013). Empowering creativity in young people through mobile learning: An investigation of creative practices of mobile media uses in and out of school. *International Journal of Mobile and Blended Learning*, *5*(3), 17–33.

Ranieri, M., Manca, S., & Fini, A. (2012). Why (and how) do teachers engage in social networks? An exploratory study of professional use of Facebook and its implications for lifelong learning. *British Journal of Educational Technology*, *43*(5), 754–769.

Raynes-Goldie, K., & Walker, L. (2008). Our space: Online civic engagement tools for youth. In L. W. Bennett (Ed.), *Civic life online. Learning how digital media can engage youth* (pp. 161–188). Cambridge, MA: The MIT Press.

Rheingold, H. (1993). *The virtual community: Homesteading on the electronic frontier*. Cambridge, MA: The MIT Press.

Rheingold, H. (2008). Using participatory media and public voice to encourage civic engagement. In L. W. Bennett (Ed.), *Civic life online. Learning how digital media can engage youth* (pp. 97–118). Cambridge, MA: The MIT Press.

Robelia, B., Greenhow, C., & Burton, L. (2011). Environmental learning in online social networks: Adopting environmentally responsible behaviors. *Environmental Education Research*, *17*(4), 553–575.

Schuck, S., Aubusson, P., & Kearney, M. (2010). Web 2.0 in the classroom? Dilemmas and opportunities inherent in adolescent Web 2.0 engagement. *Contemporary Issues in Technology and Teacher Education, 10*(2), 234–246.

Selwyn, N. (2011). *Education and technology: Key issues and debates*. New York, NY: Continuum International Publishing Group.

Siemens, G. (2005). Connectivism: A learning theory for the digital age. *International Journal of Instructional Technology and Distance Learning, 2*(10), 3–10.

Siemens, G., & Weller, M. (2011). Higher education and the promises and perils of social networks. *Revista de Universidad y Sociedad del Conocimiento, 8*(1), 164–170.

Smith, A. (2013). *Civic engagement in the digital Age*. Pew Internet and American Life Project Report.

Stahl, G., Koschmann, T., & Suthers, D. (2006). Computer-supported collaborative learning: An historical perspective. In R. K. Sawyer (Ed.), *The Cambridge handbook of the learning sciences* (pp. 409–425). New York, NY: Cambridge University Press.

Theocharis, Y. (2012). Cuts, tweets, solidarity and mobilisation: How the Internet shaped the student occupations. *Parliamentary Affairs, 65*(1), 162–194.

Trinchero, R., & Tordini, M. L.(2011). *Responsabilità e disagio* [Responsibility and discomfort]: *Una Ricerca Empirica sugli Adolescenti Piemontesi* [An Empirical Research on Adolescents Piedmont]. Milano, IT: Franco Angeli.

Valenzuela, S., Park, N., & Kee, K. F. (2009). Is there social capital in a social network site?: Facebook use and college students' life satisfaction, trust, and participation. *Journal of Computer-Mediated Communication, 14*(4), 875–901.

Wenger, E. (1998). *Communities of practice: Learning, meaning, and identity*. London, UK: Cambridge University Press.

CHAPTER 13

DIGITAL CITIZENSHIP

Communication Capabilities and Technological Literacy

Carolyn M. Cunningham

ABSTRACT

The rapid diffusion of social media in the 21st century broadens our conceptualizations of civic participation. Because of the democratic potential of social media, bridging the physical digital divide is seen as only a first step in achieving equality. Teaching citizens how to effectively use these media to better their lives is an additional challenge (Hargittai, 2010). Educational efforts have focused on increasing students' technological literacy, defined as "the ability to use, manage, assess, and understand technology" (International Technology Education Association, 2002, p. 13).Technological literacy emphasizes adaptability, fluency, and an awareness of the role of technology in society. This chapter argues for a reframing of technological literacy to integrate Sen's (1999) notion of capabilities. Capabilities examine the freedoms individuals have to pursue their own potential. Communication capabilities are especially important for achieving equality. This chapter provides a theoretical framework for communication capabilities and analyzes the standards developed by the International Society for Technology

E-Learning and Social Media:
Education and Citizenship for the Digital 21st Century, pp. 275–295

Education (ISTE), the leading organization for assessing technological literacy. In the end, this chapter argues these standards should be expanded to include communication capabilities, including self-representation, freedom to achieve what one values, and learning to communicate about technology.

INTRODUCTION

Social media such as Facebook, Twitter, and YouTube provide platforms for the creation and exchange of user-generated content, offering increased opportunities for civic participation. Social media allow users to share their opinions on political topics, contact those in government office, and organize communities for social change. In recent years, social media have been instrumental for mobilizing social movements, such as the Arab Spring and the Occupy Wall Street Movement (Gerbaudo, 2012).

The diffusion of social media has also broadened what is meant by civic participation; it has shifted from a narrow definition that stresses participation in government activities to activities that shed light on the many ways that citizens participate in the world around them, such as community volunteering, consumer activism, and involvement in local and global social causes. This expanded definition of civic participation is especially important for youth who cannot participate in formal citizenship activities such as voting (Bennett, 2008).

Despite the democratic potential of social media, there is disagreement that all can participate equally due to a number of cultural and structural issues. The digital divide, which refers to physical access to hardware and software, continues to impact who does and who does not have access to social media. In the United States, broadband penetration continues to hover around 70% (National Telecommunications and Information Administration, 2013). Globally, access is dependent on geographical location, government policies, and affordability. Africa has lowest worldwide Internet penetration, with only 15.6% of the continent's population having access to the Internet.

More recently, scholars have identified a second level digital divide, which assesses the way people use information and resources available through the Internet (Hargittai, 2010; Peter & Valkenburg, 2006). These scholars have argued that focusing on physical access ignores differences in how people navigate online. Thus, digital literacy, or the ability to critically evaluate information on the Internet, is an important indicator of how users transform access to the Internet into knowledge (Buckingham, 2006).

In addition to digital literacy, technological literacy is important for addressing the digital divide. Technological literacy, defined as the ability to use, analyze, examine, understand, and seek out appropriate technologies to achieve one's aims, is an important component of equality. Beyond critical thinking skills, technological literacy emphasizes adaptability to technological change, fluency, and an understanding of the role of technology in society. Scholars such as Kahn and Kellner (2006) argue that technological literacy will enable students' full participation in economic, political, and social life.

While technological literacy may be a component of equality, there is much variation and interpretation of what is meant by technological literacy. Most assessments of technological literacy emphasize the economic and political benefits of technological literacy. From an economic perspective, technological literacy will help students obtain jobs and increase a country's global competitiveness. From a political perspective, technological literacy can help facilitate citizens' participation in democratic processes such as voting or accessing government documents. What is missing is an assessment of how technological literacy contributes to individual development. This perspective emphasizes the importance of communication and cultural production to democratic societies.

This chapter first provides an overview of technological literacy, including the current standards used in educational assessments. Drawing from developmental democratic theory, this chapter argues that these standards should be expanded to also include the capabilities citizens need to help them achieve their own potential. These include the ability to participate in one's own self-representation and form communities of interest, the ability to communicate about technology to engage in activities that affect one's life, and the freedom to pursue individual interests.

CURRENT DEFINITIONS OF TECHNOLOGICAL LITERACY

In general, technological literacy can be defined as "the ability to use, manage, assess, and understand technology" (International Technology Education Association, 2002, p. 13). Technological literacy is seen as a set of skills students should acquire to effectively participate in everyday life. Commonly referred to as 21st century literacy, technological literacy also emphasizes multimodal forms of communication. For example, the New Media Consortium (2005), comprised of education and high-tech industry experts, defined technological literacy as,

> the set of abilities and skills where aural, visual and digital literacy overlap. These include the ability to understand the power of images and sounds, to recognize and use that power, to manipulate and transform digital media, to distribute them pervasively, and to easily adapt them to new forms. (p. 2)

Definitions of technological literacy emphasize fluency, rather than competency. As the National Research Council (1999) writes, "people fluent with information technology ... are able to express themselves creatively, to reformulate knowledge, and to synthesize new information" (p. 2). Technological literacy, then, stresses the use of appropriate technologies to address individuals' needs and the ability to adapt to technological change. For example, a technologically literate student would be able to assess the advantages and disadvantages of different types of presentation software, such as PowerPoint or Prezi, and select appropriate software for achieving his or her needs.

Technological literacy builds upon a broad notion of technology, as can be seen in the International Technology Education Association's (ITEA) (2002) definition of technology:

> From the Greek word *techne*, meaning art or artifice or craft, technology literally means the act of making or crafting, but more generally it refers to the diverse collection of processes and knowledge that people use to extend human abilities and to satisfy human needs and wants. (p. 2)

Pedagogically, technological literacy emphasizes critical thinking skills that enable citizens to analyze and understand general patterns of technology and technological change. The goal of technological literacy is to provide citizens with a better understanding of how social forces shape technology and how society is shaped by technology. In turn, educational strategies include preparing students to adapt to technological change.

The International Society for Technology Education (ISTE) is the leading organization that defines the standards for assessing technological literacy. ISTE is a professional organization for technology educators, primarily K–12 teachers, and offers professional development, publications, and curriculum to its membership. One of the goals for creating standards for technological literacy is to address pedagogical approaches that over-emphasized technological competency and skill acquisition, rather than literacy. Technological competency stresses students' usage and consumption of technology and aims to increase their skills in different technical applications, such as Microsoft Word, spreadsheets, or Adobe Photoshop. However, as Pearson and Young (2002) point out, technological competence does not guarantee technological literacy. For example, civil engineers may be very skilled in understanding how structures and materials respond to heavy loads, yet have little understanding of technologies outside of their field or how the structures they build and design affect society (Pearson & Young, 2002, p. 17). Instead, technological literacy is a capacity to understand the broader technological world rather than have a specified expertise to operate with particular pieces of it.

The National Educational Technology Standards (NETS) developed by ISTE are often used as criteria for measuring students' technological literacy. The NETS encompasses six areas: creativity and innovation, communication and collaboration, research and information fluency, critical thinking and problem solving, digital citizenship, and technology operations and concepts. Standard 1 emphasizes "creativity and innovation" especially the ability for students to generate new ideas (Brooks-Young, 2007, p. 7). Additionally, Standard 1 encourages teachers to engage students in creative works that express individual or group ideas. Standard 2 suggests the importance of "communication and collaboration" in which students should learn to use communication technologies to communicate effectively and to engage in collaborative projects with others. Standard 3 emphasizes the use of digital technologies for "research and information fluency." Students should use digital technologies to not only access information, but also develop critical literacy through analyzing, evaluating, and synthesizing the information. Standard 4 states that students should "identify and define authentic problems and significant questions for investigation" and encourages students to choose appropriate technologies to carry out these investigations (Brooks-Young, 2007, p. 7). Standard 5 promotes "digital citizenship" in which students practice both legal and ethical behavior online. Finally, Standard 6 emphasizes the understanding of technological concepts and operations.

Economic Rationales for Technological Literacy

ISTE recognizes that technological literacy has economic, political, and social benefits. However, economic frameworks of technological literacy tend to dominate policy discourse. From an economic perspective, the shift from an industrial to an information economy has radically altered the structure of the workplace, requiring that workers have basic competencies with computer hardware and software applications. An economic rationale proffers one important reason for providing government intervention to increase citizens' technological literacy. Yet, an economic rationale does not address other ways communication technologies can contribute to political and social life. From a political perspective, technologically literate citizens can use social media to access information and participate in political discussions. They can also produce cultural content that contributes to the diversity of ideas in the public sphere. Socially, technological literacy can help individuals use social media for meeting their needs, communicating with others, and adapting to new technologies as strategies for achieving autonomy. The following section provides a critique of economic rationales and advocate for an expansion of technological literacy that includes a consideration of the developmental benefits.

An economic rationale emphasizes global competitiveness, particularly in developing technological innovation and increasing educational achievement so that citizens can be prepared to enter the increasingly technological workforce. From an economic perspective, jobs increasingly require advanced computer skills. In the United States, information technology jobs continue to grow steadily. The Bureau of Labor Statistics estimates that between 2010–2020, IT jobs will grow at an average annual rate of 6.1%, compared to 2.9% growth for all industries (Csorny, 2013). However, there is much concern that Americans will not be prepared to enter technology-related fields, and that they are falling behind other countries in creating and sustaining technological innovation, as reflected in the decrease in the U.S. share of IT revenue from 75% in the 1970s to 45% in 2000 (Cooper, 2004).

The economic rationale not only offers economic solutions, but also frames benefits of technological literacy in economic terms. In an economic framework, equality is best achieved through encouraging citizens' technological training that prepares them to enter the job market and provides a certain level of technological infrastructure through government intervention. Much of the discourse surrounding technological equity and gender tends to privilege economic justifications for achieving equality. For example, research from science, technology, engineering, and mathematics (STEM) perspectives often stress the economic benefits of equality, such as increasing women's individual career advancement (Coalition for Science Afterschool, 2006; Fancsali, 2002; Ramsey & McCorduck, 2005). While economic justifications for achieving equality speak to one important goal of technological literacy, they are limited. If economics are valued over individual development, then there is a tendency to ignore those outcomes that cannot be measured in economic terms. For example, gender diversity in the STEM workforce could add better design and better technological solutions that address the particular challenges women face. Or, encouraging women and girls to become technologically literate might make them more engaged in the world around them and prepare them to influence technology policy decisions.

Economic justifications do not adequately address the full range of reasons why youth should become technologically literate or why societies should seek equality in technological literacy. Social media create what Jenkins (2006) calls "participatory culture," where youth can actively contribute their perspectives to the public sphere through their cultural production. Forms of participatory culture include mash-ups, mobilizing smart mobs, memes, and crowd mapping. Social media also offer youths opportunities to draw attention to causes that are important to them. For example, youths in Syria, through their use of cellphone cameras and social media, have been able to draw global attention to the conflict there (Kaylan, 2013). Kaylan (2013) calls the Syrian conflict the first YouTube war, where users can view the conflict in almost real time.

Technological Literacy and Educational policy

An economic rationale for technological literacy has dominated educational reform policy in the U.S. since the 1980s. *A Nation at Risk*, the 1983 report that was one of the first documents to raise the idea of technological literacy, outlined a number of economic-based reforms, such as adopting higher measurable standards for academic performance, increasing the amount of time students spent in learning environments, and aiding the professional growth of teachers (National Commission on Excellence in Education, 1983) By the 1990s, educational policy intended to increase the technological infrastructure of schools as a way of achieving technological literacy. For example, in 1995, President Clinton's "Technological Literacy Challenge" outlined four economic strategies for technological literacy: connecting schools to the Internet, providing access to computers for teachers and students, developing software and online learning resources, and providing resources for teacher training (U.S. Department of Education, 1997). The Telecommunications Act of 1996 provided affordable access to telecommunications services in schools and libraries through subsidies, discounts, and the E-rate program. All of these policies for achieving universal technological literacy emphasize technological infrastructure and assume that access to computers and the Internet will increase students' technological skills. Yet, these policies fail to address what technological literacy adds to democracy.

In 2001, Congress passed the No Child Left Behind Act (NCLB) which called for standardized testing and school accountability as a way to address educational disparities. The mandate of NCLB is "to assist every student in crossing the digital divide by ensuring that every student is technologically literate by the time the student finishes the eighth grade, regardless of the student's race, ethnicity, gender, family income, geographic location, or disability" (No Child Left Behind Act, 2001). NCLB does not define technological literacy, but instead places the burden on state education agencies and local school districts to develop their own definitions. Additionally, local and state agencies are required to determine their own criteria, standards, and curriculum for preparing students to become technologically literate. Many of them have adopted ISTE's NETS.

As these examples show, educational reform policy since the 1980s focused on macroscopic issues, such as infrastructure and accountability. However, these interventions fall short of ensuring equality, especially for girls and minority youth (Volman & van Eck, 2001). These economic-based policies fail to address other barriers to achieving equality, such as students' attitudes toward technology, lack of content that appeals to girls and minority youth, teacher expectations, and gender dynamics in the classroom.

Technological Literacy and Neoliberalism

Finally, economic rationales promote neoliberalism, emphasizing competitiveness and job growth with the assumption that if individuals are more prepared in the workplace, they will be able to acquire better jobs and advance the economic interests of the larger society. This rationale does not address the democratic potential of new digital technologies. As Petrina (2000) writes, "U.S. government policies are largely the construction of a neutralized version of technoliteracy which bolsters a conservative politics of ideological competitive supremacy" (p. 254). This emphasis on competitiveness privileges the interests of those corporations prepared to compete in the global marketplace. As Kahn and Kellner (2006) argue, by the mid-1980s, technological literacy was defined in terms of furthering the competitive and capitalist interests of private corporations. In other words, goals of technological literacy were to create a prepared workforce, not to provide citizens with necessary tools to promote democracy.

From Economics to Development

Developmental democratic theory provides guidance for how the expansion of technological literacy standards can emphasize individual development. Developmental democracy stresses the importance of individual development to democratic society. Self-development can be defined as the "process of concretely becoming the person one chooses to be through carrying out those actions that express one's purposes and needs" (Gould, 1988, p. 47). Individual development is an ongoing process of identity formation and negotiation that occurs through social interactions. "Development" also refers to the processes through which individuals meet their basic needs and build the competencies they need to contribute to their daily life. Development includes a sense of self-worth and self-esteem, a belief in the future, self-determination, self-efficacy, and social, emotional, cognitive, behavioral and moral development (Pittman, 1993) Additionally, individual development is influenced not only by how individuals come to know themselves in the social world, but also by the conditions available for them to participate (Dahl, 1989; Held, 1996).

In liberal democracy, citizens participate in self-governance and in the protection of their individual rights. Taking cue of these principles, developmental democracy takes a positive view of rights and insists that equality is achieved not only through granting political rights to citizens, but also encouraging their social and individual development (Held, 1996). Self-development becomes central to the democratic project. In the tradition of John Stuart Mill (1863) who believed that through deliberation, individuals were better able to grow their mental capacities, developmental democracy emphasizes the role of culture and communication in allowing citizens to express their experiences and better understand each other. Communication allows for inquiry and through debate with others, individuals can strengthen or change their opinions. As Dewey (1934) later pointed out, creativity and self-expression are essential for individual development because they allow individuals to better understand themselves and the world around them.

Liberal democratic theory is characterized by citizens' participation in self-governance. Participation requires that individuals are autonomous and able to participate in deliberative decision-making, primarily through communicating with others. In developmental democracy, participation contributes to self-development through not only increasing individuals' capacities, but also having an informed citizenry. Developmental democratic theory promotes an expanded notion of participation, which extends beyond participation in the political sphere, to also include "the right of participation in decision-making in social, economic, cultural and political life" (Gould, 1988, p. 212). Stressing the importance of both social and political participation is especially important for youth, who are often excluded from participating in traditional political activities, such as voting. Youth are seen as learning to become citizens through their participation in institutions, such as education. Lister (2008) calls for a thicker sense of membership for children, in which children are included as active members of their communities:

> [including children] suggests that, while at one level all children are members of the community and therefore have the status of citizens in a thin sense, recognition of children as citizens in a thicker sense of active membership requires facilitating their participation in individual decisions about one's own lives made by parents and professionals, for it also implies participation in wider collective decision-making. (p. 11)

How might technological literacy contribute to a thicker sense of membership? Social media offer avenues for youth to express themselves, and, through communication with others, they might be better equipped to make decisions about themselves. Social media create opportunities for civic engagement, whether in local communities or globally. For example, the organization DoSomething.org uses social media to launch social justice campaigns for teens, such as collecting peanut butter for local food banks, challenging teens to stand up to bullying, donating prom dresses to other teens, or creating ads that promote positive body image. Assessing technological literacy for helping children become active citizens, then, requires democratic frameworks.

Capabilities

Developmental democracy calls for an evaluation of technological literacy that considers how technological learning can increase human capabilities. An economic rationale emphasizes technologies' ability to help Americans pursue higher wage jobs, yet the measurement of income levels alone cannot account for an individual's well-being. Age, gender, and geographic location can also affect whether income contributes to well-being. Sen (1999) is critical of measures of equality that rely on assessments of material resources or individual achievements. For example, income levels are often used to measure poverty and inequality. However, there is a false assumption that equality in income will lead to the same level of equality in well-being and freedom. Rather than seeing income as an end, income should be a variable in the relationship between means and ends (Sen, 1999). Different social and physical characteristics, such as age, sex, educational attainment, and family culture, affect an individual's ability to achieve. In other words, some people have more freedom than others based on social and physical characteristics. For example, even if a disabled worker and an able-bodied worker receive the same income, they have quite different abilities to translate this income into freedoms.

Measuring inequality in terms of income levels overlooks inequalities in freedom. There is a need to examine what people can *do* rather than what people can *buy* (Saito, 2003). Access to the same technology does not ensure equality of opportunity, which can be evidenced by the persistent under-representation of women and minorities in the IT workforce. When women do enter STEM fields, they may receive a high income, yet they might not have the same freedom to achieve as men because of discrimination and lack of maternity leave policies.

Capabilities encompass what Gould (1988) calls "positive freedoms," which includes "capacity for choice and its exercise, absence of constraining conditions, and the availability of means" (p. 40). Ensuring that individuals have equality of capabilities requires looking at the constraining conditions, such as discrimination, illiteracy, and poverty, which create barriers to equality.

Technological literacy can also increase one's capabilities because it provides the means to access information, adapt to the cycle of technological change, contribute one's perspective to the public sphere, and allows people to use different communication channels to draw attention to issues that may not be covered in mainstream media. Technological literacy can contribute to a person's freedom to achieve and provide choices, for example in the number of potential careers, increased opportunities for social and cultural participation, and expression of diverse perspectives. Technological literacy, then, can become a means for achieving a number of different ends. This expanded notion of technological literacy emphasizes capabilities, especially communication capabilities.

Social Media and Communication Capabilities

Communication increases human capabilities through techniques such as persuasion, dialogue, decision-making, and being taken seriously by others. Communication capabilities, such as the capability to participate in self-representation and to access relevant information to positively impact social development, are especially important for achieving equality.

Communication capabilities are essential to individual development. Social media offer several opportunities for encouraging democratic communication and increasing citizens' capabilities, especially in providing channels for producing, distributing, and receiving information. As Downing (2001) writes, democratic theorists often overlook the importance of media in achieving democracy, particularly in recognizing media's ability to create dialogue, provide a forum for civic participation, and allow for diverse perspectives and opinions. Social media can provide powerful tools for civic participation, such as community building, social networking, and the production of alternative perspectives. Social media, and communication technologies more broadly, can enable democratic processes by allowing people to "actively participate in the production of culture, ranging from dialogue and debate on public issues to the creation and expression of their own cultural forms" (Kahn & Kellner, 2006, p. 266). Cultural studies scholars such as Hall (1997) and McRobbie (2004) point out, political participation often is reflected in cultural forms. Kellner and Durham (2006) write,

> cultural texts are saturated with social meanings, they generate political effects, reproducing or opposing governing social institutions and relations of dominance and subordination ... culture can also embody specific political discourses ... advancing competing political positions on issues like the family and sexuality, masculinity or femininity, or violence or war. (p. xvi)

Cell phones, the Internet, television, and film are not only important tools for communication and cultural production, but also reflect power struggles over social values, such as whose stories are told and by whom. For example, while Latinos represent 13% of the U.S. population, only three percent of characters in primetime television are Latino (Mastro & Behm-Morawitz, 2005) When Latinos do appear in primetime television, they are often represented by stereotypes such as "the Latin lover" or the "buffoon" (Mastro & Behm-Morawitz, 2005, p. 111).

Technological literacy standards should emphasize the role of communication and cultural production to democratic societies. As political theorists such as Habermas (1989) and Dewey (1927) write, communication is a central element in encouraging political participation, enacting citizenship, and fostering democracy. The interactive nature of communication is vital for encouraging citizens to relate with each other, engage in dialogue, contribute their diverse ideas and perspectives, and form public opinions. Self-expression and creativity, then, are important for allowing individuals to develop to their full capacities and enact citizenship. Additionally, communication can facilitate political participation, an essential component of democratic societies.

Technological literacy can support communication capabilities. Individuals need to know how to effectively communicate in multimodal forms, craft messages with different audiences in mind, understand how to link to networked information, or use hashtags on Twitter to be effective. Social media are most effective when they are "spreadable" (Jenkins, Ford, & Green, 2013). Thus, technological literacy can help individuals to understand the benefits and limitations of different social media, such as Facebook, Instagram, or YouTube. Furthermore, technological literacy can help citizens understand how to protect their privacy and respond to cyber bullying or harassment.

EXPANDING TECHNOLOGICAL LITERACY STANDARDS

This section argues for the expansion of current standards to emphasize the importance of individuals' capabilities for communication. Based on developmental democratic theory, this section argues that Standard 5 of ISTE's NETS is limited and offers suggestions for expanding this standard. This section also puts forth three additional standards: learning how to communicate about technology, self-representation, and freedom to achieve what youth value.

Digital Citizenship

Communication is essential to citizenship, and technological literacy helps citizens to communicate effectively. Citizenship does not only refer to political rights granted to individuals, but also an activity that is enacted through participation in economic, political, and social life. As Lister (2008) writes, "to be a citizen, in the legal and sociological sense, means to enjoy the rights of citizenship necessary for agency and social and political participation. To act as a citizen involves fulfilling the full potential of the status" (p. 42). This active view of citizenship is especially important to youth, who have a contested relationship to citizenship. On the one hand, American youth are granted citizenship status through being born in the United States. On the other hand, youth are disqualified from adult-citizenship rights, such as voting, because of their dependence status on adults. At best, children are seen as being in the process of becoming citizens and learning how to enact citizenship through their participation in institutions, such as school. Increasing youths' capacities for communication is especially important for encouraging their social participation and giving value to their views of social, political, and cultural life.

Digital citizenship as it is currently conceptualized is limited. For example, Mossberger, Tolbert, and McNeal (2008) define digital citizenship as online participation in both economic and political activities. Their work measures the knowledge that citizens need to have to participate in these activities through indicators such as skills, access, and frequency of use.

Standard 5 of ISTE's NETS frames digital citizenship as the appropriate behaviors students should follow online (Ribble, Bailey, & Ross, 2004). Digital citizenship, then, refers to online etiquette, responsibility, safety, and security. Lenhart and colleagues (2011) focus specifically on teens and digital citizenship. However, they define digital citizenship in terms of appropriate behavior on social networking sites, such as not engaging in bullying.

In these frameworks, digital citizenship is about knowing what is "right" and "wrong" when navigating the Internet, not actively contributing to society, as is the goal of developmental democracy. Instead, digital citizenship should be measured by communication and cultural production online. Expanding Standard 5 to emphasize communication and cultural production is especially important for disenfranchised groups, including girls and minority youth, who are often hindered from communication and social participation for reasons including discrimination and limited access to resources. Women and girls have a particularly negative relationship to digital technologies, as evidenced in their low level of participation in such careers as engineering, computer science, Web design, and computer animation. Currently, women only make up about 25% of the IT workforce (Ramsey & McCorduck, 2005). Women's and girls' ambivalent experiences with communication technologies can lead to them being ill-prepared to obtain and retain jobs, access essential government services, seek out relevant information, participate in public forums, or contribute to public knowledge.

Digital citizenship, then, should move beyond simply communicating appropriately online to articulating how the digital environment promotes civic engagement, both in terms of institutional activities, such as accessing government information, and in terms of dialogue, debate, and cultural production. Encouraging diverse groups to contribute to digital content is especially important to the notion of digital citizenship because it allows for diverse voices and perspectives to circulate in the online public sphere. Because social media offer platforms for user-generated content, there are many outlets for cultural production, such as YouTube videos or Wikipedia. However, these outlets continue to privilege majority viewpoints. For example, only 15% of Wikipedia entries are authored by women, leading to a lack of public knowledge about women's contributions (Cohen, 2011).

Race and class also influence technological literacy and digital citizenship. While 82% of white children have access to computers in their homes, only 55% of Latino and African-American children have access to home computers (U.S. Census Bureau, 2008). Minority youths' limited access to computers and the Internet affect their educational success and their ability to secure future jobs (Tanno, 2003). In order to encourage minority youth's digital citizenship, especially as it relates to cultural production, technological literacy standards need to address the specific cultural and structural barriers minority youth face, including lack of relevant or appealing content, such as Spanish-language content that appeals to their interests (Slate, Manuel, & Brinson, 2002).

Learning How to Communicate About Technology

The NETS calls for the use of multiple forms of media as a strategy for helping students communicate ideas. The NETS also recommends that students take a critical approach to communication, through an understanding of how messages are created and transmitted. A developmental approach to technological literacy draws from these national standards, but also highlights the importance of communication to democratic society on an additional level. Learning how to communicate about technology is important for helping citizens to engage in discussions about technology as well as better understand the importance of technology to their lives.

Technological literacy can help people in everyday decision-making and improve individuals' lives. Technological literacy can increase the capacity of individuals to make decisions in complex social situations. Fourez (1997) speaks to this point when he writes, "understanding the spread of disease of epidemics, deep-freezing, the structures of computer software, the way to transmit a fax, or the freezing of diesel fuel, makes it possible for us to negotiate reasonable and rational decisions, when faced with a series of problems" (p. 905).

Understanding technology affords a certain level of freedom to individuals, in giving them a capacity to communicate to others about everyday life and in giving them a certain amount of independence to make a variety of informed choices about issues that affect their lives. In relation to social media, individuals might not need to know all of the ways that different social media work, but they can be fluent in thinking about the different ways these media communicate information in terms of form and content.

Fourez (1997) emphasizes communication in his definition of technological literacy. He stresses that communication is crucial not only for individuals to understand how particular technologies work, but also how to speak about technologies to others. In this way, technological literacy is not about overcoming "cognitive deficit," as tends to be highlighted in educational programs designed to increase girls' and minority youths' participation with technology, but instead to achieve a "level of interaction with scientific practices" (p. 911).

Learning how to communicate about technology encourages students to make informed choices about which technologies to use for which purposes. Communication about technology also prepares students to engage in broader conversations about technology policy issues in the digital age, such as network neutrality, privacy, and surveillance. This approach emphasizes civic engagement around the way that technology influences society and the way society influences technological development.

Self-Representation and Self-Interest

Standard 1 of the NETS identifies self-expression as an important component of technological literacy, yet the utility of self-expression is framed in terms of its benefits for increased productivity and functionality. For example, the NETS advocates for students to use technology to show originality in thought. The NETS states that students should "create original works as a means of personal or group expression" (Brooks-Young, 2007, p. 7). This standard should be expanded to also include a consideration of what self-expression adds to both individual and social development. Developmental democratic theory posits that as citizens better understand themselves, they become more actively engaged in social and cultural life.

Additionally, the concept of self-expression should be expanded to include self-representation. As Murdock and Golding (1989) write, in democratic societies individuals "must be able to recognize themselves and their aspirations in the range of representations offered within the central communications sectors and be able to contribute to developing those representations" (pp. 183–184).

Self–representation is particularly important for adolescent development (Brown & Gilligan, 1992; Markus & Nurius, 2000; Pipher, 1994). As youths navigate through the world and come to understand themselves, they need to see representations of their experiences in popular culture and be encouraged to contribute their perspectives. Research by Stern (2004) and Mazzarella (2005) shows the importance of self-expression to girls' identity development. For example, in their analyses of girls' homepages, they found that the web offered girls outlets for exploring issues relevant to their own lives, such as their feelings about their bodies or relationships, that were not available to them in mainstream media outlets.

In addition to individual development, self-representation is important for social development. Diversity in representation and in the forms of cultural production are important elements to sustaining democracy (Andren, 1993; Hamelink, 2004; Hirsch Jr., 1988) For example, Rodriguez (2001) illustrates the importance of cultural production to democracy:

> producing alternative media messages … implies having the opportunity to create one's own images of self and environment; it implies being able to recodify one's own identity with the signs and codes that one chooses, thereby disrupting the traditional acceptance of those imposed by outside sources; it implies becoming one's own storyteller, regaining one's own voice; it implies reconstructing the self-portrait of one's own community and one's own culture. (p. 3)

While cultural production is important to democratic societies, individuals may face several barriers to cultural production, such as limited access to the means of production either through low levels of technological literacy or structural issues, such as media consolidation. Additionally, as Andren (1993) writes, cultural norms can inhibit large groups of the population from expressing themselves:

> for a person to develop, entertain, and express definite beliefs and attitudes of his own, and not just reproduce those that he meets in his social environment or considers opportune, is an active undertaking that presupposes more or less considerable funds of autonomy, maturity, and in certain cases, even courage. (p. 63)

Andren (1993) illustrates his point through arguing that messages that minority groups are inferior, for example through racist and sexist stereotypes in popular culture, undermine individuals' power to act. Andren's work speaks to the importance of expanding Standard 1 to encourage diversity in online settings.

Freedom to Achieve What Youth Value

Developmental democracy takes a refined look at equality to examine the freedoms individuals have to participate in economic, social, and cultural life. These freedoms include the ability to communicate with others and to participate in community life. Drawing on developmental democratic theory, an important communication dimension of technological literacy is enabling youth with freedoms to use technological literacy in the way they value. Youths should have the freedom to use technological literacy to advance their education, participate in cultural production, or access information that they find useful. This aspect of technological literacy calls for educational programs to address the obstacles that youth have in achieving these freedoms, such as providing increased access to computers and the Internet and providing training on how to use digital technologies.

Expanding the NETS to include freedoms requires looking at structural policies in schools, such as filtering or acceptable use, that ban access to certain information. Many public schools filter access to social media, yet these are the platforms that youth can use for civic engagement and to increase their capabilities. For example, Vickery (2014) found that students' participation in after-school digital media clubs helped students to develop digital literacy. However, restrictive school policies blocked students' access to social media and video sharing sites, which meant that they were unable to share their work online or develop their social networks and social capital.

CONCLUSION

Both ISTE and ITEA define technological literacy broadly, emphasizing the mutual shaping of technology and society. These organizations recognize that citizens must take a critical approach to understanding how technology influences society and how society can influence technological development. However, standards developed by ISTE over-emphasize economic dimensions of technological literacy without articulating how communication and cultural production benefit society. Drawing on developmental democratic theory, this chapter offers a roadmap for how to expand current standards to evoke a more robust approach to civic engagement and digital citizenship.

The NETS are widely adopted in the U.S. and have a global reach, implemented in schools in Norway, Costa Rica, Malaysia, Japan, Australia, Philippines, Micronesia, Korea, and Turkey. The recognition that technological literacy is an important component of education offers an opportunity to rethink how technological literacy can lead to individual development and social change.

As social media become powerful tools for enacting citizenship, students need to become fluent in how they can use these media to effectively communicate their ideas and access information to positively impact their development. Increasing communication capabilities of girls and minority youth is especially important for creating a more equal and just society. This chapter offered some examples of how technological literacy can increase communication capabilities. In the end, this chapter may offer new ideas for educators and policymakers as they continue to develop strategies to assess technological literacy.

REFERENCES

Andren, G. (1993). A concept of freedom of expression for superindustrialized societies. In S. Splichal, & J. Wasko (Eds.), *Communication and democracy* (pp. 55–67). Norwood, NJ: Ablex.

Bennett, W. L. (Ed.). (2008). *Civic life online: Learning how digital media can engage youth*. Cambridge, MA: MIT Press.

Brooks-Young, S. (2007). *NETS for students*. Washington, DC: International Society for Technology in Education.

Brown, L. M., & Gilligan, C. (1992). *Meeting at the crossroads: Women's psychology and girls' development*. Cambridge, MA: Harvard University Press.

Buckingham, D. (2006). Defining digital literacy. *Nordic Journal of Digital Literacy, 4*(1), 263–276.

Coalition for Science Afterschool. (2006). Afterschool programs: At the STEM of learning. *Afterschool Alert Issue Brief, 26*, 1–4. Retrieved from internal-pdf:// Coalition for Science, issue_STEM_26-2617605888/Coalition for Science, issue_STEM_26.pdf

Cohen, N. (2011, January 30). Define gender gap? Look up Wikipedia's contributor list. *The New York Times*. Retrieved from http://courses.washington.edu/com201/COM%20201%20readings/Cohen-Define%20gender%20gap.pdf

Cooper, M. (2004). Expanding the digital divide and falling behind in broadband: Why a telecommunications policy of neglect is not benign. Retrieved from http://www.consumerfed.org/pdfs/digitaldivide.pdf

Csorny, L. 2013. Careers in the growing field of information technology services. *Beyond the Numbers, 2*(9). Retrieved from http://www.bls.gov/opub/btn/volume-2/careers-in-growing-field-of-information-technology-services.htm

Dahl, R. A. (1989). *Democracy and its critics*. London, UK: Yale University Press.

Dewey, J. (1927). *The public and its problems*. New York, NY: Holt.

Dewey, J. (1934). *Art as experience*. New York, NY: Capricorn Books.

Downing, J. (2001). *Radical media: Rebellious communication and social movements*. Thousand Oaks, CA: Sage.

Fancsali, C. (2002). *What we know about girls, STEM, and afterschool programs: A summary.* Washington, DC: Educational Equity Concepts. Retrieved from http://www.afterschool.org/sga/pubs/whatweknow.pdf

Fourez, G. (1997). Scientific and technological literacy as a social practice. *Social Studies of Science, 27*(6), 903–936.

Gerbaudo, P. (2012). *Tweets and the streets: Social media and contemporary activism.* New York, NY: Pluto Press.

Gould, C. C. (1988). *Rethinking democracy: Freedom and social cooperation in politics, economics, and society.* Cambridge, UK: Cambridge University Press.

Habermas, J. (1989). *The structural transformation of the public sphere: An inquiry into a category of bourgeois society.* Cambridge, MA: MIT Press.

Hall, S. (1997). *Representation: Cultural representations and signifying practices.* London, UK: Sage.

Hamelink, C. J. (2004). *Human rights for communicators.* Cresskill, NJ: Hampton University Press.

Hargittai, E. (2010). Digital na(t)ives? Variation in Internet skills and uses among members of the "Net generation". *Sociological Inquiry, 80*(1), 92–113. doi:10.1111/j.1475-682X.2009.00317.x

Held, D. (1996). *Models of democracy* (2nd ed.). Stanford, CA: Stanford University Press.

Hirsch, E. D., Jr. (1988). *Cultural literacy: What every American needs to know.* New York, NY: Vintage Books.

International Technology Education Association. (2002). *Standards for technological literacy: Content for the study of technology.* Reston, VA: International Technology Education Association.

Jenkins, H. (2006). *Convergence culture: Where old and new media collide.* New York, NY: New York University Press.

Jenkins, H., Ford, S., & Green, J. (2013) *Spreadable media: Creating value and meaning in a networked culture.* New York, NY: New York University Press.

Kahn, R., & Kellner, D. (2006). Defining technological literacy: Towards an epistemological framework. In J. R. Dakers (Ed.), *Reconstructing technoliteracy: A multiple literacies approach* (pp. 253–272). New York, NY: Palgrave MacMillan.

Kaylan, M. (2013, Sept. 27). Syria's war viewed almost in real time. *The Wall Street Journal,* Retrieved from http://online.wsj.com/news/articles/SB10001424127887324492604579083112566791956

Kellner, D., & Durham, M. G. (2006). Media and cultural studies keyworks. In M. G. Durham, & D. Kellner (Eds.), *Adventures in media and cultural studies: Introducing the keyworks* (pp. ix–xxxviii). Malden, MA: Blackwell.

Lenhart, A., Madden, M., Smith, A., Purcell, K., Zickuhr, K., & Rainie, L. (2011). Teens, kindness and cruelty on social network sites: How American teens navigate the new world of "digital citizenship." *Pew Internet & American Life Project.* Retrieved from http://www.pewinternet.org/files/old-media//Files/Reports/2012/PIP_Teens_Smartphones_and_Texting.pdf

Lister, R. (2008). Children and citizenship. In A. Invernizzi, & J. Williams (Eds.), *Unpacking children's citizenship* (pp. 9–19). London, UK: Sage.

Markus, H., & Nurius, P. (2000). Possible selves. *American Psychologist, 41*(9), 954–969.

Mastro, D. E., & Behm-Morawitz, E. (2005). Latino representation on primetime television. *Journalism and Mass Communication Quarterly, 82*(1), 110–130.

Mazzarella, S. (Ed.). (2005). *Girl wide web: Girls, the Internet, and the negotiation of identity*. New York, NY: Peter Lang.

McRobbie, A. (2004). Post-feminism and popular culture. *Feminist Media Studies, 4*(3), 255–264. doi:10.1080/1468077042000309937

Mill, J. S. (1863). *Utilitarianism*. London, UK: Parker, Son, & Bourn.

Mossberger, K., Tolbert C., & McNeal, R. S. (2008). *Digital citizenship: The Internet, society, and participation*. Cambridge, MA: MIT Press

Murdock, G., & Golding, P. (1989). Information poverty and political inequality: Citizenship in the age of privatized communication. *The Journal of Communication, 39*(3), 180–195.

National Commission on Excellence in Education. (1983). *A nation at risk: The imperative for educational reform*. Washington, DC: U.S. Government Printing Office.

National Research Council. (1999). *Being fluent with information technology*. Washington, DC: National Academy Press.

National Telecommunications and Information Administration. (2013). U.S. broadband availability June 2010–June 2012. Retrieved from http://www.ntia.doc.gov/files/ntia/publications/usbb_avail_report_05102013.pdf

New Media Consortium. (2005). A global Imperative: *The report of the 21st century literacy summit*. Retrieved from http://www.nmc.org/publications/2005-a-global-imperative

No Child Left Behind (NCLB) Act of 2001, Pub. L, No. 107-110, Stat. 1425 (2002).

Pearson, G., & Young, T. A. (2002). *Technically speaking: Why all Americans need to know more about technology*. Washington, DC: National Academies Press.

Peter, J., & Valkenburg, P. M. (2006). Adolescents' Internet use: Testing the "disappearing digital divide" versus the "emerging digital differentiation" approach. *Poetics, 34*, 269–305.

Petrina, S. (2000). The politics of technological literacy. *International Journal of Technology and Design Education, 10*(3), 181–206.

Pipher, M. (1994). *Reviving Ophelia: Saving the selves of adolescent girls*. New York, NY: Putnam Books.

Pittman, K. (1993). *Youth development and resiliency research. Making connections to substance abuse prevention*. Washington, DC: Adacemy of Educational Development.

Ramsey, N., & McCorduck, P. (2005). *Where are the women in information technology*. Boulder, CO: University of Colorado.

Ribble, M. S., Bailey, G. D., & Ross, T. W. (2004). Digital citizenship: Addressing appropriate technology behavior. *Learning & Leading with Technology, 32*(1), 6–9.

Rodriguez, C. (2001). *Fissures in the mediascape: An international study of citizens' media*. Cresskill, NJ: Hampton Press.

Saito, M. (2003). Amartya Sen's capability approach to education: A critical exploration. *Journal of Philosophy of Education, 37*(1), 17–34.

Sen, A. (1999). *Development as freedom*. New York, NY: Anchor Books.

Slate, J. R., Manuel, M., & Brinson, K. H. (2002). The "digital divide": Hispanic college students' views of educational uses of the Internet. *Assessment and*

Evaluation in Higher Education, 27(1), 75-93. Retrieved from internal-pdf://Slate, _Hispanic college students and digital divide_-3474027520/Slate, _Hispanic college students and digital divide_.pdf

Stern, S. (2004). Expressions of identity online: Prominent features and gender differences in adolescents' world wide web home pages. *Broadcast Education Association, 48*(2), 218–243.

Tanno, D. (2003). When education, media and technology converge, what do latino/a students gain? *Journal of Latinos and Education, 2*(1), 39–46.

U.S. Census Bureau. (2008). *Statistical abstract of the United States*. Retrieved from http://www.census.gov/compendia/statab/2008/2008edition.html

U.S. Department of Education. (1997). *President Clinton's call to action for American education in the 21st century*. Retrieved from http://www.clintonlibrary.gov/assets/storage/Research%20-%20Digital%20Library/Reed-Education/94/647429-sotu.pdf

Vickery, J. R. (2014). The role of after-school digital media clubs in closing participation gaps and expanding social networks. *Equity & Excellence in Education 47*(1), 78–95.

Volman, M., & van Eck, E. (2001). Gender equity and information technology in education: The second decade. *Review of Educational Research, 71*(4), 613–634.

CHAPTER 14

DIGITAL DIVERSITY AND BELONGING IN HIGHER EDUCATION

A Social Justice Proposition

Sue Timmis, Wan Ching Yee, and Emma Bent

ABSTRACT

This chapter focuses on social justice relating to undergraduate education for diverse and underrepresented students. Within mass higher education, participation and equity are increasingly critical; including the experience students have while at university. We argue that the pervasiveness of digital media offers potential for supporting diversity and belonging through informal networks and peer support. The emerging concept of digital diversity is explored before conceptualizing this as both the proliferation of digitally-mediated opportunities and the possibilities for more diverse communities to engage in digital practices that might be distinct or for different purposes. Drawing on a recent study, this chapter argues that digital technologies have a role in sustaining social networks and developing identities within academic spaces as well as affording alternative spaces and

E-Learning and Social Media:
Education and Citizenship for the Digital 21st Century, pp. 297–320

discourses. Yet such networks can also be exclusive or excluding for students whose identities may be more firmly established elsewhere. We conclude that digital diversity can help to understand the dynamics of underrepresented student experiences in a digital world. From a social justice perspective, digital diversity suggests the need to expand understandings of 'the digital university' and recognize underrepresented students as collaborators and knowledge producers in order to open up opportunities and mechanisms for participation and success.

INTRODUCTION

This chapter is about social justice in higher education in relation to the experiences of students from diverse and underrepresented backgrounds once they have begun their university education. Within the context of a discourse of mass higher education, widening participation, access and equity and "College for All," closer attention is needed, not just to who participates, but what that experience involves (Reay, David, & Ball, 2005). It can be argued that students need to integrate into the culture and practices of university life in order to sustain their engagement and become confident and successful learners who stay the course, obtain a degree, and benefit from the social and cultural experience of being a student.

Higher education institutions have a responsibility to support the students they admit under a widening participation brief, or as Tinto suggests, "access without support is not opportunity" (Tinto, 2008). Furthermore, equality of opportunity may not be enough, and we also need to pay attention to equality of experience and outcomes. Cope and Kalantzis (2000) argue that while education cannot offer equality (in other words the same outcomes for all), due to the different lifeworlds they bring, it often gives an illusion of equity in terms of life chances. It is through the way in which HE differentially engages, in theory and practice, with these lifeworlds that transformation occurs and it is these opportunities this chapter will focus on. In particular, while there are many university-led initiatives to support the integration of more diverse students, far less is understood about how informal networks and interactions might contribute to underrepresented students' integration and successful participation in higher education.

In this chapter, the role of digital media in supporting students from more diverse backgrounds through their university lifeworlds, informal networks, and interactions are explored. The pervasiveness of digital media offers potential for supporting diversity through communications, collaborations, and access to an expanded and shared social memory through the Internet, online resources, and databases, as suggested by Säljö: "Through the documentary capacities of digitized external symbolic storage systems, the social memory has expanded dramatically, and the recent developments of networking systems give us more or less constant access to these vast sources of potentially relevant information" (Säljö, 2010, p. 60).

We argue that digital media also has the potential to help foster a culture of belonging within and to the university among more diverse students while also asking questions about the role of digital media in brokering or contributing to a sense of unbelonging or dissent, and how that might sustain and empower students developing their emergent identities and finding their own voices in an academic environment. Despite these notable potentialities, digital technologies are neither neutral nor necessarily positive (Selwyn, 2011) and may also reinforce, or contribute negatively toward, some of the challenges of diversity. They therefore offer opportunities for emancipation and oppression or perhaps both.

The chapter first examines some pertinent issues relating to higher education and social justice and then considers the relationship between digital media and university life before suggesting how the concept of digital diversity can be constructed and interrogated as a proposition for empowerment and social justice. The chapter draws on an ongoing study of digital diversity, learning, and belonging in order to show some examples of how this concept relates to the lived experiences of a group of undergraduates studying in the United Kingdom. These examples are then discussed in relation to social justice and diversity concerns before presenting our conclusions.

HIGHER EDUCATION AND SOCIAL JUSTICE

Access, diversity, and social justice are all critical to the expansion of higher education globally and to changing international economic and social contexts (David, 2010). This has led to the call to move beyond an argument about equality of entry to higher education and toward what has been termed in the United Kingdom "widening participation" as a means of championing higher education "for the socially or economically disadvantaged, or social class or gender" (David, 2010, p. 5). The emphasis on participation suggests that this is about taking part, as well as gaining access to a university or higher education institution in line with a relational as well as distributive understanding of social justice where equality of outcomes, not just equality of opportunities are encapsulated (Gewirtz, 1998). Gidley, Hampson, Wheeler, and Bereded-Samuel (2010) add that the concept of social justice in higher education should go beyond social inclusion, emphasizing both participation and engagement where "its primary aim is to enable all human beings to participate fully in society with respect for their human dignity" (Gidley et al., 2010, p. 9).

Therefore, an emphasis on social justice needs to consider what the experience of higher education involves and where it leads, particularly for students from underrepresented or more diverse circumstances including non-traditional family backgrounds, first generation into higher education, those from lower socio-economic backgrounds, minority ethnic communities, women, and mature students.

In a recent U.K. study of student retention and success, Thomas and colleagues found that "a *culture of belonging*" is critical to the success and well-being of students at university (Thomas, 2012 p. 17, emphasis added). However, this may be more challenging for those who come from more diverse backgrounds who may not necessarily have the same social or cultural capital at their disposal. For example, Crozier, Reay, and Clayton (2010) found that students from lower socio-economic backgrounds had more difficulties "fitting in," and their engagement was often more sporadic. The challenges of becoming and belonging also intersect with issues surrounding ethnicity, gender, and age (see Ball, Reay, & David, 2002; Crozier, Reay, Clayton, Colliander, & Grinstead, 2008). Thomas (2002) points to the need for institutions to establish an "institutional habitus" that values diversity and difference, and does not make assumptions about prior experience and cultural capital. There are also challenges in terms of positioning oneself for a post-degree world, and students must "play the game" to take advantage of other opportunities while at university because getting a degree is no longer enough to secure graduate employment and opportunities (Bathmaker, Ingram, & Waller, 2013).

This suggests that despite the wide variety of individual, institutional, and societal benefits that increased diversity in the student population affords (Gurin, Dey, Hurtado, & Gurin, 2009), there are challenges for universities in supporting more diverse students in their university lives, and challenges for students who do get a place in fitting into university culture, sustaining their work academically, and benefitting from campus life.

THE DIGITAL UNIVERSITY?

Introduction

In this section, we consider the idea of a digital university and give an overview of some of the key areas in which technology is influencing the experience of higher education. The student experience of higher education could be seen to be increasingly digitally and physically situated, and the term digital university has become part of the policy discourse of higher education, though this is not always clearly elaborated (Jones, 2013). While such a blanket term could be argued to be over simplistic, the very large ECAR longitudinal study in the United States, which has been reporting on student trends in technology use since 2004, reported in 2013 (based on a sample of 112,000 students) that there is now almost universal student use of learner or course management systems (also known as virtual learning environments), university websites, online library systems, and e-mail (Dahlstrom, de Boor, Grunwald, & Vockley, 2011; Dahlstrom, Walker, & Dziuban, 2013). All of these technological systems and tools constitute alternative or additional educational spaces or "learnplaces" which students must learn to understand and adapt to (Ellis & Goodyear, 2010). These trends have also been echoed by studies in the United Kingdom and Europe (Sutherland, Joubert, & Eagle, 2012).

Social Media and Educational Tensions

Beyond institutionally owned educational spaces, there are opportunities through social media, online tools, and "apps" for student to establish and inhabit alternative spaces, suggesting that participation in online social networks related to university life might offer opportunities for alternative forms of student discourse and culture (see, e.g., DeAndrea, Ellison, LaRose, Steinfield, & Fiore, 2012; Selwyn, 2009). In previous research, Timmis (2012) found that undergraduates using instant messaging as part of informal studying practices supported their peers through private and longitudinal exchanges, dipping in and out of conversations over lengthy periods of time. Such conversations continually crossed the boundaries between studying and social topics facilitating the integration of their everyday lives (Timmis, 2012). This suggests that students inhabiting online spaces are not just engaged in alternative educational discourses, they also collaborate in co-constructing academic work and offer and receive empathetic support. Yet this also presents some possible conflicts with formal academic support outside of teaching, which can be slower to arrive and time limited through heavy staff workloads. Timmis found that this could lead to a sense of frustration and unrealistic expectations. Bonderup Dohn (2009) has also argued that the rise of Web 2.0 (O'Reilly, 2007) has led to increased participatory and knowledge building practices which might be regarded as "patchworking" through the regularity of re-use and appropriation of existing material available on the web which can then be creatively repurposed as a form of bricolage. She further argues that there are potential conflicts between the goals of web 2.0 practices and Education. In Web 2.0 practices, the goal *is* participation, seen as an end in itself, whereas in Education, educational goals and predetermined outcomes drive the activities, and participation is only a means to an end. Timmis, Joubert, Manuel, and Barnes (2010) suggest that there can also be conflicts when students are asked to use informal communication tools for formal educational activities. In exploring the practices of undergraduate students and researchers collaborating on a project, they found that undergraduate students involved in educational activities using social networking tools chose digital communication tools based on their friendships and communities, whereas researchers were more discerning in their choices and looked more carefully at the purpose of a particular task and the suitability of a particular tool or environment. These are examples of how technology can offer potential for informal knowledge production, communication, and collaboration, but how it can also disrupt and destabilize educational activities and purposes. Equally, the potential of technology for reframing how we do things is an opportunity for creative change, as Säljö argues, technology has a critical role to play in reconfiguring what learning *is* and in opening up possibilities for new thinking and new knowledge (Säljö, 2010).

Digital Natives and Other Myths

Jones (2013) argues that the concept of the digital university is in need of definition and he points to three areas that might need to be clarified: digital natives, digital literacies, and digital scholarship. Jones, Ramanau, Cross, and Healing (2010) have previously critiqued the idea that those entering university can be considered as "digital natives", arguing that this is a deterministic myth that needs to be challenged. One of the key arguments that Jones and colleagues make in contrast to the proposition put forward by Prensky (2001) and others (see, e.g., Oblinger & Oblinger, 2005), is that the student population is not homogeneous, not all new undergraduates are young or necessarily digitally accomplished (see also Selwyn, 2011 and Livingstone, 2008 for other arguments on the myths behind the digital native discourse). Yet, despite this myth having been largely discredited, Jones (2013) and Lea (2013) point out that it is still broadly accepted in HE policy and political circles and therefore continues to act as an influential discourse.

The evolving idea of "digital literacy" has also been the subject of much discussion and challenge, with debates over the extent to which this refers to skills or practices. Gourlay and Oliver (2013) review the different interpretations of this term which have often suggested that there is an overemphasis on the individual with the student being "seen as a 'user' of technologies; suggesting a clear division between the human and the machine, action and context, writer/reader and text, in the university and other domains of life" (p. 80). They take a position of digital literacy as socio-material practice, drawing on Brice-Heath's work on literacy events

(Brice-Heath, 1986). Digital literacies are an important aspect of the mode and form of students' engagement in digital practices, and therefore forms part of the context for our concerns in this chapter. The points raised about the relationship between people, tools, action, and context also need careful elaboration and we return to this in the next section.

While Jones (2013) acknowledges that a "digital university" remains an abstract concept, it does help to highlight that the technological landscape of higher education is increasingly integral to university life and a multi-level influence on students' lived experiences.

Interestingly, however, one area that has received limited attention in the literature on digital technologies in HE is diversity and difference in the student population and the impact of this on students' experiences with digital technologies. Studies and debates within the area of digital technologies and learning tend to suggest universal applicability or focus on individual or subject differences. It is the idea of digital technologies in relation to diversity to which we will now turn our attention, and which is of principal concern in this chapter.

DIGITAL DIVERSITY, LEARNING, AND BELONGING—AN EMPOWERMENT PROPOSITION

In this section, we develop the concept of digital diversity in relation to both learning and belonging and consider this idea as a proposition for understanding the emancipatory potential of technology in relation to more diverse and underrepresented groups. In line with similar research (Andrews & Yee, 2006; Holland, Lachicotte, Skinner, & Cain, 1998; Thomas, 2012; Timmis, 2012), we take a socio-cultural positioning which embraces interdisciplinarity and combines sociological, psychological, and anthropological perspectives as multiple levels of inquiry to investigate the social, cultural, and educational activities that students engage in as part of their university learning lives.

The Dynamic Interplay of Digital Technologies, Action, and Context

Learning from this position, is understood to emerge from social and relational activities, historically accumulated within particular cultures and communities (Cole, 1996; Lave & Wenger, 2005; Vygotsky & Kozulin, 1986). Vygotsky's socio-cultural theory included the important concept of mediation, arguing that all action is mediated by tools, including psychological and semiotic tools (Vygotsky, 1978; Wertsch, 1991, 1998).

This is particularly helpful in understanding the role of technologies as mediational means, acting in concert with the person and the context to make sense of and to facilitate actions. Within a socio-cultural positioning, context is not just the surrounding environment or the "situation," but is actively constructed by the person or persons making meaning. Therefore, context "is never universally given, nor objectively determined by the characteristics of the situation itself. What counts as a context depends on how a situation is interpreted in terms of activity to be carried out" (Van Oers, 1998, p. 481). This is important in understanding the dynamics that surround digital technologies and their influence on people and their activities. Rather than seeing digital technologies as the sole determinants of transformation, this perspective sees their role as part of a complex set of dialectical relations and enactments, which include people, language, physical tools, settings, and artefacts. It is equally important to clarify that digital technologies are also embodied; meaning that they are physical entities as well as online or virtual spaces and that engaging with digital technologies involves our bodies in multiple ways (see Bloomfield, Latham, & Vurdubakis, 2010 for an ethnographic account that offers a vivid example of this). Increasingly physical and virtual spaces and representations are also becoming interchangeable or fused. To be "present" and participating in a context no longer means that you are necessarily physically present, for example where a group of people assembled in one physical space invite others to participate in their face to face conversation via social networks such as Facebook or communications platforms through a phone or computer (Davies, 2014). This suggests a further aspect of digital media that influences the socio-cultural context, namely the spatio-temporal dimensions to our digital interactions.

Lemke (2004) reports that in western cultures, space is generally thought of as a container waiting to be filled or simply as a negative. Equally, time is often considered as immutable and independent of, or imposed on, our lives and actions. In contrast, Lemke argues that spatiality and temporality are related to action or material processes and that we experience space and time as we construct them and that they can be mobilized as resources for learning. "Our sense of place, whether immediate or virtual, is made cumulatively and progressively as we act in and move through spaces, affording ourselves of their opportunities to perceive, feel, use, act, and move" (p. 1).

For Bakhtin (1981), writing about literature and narrative in the 1920s, time and space are inextricably linked, and space is always created through time so that they are dialectically related to one another. He referred to these time/space configurations as *chronotopes* and he used this idea to explore how different forms of narrative move the scene of action from place to place and how events unfold over time. Bakhtin's concept of a chronotope has been adopted recently in theorizing on learning across contexts (Kumpulainen, Mikkola, & Jaatinen, 2014; Lemke, 2004; Ligorio, Loperfido, & Sansone, 2013). In particular, chronotopes give accounts of actions and discourses through which people make meaning and could be described as "chronotopes in action" (Ligorio et al., 2013, p. 353). A chronotope is therefore a typical pattern of organization and activities across space and time where "space becomes a place when, over time, it is attached with socially meaningful affordances" (Kumpulainen et al., 2013, p. 4). This gives us insight into how cultural groups' instantiate everyday forms of activities as trajectories across different places and over time. Space and time are therefore important dimensions to understand in relation to higher education students working, studying, and socializing within and across the physical and digital boundaries of a university. Such boundaries are permeable and flexible, yet unstable (Timmis & Williams, 2014). This suggests that further investigation into space: time configurations or chronotopes and their effects are needed, including to what extent this facilitates interactions and collaborations, and why this might be the case.

In summary, from a socio-cultural perspective, investigating how we engage with digital technologies is necessarily multi-layered; requiring understanding of the dynamic, social, semiotic, cultural, physical, and historical inter-relationships and actions across different time/space configurations (or chronotopes). It also leads us to conclude that a critical approach is necessary to investigate the purposes, social structures and constraints as well as understanding more deeply what happens. In the next section, the concept of belonging is discussed before these two strands are brought together in the third section on digital diversity.

Belonging in Higher Education

Earlier, it was highlighted that a social justice perspective on higher education involves both participation and engagement. Engagement can be considered to be simply about involvement in activities and in some policy and practice interpretations, it is suggested that this is an expectation (see Trowler, 2010). However, Harper and Quaye (2009) argue that engagement "requires feelings and sense making as well as activity." In other words, to be engaged involves both commitment and attachment (Harper & Quaye, 2009, p. 5). Engagement, therefore, is also about culture and practices and developing a sense of belonging. It is this notion of belonging and its relationship to identity that we now consider in more depth.

Thomas found in her recent study that a culture of belonging was necessary for student retention and success in higher education, and this was fostered in particular within the academic sphere and through supportive peer relationships and meaningful interactions between staff and students (Thomas, 2012, p. 17). Belonging and unbelonging are closely related to one's place and position within a community such as a university, or in networks or groups that connect to it. They are also closely related to identity, and both of these areas are now considered.

Identity and Figured Worlds

Identity has been frequently conceptualized in terms of giving a performance or "facework" (Goffman, 1959) where an individual is continually moving between publicly visible front stage arenas to backstage, where other identities are kept hidden or suppressed (Goffman, 1959; Selwyn, 2009). While this is a useful starting point, which gives a sense of shifting identities, it tends to focus on the individual, suggesting people act alone and that identity making is always under the control of the subject. Erstad and Sefton-Green (2012) highlight that identity and learning are inextricably linked, and point to the problematic and runaway nature of the concept identity. Ecclestone, Biesta, and Hughes (2010) focus on transition as a means of uncovering identity making through changing understanding of self in relation to individuals and social structures.

The concept of transition is closely aligned to our understanding of identity and belonging. Identities are formed in the process of transition through different activities in relation to others and the communities and networks in which they are situated, and in which they engage. We draw on the work of Dorothy Holland and colleagues and their idea of "figured worlds" meaning "a socially and culturally constructed realm of interpretation in which particular characters and actors are recognized, significance is assigned to certain acts, and particular outcomes are valued over others" (Holland et al., 1998, p. 52). A disciplinary community or a particular learning environment can be considered as a figured world (Solomon, 2007). Figured worlds are social encounters in which the positions of those taking part matter; they are socially organized and located in particular times and places. Through our encounters with different figured worlds over time, we gain new or changing identities "through continued participation in the positions defined by the social organisation of those worlds' activity" (Holland et al., 1998, p. 41). In other words, we begin to develop a sense of belonging and position within a particular figured world. Developing a figured identity within a learning community also involves a person's own agency through improvisational acts that help to overcome the cultural and historical constraints that powerful structures and positions embody.

Figured identities can therefore provide individuals with the opportunity to challenge positional identities through new imaginaries. We argue that digital technologies have the potential to be important mediators in opening up places and possibilities in which potentially transformative or emancipatory actions can occur.

Digital Diversity

The concept of digital diversity is not new and we begin with a brief review of some of the other uses of the concept before offering our own interpretation.

Clark (2011) shows that the term has been used quite frequently in Australia and New Zealand but, as he points out, diversity tends to be associated with technological proliferation and doing things in different ways: "Addressing diversity in styles of learning and thinking offers us new pathways for building the right knowledge and skills to adapt to constant change" (Australian Council for Computers in Education, 2010, p. 1). It is also being appropriated by commercial companies claiming to meet the demands of more dispersed and diverse communities for pervasive technologies. Clark himself argues for a wider view than this and challenges the claim to digital diversity as a normative concept including the ethical and epistemological problems associated with it, such as whether or not it is ethical to claim diversity when inequalities persist in access to and engagement with technologies.

However, not all those who have adopted this idea are claiming that digital diversity is a resolution. It is also a term adopted to update and reframe the discussion about what we previously termed the "digital divide" toward a broader and more culturally rich dialogue about global inequalities and differences. For example, Washington State University runs a course on digital diversity as part of American Studies, which looks at the ways in which the Internet and "cyberculture" reflect and represent questions of diversity. Their main aim is stated as: "We will focus on the medium of cyberspace, our ultimate topic is the larger issue of inequality in the United States and the wider world" (http://public.wsu.edu/~amerstu/475/475syl.html).

Similarly, the Developing Digital Diversity Network in the U.K. aims to "Focus more constructively on strategies that are being developed to create rich and diverse uses of online networked media and technologies both in local and global communities around the world" (http://www.digitaldiversity.org.uk).

While improving access to and participation in education are concerns of these programs, initiatives, and networks, the focus tends to be on considering equalities and inequalities on a national and international scale, rather than focusing on the practices and local educational communities such as schools, universities, or colleges. Looker and Naylor (2010) are an exception; they focus on digital diversity in relation to youth, equity, access to information and communication technologies, and the challenges young people face within the school system.

We are employing the concept of *digital diversity* to encapsulate two related ideas that draw on the wider perspectives discussed above. We see this term as dialectically relational and as problematic. It encapsulates the idea that people from more diverse and non-traditional backgrounds may engage or need to engage differently with digital cultures within university and other communities, and that there may be interrelated issues of equality and social justice that influence such engagement. Additionally, digital media are an increasing part of the landscape in which we live which in itself offers opportunities for more diverse ways of working, studying, and experiencing university life, which may or may not offer routes to empowerment and emancipation. Digital diversity also suggests an emphasis on students' agency, voice, and capacity for change, which makes it particularly helpful when investigating the role of digital media in learning and belonging in higher education.

Furthermore, the word diversity *implies* multivoicedness, and we argue that this principle also needs to underpin the approach to research. Community of inquiry and co-researcher methodologies (see Timmis & Williams, 2013) or similar forms of co-produced and participatory research are increasingly favored when seeking to encourage student voice and participation in research, rather than positioning those taking part as objects of research (Brew, 2006; Fielding & Bragg, 2003; Heron & Reason, 2001).

In the next section, in order to explore the social justice implications of digital diversity in a higher education context, we draw on a recent study—"Digital Diversity, Learning and Belonging" (DD-lab), investigating the use of digital media by students from underrepresented backgrounds, including the potential and constraints for offering additional means of support and impact on their university lives and academic progress.

DD-LAB—THE STUDY

This U.K. based study investigated undergraduate experiences and relationships with peers over the course of one academic year at a research-intensive university in South-West England. It focused on their learning and studying interactions and engagements, particularly informal activities and interactions with peers. Underrepresentation was defined through first generation university and state school attendance, Black and ethnic minority, and mature and local student community membership. Thirty-two second year undergraduates took part in the study, and informal studying practices have been documented at key points during the course of one academic year. Second year undergraduates were chosen because they may have already generated some "sense of belonging" by returning for the second year of study, and can be regarded as successful students, having avoided the key drop out periods for underrepresented students within their first year. Second, their communities of practice may have become more established in their first year of study and the picture of their learning lives would therefore be likely to be more stable.

The research questions focus on the extent to which "a culture of belonging" is experienced and how this impacts on informal support and peer relationships, how digital technologies are being mobilized, and what new forms of learning interactions are created.

The Co-Researcher Methodology

Obtaining authentic accounts of students' experiences using traditional data collection methods is challenging because of the personal nature of some of the data and the potential for intrusion (Andrews & Yee, 2006). This is particularly the case if the research investigates communications or personal experiences such as collaborations or studying practices, which might take place in a variety of different online or physical settings and in particular may occur outside of institutional walls.

The project adopted a collaborative community of inquiry research design in line with recent work on undergraduate involvement in research (Brew, 2006) and co-researcher methodology developed by one of the authors across several previous projects (Timmis, 2012; Timmis & Williams, 2013). In addition, this approach was designed to enable students to get some benefit from the research for themselves, and to see themselves as partners and co-producers rather than being positioned as objects of the research. The co-researcher methodology was also important for ensuring students were not positioned as "disadvantaged" or "needy" and for student control over their personal data. This was particularly important in a study about widening participation, learning, and belonging for students from more diverse backgrounds.

All student co-researchers were given an iPad to document their informal studying practices and the use of digital technologies within their learning lives (Erstad & Sefton-Green, 2012) using an application called Evernote, which enables the collection of a variety of multimodal data across contexts. For example, students uploaded screenshots, photos, video, audio files, texts, and links to YouTube clips to illustrate and comment on their accounts. They were asked to upload documentaries approximately twice weekly throughout a four-week period in November, February, and April in order to get an understanding of their learning lives throughout the year and how things changed over time.

The co-researcher approach to data collection can be argued to support the collection of more authentic life history accounts and offered an enrichment of the students' learning experiences at university. Not only were students able to provide examples and direct links, but this approach offered greater insight and access to their lives, thoughts, backgrounds, social contexts, and homes. Students have also had the opportunity to take part in preliminary thematic analysis and contribute to dissemination and presentation of findings.

Dimensions of Digital Diversity, Learning and Belonging

Analysis of the co-researcher documentaries identified many opportunities where the students were found to have mobilized digital technologies for educational, cultural, and social purposes. These included the integration of different aspects of their lives, mobilizing student voice for action and dissent, using alternative sources for advice and guidance to tutors and formal teaching, maintaining connections with home, family, and friends, the organization of events, and knowing what is going on and validating their own understanding and sense of self. Here we report on three dimensions, which illustrate how digital diversity can be understood in relation to learning and belonging within the context of a university setting.

These center on communication and connections, creative appropriation, challenges and control of space/time configurations. As these dimensions are all interrelated, the following section takes each in turn, but with necessary overlaps.

In this study, we found that digital diversity was particularly evident in communications and connections within and outside the university. For some working class students or those from minority ethnic communities, university produced mixed feelings of belonging. While being keen to adapt and integrate, maintaining connections to home and other friends was particularly important once they were at university, and social media were used frequently, sometimes on a daily basis, to sustain those connections. Furthermore, for those whose families were some distance away, the costs of travelling back home made this an infrequent option for many, and in such cases communications through social networks to home, extended family, and outside friends were found to be essential. One student used Skype to talk to her friend from home who was studying elsewhere every day. Her friend was further on in her university studies and she acted as a sounding board and a mentor. Many other students in the study also reported that friends and family members acted as mentors or advisors, and provided emotional support through digitally mediated communications such as text messaging, mobile calls, Skype, and Facebook. Most students reported that the first year (they were all second year students) had been particularly challenging for them and that this had improved over the first 12 months and they were becoming less reliant on support from home. However, for some students, their sense of where they belonged and their relationship to the university appeared to be shifting over time as new friendships developed and they gradually became more integrated into the practice and culture of university. Some people reported that as they became more integrated into university, this was changing the place they felt was really "home," and that going back home became more like a visit.

Another aspect was that in this group of students from more diverse backgrounds and contexts, there were many who had caring responsibilities for others or paid work which made integrating into university life more challenging. Digital media and online systems helped students to meet studying commitments remotely and maintain contacts with the university while fulfilling other commitments. The notion of *belonging* can therefore be seen to be a complex web of diverse identities, commitments, and attachments, and belonging to the university needs to be seen in relation to other forms of belonging and identity. Digital media can broker more persistent communications and emotional support through constant connectedness (Timmis, 2012) but what is less clear is whether this fosters a culture of university belonging.

The second dimension concerns the creative appropriation of technology to achieve particular purposes. Students in the study were mobilizing social media, especially Facebook, on a regular basis for social interactions as might be expected. However, they were also using Facebook and file sharing apps such as Dropbox for setting up informal group spaces, which worked in parallel to the formal work of the program or course. This was particularly the case on programs with large cohorts of students, suggesting that there was perhaps less need for such brokerage on smaller, more intimate programs. These were used for questions and informal discussions, sharing notes, and lecture recordings widely throughout the cohort and were mostly unofficial and unseen by academics. In fact, Dropbox was not officially supported by the university and positively discouraged, and yet formed part of a "hidden curriculum" and informal support network for students. Several students also reported that they were using YouTube to supplement lectures where they felt lecturers were not making things clear enough, or where they did not understand some aspects of the lecture. The proliferation of video-based materials meant that it was always possible to find the topic in question and if one video was not suitable, they could find others that were. In addition, student voice and dissent was mobilized by one of the students who was a course representative. He initiated an online survey to gather further detail and opinions to feedback on a course unit after students in the cohort had gone to them with negative feedback about a specific lecture and lecturer. This strengthened the position and authority that the co-researcher was able to bring to the group's dissenting voices when feeding back to the unit organizers.

There were also examples of more individually focused appropriation, particularly among the mature students who showed considerable initiative in their uses of technology, such as using the Internet very creatively for their own individual needs and to support their studies. In particular for advocacy, research, independent, and private validation of one's understanding and providing alternative sources of advice and guidance to support limitations in understanding or poor teaching. Thus, there was evidence of students mobilizing digital technologies to create alternative educational spaces that offer a means of personal validation, augmented understanding, voicing dissent, and shared concerns as well as more practical activities such as file and notes sharing.

The third dimension concerns the dynamics and challenges of space and time. As discussed above, many students in the study highlighted frequent working and communicating online across different times and spaces, engaging in and creating alternative learning spaces that involved changes in time/space possibilities, and the benefits of flexibility and sharing that accrued. However, the challenges of time and space were especially notable in the experiences of mature students (over 22 years) living in their own homes within daily traveling distance of the university. Such students may appear to be local and indeed, in the university in question, this is how they were categorized, however this study found that they could be more isolated. As well as feeling different to the younger students through age, they are sometimes isolated geographically, in that they have further to travel than those living on campus or in the city, and can't take part in social activities. Many of the mature students also reported a lack of social interaction with other students and that this limited their sense of belonging. Furthermore, there was little evidence that social networks or online communications were helping to mediate this, and sometimes added to the distance experienced by local mature students. Therefore, while social networking and use of Facebook were very common, this was sometimes exclusive and excluding, especially for mature students who were not part of these networks. Furthermore, some (though not all) of the mature students were the least comfortable using technology, making exclusion more pronounced. By contrast, if they had worked prior to starting at university, sometimes mature students felt the university systems were poor, and were intolerant of delays or bureaucratic issues concerning technological systems because they had had previous experiences to compare with. They expected more timely responses and more consistency across digital spaces and this constrained a sense of belonging to a joined up university.

DISCUSSION

The study findings outlined above show some examples of how digital technologies were found to help in fostering a sense of belonging, particularly through academic interactions with their peers (Thomas, 2012) and through the creative appropriation of digital space for self validation and the development of alternative communities, which are fluid and dynamic. Social networking and communications tools were important mediators which helped to maintain the connectedness and constancy of communications with others (Timmis, 2012). Nevertheless, social media and online interactions are not necessarily inclusive of all students, and the findings also show how some underrepresented groups might continue to feel isolated and excluded and how online social interactions can sometimes reproduce existing inequalities (Boyd, 2011). As Hughes (2009) suggests, we should temper our "enthusiasm for the new technologies ... with an appreciation that identity and belonging to learning communities are complex and often unresolved issues for learners" (p. 291).

The findings also beg the question of "Belonging to what?" and whether there are multiple modes of belonging and even a sense of unbelonging or retaining existing identities that are important if diversity is to be acknowledged. The students in this study overwhelming valued the support of family, friends, and outside groups to which they belonged in supporting them with their studies, although over time, their sense of belonging to the university was also increasing, particularly as they moved through the transition from first to second year which in turn changed their sense of belonging elsewhere. Equally the findings show how a sense of belonging can develop among peers at university through personal development and over time, but this does not necessarily apply to the university as an institution or even to the formal academic environment.

While almost all students reported an increasing sense of belonging to university life, belonging elsewhere was also critical. In some cases, for example, through part time work and ongoing family responsibilities, other identities were constructed or maintained which offered different positionings within alternative figured worlds (Holland et al., 1998) which could be marshaled positively among underrepresented or more diverse students to promote other forms of engagement elsewhere. Social networking, digital communications, and online spaces can help to sustain engagement in different figured worlds simultaneously through the possibilities they afford for alternative chronotopes or time/space configurations that enable working across physical and digital spaces simultaneously or continuing to engage in spaces with peers or others, but at different times and physically separate to other people (Davies, 2014; Kumpulainen et al., 2014; Lemke, 2004).

We also found that belonging in the academic sphere did not necessarily mean in formal lectures and organized teaching spaces. There were many examples of students initiating and participating in digitally mediated interactions and sharing of resources among friends or the whole cohort of students. Equally working with peers in social spaces and sharing work in digital and face-to-face settings were also commonplace among these students. These improvisations were designed to overcome the challenges that were felt in being members of large groups of students who were not always physically co-located.

Spaces were mobilized and constructed as cultural resources to support their learning (Holland et al., 1998; Lemke, 2004). Such spaces are social and pedagogical hybrids in which private and public contributions can merge and impact on each other. The active construction of spaces can also be understood within the social networking culture of student life, where Facebook and other social networking platforms were reported to be integral to daily life (Selwyn, 2009). This is also important in terms of the agency of students in mobilizing technologies to meet their own needs.

In university-owned digital spaces such as learner management systems (or virtual learning environments), students do participate in formal, required activities based on academic directives and the design of tasks and curriculum. However, students do not generally have the possibility to establish their own spaces within formal environments, and these are usually set up for them for a specific purpose. Previous work by Timmis (2012) has shown that because social networking and online communications are participatory practices with an "always on" and "always active" set of cultural norms, this creates conflicts in expectations in institutionally-owned environments. The lack of integration, control, and spontaneity encountered can lead to a sense of frustration at the loss of agency, which in turn limits participation (Timmis, 2012). By establishing alternatives to formal study spaces, it can be argued that students are able to capitalise on their own cultural resources and regain a sense of agency, as well as creating opportunities for sharing and networking. It is important to emphasise that such activities cannot be claimed to be particular to underrepresented students, but rather that these kinds of hidden activities are particularly helpful for students in developing a wider sense of belonging to the university as a community of peers through collective action.

Säljö (2010) argues that the Internet offers new possibilities for learning through an extended and shared social memory, expanded resources, and alternative access to expertise. This form of diversity suggests further opportunities for individual and collective empowerment and arguably for students from more diverse backgrounds with more limited cultural capital, this suggests that such resources in themselves can be mobilized as supports. Students in the DD-lab study (in particular, mature students) were capitalizing on this potential including alternative sources of advice and expertise to their academic tutors or lecturer notes. They also showed in their documentaries numerous examples of the creative possibilities that web 2.0 participatory practices afford (Bonderup Dohn, 2009) for working with others and individually to construct and reconstruct digital resources using multiple sources and combinations, examples of what Dohn refers to as "patchworking."

In summary, dimensions and modes of digital diversity were found in the reported experiences of the students in the DD-lab study, which offers some indications of how digital diversity might be considered in relation to both a sense of belonging within higher education settings but, more importantly, as a means to empowerment through multiple forms of communication and co-construction of hybrid pedagogic and social spaces, together with access and engagement in sharing, support, and expertise.

CONCLUSIONS

This chapter has considered the concept of digital diversity and how this might be developed for understanding and investigating widening participation in higher education alongside the experiences of underrepresented groups such as students from more diverse backgrounds. The concept has been shown to have different meanings and uses in different contexts, and therefore to be something of a "fuzzy" concept. Nevertheless, this chapter has shown how this can be helpful in understanding the dynamic interplay of digital proliferation and diverse communities, and that diversity encapsulates the idea of multivoicedness and opportunities for alternative and divergent routes to studying.

It is important to note that the digital practices of students from diverse backgrounds are not necessarily different to other students, and underrepresented groups are not necessarily those who make more use of such technology; rather we are arguing that these mobilizations of particular forms of social and cultural capital may be particularly important for students whose identities are more fragile or fragmented, or where personal, social, or economic circumstances are more challenging. Digital technologies can offer ways to enhance the voice and agency of underrepresented groups and afford opportunities for retaining connections and developing social interactions, but do not necessarily do this for all students. Yet even where the social dimensions and sense of belonging are more challenging, there are opportunities for individual empowerment through the expanded social memory of the Internet and creative knowledge construction afforded by Web 2.0 practices.

In conclusion, from a social justice perspective, we need to ask in what ways universities can capitalize on these potential benefits and support increased belonging and empowerment, particularly for disadvantaged students. We argue that universities need to recognize students as collaborators in the co-construction of their university, as active knowledge producers, rather than seeing them as consumers of pedagogic interventions and transmitted knowledge (Neary & Winn, 2009). A key part of this includes expanding participation within the "digital university" (Jones, 2013) to encompass students taking initiative using digital technologies and not just acting as passive receivers. These mobilizations are even more critical for students who come from more diverse lifeworlds because through these active engagements, students can increase their social and cultural capital and develop their sense of belonging across the various dimensions of university life. Digital diversity as a social justice and empowerment proposition also suggests the need to account for value, and celebrate difference and the different offerings people bring to higher education. This will necessarily include multiple forms of belonging, creative improvisation, and cultural engagement at an individual and social level that can open up opportunities and mechanisms for participation, retention, and success.

ACKNOWLEDGMENTS

We wish to thank all of the 31 students who took part in the study referred to in this chapter for their inspiration and invaluable contributions to this work. We also acknowledge the support of the University of Bristol's Widening Participation Research Initiative who funded the DD-lab study.

REFERENCES

Andrews, J., & Yee, W. (2006). Children's "funds of knowledge" and their real life activities: Two minority ethnic children learning in out-of-school contexts in the UK. *Educational Review, 58*(4).

Australian Council for Computers in Education. (2010). Biennial conference: Digital Diversity. Conference website. Melbourne, April. http://acec2010.acce.edu.au

Bakhtin, M. (1981). *The dialogic imagination: Four essays by M. M. Bakhtin* (C. Emerson & M. Holquist, Trans.). Austin, TX: University of Texas Press.

Ball, S. J., Reay, D., & David, M. (2002). "Ethnic Choosing": Minority ethnic students, social class and higher education choice. *Race Ethnicity and Education, 5*(4), 333–357. doi:10.1080/1361332022000030879

Bathmaker, A. M., Ingram, N., & Waller, R. (2013). Higher education, social class and the mobilisation of capitals: Recognising and playing the game. *British Journal of Sociology of Education, 34*(5-6), 723–743. doi:10.1080/01425692.2013.816041

Bloomfield, B. P., Latham, Y., & Vurdubakis, T. (2010). Bodies, technologies and action possibilities: When is an affordance? *Sociology, 44*(3), 415–433. doi:10.1177/0038038510362469

Bonderup Dohn, N. (2009). Web 2.0: Inherent tensions and evident challenges for education. *International Journal of Computer-Supported Collaborative Learning, 4*, 343–363.

Boyd, D. (2011). White flight in networked publics? How race and class shaped American teen engagement with MySpace and Facebook. In L. Nakamura & P. Chow-White (Eds.), *Race after the Internet* (pp. 203–222). London, UK: Routledge.

Brew, A. (2006). *Research and teaching: Beyond the divide*. Basingstoke: Palgrave Macmillan.

Brice-Heath, S. (1986). Critical factors in literacy development. In K. Egan, S. de Castell, & A. Luke (Eds.), *In literacy, society, and schooling* (pp. 209–229). Cambridge, UK: Cambridge University Press.

Clark, J. A. (2011). Digital diversity and education: Some philosophical problems. *Computers in New Zealand Schools: Learning, Teaching, Technology, 23*(2), 114–125.

Cole, M. (1996). *Cultural psychology: A once and future discipline*. Cambridge, MA: Harvard University Press.

Cope, B., & Kalantzis, M. (2000). *Multiliteracies: Literacy, learning and the design of social futures*. London, UK: Routledge.

Crozier, G., Reay, D., & Clayton, J. (2010). The socio-cultural and learning experiences of working class students in higher education. In M. David (Ed.), *Improving learning by widening participation in higher education* (pp. 62 –74). London, UK: Routledge.

Crozier, G., Reay, D., Clayton, J., Colliander, L., & Grinstead, J. (2008). Different strokes for different folks: Diverse students in diverse institutions—experiences of higher education. *Research Papers in Education, 23*(2), 167–177. doi:10.1080/02671520802048703

Dahlstrom, E., de Boor, T., Grunwald, P., & Vockley, M. (2011). *The ECAR national study of undergraduate students and information technology*, Boulder, CO: EDUCAUSE Center for Applied Research. Retrieved from http://www.educause.edu/2011StudentStudy

Dahlstrom, E., Walker, J., & Dziuban, C. (2013). *The ECAR study of undergraduate students and information technology* (Vol. 2010). Louisville, KY: EDUCAUSE Center for Analysis and Research. Retrieved from http://www.educause.edu/ecar

David, M. (2010). Introduction to the dilemmas of widening participation in higher education. In M. David (Ed.), *Improving learning by widening participation in higher education* (pp. 3–27). Abingdon, Oxon: Routledge.

Davies, J. (2014). (Im)material girls living in (im)material worlds: Identity curation through time and space. In C. Burnett, J. Davies, G. Merchant, & J. Rowsell (Eds.), *New literacies around the globe: Policy and pedagogy*. London, UK: Routledge.

DeAndrea, D. C., Ellison, N. B., LaRose, R., Steinfield, C., & Fiore, A. (2012). Serious social media: On the use of social media for improving students' adjustment to college. *The Internet and Higher Education, 15*(1), 15–23. doi:10.1016/j.iheduc.2011.05.009

Ecclestone, K., Biesta, G., & Hughes, M. (2010). *Transitions and learning through the lifecourse* (p. 240). Abingdon, Oxfordshire: Routledge.

Ellis, R., & Goodyear, P. (2010). *Students' experiences of e-learning in higher education: The ecology of sustainable innovation* (Open & Flexible Learning Series). Abingdon, UK: Routledge.

Erstad, O., & Sefton-Green, J. (2012). *Identity, community, and learning lives in the digital age* (p. 237). Cambridge, UK: Cambridge University Press.

Fielding, M., & Bragg, S. (2003). *Students as researchers: Making a difference—Consulting pupils about teaching and learning.* Cambridge, UK: Pearson.

Gewirtz, S. (1998). Conceptualizing social justice in education: Mapping the territory. *Journal of Education Policy, 13*(4), 469–484. doi:10.1080/0268093980130402

Gidley, J. M., Hampson, G. P., Wheeler, L., & Bereded-Samuel, E. (2010). From access to success: An integrated approach to quality higher education informed by social inclusion theory and practice. *Higher Education Policy, 23*(1), 123–147. doi:10.1057/hep.2009.24

Goffman, E. (1959). *The presentation of self in everyday life.* New York, NY: Anchor Books.

Gourlay, L., & Oliver, M. (2013). Beyond "the social": Digital literacies as sociomaterial practice. In R. Goodfellow & M. Lea (Eds.), *Literacy in the digital university: Critical perspectives on learning, scholarship, and technology* (pp. 79–94). Abingdon, Oxfordshire: Routledge.

Gurin, P., Dey, E. L., Hurtado, S., & Gurin, G. (2009). Diversity and higher education: Theory and impact on educational outcomes. *Harvard Educational Review, 72*(3), 330–367. Retrieved from http://her.hepg.org/content/01151786u134n051/

Harper, S. R., & Quaye, S. J. (2009). Beyond sameness, with engagement and outcomes for all: An introduction. In S. R. Harper & S. J. Quaye (Eds.), *Student engagement in higher education theoretical perspectives and practical approaches for diverse populations* (pp. 1–15). London, UK: Routledge.

Heron, J., & Reason, P. (2001). The practice of co-operative inquiry: Research with rather than on people. In P. Reason & H. Bradbury (Eds.), *Handbook of action research: Participative inquiry and practice* (pp. 179–188). London, UK: Sage.

Holland, D., Lachicotte, W., Skinner, D., & Cain, C. (1998). *Identity and agency in cultural worlds.* Cambridge, MA: Harvard University Press.

Hughes, G. (2009). Social software: New opportunities for challenging social inequalities in learning? *Learning, Media and Technology, 34*(4), 291–305.

Jones, C. (2013). The digital university: a concept in need of definition. In R. Goodfellow & M. Lea (Eds.), *Literacy in the digital university: Critical perspectives on learning, scholarship, and technology* (pp. 162–172). Abingdon, Oxfordshire: Routledge.

Jones, C., Ramanau, R., Cross, S., & Healing, G. (2010). Net generation or digital natives: Is there a distinct new generation entering university? *Computers & Education, 54*(3), 722–732.

Kumpulainen, K., Mikkola, A., & Jaatinen, A. M. (2014). The chronotopes of technology- mediated creative learning practices in an elementary school community. *Learning, Media and Technology, 39*(1), 53–74. doi:10.1080/17439884.2012.752383

Lave, J., & Wenger, E. (2005). Practice, person, social world. In H. Daniels (Ed.), *An introduction to Vygotsky* (2nd ed., pp. 149–156). London, UK: Routledge.

Lea, M. (2013). Academic literacies in the digital university: Integrating individual accounts with network practice. In R. Goodfellow & M. Lea (Eds.), *Literacy in the digital university: Critical perspectives on learning, scholarship, and technology* (pp. 137–148). Abingdon, Oxfordshire: Routledge.

Lemke, J. (2004). Learning across multiple places and their chronotopes. In *AER 2004 Symposium*. San Diego, CA. Retrieved from http://www.personal.umich.edu/~jaylemke/papers/aera_2004.htm

Ligorio, M., Loperfido, F., & Sansone, N. (2013). Dialogical positions as a method of understanding identity trajectories in a collaborative, blended university course. *International Journal of Computer-Supported Collaborative Learning*, *8*(3), 351–367. doi:http://link.springer.com/article/10.1007%2Fs11412-013-9174-3

Livingstone, S. (2008). Internet literacy: Young people's negotiation of new online opportunities. In T. McPherson (Ed.), *Digital young, innovation, and the unexpected: The John D. and Catherine T. MacArthur Foundation Series on Digital Media and Learning* (pp. 101–122). Cambridge, MA: MIT Press. doi:10.1162/dmal.9780262633598.101

Looker, E. D., & Naylor, T. D. (Eds.). (2010). *Digital diversity: youth, equity, and information technology.* Waterloo, Ontario: Wilfrid Laurier University Press.

Neary, M., & Winn, J. (2009). The student as producer: reinventing the student experience in higher education. In L. Bell, H. Stevenson, & M. Neary (Eds.), *The future of higher education: Policy, pedagogy and the student experience* (pp. 192–210). London, UK: Continuum.

O'Reilly, T. (2007). What is Web 2.0: Design patterns and business models for the next generation of software. *Communications & Strategies*, *65*(1), 17–37. Retrieved from http://papers.ssrn.com/abstract=1008839

Oblinger, D. G., & Oblinger, J. L. (2005). *Educating the net generation*. Washington, DC: Educause.

Prensky, M. (2001). Digital natives, digital immigrants. *On the Horizon*, *9*(5), 1–6.

Reay, D., David, M., & Ball, S. J. (2005). *Degrees of choice: Class, gender and race in the higher education choice process*. Stoke on Trent, UK: Trentham Books.

Säljö, R. (2010). Digital tools and challenges to institutional traditions of learning: Technologies, social memory and the performative nature of learning. *Journal of Computer Assisted Learning*, *26*(1), 53–64. doi:10.1111/j.1365-2729.2009.00341.x

Selwyn, N. (2009). Faceworking: Exploring students' education-related use of Facebook. *Learning, Media and Technology*, *34*(2), 157–174.

Selwyn, N. (2011). *Education and technology: Key issues and debates*. London, UK: Continuum.

Solomon, Y. (2007). Not belonging? What makes a functional learner identity in undergraduate mathematics? *Studies in Higher Education, 32*(1), 79–96.

Sutherland, R. J., Joubert, M., & Eagle, S. (2012). *A vision and strategy for technology enhanced learning: Report from the STELLAR Network of Excellence*.

Thomas, L. (2002). Student retention in higher education: The role of institutional habitus. *Journal of Education Policy*, *17*(4), 423–442. doi:10.1080/02680930210140257

Thomas, L. (2012). *Building student engagement and belonging in higher education at a time of change: Final report from the What Works? Student retention and success programme*. York, UK. Retrieved from http://www.heacademy.ac.uk/assets/documents/retention/What_works_final_report.pdf

Timmis, S. (2012). Constant companions: Instant messaging conversations as sustainable supportive study structures amongst undergraduate peers. *Computers & Education, 59*(1), 3–18. Retrieved from http://dx.doi.org/10.1016/j.compedu.2011.09.026

Timmis, S., Joubert, M., Manuel, A., & Barnes, S. (2010). Transmission, transformation and ritual: An investigation of students' and researchers' digitally mediated communications and collaborative work. *Learning, Media and Technology, 35*(3), 307–322. Retrieved from http://dx.doi.org/10.1080/17439884.2010.509354

Timmis, S., & Williams, J. (2013). Students as co-researchers: A collaborative, community- based approach to the research and practice of technology enhanced learning. In E. Dunne & D. Owen (Eds.), *The student engagement handbook, practice in higher education* (pp. 509–525). Bingley, UK: Emerald.

Timmis, S., & Williams, J. (2014). Lost in transition? Making sense of space:time configurations across workplace and educational boundaries. In S. Bayne, C. Jones, M. De Laat, T. Ryberg, & C. Sinclair (Eds.), *Proceedings of the 9th International Conference on Networked Learning 2014* (pp. 288–295). Edinburgh, SCT.

Tinto, V. (2008). Access without support is not opportunity. In *Keynote address at the 36th Annual Institute for Chief Academic Officers, The Council of Independent Colleges,*. Seattle, WA. Retrieved from http://faculty.soe.syr.edu/vtinto/Files/CouncilofIndependentColleges2008Keynote.pdf

Trowler, V. (2010). *Student Engagement Literature Review* (p. 74). York, UK. Retrieved from http://www.new2.heacademy.ac.uk/assets/documents/studentengagement/StudentEngagementLiteratureReview.pdf

Van Oers, B. (1998). From context to contextualizing. *Learning and Instruction, 8*(6), 473–488. doi:10.1016/S0959-4752(98)00031-0

Vygotsky, L. S. (1978). *Mind in society: The development of higher psychological processes*. Cambridge, MA: Harvard University Press.

Vygotsky, L. S., & Kozulin, A. (1986). *Thought and language*. Cambridge, MA: MIT Press.

Wertsch, J. V. (1991). *Voices of the mind: A socio-cultural approach to mediated action*. Cambridge, MA: Harvard University Press.

Wertsch, J. V. (1998). *Mind as action*. New York, NY: Oxford University Press.

CHAPTER 15

VIDEO CONNECTIONS

Media Education and Global Citizenship a New Form of Alliance

Alessia Rosa

ABSTRACT

Global citizenship requires a new commitment from the education community. Though media systems provide opportunities to communicate quickly, not everyone has free access to media or adequate media literacy. "Video connection" is a media education research project realized between a group of Italian and Kenyan youth. For the Kenyan youngsters, the "video connections project" was a tool to analyze and share their personal perspectives of life in their country. The Italian component of the project was used as an instrument to raise awareness of authentic life in Kenya. An inductive learning approach was used to assist the students in developing an awareness of the importance of global active citizenship. Video production (digital storytelling and cartooning) was implemented because it represented a space for sharing and growth among all study participants. These activities were based on a peer-to-peer approach. The boys and girls in Kenya directly presented their daily life, providing not only a new awareness of and a common response to cultural mobilization.

E-Learning and Social Media:
Education and Citizenship for the Digital 21st Century, pp. 321–342

VIDEO CONNECTIONS. MEDIA EDUCATION AND GLOBAL CITIZENSHIP A NEW FORM OF ALLIANCE

Migration flows, progress in information technologies and growing economic interdependence make the world a smaller place (Giddens, 2003; Spiro, 2007), and concepts of citizenship and participation evolve into a global perspective (Morley & Robins, 1995).

In such a deeply interconnected environment, it is possible to approach the concept of citizenship from two different perspectives (Myers, 2010): on one hand, within the nation state, the concept of citizenship has become progressively plural[1] as diverse social and ethnic groups affirm their rights (Kymlicka, 2007); on the other hand, from a supranational perspective, individuals increasingly take on global affiliations that extend beyond a single nation (Heater, 2002; Kivisto & Faist, 2007). Both these perspectives recognize the concept of citizenship as a personal and flexible construction (Held, 2002; Kennedy, 2007). Today it's possible to attribute an important role to the media system in the development of the concept of citizenship (Dahlgren, 2005; Tremayne, 2007). As Castells (2008, p. 89) underlines, "The contemporary global public sphere is largely dependent on the global/local communication media system." The convergence of media and technology in a global culture is changing the way we learn about the world (Thoman & Jolls, 2004) and at the same time these technologies are increasingly strengthening our ability to connect to the rest of the world (Bennett 2004; Dahlgren, 2005; Tremayne, 2007). Digital media channels constitute new spaces for socialization, in which individuals can become effective members of an extended, geographically spread community, which does not require adherence to rigidly codified systems of meaning or models of behavior. Non-coercive social relationships and a non-linear type of learning characterize these new systems (Rosa & Torre, 2014).

We experience a reconfiguration of the relations between media texts, producers, and consumers. Compared with a not-so-distant past, we are witnessing new and unpredictable phenomena. Until a few years ago anyone coming into contact with the media (in a non-professional capacity) was limited to the role of mere consumer, whereas today technological simplification makes it increasingly possible to create and share content and, with it, ideas, perspectives, and values. We are witnessing an epochal transition from being mere consumers of media content to being potential producers (Benkler, 2006; Tremayne, 2007; Rice, 2002).

Deuze (2006) argues that the emerging practices of participation in new media contexts have three ways in which individuals engage with media. He summarizes these three forms of engagement as follows: participation, when individuals are active agents in the process of meaning-making; remediation, when we adopt but at the same time modify, manipulate, and thus reform consensual ways of understanding reality; and bricolage, when we reflexively assemble our own particular versions of such reality (Deuze, 2006, p. 66). This does not merely entail the acceptance of predefined values but also the need to participate in their definition even in everyday life.

Citizenship can be practised as much through everyday life, leisure, critical consumption, and popular entertainment as through debate and engagement with politics (Burgess, Foth, & Klaebe, 2006; Rheingold, 2002).

This transition puts new responsibilities in the hands of the broader public, which needs to become aware and educated for this active role (Keane, 2003; Tremblay, 2002). This cultural and technological evolution requires more complex media literacy and a body of competences *to critically interpret the powerful images of a multimedia culture.* To live successfully and freely in a globalized world, people must develop the appropriate skills, knowledge, attitudes, and perspectives (Zhao, 2010) both in relation to their local situation and to other realities (virtual or real).

As Luke (2000) observed,

> unless educators take a lead in developing appropriate pedagogies for these new electronic media and forms of communication, corporate experts will be the ones to determine how people will learn, what they learn, and what constitutes literacy. (p. 71)

Media Education and Critical Thinking

Media education is the process of teaching and learning about media. The outcome of this process is media literacy (Buckingham, 2003). Media literacy is generally defined as the ability to access, analyze, evaluate, and communicate messages in different forms (European Commission, 2007; Potter, 2010; Aufderheide, 1993). In a few words, the competence of "reading" and "writing" the media (Silverblatt, Ferry, & Finan, 2009). In accordance with this definition, Koltay (2011) underlines that the various levels of media literacy include:

- feeling comfortable with all existing media exploiting their potential for entertainment, access to culture, intercultural dialogue, learning and daily-life applications
- having a critical approach to media as regards both quality and accuracy of content
- using media creatively, to create and disseminate images, information, and content

- understanding the media economy and the difference between pluralism and media ownership
- being aware of copyright issues which are essential for a "culture of legality," especially for the younger generation in its double capacity of consumers and producers of content

Media literacy is not only a form of information's decoding but it may be thought of as the ability to create personal meaning from and through media messages. People should be critical thinkers who can understand and produce in the media culture (Adams & Hamm, 2001). Media education, therefore, aims to develop both critical understanding and active participation. It enables young people to interpret and make informed judgments as media consumers, but it also enables them to become producers of media (Masterman & Mariet, 1994).

Developing literacy toward media represents an important instrument to overcome the digital gap due to unequal technical and social access to media. This element is important from a global perspective but is fundamental for economic and social growth in the developing countries (Ranieri, 2010; Sartori, 2006).

Today, media literacy represents a necessary condition to enable people to participate in the local, national, and global economy, culture, and politics. Hence, without developing adequate literacies, digital gaps cannot be overcome and big groups of people will be left out of the emerging global economy, networked society, and culture.

People must be able to negotiate meanings, locate misrepresentations and under representations, and produce their own messages to develop a true global village (McLuhan, 1997).

> Addressing issues of inequality and injustice in media representations can be a powerful starting place for problem-posing transformative education. Critical media literacy offers the tools and framework to help students become subjects in the process of deconstructing injustices, expressing their own voices, and struggling to create a better society. (Kellner & Share, 2005, p. 381)

The acquisition of these skills becomes an essential tool with which to fight against cultural and economic imperialism (Shachaf, 2008) and to support the development of active participation in global citizenship. The term cultural imperialism refers most broadly to the exercise of domination in cultural relationships in which the values, practices, and meanings of a powerful foreign culture are imposed upon one or more native cultures (Tomlinson, 1991). The shared commitment to global citizenship means to assure the cultural mutual respect and enrichment in a global system of critical solidarity (Ferguson, 2001).

For this to happen it is not enough to merely identify the connection that already exists with technology; young people need to understand the implications of this connection and react through the same technology in order to develop forms of global citizenship.

To reach this ambitious goal, media education should:

- involve critical analysis and creative production
- take place in formal and informal settings
- promote the sense of community and social responsibility, as well as individual self-fulfillment

Intercultural exchanges via technologies can educate students around the world to become culturally sensitive global citizens. In order to achieve this, the youngest need to have the opportunity to use media competences related with reading and writing media languages, otherwise they risk being caught in the whirl of the media system. In addition, they need free access to the media system and the possibility to interact freely, not only as consumers but also as producers.

Teaching Approach

The development process of "media competences" requires deep work on people's skills and, at the same time, a serious reflection on the use of those skills in the media world, as well as in the real world. For this reason media education activities should start from the knowledge/experience students already have about the media and subsequently an educator can suggest interpretative models and action strategies, supporting people in building up and experimenting with new interpretations and actions, and stimulating them to reflect systematically on their own interpretation and actions.

The literature about media education has identified a repertoire of teaching techniques that are suited to a specific context or areas of interest. More common examples of these techniques are: textual analysis, contextual analysis, case studies, translations, simulation, and production. These techniques can complement each other and also be integrated with other educational approaches.

In the video connection project case studies, simulation and production were used. All these techniques have been integrated in the experiential learning cycle proposed by Pfeiffer and Jones (1985) for the construction of teaching units in the school context and then revised by Trinchero (2010) in the media education curriculum for secondary school. The cycle shown in Figure 15.1 begins with the proposal of a meaningful open problem in a playful perspective.

Figure 15.1. The Pfeiffer and Jones (1985) model of the experiential learning cycle.

More specifically the problem must be: (a) open, which means that it involves different possible solutions, each one with both strong and weak points; (b) significant to people who have to face it, which implies that it should be challenging and generate satisfaction once solved; (c) solved alone, in pairs, or in small groups, but always counting on interaction with classmates, the teacher, and the consultation of school materials (Trinchero, 2010). Solutions must then be shared verbally within the group, in the phase called Publishing, in order to analyze weaknesses and strengths. In this stage the teacher-mediator has a key role, in order to allow everyone to express opinions and concerns in a respectful and explorative climate. Finally, the teacher, the group, or one of the students summarizes the strengths of all solutions that emerged. This final stage can be thought of as the fulcrum or the pivotal step in experiential learning since it is the systematic examination of commonly shared experiences. This is the 'group dynamics' stage of the cycle, in which participants essentially reconstruct the patterns and interactions of the activity from the published individual reports (Pfeiffer, 1998, p. 5).

The aim is to produce one or more optimal solutions and extrapolate general principles useful to the solution (or solutions to similar problems in the future); this activity is called generalizing.

If learning is transferring knowledge to the "real world," it is important for the participants to be able to extrapolate the experience from the training setting to the outside world. An inferential leap has to be made at this point in the structured experience from the reality inside the activity to the reality of everyday life (Pfeiffer, 1998, p. 6).

At the end, the teacher suggests a simulation where these principles should be applied and this will start a new cycle of experiential learning.

Media were central in each problem proposed in this project and in all the related educational activities. The traditional media system offers a specific point of view on reality; web and social networks on the other hand can offer a new means of sharing ideas and perspectives.

The Aim of the Project

Life conditions in Africa are often mentioned by the media world, but the perspective of the story is usually given from the Western point of view. For a group of young people, the "Video Connections Project" has been a reflection activity about the common idea of African frailty in Italy, while in Kenya it has been a tool to show their everyday reality.

The common theme was the media representation of life in Africa, especially in Kenya. The aim of the "Video Connection Project" was the realization of a media education activity shared by a group of Italian children together with a group of street boys from Kenya. The objective was to know each other, compare different points of views, and finally develop a common value of belonging to a single global civilization.

The activities of the project have been structured in three phases, such as analysis of media languages, video production, and contact and exchange between Italian and Kenyan children. The main purpose of the project was to empower the students, strengthen their identity, and allow the growth of the individual through a more authentic comparison with other realities.

The Project Partners

The project was realized through the cooperation of AMREF[2] Italy and a media educator belonging to the Italian Association of Media Education (MED).[3]

With the support of international broadcasters and institutions AMREF has been implementing a participatory video project named "Different

Perspective." The project has worked out both as an educational tool during the rehabilitation of street children and as a communication and advocacy instrument for, and as part of, the AMREF Dagoretti Child in Need Project. AMREF participatory video products (documentaries, reportages, short fiction, advocacy clips, news magazines) are broadcast worldwide, have received international awards, and are screened in international congresses and film festivals. It has been considered a Good Practice by the United Nations.

The Different Perspective Project emerged from a critical review of the role and means of information on the issue of African problems. Mainstream media traditionally focuses on African emergencies and extreme circumstances, depriving the object of their interest of dignity and vitality. What is new in AMREF's approach is the double aspect of its products: binding together the social importance of the process with the artistic result of the products. They give voices to the voiceless along with returning the dignity and the initiative to the protagonists. Such added value reveals the enormous potential of this approach in spreading the message and stimulating action on a large scale, from the perspective of global citizenship.

The Different Perspective Project has shown also a real value in terms of rehabilitation of children. Through the video training, the actual work of filming in the slums, and having to clearly define issues, a growing number of boys and girls have been able to acquire a greater degree of awareness and self-confidence, which has greatly helped them in moving away from the streets. The Different Perspective team has proved to be a strong promotion tool and a proof that the marginalized can be empowered to communicate and advocate their rights, to fight stereotypes. It is in this very context that the "Video Connection Project" was born.

The Project Attendees

The project involved two different groups:

- 23 children, 10 years old, attending the same class in a school in Milan;
- 16 teenagers (from 13 to 18 years old), part of AMREF's Dagoretti Child in Need Project.[4]

Pupils in the Italian school were from different nations and came from families with different social and cultural backgrounds. The Kenyan teenagers were a group of street boys and girls from Nairobi's slums.

The Narrative Productions

Media education focuses the attention on different languages and tools. For this specific project, two narrative products were chosen for media education production activity: the cartoon language in Milan and the digital storytelling activity in Kenya

The interest was not only in narrative products but also, and especially, in narrative processes and their educational role. Bruner (1986, 1990) underlines that it is through narrative thought that we can know and that stories constitute authentic models through which reality can be interpreted. In others words, it is possible to affirm that as a result of the process of reflection activated by narrative processes, individuals are placed in a position to understand their own reality, and in particular their own experiences, attributing to them a specific meaning that is instrumental to the attribution of sense. Experience no longer represents a random sequence of events but acquires an order that serves to understand it. The individual storyteller necessarily places between him/herself and the events narrated the necessary distance to look at them "from another point of view": this enables an interpretation that is different from reality as experienced, which helps the subject not only to understand aspects and elements which still have not been understood until that moment but also, through that very attribution of sense, to acquire energy and awareness of his/her own capacities and potential. Narrating stimulates a process of self-empowerment. The use of two different languages is due to theoretical and practical reasons.

Video production was used because it was closer to what AMREF had already promoted in Kenya. Since in Italy the participants were younger and less experienced, cartoons seemed to be the most appropriate language (even because it is a form of visual art that they already know). In a school context, cartoons production does not require any acting skills, and this is an additional advantage.

In Kenya, the digital storytelling[5] was used because digital stories revolve around a chosen theme presented by the specific viewpoint of the participants. The stories are typically just a few minutes long and have a variety of uses, including the telling of personal tales (Robin, 2008). These features make the digital storytelling a tool of simple construction and with great communicative potential.

The Project Structure

The project is articulated into three different phases, where media education plays the role of providing several opportunities to improve the intercultural reflection. The total duration was one year but the educational institutions involved in the project are still cooperating and promoting exchanges and online meetings.

The first phase took place in a school in Milan, where AMREF and MED staged media education activities about the representation of the value of water resources in the media system.

The second phase was carried out in Kenya, where a group of street boys and girls from Nairobi's slums were trained in the digital storytelling language. They produced a series of digital stories where the protagonists are the Kitui's communities participating in the experiences of community wells and gardens.

Last, the video productions realized in Kenya and in Italy were shared, so creating a common knowledge and highlighting the effectiveness of this activity in order to increase awareness about different points of views about the world.

The activities in Italy and in Kenya were managed by a MED media educator. All the videos produced within the project will be exhibited during the "Expo of the Peoples" in 2015.[6]

Activity in Milan

The activity began in Milan where children were invited to make a drawing of how they imagined the lives of their peers in Kenya and in Africa more in general. The drawings collected showed a rather sad and stereotyped Africa where poverty was the predominant theme. Only two children drew a colorful market and a white beach. The children were asked to describe their designs and also explain what type of sources they used for inspiring their picture about Africa. The main sources mentioned were: the TV news, advertisements for fundraising charities and movies. Children who had designed a colorful Africa were one of African descent and the other who had been to Africa on holiday with his parents. The media educator asked children who could help their peers in need and how. All responses show a certain estrangement regarding the conditions of their peers; children identified donating money as the only possible solution and did not recognize in the involved people any chance to improve their condition without the help from Western countries. The representation of the value of water resources in the media system was the first "meaningful open problem" chosen to start the experiential circle. This apparently simple element had been chosen to gradually introduce the media representation of African culture in a very different context. More in detail, eight activities were prepared using the structure of the experiential cycle. Children were asked to collect all videos or pictures linked to water they met in a week.

The images became the object of reflection and sharing, in order to identify the recurrent way the media represents water. After that, they were asked to fill in a logbook about their daily use of water (drinking, bathing, playing, and so on). Also in this case the different experiences were shared, trying to identify which habits determined waste of water. The last request was very demanding for children, since the media educator asked them to identify themselves with a situation where water is not largely available as it is in Western countries.

A role-play game was organized to help them to identify themselves with a situation far from their reality.

Table 15.1. Example of a Conversation With Children

"If you're on a desert island, what are the first things you'll do to survive?"
"I'll look for water" is the main answer."
"Maybe you're not lucky because there's little water or it is poisonous, what would you do?"
"I'll try to buy the water" is one of the answer.
"How would you organize your community?"
"I don't know, adults should do it" is one of the answer.

The children understood the water is crucial for surviving; however, they think at it as something "available" and not difficult or impossible to find. The class, divided into groups, analyzed the several problems that their African peers are familiar with. The task presented was very simple; however, in many cases the children said they were unable to find a solution. The media educator to the children that their peers in Kenya have to deal with lack of water daily and constantly face issues related to poverty. Once again, children were asked to collect images and videos, this time the subject of the research was Africa.

Following the experiential cycle, the materials found were analyzed by the students together with the media educator, in order to understand (sketching on a billboard) which idea of Africa and specifically of Kenya, was provided by such images (videos and pictures mainly from advertising and newspapers). Finally, some *Millennium News* episodes, a series of eight television breaking news segments on the Millennium Development Goals, written and filmed by former street boys and girls from Nairobi, were presented.

For a group of young Africans, the *Millennium News* project has been a tool to show their personal attitude towards their own country. In this regard, AMREF organized different awareness-raising activities, and an online teaching guide has been created with the support of a media educator. The teaching guide gives educational suggestions and proposals about the uses of Millennium News production. However, to watch videos is not enough. It is necessary to reflect, compare ideas with each other, and finally act. By listening to the voices and the perspective of their African peers, students could understand how priceless water is. Finally, they produced a rhyming cartoon in stop motion to share their reflections about the value of water resources. In the cartoon a girl heroine, thanks to the support of local communities, finds the solution to every problem. The style was magical and imaginative, even if what has been achieved by Lara, the protagonist of the cartoon, is what AMREF is actually doing in Kenya (see Figure 15.2).

Figure 15.2. Snapshot from "Lara va in Africa" ("Lara goes to Africa") cartoon.

Three months after the conclusion of the project, media educators asked the children again to draw a picture about Africa. It was possible to detect that every imagined location was possible; all the drawings represented African characters committed to their territory, five represent themselves intent on helping in some activity. Therefore, a focus group was carried out in which the children were asked what their commitment could be in order to ensure a sustainable development .

All children have identified aspects of civic engagement. Their possible initiatives were mainly related to the reduction of waste (food and water). Three children have mentioned education as a central aspect to improve the future of peers. Water was recognized as a common good. Compared to the initial scarcity of ideas, proposals have been able to detect the capture of engagement with peers.

At the end of the project, this cartoon was used as an instrument to increase awareness in other children about the issue of water saving and as the start up in a digital storytelling project in Africa.

Activity in Nairobi

The second phase was carried out in Kenya and lasted about 10 days. The same approach used in the Italian context was adopted. The first topic was the representation of young people from the African newspapers; magazines with representations of teenagers were distributed to the kids. Several newspapers representing teenagers' lifestyles were provided. In several cases the lifestyles presented were closer to teens from European or African rich families but very distant from the street kids.

The teens identified recurring representations in the press and reflected on aspects they shared and those they considered not true. These data were collected through individual interviews and then with a focus group because the limited literacy of the group would have made it difficult for the administration of a written questionnaire. The element on which all the boys agreed on was that the media representations were related to how they wanted to be and not how they actually were. Two boys pointed out that many newspapers connect violent illegality with poverty. One boy has shown that the representations proposed by the newspapers analyzed were functional to their audience, to which they did not belong. He then asked the boys if they wanted to present their reality of life and the reactions were not enthusiastic, three said no without explanation; four reported that they feel ashamed; three argued that their life was not of interest to anyone, given that the rich and the West were not interested and the other slum dwellers already knew about their life; and only six kids said they would talk about themselves (see Figure 15.3).

They all shared, however, a strong desire to measure themselves with the media and tell their stories, maybe not the most personal ones. The structure and language of digital storytelling was then presented using products available on the web. The Seven Elements of Digital Storytelling, which are often mentioned as a useful starting point for anyone working with digital stories, had been emphasized. Then, children were asked to plan digital storytelling in which they introduce themselves through five common objects (keys, clothes, plastic bags).

The help from Dagoretti Centre educators' had been crucial both to translate the lessons from English into Swahili for the kids and to help them write their narrative. The result was interesting. The objects chosen by the youth were not trivial or obvious: one used an egg to talk about himself because the shell is hard but at the same time easy to break, and

Figure 15.3. Media literacy activities in Dagoretti Center.

because the inside is soft and colorful (these were the words used by the boy). Other items mentioned were plastic bags, keys, flashlights, shoes, drawings and so on.

Digital stories were shown to the group, but the products made by attendees were original; they did not copy the contents or structure of the viewed products. The soundtracks chosen instead showed a lack of competence and the boys simply used their favorite songs without assessing the relevance to the content of the digital storytelling products.

For the production, teens were taught how to use an easy free editing program and the result was definitely good. Through the use of pictures, the Italian media educator was able to communicate in a deep way with these guys. Any cultural or linguistic barriers had been overcome (see Figure 15.4).

A second focus group was organized aiming to decide how to use the digital stories created by teens. The initial fear seemed to have disappeared, and all the boys were unanimous in wanting to share their products with as many people as possible. They considered the experience rewarding and worth being shared.

It was then asked if they thought that their digital stories could be of interest to someone. The responses were mixed, two continued to think that nobody was interested, but it was still fun to be seen; six have argued that it could be attractive to operators of AMREF; and eight said that if we put the digital stories on the web, maybe someone else would be concerned, even if they were not able to define the audience.

Figure 15.4. Media literacy activities in Dagoretti Center.

A girl then made a statement about which many have agreed, saying that she often watched other videos which initially seemed uninteresting and then after all she liked them. With regards to issues related to the possibility of sharing, such as the language, only one guy proposed to insert subtitles.

The teens were amazed and ready for the last part of the project, whose aim was to realize some digital storytelling with the Kitui's communities participating in the experiences of community wells and gardens. Kitui is a county in the former Eastern Province of Kenya.

The community operators support the social change within communities and improve their life quality in the area. They work on a voluntary basis (or with little funding for living expenses) with individuals, families, and entire communities in order to strengthen their skills. Most of time they are very important because they create a connection between communities and local authorities to tackle inequality and facilitate the work of development. They actively involve the community, helping them to better understand the issues that affect their lives, they answer problems and needs through empowerment and active participation. An important factor is that the community operator is chosen by the community itself. Community operators have cultural awareness and are accepted by other members with recognized expertise. There are also specialized community operators—such as community health workers, focused on providing basic health and medical care—they are recognized, trained, and registered by the government and they are, therefore, paid for the work they do.

The activity of writing, collecting, and selecting six stories for the reportage represents an important praxis of media education as well as a form of participation in global citizenship.

Particularly in Kitui, digital storytelling activities offered several opportunities to:

- realize a participatory video in which a group or community creates its own digital story
- bring people together to explore issues, voice concerns, or simply to be creative and tell stories
- reflect about their experience in AMREF project
- share the opportunity to develop: environmental sustainability, dissemination of socioeconomic well-being, and health from increased access to drinking water
- show their personal thinking through their own language
- explain how such millennium goals are pursued, through their own stories.

At the end, Video Connection Projects encouraged people to take concrete action in order to support cultural diversity through cultural exchanges, to present their own point of view, to preserve the planet.

The project was presented in a meeting with the participation of all the Community operators.

They were asked to present their work through five objects representing their commitment. Everyone thought about it individually and then shared the result with the Dagoretti's team.

Also, in this case the result was very interesting because the operators chose not trivial objects. For example, they represented their job such as: a broom able to help people to wipe out the problems; an umbrella useful to protect us from the rain and sun; and as salt that gives flavor to food, but also preserves it. The videos were shot in the local language and translated and edited by the teens (see Figure 15.5).

At the end of the activity several focus groups were organized with social operators and one with social operators and the teens.

- The group idea about the possible use of their digital stories was explored.
- Adults recognized an important role in this video production as an educational instrument for other operators and also as tools to increase AMREF donors' awareness.
- There were conflicting ideas about the usefulness of diffusion of digital stories.

Figure 15.4. Media literacy activities in Dagoretti Center.

- Only half of group thought that the diffusion was a way to show an authentic side of Africa.
- The other half of the group considered digital storytelling as "'a grain of sand in the desert."

The six participants pointed out that the production of these products was mainly served to them as a reflection on their role in the community. Two women claimed that this product could be used as a tool for the acceptance of their role by some men of the village. The moment of comparison between social operators and the young was remarkable, as it represented a cross generational exchange.

All the guys were thrilled with the work done and were sure that the diffusion would be an important element to allow others (mainly non-Africans) to learn about the great work done by social workers. The boys said that before this activity, they also only superficially knew these activities. In this case, the adults had no objections. Maybe guys' enthusiasm has been contagious.

CONCLUSION

The limited duration of the project does not allow us to claim that the results can be said to be long-term. It can be assumed that in Africa, the involvement of local groups in the design would have a limited initial resistance. In Italy, however, the involvement of families might have optimized the development of the acquired skills. Nevertheless, in both contexts, the statements in the focus groups, the answers given during individual interviews, and the video production all demonstrated that children are able to make media values explicit, to reflect on and acquire other values and welcome others' point of view on the topic.

In addition with regards to video production, children have shown to be able to explore the media logic. Practical, hands-on use of video technology offered the most direct and effective way of exploring the media logic, and to understand the inherent social character of media production and the opportunity to express themselves freely.

They worked collaboratively to achieve their shared vision of the film and the video production. Boys and girls supported each other voluntarily in their different responsibilities, and the students quickly recognized the benefits of teamwork. An important element emerged from the final interviews, since all the involved teens recognized that their commitment to the development of a global citizen was important.

Back in Italy, a public presentation of the digital stories and cartoon was organized. Italian and Kenyan children kids showed great interest for each other's opinions about the activities carried out, highlighting the effectiveness of this activity. For this reason, a twinning project in which media education productions are exchanged between Italian and Kenyan schools is now under development by AMREF. Activities are based on a peer-to-peer approach. The boys and girls in Kenya directly call on young people, demanding not only a new awareness but also a common response and a cultural mobilization. Today, for the kids involved in the project, some of the Africans' problems have a face. Now, to Italian children, these are not problems of someone else who lives very far away, these problems are the real life that deserves to be shared for attention and respect, the ordinary approach for a global citizen. Though this was just a small project, video production proved to be an effective tool to develop new forms of emancipation and participation. Internet gives us the opportunity to share videos globally, the best of which could become viral. Also, through mass media, the new key words could be "action" and "participation."

NOTES

1. In every country, there are *local civil society actors* who defend local or sectoral interests, or specific values but some analysts, particularly Putnam (2000), even argue that this form of civic engagement is on the decline.
2. AMREF is an international African organization headquartered in Nairobi, Kenya. AMREF's vision is for lasting health change in Africa and consists of providing communities with the knowledge, skills and means to maintain

their good health and break the cycle of poor health and poverty. AMREF Italia has been supporting Kenyan communities through several activities, among them participatory video projects and general media education offers. URL: www.amref.org.

3. MED was founded in 1996 in Rome by a group of university professors, school teachers, and media professionals. Its mission is to create a network among all the people who are interested in the relationship between media and children/adult education. URL: www.mediaeducationmed.it.
4. AMREF's Dagoretti Child in Need Project is a model for community-based child-care and support for street children, as well as for children from slums and other disadvantaged backgrounds. The project involves a process known as the 4-Rs: Rescue, Rehabilitation, Resocialization, and Reintegration. See more at: http://amref.org/about-us/dagoretti-child-in-need-project/#sthash.wapMXtEp.dpuf.
5. 5. There are many different definitions of "Digital Storytelling," but in general, they all revolve around the idea of combining the art of telling stories with a variety of digital multimedia, such as images, audio, and video. Just about all digital stories bring together some mixture of digital graphics, text, recorded audio narration, video, and music to present information on a specific topic (Robin 2006).
6. Expo Milano 2015 is a non-commercial Universal Exposition with some very unique and innovative features. Not only is it an exhibition but also a process, one of active participation among a large number of players around the theme of Feeding the Planet, Energy for Life. It is sustainable, technological, thematic, and focused on its visitors. Open from May 1 to October 31, 2015, the Expo will host over 130 participants. Running for 184 days, this giant exhibition site, covering one million square meters, is expected to welcome over 20 million visitors http://www.expo2015.org/ .

REFERENCES

Adams, D., & Hamm, M. (2001). *Literacy in a multimedia age*. Norwood, MA: Christopher-Gordon.

Aufderheide, P.(1993). *Media literacy: A report of the National Leadership Conferenceo n Media Literacy*. Aspen, CO: Aspen Institute.

Bennett, W. L. (2004). Global media and politics: Transnational communication regimes and civic cultures. *Annual Review of Political Science, 7*(1), 125–48. doi:10.1146/annurev.polisci.7.012003.104804

Benkler, Y. (2006). *The wealth of networks: How social production transforms markets and freedom*. New Haven, CT: Yale University Press.

Bruner, J. (1986). *Actual minds, possible worlds*. Cambridge, MA: Harvard University Press.

Bruner, J. (1990). *Acts of meaning*. Cambridge, MA: Harvard University Press.

Buckingham, D. (2003). *Media education: Literacy, learning, and contemporary culture*. Cambridge, MA: Polity in association with Blackwell.

Burgess, J. E., Foth, M., Klaebe, H. G. (2006, September). *Everyday creativity as civic engagement: A cultural citizenship view of new media*. Paper presented at Communications Policy & Research Forum, Sydney, AU. Retrieved from http://eprints.qut.edu.au/5056/

Castells, M. (2008). The new public sphere: Global civil society, communication networks, and global governance. *The ANNALS of the American Academy of Political and Social, 616*(1), 78–93. doi:10.1177/0002716207311877

Dahlgren, P. (2005). The Internet, public spheres, and political communication: Dispersion and deliberation. *Political Communication, 22*(2), 147–62. doi:10.1080/10584600590933160

Deuze, M. (2006). Participation, remediation, bricolage: Considering principal components of a digital culture. *The Information Society: An International Journal, 22*(2), 63–75. doi:10.1080/01972240600567170

European Commission. (2007). *A European approach to media literacy in the digital environment*. Retrieved from http://www.cedefop.europa.eu/EN/news/7621.aspx

Ferguson, R. (2001). Media education and the development of critical solidarity. *Media Education Journal, 30*, 37–43.

Giddens, A. (2003). *Runaway world: How globalisation is reshaping our lives*. New York, NY: Routledge.

Heater, D. (2002). *World citizenship: cosmopolitan thinking and its opponents.* London, UK: Continuum.

Held, D. (2002). The transformation of political community: rethinking democracy in the context of globalization. In N. Dower, J. Williams, & O. O'Neill (Eds.), *Global citizenship: A critical reader* (pp. 92–100). Edinburgh, SCT: Edinburgh University press.

Keane, J. (2003). *Global civil society?* Cambridge, UK: Cambridge University Press.

Kellner D., & Share J. (2005). Toward critical media literacy: Core concepts, debates, organizations, and policy discourse. *Studies in the Cultural Politics of education 26*(3), 369–386. doi:10.1080/01596300500200169

Kennedy, K. J. (2007). Student constructions of "active citizenship": What does participation mean to students? *British Journal of Educational Studies, 55*(3), 304–324. doi:10.1111/j.1467-8527.2007.00381.x

Kivisto, P., & Faist, T. (2007). *Citizenship: discourse, theory, and transnational prospects.* Malden: Blackwell.

Koltay T. (2011), The media and the literacies: Media literacy, information literacy, digital literacy. *Media Culture Society, 33*(2), 211–221. doi:10.1177/0163443710393382

Kymlicka, W. (2007). *Multicultural odysseys: navigating the new international politics of diversity.* Oxford, UK: Oxford University Press.

Luke, C. (2000). Cyber-schooling and technological change: Multiliteracies for new times. In B. Cope & M. Kalantzis (Eds.), *Multiliteracies: Literacy, learning & the design of social futures* (pp. 69–105). Melbourne, Australia: Macmillan.

Masterman, L., & Mariet, F. (1994). *Media education in 1990s Europe: A teachers guide.* Strasbourg, FR: Council of Europe.

McLuhan, M. (1997). *Understanding media: The extensions of man.* Cambridge, MA: MIT Press.

Morley, D., & Robins, K. (1995). *Spaces of identity: Global media, electronic landscapes and cultural boundaries.* London, UK: Routledge.

Myers, J. P. (2010). "To benefit the world by whatever means possible": Adolescents' constructions of global citizenship. *British Educational Research Journal, 36*(3), 483–502. doi:10.1080/01411920902989219

Pfeiffer, J. W., & Jones, J. E. (1985), *A handbook of structured experience for human relation training* (pp. 1–10). San Diego, CA: University Associates.

Pfeiffer, J. W., (1998). *Pfeiffer and company library* (Vol. 21). San Francisco, CA: Pfeiffer Jossey-Bass.

Potter, W. J. (2010), The state of media literacy, *Journal of Broadcasting & Electronic Media, 54*(4), 675–696. doi:10.1080/08838151.2011.521462

Putnam, R. D. (2000). *Bowling alone: The collapse and revival of American community.* New York, NY: Simon & Schuster

Ranieri, M. (2010), Digital competence assesment in secondary education. In X. Xu, G. Cappello, & C. Socol (2010), *Media education sans frontiers: Common challenges, shared solutions for China and Italy* (pp.100–111). Trento, IT: Centro Studi Erickson.

Rheingold, H. (2002). *Smart mobs: The next social revolution.* Cambridge, MA: Perseus.

Rice, R. E. (2002). Primary issues in internet use: Access, civic and community involvement, and social interaction and expression. In L. Lievrouw, & S. Livingstone (Eds.), *Handbook of new media: Social shaping and consequences of ICTs* (pp. 105–129). London, UK: Sage.

Robin, B. (2006). The educational uses of digital storytelling. In C. Crawford et al. (Eds.), *Proceedings of Society for Information Technology & Teacher Education International Conference 2006* (pp. 709–716). Chesapeake, VA: Association for the Advancement of Computing in Education (AACE). Retrieved from http://www.editlib.org/p/22129.

Robin, B. R. (2008) Digital storytelling: A powerful technology tool for the 21st century classroom. *Theory Into Practice, 47*(3), 220–228. doi:10.1080/00405840802153916

Rosa, A., & Torre, E. (2014). *Media e Scuola tra Forma Mentis e Modus Operandi: Analisi Teorica e Dati di Ricerca* [Media and school between "Forma Mentis" and "Modus Operandi": Theoretical analysis and research data]. Roma Aracne.

Sartori, L.(2006). *Il divario digitale* [The digital divide]. Bologna, Italy: Mulino.

Shachaf, P. (2008). Cultural diversity and information and communication technology impacts on global virtual teams: An exploratory study. *Information & Management, 45*(2), 131–142.

Silverblatt, A., Ferry, J., & Finan, B. (2009). *Approaches to media literacy: A handbook.* Armonk, NY: Sharpe.

Spiro, P. J. (2007). *Beyond citizenship: American identity after globalization.* New York, NY: Oxford University Press.

Thoman, E., & Jolls, T. (2004). Media literacy: A national priority for a changing world. *American Behavioral Scientist, 48*(1), 18–29. doi:10.1177/0002764204267246

Tomlinson, J. (1991). *Cultural imperialism.* Baltimore, MD: John Hopkins University Press.

Tremayne, M. (2007). *Blogging, citizenship, and the future of media.* New York, NY: Routledge.

Tremblay, G. (2002). Global media and cultural diversity. In R. S. Robin Mansell, R. Samarajiva, & A. Mahan (Eds.), *Networking knowledge for information societies: Institutions and intervention* (pp. 292–297). Netherlands: Delft University Press.

Trinchero, R. (2011). Developing and assessing media competence. In A. Parola, M. Ranieri (Eds.), *Media education in action: A research study in six European countries* (pp. 37–54). Firenze: Firenze University Press.

Zhao, Y. (2010). Preparing globally competent teachers: A new imperative for teacher. *Education, Journal of Teacher Education, 61*(5), 422–431. doi:10.1177/0022487110375802

CHAPTER 16

WHAT TEACHERS BELIEVE ABOUT DEMOCRACY AND WHY IT IS IMPORTANT—HOW (SHOULD) WE PREPARE STUDENTS FOR DEMOCRACY AND CITIZENSHIP

Lessons From Australia

David Zyngier

ABSTRACT

Democracy means many things to many people. There is much discussion that democracy is in now in decline or even in crisis citing apparent youth apathy and disengagement. The research which this chapter reports on seeks a more robust, critical, or thicker interpretation of what democracy is; what it should be; and, significantly, how it can be beneficial to all peoples. The traditional approach in civics and citizenship education focuses on understanding

E-Learning and Social Media:
Education and Citizenship for the Digital 21st Century, pp. 343–368

political structures, often isolated to a single unit of study on and teaches *about* democracy not necessarily *for* democracy. This chapter argues that a broader, more participatory, critical, and relevant educational experience that includes a critical use of social media and critical digital literacy is fundamental to facilitating a process of meaningful societal transformation through *thick* democracy. Three questions related to democracy are framed within the context of empirical and qualitative data gathered from a study of over 600 teachers. This chapter uses a critical framework to elucidate the potential for transformation of our individual and collective sense of democracy and builds on previous studies in the U.S. and Canada together with research being conducted in over 25 countries with educators internationally through the Global Doing Democracy Research Project.

INTRODUCTION

> Negative stereotyping of younger generations as apathetic, apolitical and disengaged is mad, bad and dangerous for the health of Australian democracy. (Evans, Halupka, & Stoker, 2014)

Democracy means many things to many people. There is much discussion that democracy is in now in decline (Diamond, 2015) or even in crisis (Ercan & Gagnon, 2014). The research which this chapter reports on seeks a more robust, critical, or thicker interpretation of what democracy is; what it should be; and, significantly, how it can be beneficial to all people (Carr, 2010). The traditional approach in civics and citizenship education (CCE) in schools focuses on understanding formal political structures and is often problematically isolated to a single unit of study on government in both primary (elementary) and secondary (high) school education (Brophy & Alleman, 2009) and it teaches *about* democracy not necessarily *for* democracy.

The notion of normative democracy is simultaneously highly contested and often benignly accepted. Beyond the hegemonic zeal that proclaims that elections equate to democracy, replete with political parties, fundraising, polling, media manipulation, and other components that frame a *thin* conceptualization of democracy, this chapter argues that a broader, more participatory, critical, and relevant educational experience that includes a critical use of social media and critical digital literacy is fundamental to facilitating a process of meaningful societal transformation through *thick* democracy. Three questions related to democracy are framed within the context of empirical and qualitative data gathered from a study of over 600 teachers across a diverse range of schools in Victoria (Zyngier, 2013b). While considering specific concerns, issues, and themes raised by participants in the study, this chapter uses a critical framework to illustrate and elucidate the potential for transformation of our individual and collective sense of democracy. I ask "How do educators understand democracy? How do they connect democracy and education? What are their concerns and proposals for enhancing democracy in and through education?"

This research builds on previous studies in the U.S. and Canada (Zyngier, 2013a) together with research being conducted in over 25 countries with teachers as well as education students conducted internationally through the Global Doing Democracy Research Project.[1]

Attempting to determine the salience of a linkage between education and democracy **beyond** the civics classroom is important as it may have implications for the conceptualization and delivery of teaching and learning in relation to democracy (Westheimer & Kahne, 2004) both in the classroom and in the education academy. Indeed as the mantra of "every teacher is a teacher of literacy and numeracy" spread through education systems worldwide, followed by "every teacher is a teacher of ICTs," it is also critical that *every teacher become a teacher* ***of and for*** *democracy*. The need to critically interrogate and understand the perspectives, experiences, and perceptions of teachers in relation to democracy in education informs the context of this research (Carr, 2007, 2008).

The Perspectives, Experiences and Perceptions of the Young In Relation To Democracy In Education

> Young people are the sail and not the anchor of [Australian] democracy and not as is so often thought disenchanted but are more active than any other generation in terms of social media use, in terms of collective action through the internet—they are information activists—they share information and debate public policy in a degree of detail that leaves the Australian parliament to shame. (Alberici, 2014)

There have been detailed studies of students' attitudes to democratic values and participation in society that conclude that while Australian students have a well-developed set of democratic values, they adopt a passive rather than an active style of engaging in conventional citizenship activities. They will participate formally through voting and they will pursue issues where they see some community benefit, but they do not see themselves exercising an effective presence in the formal political system (Mellor & Kennedy, 2003).

New research commissioned by the Museum of Australian Democracy (2014) shows that young people are increasingly politically active online, rather than channelling their energies into traditional party politics. However, it all depends on how you define political engagement. If measuring traditional actions like joining political parties or street protests or writing a letter to a parliamentarian, young people are more disengaged than ever. This is discussed in detail below in the next section.

But if online activities such as joining advocacy groups or engaging with campaigns or issues by sharing or commenting on Facebook, YouTube or Twitter are included, then youth political engagement soars. These traditional forms have really fallen to the wayside but in their place these new forms, which the youth seems to be a lot more comfortable with, have really picked up in their place (Evans et al., 2014).

School education can and does contribute to the production of citizens' identities as the IEA-CIVED[2] studies indicate, but such contribution cannot be controlled or measured in the same way systems assess how much a student has learned about mathematics or literacy in any given year. Citizenship education is: "Always an educationally unfinished project, an unsolvable tension, that cannot be learned and understood through conscious rationality alone and thus not solved through the delivery of explicit instruction on what democracy is and how a good citizen should act" (Fischman & Haas, 2012, p. 174).

Hahn's (1998) study shows schools are implicated in promoting civic education through certain types of political experiences. Schools and classrooms can play a part in the education of democratic citizens through the way they are organized. However, the opposite is also true—if schools and classrooms are not democratically organized they are also helping to shape a more authoritarian one. This highlights the discrepancy between what the CIVED data show and what is possible in schools that establish effective practices including debating controversial issues, lobbying politicians, raising money for charities, interviewing community figures, and volunteering in community organizations and international agencies.

What students experience in schools—what topics they discuss and how they are discussed—and their attitudes and beliefs concerning a particular range of political issues are of fundamental importance in their civic development. What takes place in schools, not just in the classroom but also in the school lunchroom or cafeteria, the corridors, playground, gymnasium, assembly areas, and elsewhere within the school, apart of course from the classroom, will have a determining effect on students (Hyslop-Margison & Thayer, 2009). Is there bullying, racism, sexism, homophobia, marginalization, a detrimental hidden curriculum, meaningful parental involvement, engaging school trips, guest visitors, or something else? What happens, and what does not happen or is omitted, is important. How issues are presented and discussed, and how they are open or closed to diverse epistemological vantage points is also critical. In sum, students learn explicitly, but also in a very significant implicit way to develop their own sense of democracy and it is here where our teacher research could have a lasting effect on broadening or restricting the reach of democratic knowledge, engagement, and action in our students now and in the future.

The focus on education provides a more distinct linkage into how democracy is constructed within schools and the broader education field. The formative years of public education can represent the platform for future development of what has been termed the active citizen which stems, in large part, from social experience and learning within the first two decades of a person's life.

HAS GEN Y REALLY GONE OFF DEMOCRACY?

> The health of a democracy depends on the largest number of people engaging in it, taking an interest and participating in it and if we have significant groups of people that don't so that then potentially if we have a crisis in democracy, if there are some economic problems or there is some threat to democracy then this can become a real problem. They can look to charismatic leaders, to protest parties and they can turn away from the major established political parties which are the ones that provide the long term stability in our political system. (O'Neill, 2014)

A 2014 national survey in Australia found that young Australians are ambivalent toward the democratic system of government and that they have lost faith in Australia's democracy. Over the last three years, polling has uncovered a surprising ambivalence amongst Australians about the value of democracy, despite Australia being one of the oldest continuous democracies in the world. In 2014, only 60% of Australians believe that "democracy is preferable to any other kind of government." This confirms previous findings, with only 42% of 18–29 year-olds in 2014 view democracy as preferable to any other kind of government, compared with 65% of those 30 years and over.

When asked the question "if you had to choose between a good democracy or a strong economy for Australia, which one would you personally choose?", only a small majority (53%) choose a "good democracy," with 42% opting for "a strong economy."

To those Australians who have indicated in the Lowy polling that they do not believe democracy is preferable to any other kind of government, they posed five propositions in the 2014 poll and asked whether each was a "major" or "minor" reason for their views. In responding, 45% say "democracy only serves the interests of a few and not the majority of society" is a major reason for not preferring democracy. For 42%, the proposition that "democracy is not working because there is no real difference between the policies of the major parties" is cited as a major reason for not preferring democracy. The third strongest response is that "I have become disillusioned with Australian politics and think another system might work better" (36%).

Twenty percent cite as a major reason for not preferring democracy that "a more authoritarian system where leaders can make decisions without the processes of democracy achieves better results." Similarly, it does not appear that Australians' equivocal support for democracy can be ascribed to mere apathy. Only 21% say that "democracy is the usual form of government now and always will be, so I don't worry about it."

The problem is not mere apathy, but genuine misgivings about Australian democracy with 33% believing "in some circumstances, a non-democratic government can be preferable" because "democracy only serves the interests of a few and not the majority" and a further 19% saying it does not matter what kind of government we have. Of concern was the fact that 21% believe "a more authoritarian system where leaders can make decisions without the processes of democracy achieves better results." Only 42% believe that "democracy is preferable to any other kind of government" (Oliver, 2014). These misgivings are replicated in the teachers in this research.

These findings are replicated by the recent Scanlon Report (Markus, 2014) Mapping Social Cohesion (Markus, 2014) which has, for a number of years, sought to enhance the evidence base available for interpreting Australian opinion on government. Their findings confirm "research … revealing a sharp drop in satisfaction with the political system." Since 2007 the Scanlon Foundation surveys have included a question on trust in government. Respondents are asked: "How often do you think the government … can be trusted to do the right thing for the Australian people?" and are presented with four response options: "almost always", "most of the time," "only some of the time," and "almost never." The highest proportion indicating the first or second response, "almost always" or "most of the time," rose from 39% to 48% in 2009; this was followed by a sharp fall to 31% in 2010, in the context of a loss of confidence in the then government. A low point of 26% was reached in 2012, representing a decline of 21 percentage points since 2009, followed by stabilization in 2013. There was an expectation that in 2014 there would be significant upward movement, in the first year of the newly elected Abbott government, on the pattern of the increase in confidence in the early period of the Rudd government. This expectation has not, however, been realized. While the level of trust has increased, it is by less than three percentage points. Analysis by age group finds a relatively high level of trust amongst those aged 18–24 and 65 and over, with the lowest level amongst those aged 35–54. Later polls in 2014 and 2015 indicate a further dramatic decline for these figures.

Clearly there is a malaise that is not to be explained purely in terms of political alignment, identification, or lack of identification with the party in government. A further concern is indication of a decline in participation in political life: in 2009, 87% indicated that they had voted in an election over the last three years; in 2014, a lower 82%; in 2009, 56% indicated that they had signed a petition over the last three years; and in 2014, 48%. Contact with a member of parliament was down from 27% to 23%.

When asked to consider systems of government other than democratic, a substantial minority indicated approval. Thus 49% agreed with a system in which "experts, not government, make decisions according to what they think is best for the country," and almost one in four respondents (26%) agreed that it was good to have a system of government in which a "strong leader … does not have to bother with parliament and elections." This finding is consistent with the understanding that a substantial proportion of the population lacks firm or reasoned views on political systems and may not be aware that they are indicating agreement to contradictory propositions.

The 2013 national survey (Markus, 2014) found that federal parliament and political parties were the lowest ranked among people to trust. In 2014 Federal parliament again was ranked last, with just 5.3% indicating "a great deal of confidence." The survey also asked respondents if the present system of Australian government works well or is in need of change. Just 15% indicated that it "works fine as it is"; 48% considered that it needed minor change; 23% major change; and 11% that it should be replaced—close to the 9% who disagreed with the view that democracy, despite its faults, "is still the best form of government."

Further an ANU-SRC poll released in August 2014 focused on views of government. A key finding was that

> satisfaction with democracy remains at a low level of 72% in comparison to the 2007 when it was 86%, although it was relatively high by international standards, at the same level as Canada and Germany. Only 56% believed that their vote mattered down from 68% in 2007.

Only 43% believed that it made a difference whichever party was in power, the lowest level recorded, and only 56% considered that their vote made a difference, compared to 70% in 1996. Contrary to the view that young people lacked confidence in institutions, the ANU Poll reported that "overall, younger people have the same level of confidence in institutions compared to the rest of the population."

If these figures are alarming, it is also relevant to point out that at the last federal election (2013) almost 20% *opted-out* from voting—they did not enrol, did not show up, or voted informally—that is 20% of the eligible voters.[3] As disenchantment rises, this percentage tends to increase especially among the young, poor, less educated, and those living in outer metropolitan and rural areas. However, there is a significant difference between *disenchantment* and *disengagement* or apathy. Disenchantment means that people take a conscious decision believing that somehow the system is failing them—that democracy is only serving the interests of the few not the majority, where *ordinary people* have been shut out of the conversation by politicians and the media. Something from 80–90% of Australians believe they have little or no influence over national decision making.[2]

Such negative stereotyping of younger generations as apathetic, apolitical, and disengaged is "mad and dangerous for the health of Australian democracy" (Evans et al., 2014, p. 9). "Our research shows that young Australians passionately believe in democratic values, possess strong political views and are actively engaged in democracy. They simply do not like the current politics on offer." But the research shows that 19% of Gen Y Australians are dissatisfied with the way democracy works in Australia, making them the most dissatisfied generation in comparison to Generation X (15%) and Baby Boomers (%). In the research, 30% of those surveyed had negative views on compulsory voting. Younger generations were more likely to have negative views with 39% of Generation Y and 36% of Generation X against compulsory voting. This compared with Baby Boomers (27%) and the older Builders (16%). Negative views on compulsory voting include that the government should not be able to force people to vote, or that it forces voters to make uninformed decisions just to avoid fines (Museum of Australian Democracy, 2014).

Democratic Deficit or Democratic Disengagement: Teaching About But Not For Democracy

> Democracy cannot go forward unless the intelligence of the mass of people is educated to understand the social realities of their own time. (Dewey, 1936)

The debate over democracy in education (Lund & Carr, 2008) has been characterized in terms of *representative* versus *participatory* democracy,[4] with the former highlighting electoral processes—*thin* democracy—and the latter focusing on critical engagement and social justice, or *thick* democracy. *Thin* democratic teaching focuses on activities such as students contributing food to a food drive or in a more active participatory manner organizing a food drive for the poor while *thick* democratic teaching would explore why people are hungry, and then empower students to act to make decisions about and to solve its root causes (Westheimer & Kahne, 2004).

The research of the author and his associates over the past several years has raised the pivotal concern of the role of education in forming, buttressing, cultivating, and sustaining a meaningful, critical, democratic experience for all sectors of society (Banks, 2004; Lund & Carr, 2008; Westheimer & Kahne, 2004b). The shift and acceptance toward market-based policies in education has had a wide range of effects and consequences on society which are well documented and accepted (Porfilio & Carr, 2010).

According to Crick (2000), democracy is a *promiscuous* word, archetypically difficult to pin down with as many meanings as there are uses for the term because of its conceptual complexity this article clearly preserves the contested nature of the term. The notion of *thick* and *thin* democracy (Gandin & Apple, 2002), builds on the seminal work of Barber (1984, 2004) who raised pivotal questions on the saliency of liberal democracy, including the tension between individualism and the rights of all citizens framed by concepts of shallow and deep democracy (Furman & Shields, 2005) suggesting that participatory citizenship demands every member of the community to participate in self-governance which leads to a strong(er) democracy.

What Furman and Shields (2005) call "deep democracy" attaches "significant value to such goods as participation, civic friendship, inclusiveness and solidarity" (p. 128). Deep democracy espouses a number of principles that champion individual rights and responsibilities within diverse cultural communities in the interests of the common good.

Discussions on democracy often result in platitudinous affirmations that it is naturally desirable, and, as a corollary, anything that is not democratic is considered virtually irrelevant. Kahne and Westheimer (2003) found that schools and teachers largely teach a *thin democracy* which "emphasiz[es] individual character and behaviour [but] obscures the need for collective and often public-sector initiatives" (p. 36). In their research, they conclude that each vision of citizenship reflects a relatively distinct set of theoretical and curricular goals. Significantly, they claim that these visions as delivered in programs are not cumulative. The core assumptions behind each of the different perspectives reflect a particular approach to problems and solutions in society: the *personally responsible citizen* solves social problems and improves society, by having a good character; they must be honest, responsible, and law-abiding members of the community. The *participatory citizen* solves social problems and improves society through active participation and leadership within established systems and community structures. Finally, the *justice oriented citizen* solves social problems and improves society by questioning, challenging, and changing established systems and structures when they reproduce patterns of injustice over time.

Through the notion of *thin* versus *thick* democracy, we can conceptualize the visible tension between the superficial features often associated with teaching *about* democracy and the fundamental scaffolding which permits people to appropriate the deeper meaning of teaching for democracy. Bolstering efforts to teach through the academic disciplines—whether pursued through high-stakes exams or well-crafted curriculum frameworks—is insufficient to further the goals of teaching *for* democracy (Davies & Issitt, 2005).

Carr (2010) has further developed the notion of (thick) democracy, infusing it with social justice and political literacy and the notion of how knowledge is constructed into a spectrum of possibilities, potential, experiences and realities in relation to how we can consider and conceptualize democracy in education. (See Table 16.1).

Table 16.1. Thick-Thin Democratic Continuum

THIN<--	-->THICK
Voting and elections are the key to democracy	Voting and elections are but one component to democracy, and must be problematized
Studying mainstream political parties, processes and structures forms the core of teaching about democracy	Studying about democracy necessarily involves preparing (and engaging) for democracy, including dialectical critique, and a focus on power
Democratic education is generally concentrated within a single class or subject (i.e., Government, and/or Social Studies)	Democratic education is infused across the curriculum, and involves all aspects of how education is organized (i.e., assemblies, extra-curricular, staff meetings, parental involvement, community linkages)
Weak connection between democracy and education	Explicit, engaged connection; democracy must involve a politically literate populace
Support for democracy involves an uncritical assessment of foreign policy, militarization, conflicts, neo-liberalism and patriotism	Foreign interventions, war, conflicts, racism, injustice and human rights abuses are critically interrogated, linking local issues/concerns with the international/global context
Politics generally pertains to elections, the predominant political parties, and the agenda set by the mainstream media	Politics pertains to all aspects of education, including decision making, oppression, marginalization and power (what is omitted is as equally important)
Concern that teaching for and about democracy may be contentious, and could even be considered indoctrination	To not teach about and for democracy in a critical fashion is to privilege dominant hegemony; avoiding contentious matter and concepts can lead to great harm (racism, war, injustice, poverty, etc.)
Weak linkage between school experience and the broader societal experience	Education is linked to society, and should seek to understand, and, in some cases, to transform it
Limited formal curriculum on the vastness, richness, and complexity of democracy, with limited opportunities to experience democracy outside of the voting process	Formal and informal opportunities to cultivate, stimulate and inculcate democracy and democratic practices; what is most important here is that knowledge is constructed, not merely conveyed or transmitted (as in the "banking model")

(Table continues on next page)

Table 16.1. (Continued)

THIN<--------------------	-------------------->THICK
Narrow engagement with alternative visions, movements, concepts and phenomena outside of formal curriculum and mainstream hegemony	Seeking to understand political and social movements not mentioned in mainstream media and the formal curriculum is important; linking what we know with what we do is encouraged
Diversity is generally understood in an essentialized way, with limited linkages to White power and privilege, and inequitable power relations	Democracy cannot be understood without a critical linkage to social justice, which problematizes identity, diversity and social change, including intersecting forms of power and privilege
Curriculum is generally prescriptive, with limited emphasis on critical analysis and engagement, and assessment often suffocates dynamic and complex interplay between groups and power-structures; formal democratic education avoids political nature of education	Assessment is not the focus of thick democratic education; seeking critical engagement with authentic encounters, understanding that knowledge is constructed, and accepting that teachers do not have all of the answers are key; Freire's generative themes and Dewey's progressive education underscore notion that education is a political project
Discussion about and for democracy is limited, contrived and aims for comfort and reassurance rather than questioning complicity, change, and power	Deliberative democracy must be made more authentic with engagement with a broad range of groups/interests/concerns; students should be encouraged to question and challenge problems
Literacy is constructed in a limited way, often focused on skills and knowledge considered relevant for employment	Political and media literacy are fundamental pillars, seeking what Giroux calls "emancipatory literacy" and democratic conscientization

Source: Carr (2010, p. 19)

Using the thick-thin[5] democratic education model (Carr, 2010, p. 19) as a framework to understand the potential for critical, transformative democratic work in and through education, this research underscores the myriad difficulties, barriers, problems, issues, and complexities to doing thick democracy within institutional and school environments in education. It would appear that a large percentage of participants in my study, as is the case in the previous studies, had a less than enviable democratic experience in their own education, which includes after the formative years to comprise, as well, teacher education experience. There has been a great deal of research focused on the shortcomings of teacher education programs, highlighting the obsession with standards, expectations, and outcomes while overlooking social justice, power relations, and political literacy (Kincheloe, 2008).

A CONSERVATIVE AGENDA PROMOTED BY RHETORIC OF ACTIVE PARTICIPATION

The 1990s saw the implementation and uptake of what have been termed neo-liberal policies in the guise of privatization of state concerns; the selling of public resources; and deregulation of private companies and their business practices. This resulted in the accelerated privatization of education in many countries.

Democratic and social advances are now seemingly under attack with the rising influence of neo-liberalism in education policy as documented by Pasi Sahlberg through what he calls the *GERM,* the Global Education Reform Movement. When states began to slow and then reverse their commitment human rights, civil rights, diversity, and equality, they began also to reverse support for public education and moved more toward supporting market-driven imperatives in society and education. The well-documented struggle over the development of suitable content for history and civic education curricula—what some countries have called "the history wars"—for example is part of this influence.

The International Association for the Evaluation of Educational Achievement (IEA) (Torney-Purta, Schwille, & Amadeo, 1999) examined the civic knowledge, engagement, and attitudes of 14-year-old students in 28 democratic countries. Its results support the notion that democracy is understood by both teachers and students in a thin way, focused on the notion that young people should (and do) believe that good citizenship includes the obligation to vote and to obey the law. However, four out of five students do not intend to participate in conventional political activities, such as joining a political party, writing letters to newspapers, or being a candidate for a local office. Nevertheless, students are willing to become engaged in other forms of civic life, such as collecting money for a social cause or charity, and they believe it is important for adult citizens to participate in community and environmental groups.

The IEA study also found that schools that model democratic practices in classrooms, by creating an open climate for discussing issues, are most effective in promoting civic knowledge and engagement among students developing the potential for democracy to be understood in a *thick* way that includes participation and transformation of society.

However, across many countries, many students do not experience this positive type of classroom environment. In practice, thin democracy is exemplified in activities such as students contributing food to a food drive or in a more active participatory manner by organizing a food drive for the poor. Thick democracy in the classroom would, however, explore why people are hungry, and significantly act to solve the root causes (Westheimer & Kahne, 2004) so that students know that civic engagement is not an individual, private endeavour. Kahne and Westheimer (2003) conclude that bolstering efforts to teach the academic disciplines—whether pursued through high-stakes exams or well-crafted curriculum frameworks—is insufficient to further the goals of teaching democracy. Carr (2010) has further argued that the institutionalization of mainstream or thin democracy has made it difficult to problematize inequitable power relations but the (critical pedagogical) effort consecrated to validate diverse epistemological and lived experiences can lead to a greater sense of inclusion, participation and engagement, which is at the base of a thicker democratic experience.

In Australia, public discussion about citizenship, democracy, and education is over 20 years old, beginning with a Senate inquiry in 1988. This resulted in recommendations for improvement in school curricula, pedagogy, and teacher preparation. While the federal government had no direct responsibility for these issues (as they are constitutionally devolved to the States), it formed a civic experts group that prepared a strategic plan for a national program resulting in the development and implementation of the *Discovering Democracy*[6] curriculum program (DD).

The CCE project in Australia, like others elsewhere, places a "growing emphasis on the promotion of civic awareness and individuals' rights and responsibilities embedded in discourses of citizenship" (Garratt & Piper, 2008, p. 486), highlighting the conflicting discourses in approaches to citizenship education (Criddle, Vidovich, & O'Neill, 2004) which "permeate both policy production and policy practices across all levels" (p. 32) of the DD project. On the one hand, there is an emphasis on passive consumption of knowledge about citizenship with a strong historical focus—*thin democracy*—and, on the other, critical and active participation in change, which is labelled as an "active citizenship"—*thick democracy*. This confusion is even found at a ministerial level. Criddle and colleagues (2004, p. 32) suggest that at the school level the "narrow historical knowledge version" was often contested by individual teachers. Further, despite the narrow or thin objectives for CCE at the Commonwealth government level, these were resisted by so-called "trainers" who were "determined to impress their own agenda ... to encourage critique of government in a more comprehensive 'active citizenship' model" (p. 32) of CCE. According to the teachers surveyed, they perceived that the knowledge *and* activity components were equally important. While CCE in Australia has been largely a *top-down* process, at the macro-level it is "doubtful that policy initiators ... achieved what they expected" as a result of teachers "actively interpreting the policy to suit their own needs" (Criddle et al., 2004, p. 33). As a result, a counter-resistance occurred at a micro (classroom) level where teachers "pick and choose" and "completely rejected any notion of a prescribed curriculum" (Criddle et al., 2004, p. 35). Despite this resistance, the teachers interviewed in this research were still pessimistic that their attempts to imbue a more active component into CCE were efficacious.

The so-called crisis of civic engagement was used by politicians from 1988 onwards to gain support for the nation state under a perceived threat from globalization; where "greater diversity is met by calls for cohesiveness; disengagement is responded to with a call for understanding of how things currently work" (Davies & Issitt, 2005, p. 394). A broadly neo-conservative or neo-liberal agenda was promoted through most of the materials produced by the *Discovering Democracy* project. Significantly, it is claimed that the new CCE was used to ensure that "radical intentions are not carried forward" (Kennedy, 1998, p. 394). The rhetoric of active participation found in these programs and in various ministerial statement about CCE are usually "not achieved in the activities that are provided for school students"[10] (Davies & Issitt, 2005, p. 404).

Dejaeghere and Tudball (2007) conclude that most recent assessments of the CCE suggest "further work is required to promote depth and breadth" (p. 41) and propose an alternative to the thin democracy espoused in the neo-liberal CCE. They argue for a compromise(d) pragmatic "Critical Citizenship" as an "expanded conceptualization of citizenship education [that] is being enacted in many schools" that would include investigation of and participation in activities that "support sustainable practices, social justice and underpin the future well-being of societies from a local to a global level" (Dejaeghere & Tudball, 2007, p. 44). What in their view, would a maximalist *critical citizenship* look like? They eschew the *minimalist* content led focus on civic knowledge confined to promoting the "good" citizen—which Print (2000) described as "either a direct or implied goal of civic education, [and] was generally seen as one who contributes to society" (p. 16), to focus on *critical* citizenship. Dejaeghere and Tudball draw from Kahne and Westheimer's three forms of citizenship (2003) to prepare and motivate students to address social problems, but still they do not see the necessity for students to act. While stating it is necessary for "students and teachers [to be] involved as proactive agents of change" (Dejaeghere & Tudball, 2007, p. 49), this is confined to participation in "Decision making processes, [to] critically analyze knowledge and what happens when that knowledge is put into practice ... including an examination ... of the structures of social injustice. The goal of critical citizenship is to provide the conditions for collective social change." (p. 49)

Asserting the importance of student participation in school democratic processes, they suggest these include items like peer support and community service—including "greater participation in school governance ... developing students' understanding of critical concepts" (p. 50); this leaves the students to learn about agency without being agentic. Once again we are left with students *play acting* and pretending to develop solutions but not enacting them as Freire's praxis suggests is necessary (Freire, 1973).

Schwille and Amadeo (2002), in their analysis of the IEA-CIVED Civic Education Study (Torney-Purta, Schwille, & Amadeo, 1999), argue that "as long as parts of the political system aspire to foster active, informed and supportive citizens, schools will be considered a possible means to this end" (p. 105). However, they add, as a rider "their success in this respect has been mixed" (Schwille & Amadeo, 2002, p. 105).

The Australian analysts of the IEA-CIVED Study (Print, Kennedy, & Hughes, 1999) have become preeminent in discussions of the CCE project, publishing multiple papers about both the IEA-CIVED study and the subsequent DD project and related CCE in Australia. Significantly in their IEA-CIVED initial study, the authors already understand that this is about education for a *thin* democracy "where the teacher provides information and discusses with students in a structured classroom environment" (Print et al., 1999, p. 48) that involve activities but not any action component. This raises significant questions, such as; do students learn about democracy by experiencing democracy, do teachers use democratic pedagogies, are students encouraged to be responsible for their school and wider community (Torney-Purta et al., 1999)?

Schwille and Amadeo (2002) conclude that there is little evidence of adoption of this 'radical challenge' because the issue for schools (and democracy) is, "how much freedom and autonomy can citizens enjoy without undermining the social order" (p. 117). Their argument, however, is still about a *thin* democracy that deals with "attitudes, dispositions, and behaviour" so that teaching about democracy will "allow debate over controversial issues" (p. 127) so that students are "learning to become competent democratic citizens"(p. 125, emphasis added).

In 2003, Print and Coleman repeat that the "primary goal of CE is to prepare the next generation of citizens for enlightened political engagement" (Print & Coleman, 2003, p. 130, emphasis added). Parker (2001) singularly contends that such political engagement requires the purposeful involvement of students in schools in "contacting public officials ... campaigning ... civil disobedience, boycotts, strikes, rebellions and other forms of direct action" (Parker, 2001, p. 99). Print and Coleman dismiss this suggesting "in practice CCE is considered to be the school based experience for the **preparation** of democratic citizenship" (Print & Coleman, 2003, p. 130, emphasis added). Print, both here and in other articles, repeats that the primary goal of CCE in schools is about the preparation for the real world but never actually suggests that it might be necessary for such education—significantly for students—to actually engage with the real world except for added on "practice" through the informal curriculum. This practice, he suggests, is for future participation as adults, in other words this could be seen as *playing* at a pretend democracy. For Print and Coleman, the "problem of low and declining voter participation by young people" (Print & Coleman, 2003, p. 135) is the key or significant feature of political engagement and the future of democracy (Print, 2007). They argue that CCE in so-called divided societies plays an "apparently passive role through the manipulation" of "truth" within schools which they characterise as "cultural forgetting" where the goal "is to prevent open learning" (Print & Coleman, 2003, p. 141). However, they also envisage that the CCE should "generate cooperation, networking, trust and cohesiveness" (Print & Coleman, 2003, p. 136), but in reality CCE is promoting compliance and homogeneity in Australian schools.

Similarly Kennedy (2003)—writing in the context of global terror post the Bali and Twin Towers attacks of 2001—emphasizes that if Australia is to protect democracy there is a powerful need to know *about* democracy, and that the new CCE has not delivered a "great depth of civic knowledge for many students" (p. 56). Kennedy asks "what, though, should they know" (p. 57)? Focussing on the neo-liberal individual contribution, she calls for a "willingness to support those institutions and values that allow individual interests to flourish" (p. 58). Kennedy refers to the need to develop "civic capacity" which ensures that future citizens know how to act, but significantly not to act while they are in school, but only in the future. In agreement with Print and Coleman (2003), Kennedy argues that CCE has three objectives—building cohesion, inclusion, and trust; tolerance and respect; critical thinking and problem solving—again more about compliance and homogeneity. These authors see that practice in the sense of the "add-ons" of student councils and perhaps open classroom dialogue where students *play* at being democratic. Kennedy (2003) concludes that CCE while:

> Cannot consist of the passive reception of decontextualized information it must allow students to engage with both the knowledge they are expected to learn, and which is necessary to equip and active citizenry, and with activities that will give them experience with the practice of democracy. (p. 65)

Mellor and Kennedy (2003), reporting on the 1999 IEA-CIVED survey, state that while Australian students expressed commitment to traditional values associated with a democracy they do not participate in "conventional forms of political participation"; activities that they suggest epitomise active citizenship—joining political parties, running for office, or writing to newspapers about issues of social concern. Mellor and Kennedy conclude that students are not engaging in the "very political system that guarantees [democratic] values" (p. 535), but that this reluctance is not reproduced "when it comes to participating in broader social movements" (p. 535).

They explain this as the result of either the lack of adequate understanding of the "relationship between the formal political system and their freely expressed democratic values" or as a result of a "sense of alienation because of a perceived lack of self–efficacy" (p. 535). Raising the neo-liberal spectre of future threats to democracy post Bali and Twin Towers, they conclude by saying that "citizens need to know what is worth protecting from either internal or external forces" (p. 536). In addition, their suggested *panacea* is for students to be engaged in more role-*play* acting "in activities outside their classrooms such as Student Councils." This is described elsewhere as extending "the culture of performativity, with a concomitant focus on adult-led prescription, formalized assessment and top-down imposition" (Garratt & Piper, 2008, p. 488). Acknowledging that passive reception of decontextualized information does not work, they call for students to engage with "knowledge that they are expected to learn to equip an active citizenry, and with activities that will give them the experience with the practice of democracy" (p. 537).

Print (2007) argues that the challenge to democracy is not from an external or internal enemy but from its own citizens "who have grown distrustful of politicians, sceptical about democratic institutions and disillusioned about how the democratic process functions" (p. 325). However, he points to the paradox of over 20 years of CCE "as the demand for democratic citizenship grows, youth participation in formal democracy is declining" (p. 326). He reiterates the importance of "learning about participation... developing of political engagement ... to learn about democracy, government and citizenship ... to acquire civic knowledge, and skills and values" (p. 336). He concludes that this may "enhance political knowledge and probably political engagement" (p. 336) "[and] can influence engagement and participation" (p. 337) in the future. Criticizing "participatory pedagogy" (p. 338) as being weak in schools, Print defines this pedagogy in *thin* terms of "class voting, group inquiry, simulations, fieldwork and co-operative learning" which he also calls "engaged or conversational pedagogy" which he claims has a strong correlation with future civic engagement which he understands is epitomized by casting a vote.

LEARNING ABOUT BUT NOT DOING DEMOCRACY: RHETORIC OF ACTIVE PARTICIPATION

What seems to emerge as a policy response is a call for students to learn *about* democracy but to not—at least in a serious way—*do* democracy. Giroux (2000) suggests that "there has been a shift from responsibility for creating democracy of citizens to producing a democracy of consumers" and that: "When public education becomes a venue for making a profit, delivering a product, or constructing consuming subjects, education reneges on its responsibilities for creating a democracy of citizens by shifting its focus to producing a democracy of consumers" (Giroux, 2000, p. 173).

Missing in this debate was a thorough understanding of what a good citizen is—the civics versus citizenship debate can be seen in terms of the struggle between *thin* and *thick* democracy. Producing curriculum materials will not in itself deliver the results expected or intended.

The approach to CCE through the Discovering Democracy project (DD) was to produce material without teacher input with the focus only on civic knowledge which was to be "ineffective in achieving its own goal in citizenship education programmes of encouraging students in effective participation" (Prior, 2006, p. 125). Teachers were very negative about the attempts by government to influence and impose one view of citizenship because "the culture of their practices and beliefs [was not] taken into account by policy makers" (p. 125). Prior concludes that the existence of stand-alone unlinked or de-contextualized one-off programs did not provide the lasting affects planned for, while the schools were accused by students of "*talking the talk but not walking the walk*" because teachers were not able to model good citizenship in their practices.

THICK DEMOCRACY—ACTION AND PRAXIS

Thick[6] democracy goes beyond the championing of electoral and legislative processes, rule of law, and basic civil rights (Howard & Patten, 2006). It acknowledges the legitimacy of collective citizen and civil action as external to government and business. Such a citizenship would be more inclusive as were the various social movements that contested past forms of domination. It is a commitment to individual and collective agency that ensures inclusiveness. *Thick* democracy envisages a "social citizen"—an individual always in relationship with others—capable of reflexive agency (Giddens, 1994) where *recognitive* justice is more important than the *redistributive* justice that has been in contest with the neo-liberal *retributive* discourse (Gale, 2000; Gale & Densmore, 2002; Young, 1990). Paradoxically, as Giddens (1994) argues, many of the democracy exporting countries are experiencing crises of democracy at home. Active citizenship is based on a "social activist, the doer of public good within the collectivist decision making process" (Seddon, 2004, p. 177) and involved in capacity building and community development.

In contradistinction the active citizen of neo-liberalism is conceived as an entrepreneur and a "*can do achiever*" to primarily benefit the individual. While schools are expected to prepare students to live in a diverse democratic societies (Furman & Shields, 2005), school practices remain largely undemocratic (Duignan, 2005). Therefore, what is required is a fostering of public debate, thoughtful critique of existing social and political institutions, and a respect for the value of political action "ranging from public service to community action to protest politics" (Howard & Patten, 2006, p. 470). This is the antithesis of the neo-liberalized CCE currently promoted in Australia (and elsewhere) which increasingly adopted the narrative of humans as inherently competitive and self-interested, and resulted in the mitigation of reflective and reflexive human agency.

Howard and Patten (2006) explain that despite the common rhetoric of active citizenship there are two perceptible trends within the new civics —the *thin* neo-liberal and the *thick(er)* radical democratic trends. They suggest that the latter is motivated by egalitarian commitments and "the desire to extend democracy while enhancing the political agency of once marginalised citizens" (p. 459). Being active in this sense means being "socially engaged and committed to collective problems solving at all levels of the political community" (p. 460). Politics, then, is more than elections, and includes all power structured social relationships. In essence, they explain that this requires the ability to "navigate and influence the power-structured social relations that characterize the politics of civil society" (p. 460). Educators must acknowledge that what is necessary is an equalisation of agency for students, otherwise this is not possible.

Thick democracy actively challenges the view that "unregulated markets are by definition realms of freedom that produce equality of opportunity" (Howard & Patten, 2006) with "extensive social and cultural citizenship rights" (p. 461) associated with a politicized empowerment in the social processes that shape society where all are visible and heard despite their social status. Thick democracy must be about "voice, agency, inclusiveness and collective problem solving" that is "rooted in the capacity to see oneself reflected in the cultures of society" (Howard & Patten, 2006, pp. 462–463), and not in the freedom to pursue one's own individual self-interest. Therefore thick democratic teaching will be concerned with a recognitive, not just redistributive, social justice (Gale & Densmore, 2002). Recognitive social justice is incorporated in Westheimer and Kahne's vision that goes beyond the *personally responsible citizen* of the so-called "critical democracy" urged by Dejaeghere and Tudball (2007) to incorporate both the *participatory* and *justice orientated citizen*. Nevertheless, Westheimer and Kahne warn:

> While pursuit of both goals may well support development of a more democratic society, it is not clear whether making advances along one dimension will necessarily further progress on the other. Do programs that support civic participation necessarily promote students' capacities for critical analysis and social change? Conversely, does focusing on social justice provide the foundation for effective and committed civic actors? Or might such programs support the development of armchair activists who have articulate

> conversations over coffee, without ever acting? (Westheimer & Kahne, 2004, pp. 242–243)

Thick democracy is not easily achieved, in either society generally or in schools in particular. As the agents of society in which they exist, teachers (rightly) can claim they are therefore restricted in what they alone can achieve as the national agendas and budgets are nationally and state controlled.

CONCLUSIONS

Dobozy (2007) asks if it is possible to educate tomorrow's citizens to create a more democratic society without democratizing education. How authentic is the student experience in exercising democratic decision-making? How are students encouraged to be active citizens of their school? This chapter has argued that schools and teachers play an important role in preparing individuals for democratic citizenship (Kennedy, 2001a, 2001b; Sachs, 2001). Schools and teachers provide one of the first opportunities to introduce children to democratic principles and practices.

Civics related knowledge is necessary but not sufficient for "becoming a competent democratic citizen" (Schwille & Amadeo, 2002, p. 125). Thick democracy has the potential to become the site of struggle for social justice and equity, and not necessarily assimilationism (Taylor, 1996). The pedagogical framework as expressed in CCE is "fundamentally anti-democratic because it denies legitimacy to educational debate about the form and content of education" (Armstrong, 2006, p. 4).

Thick democracy goes beyond the championing of electoral and legislative processes, rule of law, and basic civil rights (Howard & Patten, 2006). It encourages and facilitates the legitimacy of collective citizen and civil action. Thick democracy envisages a "social citizen"—an individual always in relationship with others—capable of reflexive agency (Giddens, 1994).

Research into how democracy is understood, experienced, cultivated, and demonstrated among educators therefore is extremely important. Such research can have great benefit to educators, scholars, decision-makers, and others in developing, implementing, and assessing democratic education programs, practices, and pedagogy in schools (Zyngier, 2013a, 2013b).

Teacher who held a *thin* perspective of the role of democracy in society would include cultivating voting, explaining the mechanics and the virtues of election as the focus; linkages to the community are not undertaken with a view to addressing problems; when there is service-learning, there is real no connection to the curriculum and the educational experience. Concern about "taking sides," being "biased," "indoctrination," or "being political" would be evident, and lead to omitting, avoiding, and/or downplaying controversial issues. Those minority of teachers with a *thicker* understanding would acknowledge that knowledge is constructed, reject the "banking model" of education, and would make an effort to have students engage with diverse groups, problems, realties, and so on, outside of the mainstream media lense of society; service-learning, for example, would link to the educational experience, and not simply be an add-on with little pedagogical and epistemological value. In this case they understood that to be neutral is to side with hegemonic powers, and that discussing controversial issues does not equate to indoctrination; avoiding critical discussions can lead to passive acceptance of injustice, war, and hatred, and also cultivate compliance and docility among students.

But can this be done without facilitating students' "understanding of the value of social justice" without "education *in* and *for* democracy" (Dobozy, 2007, p. 116). School students cannot acquire the knowledge, attitudes, and skills to successfully become agentic citizens in Australia without the simultaneous democratization of pedagogy, schools, and school systems. The role-playing of democracy and pretend parliaments—extolled in CCE and reflected by the majority of teachers (Zyngier, 2013b)—means too often that students are involved in decision making on "an abstract and often detached level" (Dobozy, 2007, p. 118). Programs associated with a *thin* democracy are unable to take the "social organisation of specific schools and the everyday life of individual students into consideration" (p. 118). The responses of the teachers in this research indicate that it requires a change in educational practice to "inspire political empowerment" beyond the implementation of off the shelf products or programmes.

RECOMMENDATIONS

Civics related knowledge is necessary but not sufficient for "becoming a competent democratic citizen" (Schwille & Amadeo, 2002). However, thick democracy has the potential to become the site of struggle for social justice and equity (Taylor, 1996). While neo-liberalism seemingly has a stranglehold on education in many of the countries studied so far, it is potentially at least vulnerable—educators have an opportunity to construct a transformative curriculum that includes the following possibilities for advancing education for democracy through:

- A revised curriculum based on social justice as part of the democratic process

- A move away from viewing students as insecure "objects" to agentive "subjects"
- Understanding and promoting democracy at both super-structural and micro-structural levels
- Centralizing the participation of "critical citizens" in the process of becoming more democratic
- Working for both conceptual and practical understandings of democracy in schools;
- Furthering the awareness of the power of "reflection-action" and praxis
- The generation of contextual teaching spaces
- Analysis of mass-media as part of political/democratic literacy

Ongoing research will not only enable the development of a framework for conceptualizing democracy in education, highlighting, in particular, what educators can do to become more critically aware and engaged in democracy within their teaching, but will also be able to better understand any correspondence between teacher habitus, their cultural and social capital, and their perceptions and beliefs.

Instead of education reproducing the current *thin* democracy that leads to disengaged citizens (Dejaeghere & Tudball, 2007), examples of excellent teacher practice would enable the development of an educational framework of teaching for thick democracy leading to a more participatory, empowered and engaged citizenry and a more inclusive participation in, and therefore safeguarding of, democratic society.

A more holistic and dynamic approach—pedagogical, experiential, political, social, economic, and cultural—is a necessary step to attaining a more decent society to produce citizens who are engaged, critical, and productive agents of positive change.

ACKNOWLEDGMENT

This research is funded by the Australian Research Council grant 2013-2016 *Can Educators Make a Difference: Experiencing Democracy in Education.*

NOTES

1. Retrieved from http://doingdemocracy.ning.com/
2. Museum of Australian Democracy and the Institute for Governance has an online survey http://www.sbs.com.au/powerof1/ *Does Your Vote Count:* Discover

the changing nature of Australian democracy and the power of your voice within it. See Appendix 1 for details

3. Voting is compulsory for all above 18 years of age in Australia
4. Others have referred to democratic binaries such as weak and strong Swift (2002), passive and active (Criddle, Vidovich, & O'Neill, 2004), minimalist and maximalist (McLaughlin, 1992).
5. The notion of *thick* and *thin* democracy is attributed to Gandin and Apple (2002), who build on the seminal work of Benjamin Barber (1984). Barber raises pivotal questions on the saliency of liberal democracy, including the tension between individualism and the rights of all citizens within concepts of *shallow* and *deep* democracy. Others have referred to democratic binaries such as *weak* and *strong* Swift (2002), *passive* and *active* (Criddle, Vidovich, & O'Neill, 2004), *minimalist* and *maximalist* (McLaughlin, 1992).
6. See http://www.civicsandcitizenship.edu.au/cce/discovering_democracy_curriculum_resources,9067.html for background and http://www1.curriculum.edu.au/ddunits/ for details and examples of the materials

REFERENCES

Alberici, E. (2014, November). Voters want reform. *Lateline*. Retrieved from http://www.abc.net.au/lateline/content/2014/s4126509.htm

Armstrong, D. (2006). Dreaming our future: Developing democratic professional practice? *Australian Educational Researcher, 33*(3), 1–11.

Banks, J. A. (2001). Citizenship education and diversity: Implications for teacher education. *Journal of Teacher Education, 52*(1), 5–16. doi:10.1177/0022487101052001002

Barber, B. R. (2004). *Strong democracy: Participatory politics for a new age* (20th anniversary ed.). Berkeley, CA: University of California Press.

Brophy, J., & Alleman, J. (2009). Meaningful social studies for elementary students. *Teachers and Teaching, 15*(3), 357–376. doi:10.1080/13540600903056700

Carr, P. R. (2007). Experiencing democracy through neo-liberalism: The role of social justice in education. *Journal of Critical Education Policy Studies, 5*(2), 307–341. Retrieved fro http://www.jceps.com/index.php?pageID=article&articleID=104

Carr, P. R. (2008). Educators and education for democracy: Moving beyond "thin" democracy. *International Journal of Education and Democracy, 1*(2), 147–164.

Carr, P. R. (2010). *Does your vote count? Critical pedagogy and democracy*. New York, NY: Peter Lang.

Crick, B. (2000). *Essays on citizenship*. London, UK: Continuum.

Criddle, E., Vidovich, L., & O'Neill, M. (2004). Discovering democracy: An analysis of curriculum policy for citizenship education. *International Journal of Research & Method in Education, 27*(1), 27–41.

Davies, I., & Issitt, J. (2005). Reflections on citizenship education in Australia, Canada and England. *Comparative Education, 41*(4), 389–410.

Dejaeghere, J. G., & Tudball, L. (2007). Looking back, looking forward: Critical citizenship as a way ahead for civics and citizenship in Australia. *Citizenship Teaching and Learning, 3*(2), 40–57.

Dewey, J. (1936, November). Dewey Urges instruction in "realities." *Columbia Daily Spectator*. Retrieved from http://spectatorarchive.library.columbia.edu/cgi-bin/columbia?a=d&d=cs19361116-01.2.26#

Diamond, L. (2015). Facing up to the democratic recession. *Journal of Democracy, 26*(1), 141–155.

Dobozy, E. (2007). Effective learning of civic skills: Democratic schools succeed in nurturing the critical capacities of students. *Educational Studies, 33*(2), 115–128.

Duignan, P. A. (2005). Socially responsible leadership: Schools for a more just and democratic society. *Leading and Managing, 11*(1), 1–13.

Ercan, S. A., & Gagnon, J. P. (2014). The crisis of democracy: Which crisis? Which democracy? *Democratic Theory, 1*(2), 1–10. doi:10.3167/dt.2014.010201

Evans, M., Halupka, M., & Stoker, G. (2014). Young citizens—A sail and not an anchor for the ship of Australian democracy (p. 10). Canberra ACT: Australian School of Governance.

Fischman, G. E., & Haas, E. (2012). Beyond idealized citizenship education embodied cognition, metaphors, and democracy. *Review of Research in Education, 36*(1), 169–196. doi:10.3102/0091732X11420927

Freire, P. (1973). *Education for liberation*. Melbourne, Australian: Australian Council of Churches Commission on Christian Education.

Furman, G. C., & Shields, C. M. (2005). How can educational leaders promote and support social justice and democratic community in schools. In W. A. Firestone & C. Riehl (Eds.), *A new agenda for educational leadership* (pp. 119–137). New York, NY: Teachers College Press.

Gale, T. (2000). Rethinking social justice in schools: How will we recognize it when we see it? *International Journal of Inclusive Education, 4*(3), 253–269.

Gale, T., & Densmore, K. (2002). Student success and failure: As a matter or fact or just how they are portrayed? *Asia-Pacific Journal of Teacher Education, 30*(1), 7–23.

Gandin, L. A., & Apple, M. W. (2002). Thin versus thick democracy in education: Porto alegre and the creation of alternatives to neo-liberalism. *International Studies in Sociology of Education, 12*(2), 99–116.

Garratt, D., & Piper, H. (2008). Citizenship education in England and Wales: Theoretical critique and practical considerations. *Teachers and Teaching: Theory and Practice, 14*(5), 481–496.

Giddens, A. (1994). *Beyond Left and Right: The Future of Radical Politics*. Cambridge, UK: Polity Press in association with Blackwell.

Giroux, H. A. (2000). *Stealing innocence: Youth, corporate power and the politics of culture*. Basingstoke, UK: Palgrave.

Hahn, C. (1998). *Becoming political: Comparative perspectives on citizenship education*. Albany, NY: State University of New York Press.

Howard, C., & Patten, S. (2006). Valuing civics: Political commitment and the new citizenship education in Australia. *Canadian Journal of Education, 29*(2), 454–475.

Hyslop-Margison, E. J., & Thayer, J. (2009). *Teaching democracy: Citizenship education as critical pedagogy* (Vol. 42). Rotterdam, The Netherlands: Sense.

Kahne, J., & Westheimer, J. (2003). Teaching democracy: What schools need to do. *Phi Delta Kappan, 85*(1), 34–68.

Kennedy, K. (2001a). *Conversations about civics: Practitioner realities and worldviews about civic education in schools and classrooms.* Paper presented at the Symposium on Citizenship Education, Annual Conference of the Australian Association for Research in Education.

Kennedy, K. (2001b). *The Western imagination and local values: How should civic education be constructed?* Paper presented at the Symposium on Citizenship Education, Annual Conference of the Australian Association for Research in Education.

Kennedy, K. (1998). Policy contexts for civics education in Australia: Can social reconstruction and neoconservatism exist [Electronic Version]. *University of Canberra.* Retrieved from http://www.canberra.edu.au/civics/papers/policy_contexts. html

Kennedy, K. (2003). Preparing young Australians for an uncertain future: New thinking about citizenship education. *Teaching Education, 14*(1), 53–67.

Kincheloe, J. L. (2008). *Knowledge and critical pedagogy.* Berlin, Germany: Springer.

Lund, D. E., & Carr, P. R. (2008). *Doing democracy: Striving for political literacy and social justice.* Berlin, Switzerland: Peter Lang.

McAllister, I. (2014). Voters want reform (I. McAllister, Trans.). In M. O'Neill (Ed.), *Lateline.* Sydney: Australian Broadcasting Corporation

McLaughlin, T. H. (1992). Citizenship, diversity, and education: A philosophical perspective. *Journal of Moral Education, 21*(3), 235–250.

Markus, A. (2014). *Mapping Social Cohesion 2014: The Scanlon Foundation Surveys Report.* Melbourne, AU: Scanlon Foundation & Monash University.

Mellor, S., & Kennedy, K. (2003). Australian students' democratic values and attitudes towards participation: Indicators from the IEA Civic Education Study. *International Journal of Educational Research, 39*(6), 525–537.

Museum of Australian Democracy. (2014). *"Not happy Jan"—Young Australians engaged but not impressed with politics.* Australia: Author.

Oliver, A. (2014). *The Lowy Institute Poll 2014* (Vol. 10). Sydney: Lowy Institute for International Policy.

O'Neill, M. (2014). Apathetic Aussies. *Lateline.* Retrieved from http://www.abc.net.au/lateline/content/2014/s4065314.htm

Parker, W. C. (2001). Toward enlightened political engagement. In W. Stanley (Ed.), *Critical issues in social studies research for the 21st Century* (pp. 97–118). Greenwich, CT: Information Age Press.

Print, M. (2000). Curriculum policy, values and changes in civics education in Australia. *Asia Pacific Journal of Education, 20*(1), 21–35.

Print, M. (2007). Citizenship education and youth participation in democracy. *British Journal of Educational Studies, 55*(3), 325–345.

Print, M., & Coleman, D. (2003). Towards understanding of social capital and citizenship education. *Cambridge Journal of Education, 33*(1), 123–149.

Print, M., Kennedy, K., & Hughes, J. (1999). Reconstructing civic and citizenship education in Australia. In J. Torney-Purta, J. Schwille & J. A. Amadeo (Eds.),

Civic education across countries: Twenty-four national case studies from the IEA Civic Education Project. Amsterdam, NL: IEA Secretariat.

Prior, W. (2006). Civics and citizenship education. *Ethos, 14*(4), 6–10.

Sachs, J. (2001). *Curriculum control: The cost to teacher professionalism*. Paper presented at the Annual Conference of the Australian Association for Research in Education.

Schwille, J., & Amadeo, J. A. (2002). The paradoxical situation of civic education in schools: ubiquitous and yet exclusive. In *International Perspectives on Education and Society* (Vol. 5, pp. 105–136). Bingley, UK: Emerald Group Publishing Limited.

Seddon, T. (2004). Remaking civic formation:Towards a learning citizen? *London Review of Education, 2*(3), 171–186.

Taylor, A. (1996). Education for democracy: Assimilation or emancipation for Aboriginal Australians? *Comparative Education Review, 40*(4), 426–438.

Torney-Purta, J., Schwille, J., & Amadeo, J. A. (Eds.). (1999). *Civic education across Countries: Twenty-four national case studies from the IEA Civic Education Project*. Amsterdam, NA: IEA Secretariat.

Westheimer, J., & Kahne, J. (2004a). What kind of citizen? The politics of educating for democracy. *American Educational Research Journal, 41*(2), 237–269.

Westheimer, J., & Kahne, J. (2004b). Educating the "good" citizen: Political choices and pedagogical goals. *PS: Political Science and Politics, 37*(02), 241–247. doi:10.1017.S1049096504004160

Young, I. M. (1990). *Justice and the politics of difference*. Princeton, NJ: Princeton University.

Zyngier, D. (2013a). Democracy will not fall from the sky. The global doing democracy research project: Seeking to understand the perspectives, experiences and perceptions of teachers in relation to democracy in education. *World Studies in Education, 14*(2).

Zyngier, D. (2013b). The struggle for "thick" or transformative citizenship and democracy in Australia: What future teachers believe and why it is important. *Sisyphus—Journal of Education, 1*(2), 100–126.

ABOUT THE AUTHORS

THE EDITORS

Elinor L. Brown is an Associate professor in the College of Education at the University of Kentucky, United States. She is internationally recognized in equity and social justice education through her: series co-editorship of *International Advances in Education: Global Initiatives for Equity and Social Justice*; publications in distinguished national and international refereed journals; numerous national and international refereed presentations; invited international workshops; and for hosting an international conference on cultural identity for scholars from Western and Eastern Europe, Russia, East Asia, Africa, and the United States. Additionally, numerous awards for teaching and service evidence her continued commitment to academic excellence. Her research interests focus on the development of equitable education opportunities for disenfranchised and displaced populations to maximize productive non-exploitive 21st century global citizenship. elinorlbrown@gmail.com

Anna Krasteva is doctor honoris causa of University Lille 3, France and professor at Department of Political Sciences, New Bulgarian University. She has authored and edited 29 books and published numerous articles in 15 countries. Among her recent publications: *La rue et l'e-rue* (co-ed, in print in Paris), *Migrants and Refugees: Equitable Education for Displaced Populations* (co-ed, Information Age Publishing, United States: Information Age Publishing, 2013), *E-citoyennetes* (ed, Paris: Harmattan, 2013). She has been guest professor at numerous universities. She is editor-in-chief of *Southeastern Europe* (Brill), member of the editorial boards of *Nationalism and Ethnic Politics* (Routledge), *REPCEE*, and *Europeana* (Shangai and Paris). Anna Krasteva is member of the Board of the Diplomatic Institute and vice-president of the Bulgarian political sciences association.

Maria Ranieri, PhD in "Telematics and Information Society," is an Associate Professor of Educational Methods and Technology at the Department of Education and Psychology, University of Florence (IT). Her main research areas include theory and methodology relating to media and technology in education, as well as work around teachers' practices and students' learning. Her publications include some more than 40 papers/chapters on these topics and 7 books on learning methods and technologies. She is member of SIPED (Italian Society of Pedagogy) and of the executive council of MED (The Italian Association of Media Education).

THE AUTHORS

Mónica Aresta is an independent researcher in the area of digital identity. With a PhD in Multimedia in Education (University of Aveiro), her research interests are related with the adoption of Web 2.0 tools in learning environments and in the construction of identity in formal and informal digital environments. Her academic work can be found at: https://aveiro.academia.edu/maresta

Zehlia Babaci-Wilhite is a multilingual and international scholar. Currently a Visiting Assistant Professor at the University of California-Berkeley affiliated to the Norwegian Center for Human Rights at the University of Oslo, Norway and an Adjunct Professor at the University of San Francisco. She has taught courses in the USA, Norway, Japan, India, France & Nigeria on issues related to language and culture, development & human rights. Her research interests include Language in STEM as a Human Right in Education. She is the author of many published articles in tier one academic journals, book chapters and has previously published four books on Linguist Rights in Education. She is fluent in French, English, Norwegian, Japanese and Berber with knowledge of Arabic, Portuguese, German, Spanish, Swahili and Igbo. Her email is: z.b.wilhite@berkeley.edu and z.b.wilhite@nchr.uio.no

Ben Bachmair, until his retirement in 2008, was professor of pedagogy, media education and technology enhanced learning at the University of Kassel, Germany, and former dean of the faculty of humanities. Currently he is honorary professor at the UCL Institute of Education, University College London, and University of London.

Emma Bent is a Research Assistant and Lecturer at the Graduate School of Education, University of Bristol. Her background is in Primary Education and her PhD considered the role of oral language in literacy development. She is a researcher on the Digital Diversity: Learning and Belonging project (DD-lab) exploring the role of digital media in the lived experiences of undergraduates from non-traditional and diverse backgrounds. Current research interests include widening participation, raising aspirations, identity and agency.

Kennesha S. Bracely is currently the Director of Education for Ontario Center for Special Education in Doha, Qatar. She is also an Associate Online Professor in Special Education at Grand Canyon University. Dr. Bracely holds an EdD from Argosy University in Educational Leadership in Higher Education. Since 2003 her teaching experiences have included K–12 Special Education instructor, Lead Teacher of Special Education, Assistant Professor of Secondary Education, Assistant Professor of Elementary Education, and Assistant Online Professor in Business Administration. Her research interests include culturally relevant pedagogy in special education, and global educational leadership practices.

Carolyn M. Cunningham is an Assistant Professor in the Masters Program in Communication and Leadership Studies at Gonzaga University where she teaches courses on communication theory and research, communication technology, and communication pedagogy. Her research looks at the intersections of gender and technology and her work has been published in outlets including *New Media & Society* and the *Journal of Children and Media*. She also is the editor of *Social Networking and Impression Management: Identity in the Digital Age* published in 2012 by Lexington Books.

Chris Fowler is a honorary fellow in the School of Computer Science & Electronic Engineering at the University of Essex. His first degree and doctorate are in Psychology. From 2010 to 2013 he was the Professor of Education at the University of the West Indies (UWI). Before joining UWI, he was Professor and Coordinator for Research & Evaluation at the Institute of Distance Education, University of Swaziland. Between 2002 and 2009 he was the Professor and Director of Chimera, the Institute of Socio-technical Innovation and Research at the University of Essex, and before that he worked for British Telecom's (BT) Research Department for over 10 years.

Yuqing Guo, PhD, assistant professor, got her MS in area of Computer Networking from INSA-Lyon in 2005 and her PhD in area of Educational Technology from East China Normal University in 2011. Since September 2011, Dr. Guo has been working at Institute of Educational Technology, College of Education, Zhejiang University. Her research interests include distance education, educational data mining, social computing, and so on.

Maria Antonietta Impedovo graduated in Psychology and Communication Organization. She holds a PhD in Theory, Technology and History of Education. Currently, she is pursuing Post doc at Aix-Marseille Université in France in the Technology of Education (research group: EA4671 ADEF, ENS de Lyon). Her research interests include formative processes mediated by technology and interactions in learning communities. Maria Antonietta Impedovo is the corresponding author and can be contacted at: maria-antonietta.IMPEDOVO@univ-amu.fr

Sun Hee (Sunny) Jang, PhD, is an Associate Lecturer in the Bachelor of Dementia Care, Wicking Centre, University of Tasmania. Her Online teaching expertise has been recognised with the award of University Teaching Merit Certificates in 2014 and 2015. Sunny's research interests include the use of technology in teaching and learning, student online engagement in distance courses, participatory culture in social media, and TESOL. She has published in these areas and is currently investigating beginning student use of technology in blended courses.

Anna Krasteva is director of CERMES (Centre for Refugees, Migration and Ethnic Studies) at the New Bulgarian University in Sofia. She is *doctor honoris causa* of University Lille 3, France. She has edited 21 books and published numerous articles in Bulgaria, USA, France, UK, Belgium, Russia, Switzerland, Germany, FYROM, Slovakia, Greece, Serbia, Turkey, Italy, the Netherlands, and Romania. She worked as fellow at the Institute for advanced studies in Nantes, France (January-June 2010) and lectured at several universities in Europe. Her main fields of research are post-communist democratization, migration, ethnicity, e-citizenship, digital democracy. She is editor-in-chief of the international journal *South Eastern Europe* (Brill), member of the editorial boards of one American *Nationalism and ethnic politics*, (Routledge), one French (REPCEE) and one Chinese 欧洲评论 (*Europeana*, Shangai, China) journal. She is member of a number of international scientific boards, for example, of the Institute of Central, Eastern and Balkan Europe of the University of Bologna, of the Reseau des Maisons des Sciences de l'homme in France (2008–2012. She has been awarded the Palmes Academiques of France and is president of Amopa-Bulgarie (Association of the members of the Palmes academiques). Anna

Krasteva is member of the National Board of the Diplomatic Institute. akrasteva@nbu.bg anna.krasteva@gmail.com

Katura M. Lesane is an Associate Online Professor in Educational Leadership with Grand Canyon University. She holds a PhD from Capella University in Educational Leadership & Administration. Since 1993 her teaching experiences have included K–12 instructor, Reading & Language Arts Instructional Coach, Assistant Principal, Assistant Professor of English, and Associate Online Professor in Educational Leadership. Her research interests include differentiated pedagogy in K–12 and higher education and andragogy for distance learning instructors.

Yan Li, PhD professor, got her PhD in area of web-based distance education from Texas A&M University in 2004. Since September, 2004, Dr. Li has been working at Institute of Educational Technology, College of Education, Zhejiang University. Her research interests include distance education, ICT education, media education, diffusion of educational innovation, and and so forth.

Min Li, MS, is Director of the Educational Resources Center of Xia Cheng District, Hangzhou Bureau of Education. She has many years of experiences in area of ICT education in Chinese urban K–12 schools.

Stefania Manca is a researcher at the Institute of Educational Technology of the National Research Council of Italy (CNR). Her major interests include the analysis of social and cognitive processes in Computer-Supported Collaborative Learning environments and the analysis of specific linguistic features used to express and construct social dimension in asynchronous-based learning environments. She is currently investigating the value of social networking sites for formal and informal learning purposes and in teacher and professional development.

Kshama Pandey has been working as an Assistant Professor in the Department of Foundations of Education. She has more than 10 years teaching experience. She has been awarded her D.Phil. Degree from University of Allahabad. Her research interests include ICT based Education, Innovative Learning Pedagogy & Peace Education. Her area of research is to prepare the students for a techno-oriented society without uprooting them from their values and cultural moorings. Her various chapters have been published in edited books with national and international repute like NCRERT, Springer, IGI Publication, USA, etc. An international edited book *Handbook of Research on Promoting Global Peace and Civic Engagement through Education* has been published by IGI Publication, USA & also Section Editor of an edited book entitled *A Handbook of Mobile Learning* published by Springer.

Gisella Paoletti is an Associate Professor in Experimental Pedagogy in the Department of Humanities at the University of Trieste. She teaches courses in Education and Academic Assessment and Information Technologies for Education and Learning. She has conducted extensive research on the understanding and study of written texts and multimedia, analyzing the variables that facilitate access to information and the integration of text and figures in multimedia, websites, on the use of managerial presentations in a classroom and on multitasking in the classroom and when studying.

Luis Pedro is an assistant professor in the Communication and Arts Department, University of Aveiro, Portugal. He is engaged in teaching activities in the Communication Sciences and Technologies field namely in the New Communication Technologies degree, in the Multimedia Communications MSc, and in the Multimedia in Education and in the Information and Communication in Digital Platforms Doctoral Programmes. His research interests are related with social media development and integration in educational and training contexts. His personal web page can be found at: http://about.me/lpedro

Maria Ranieri, PhD in "Telematics and Information Society," is an Associate Professor of Educational Methods and Technology at the Department of Education and Psychology, University of Florence (IT). Her main research areas include theory and methodology relating to media and technology in education, as well as work around teachers' practices and students' learning. Her publications include some more than 40 papers/chapters on these topics and 7 books on learning methods and technologies. She is member of SIPED (Italian Society of Pedagogy) and of the executive council of MED (The Italian Association of Media Education). She is currently investigating the interplay between mobile learning and social networking in formal and informal contexts of learning.

Alessia Rosa is an adjunct professor in educational technology, University of Turin. She is a media educator and an educational designer. She is member of MED. Her research interests include media education in formal and informal learning contexts, the use and production of educational videos as well as videogame education. On these topics she published some papers and books. She also manage projects, in collaboration with many ONG, Universities and other Government Department focused on sharing media education values in all the educational range. She is passionate about giving a voice to young people, especially in multicultural context.

Carlos Santos is an assistant lecturer. With a PhD in Information and Communication in Digital Platforms (University of Aveiro and University of Porto), he is the executive coordinator of the SAPO Campus research project (http://campus.sapo.pt) and his research interests are related with PLEs and promotion of Web 2.0 tools in educational contexts.

Neetu Singh is an Assistant Professor in Faculty of Education, Dayalbagh Educational Institute (Deemed University) Agra. Her 28 research paper and chapters have been published in various books and journals with national/international repute. She has participated in various national/ International conferences/workshops/Ten Days Research Methodology Training Program. She is the member of AIAER Research organization, PYIRC, Shimla and an NGO "Pahal Welfare Society." She is member of review committee of an international "Handbook of Research on Promoting Global Peace and Civic Engagement through Education" Published by IGI Global Publication, USA 2016. She has a good academic record as M.Ed., M.A. (Economics), M.A. (Education) and UGC JRF NET in Education. Her research interests include Economics teaching, ICT based Innovative Learning Pedagogy, Special Education and Educational Research.

Sue Timmis is Senior Lecturer in Technology Enhanced Learning and Co-ordinator of the Centre for Learning, Knowing and Interactive Technologies, Graduate School of Education, University of Bristol, UK. Her research investigates the learning lives of higher education students and the role of digital media in learning, empowerment, identity and student agency. She is particularly interested in the potential of digital media for furthering social justice in education. She currently leads the DD-lab project on digital diversity learning and belonging and has pioneered community of inquiry and co-researcher methodologies, working alongside undergraduate students across many projects.

Marquita Walker has been with the IUPUI School of Social Work in the Labor Studies Program since August, 2008 and is responsible for teaching and coordination of credit and training classes within the Labor Studies Program. Dr. Walker holds a PhD in Educational Leadership and Policy Analysis from the University of Missouri–Columbia, an MA in Public Affairs from the Harry Truman School of Public Affairs, University of Missouri, Columbia, an MA in English from Southwest Missouri State University in Springfield, Missouri, and a BS in English from Drury University in Springfield, Missouri. Dr. Walker's research interests lie in issues involving state and federal policies concerning workers and workers' education, social stratification, poverty, and e-learning in a distributed learning environment.

John Williamson is Dean and Professor of Education at the Faculty of Education, University of Tasmania, Australia. His recent work has explored the nature of decision making in schools and the perceptions of principals and teachers to a more distributed and shared process, teachers' work lives in a turbulent policy context, and the initial preparation of teachers. He has served on advisory groups of several Australian states and has been involved with projects for the OECD.

Yang Yang completed his PhD in 2012 and is a staff member in the Faculty of Education, University of Tasmania, Australia. He has been involved in teaching digital technologies to pre-service teachers, supervising research students, and collaborative research across educational disciplines using both qualitative and quantitative techniques. His research interests include Community of Practice, ICT in Higher Education, and Critical Discourse Analysis. Currently he is researching the potential of learning communities in academic and business contexts in different cultures.

Ching Wan Yee is a Research Fellow and Research Ethics Co-ordinator at the Graduate School of Education, University of Bristol. Her background includes teaching in Higher Education, Further Education, Youth Training Schemes and research in local government and the voluntary sector. Her research interests are wide ranging and encompass informal learning and the relationship between home and school, research ethics, widening participation, higher education, ethnic minority achievement and digital media.

David Zyngier is a former teacher and principal and is a senior lecturer in the faculty of education at Monash University. His research focuses on teacher pedagogies that engage all students but in particular how these can improve outcomes for students from communities of disadvantage focusing on issues of social justice and social inclusion. He is co-founder and co-director (with Paul Carr) of the Global Doing Democracy Research Project an international project examining perspectives and perceptions of democracy in education to develop a robust & critical democratic. He was awarded an Australian Research Council grant 2013–2016 *Can Educators Make a Difference: Experiencing Democracy in Education*.

TECHNOLOGY VOLUME EXTERNAL REVIEWERS (7-12-15)

1. Vincenza Benigno, Institute for Educational Technology, Italian National Research Council Rome, IT.
2. Alison Blair, Australian Catholic University, McAuley at Banyo, Brisbane, AU.
3. Gianna Cappello, University of Palermo, Palermo, IT.
4. Alona Forkosh-Baruch, Levinsky College of Education, Tel Aviv, IL.
5. Barbara Gerner de Garcia, Gallaudet University, Washington DC, United States.
6. Stefania Manca, Institute for Educational Technology, Italian National Research Council, Rome, IT.
7. Faith Prather, The College of Brockport/SUNY, Rochester, NY, United States.
8. Giuliano Vivanet, University of Cagliari, Cagliari, IT.
9. Karen Schuhle-Williams, The College at Brockport/SUNY, Brockport, NY, United States.
10. David Zyngier, Monash University Penninsula Campus, Victoria, AU.

www.ingramcontent.com/pod-product-compliance
Lightning Source LLC
LaVergne TN
LVHW052223200926
848481LV00001B/198